EXPERIMENTAL AND THEORETICAL STUDIES OF CONSCIOUSNESS

The Ciba Foundation is an international scientific and educational charity. It was established in 1947 by the Swiss chemical and pharmaceutical company of CIBA Limited—now Ciba-Geigy Limited. The Foundation operates independently in London under English trust law.

The Ciba Foundation exists to promote international cooperation in biological, medical and chemical research. It organizes about eight international multidisciplinary symposia each year on topics that seem ready for discussion by a small group of research workers. The papers and discussions are published in the Ciba Foundation symposium series. The Foundation also holds many shorter meetings (not published), organized by the Foundation itself or by outside scientific organizations. The staff always welcome suggestions for future meetings.

The Foundation's house at 41 Portland Place, London W1N 4BN, provides facilities for meetings of all kinds. Its Media Resource Service supplies information to journalists on all scientific and technological topics. The library, open five days a week to any graduate in science or medicine, also provides information on scientific meetings throughout the world and answers general enquiries on biomedical and chemical subjects. Scientists from any part of the world may stay in the house during working visits to London.

EXPERIMENTAL AND THEORETICAL STUDIES OF CONSCIOUSNESS

A Wiley-Interscience Publication

1993

JOHN WILEY & SONS

Chichester · New York · Brisbane · Toronto · Singapore

Published in 1993 by John Wiley & Sons Ltd
Baffins Lane, Chichester
West Sussex PO19 1UD, England

Other Wiley Editorial Offices

John Wiley & Sons, Inc., 605 Third Avenue,
New York, NY 10158-0012, USA

Jacaranda Wiley Ltd, G.P.O. Box 859, Brisbane,
Queensland 4001, Australia

John Wiley & Sons (Canada) Ltd, 22 Worcester Road,
Rexdale, Ontario M9W 1L1, Canada

John Wiley & Sons (SEA) Pte Ltd, 37 Jalan Pemimpin #05-04,
Block B, Union Industrial Building, Singapore 2057

Suggested series entry for library catalogues:
Ciba Foundation Symposia

Ciba Foundation Symposium 174
ix + 316 pages, 23 figures, 6 tables

British Library Cataloguing in Publication Data
A catalogue record for this book is
available from the British Library

ISBN 0 471 93866 1

Phototypeset by Dobbie Typesetting Limited, Tavistock, Devon.
Printed and bound in Great Britain by Biddles Ltd, Guildford.

Contents

Participants

B. J. Baars The Wright Institute, 2728 Durant Avenue, Berkeley, CA 94704, USA

M. A. Boden School of Cognitive & Computing Sciences, University of Sussex, Falmer, Brighton BN1 9QH, UK

T. H. Carr Department of Psychology, Michigan State University, East Lansing, MI 48824-1117, USA

D. C. Dennett Department of Philosophy, Center for Cognitive Studies, Tufts University, Medford, MA 02155, USA

P. Fenwick Department of Psychiatry, Section of Clinical Neurophysiology, Institute of Psychiatry, De Crespigny Park, Denmark Hill, London SE5 8AF, UK

M. S. Gazzaniga Center for Neuroscience, University of California, Davis, CA 95616, USA

J. A. Gray Department of Psychology, Institute of Psychiatry, De Crespigny Park, Denmark Hill, London SE5 8AF, UK

S. R. Harnad Department of Psychology, Princeton University, Princeton, NJ 08544, USA

N. K. Humphrey Darwin College, Cambridge CB3 9EU, UK

J. F. Kihlstrom The Amnesia & Cognition Unit, Department of Psychology, University of Arizona, Tucson, AZ 85721, USA

M. Kinsbourne Center for Cognitive Studies, Tufts University, Medford, MA 02155, USA

B. Libet Department of Physiology, University of California at San Francisco, School of Medicine, San Francisco, CA 94143-0444, USA

M. Lockwood Department for Continuing Education, University of Oxford, Rewley House, 1 Wellington Square, Oxford OX1 2JA, UK

A. J. Marcel MRC Applied Psychology Unit, 15 Chaucer Road, Cambridge CB2 2EF, UK

C. McGinn Department of Philosophy, Rutgers State University, New Brunswick, NJ 08903, USA

T. Nagel (*Chairman*) Department of Philosophy, New York University, 503 Main Building, Washington Square, New York, NY 10003, USA

W. T. Newsome Department of Neurobiology, Stanford University School of Medicine, Sherman Fairchild Science Building, Stanford, CA 94305-5401, USA

Y. Rossetti (*Bursar*) Vision et Motricité, INSERM Unité 94, 16 Avenue du Doyen Lepoine, F-69500 Bron, France

J. R. Searle Department of Philosophy, University of California at Berkeley, Berkeley, CA 94720, USA

H. Shevrin Department of Psychiatry, University of Michigan, Riverview Building, 900 Wall Street, Ann Arbor, MI 48109-0722, USA

S. Shoemaker The Sage School of Philosophy, 218 Goldwin Smith Hall, Cornell University, Ithaca, NY 14853-3201, USA

J. L. Singer Department of Psychology, Yale University, PO Box 11A, Yale Station, New Haven, CT 06520-7447, USA

E. Strain (*Bursar*) Department of Psychology, University of Nottingham, Nottingham NG7 2RD, UK

G. Underwood Department of Psychology, University of Nottingham, Nottingham NG7 2RD, UK

R. Van Gulick Cognitive Science Program, Syracuse University College of Arts and Sciences, 541 Hall of Languages, Syracuse, NY 13244-1170, USA

M. L. Velmans Department of Psychology, Goldsmiths' College, University of London, New Cross, London SE14 6NW, UK

P. D. Wall Department of Anatomy & Developmental Biology,
University College London, Gower Street, London WC1E 6BT, UK

B. Williams Corpus Christi College, University of Oxford,
Oxford OX1 4JF, UK

What is the mind-body problem?

Thomas Nagel

Department of Philosophy, New York University, New York, NY 10003, USA

Abstract. The mind-body problem exists because we naturally want to include the mental life of conscious organisms in a comprehensive scientific understanding of the world. On the one hand it seems obvious that everything that happens in the mind depends on, or is, something that happens in the brain. On the other hand the defining features of mental states and events, features like their intentionality, their subjectivity and their conscious experiential quality, seem not to be comprehensible simply in terms of the physical operation of the organism. This is not just because we have not yet accumulated enough empirical information: the problem is theoretical. We cannot at present imagine an explanation of colour perception, for example, which would do for that phenomenon what chemistry has done for combustion—an explanation which would tell us in physical terms, and without residue, what the experience of colour perception *is*. Philosophical analyses of the distinguishing features of the mental that are designed to get us over this hurdle generally involve implausible forms of reductionism, behaviouristic in inspiration. The question is whether there is another way of bringing mental phenomena into a unified conception of objective reality, without relying on a narrow standard of objectivity which excludes everything that makes them interesting.

1993 Experimental and theoretical studies of consciousness. Wiley, Chichester (Ciba Foundation Symposium 174) p 1–13

A discussion that brings philosophers together with empirical investigators of the mind and brain may give us all a better idea of the obstacles facing a scientific account of consciousness and of the prospects for overcoming those obstacles. In these introductory remarks (designed to establish my lack of impartiality before assuming the function of chairman), I shall express an opinion about how the scientific and philosophical approaches to the subject are related: I believe their problems are strongly interdependent.

The mind–body problem emerges in philosophy as the direct result of a modern ambition of scientific understanding—the desire to understand the world and everything in it as a unified system, so that the manifest diversity of natural phenomena is explained in terms of a much smaller number of fundamental principles. The special character of conscious mental processes makes it difficult to see how this ambition might be carried out with regard to them, despite the evident close dependence of what happens in the mind on what happens in the brain—a physical system composed of the same elements as any other.

The problem is not just the lack of empirical information about the physical conditions of consciousness; it is that we lack a way of thinking about consciousness that would enable us to say what this empirical information signifies, in particular whether it tells us what consciousness is. The aim of science is to acquire not just information, but understanding—of what things are and why they happen. In the case of consciousness, it is obscure what might provide such understanding. We lack a framework within which to interpret the information we already have, and through which to direct our search for further information that will provide fuller understanding.

The problem is that the defining features of consciousness—subjectivity, intentionality and specific experiential qualities—lack any obvious physical interpretation which further empirical investigation might enable us to refine. The facts of consciousness are facts about how things are *for* some conscious subject, whereas physical facts are facts about how things are, full stop. By contrast, even something as complicated as embryonic development is clearly a physical process, and we have a general idea of what it would be to understand it better in physical terms. That is, we possess the logical framework of biochemical analysis, even if we have not the faintest idea of how the actual physicochemical story goes. Our situation is completely different with respect to visual perception, for example. Perceiving is evidently something that physical organisms do; we already know a great deal about its external physical causes, its neurophysiological conditions and its effects on observable behaviour, as well as its interactions with other mental processes. But all this knowledge surrounds it, so to speak, without providing the kind of internal understanding that would be needed to bring perception into a unified scientific world view.

Many philosophers do not agree with this reading of the situation and much recent work in the philosophy of mind has been devoted to opposing it. This work is based on an assumption of physicalism and proceeds by trying to discover an interpretation of the characteristic features of consciousness which either shows them to be consistent with physicalism or dismisses them as prescientific errors. By physicalism, I mean, in this instance, not a specific view on the mind–body problem but the more general position that the world is a gigantic and complicated physical system and nothing else—at least, the world of space, time and events. So even if many of the things we say about the world do not employ explicitly physical concepts, the fundamental facts are physical facts, the most complete description of everything that exists or happens is physical, and anything else that is true must in some way depend on those facts—not just causally but ontologically.

There are various ways in which one might try to find room for conscious mental processes in such a world. One might identify them with events in the brain or with behavioural dispositions or, in the most common strategy, with functional states of the living organism. Each functional state is supposed to be defined in terms of its characteristic role in a system of internal states which controls the operation of the organism and its behavioural interaction with the environment, and the functional organization is in turn realized in the central nervous system (Lewis 1966, Putnam 1967, Dennett 1991). Great ingenuity has been expended on the attempt to provide reductionist analyses of this sort for the most intractable aspects of consciousness, specifically intentional content and phenomenological qualia (for example, that a visual perception is 'of' a dollar bill and that that shade of green looks to me the particular way it does). However, I believe that these attempts have not succeeded and have no hope of succeeding: if scientific progress in understanding consciousness depends on the success of some kind of reductionism, we are in a discouraging situation. (A more sanguine opinion, of the resources of functionalism in particular, will no doubt be expressed by others at this meeting.)

Yet, my wider outlook is not pessimistic. In some way, conscious mental life obviously must be explained by what happens in the brain, and if we cannot account for this through a reduction of the mental designed to show its compatibility with physicalism, we should be looking for another way to do it. We should begin, I believe, with a less limiting conception of what it is to admit something as part of objective reality. Without resorting to any kind of reductionist analysis, we can say that the existence of conscious mental events is an objective fact, and that the characteristics of these events can be established by different observers, who can correct one another's descriptions fully as much as physical observers can correct one another's measurements. Conscious mental events differ from other objective facts because they are the objects not only of observational or inferential awareness but also of immediate first-person awareness. However, others can know that I am perceiving a dollar bill as well as I can; they can know that it looks green to me, and that the perception of that precise shade has some particular subjective quality for me, even if it remains unclear what exactly they can know about what that quality is.

Some defenders of functionalism (Shoemaker 1975, Van Gulick 1985, Loar 1990) have applied it to the analysis of introspective first-person awareness itself, in an attempt to explain the special character of mental concepts within a theory that employs only the kinds of objective ideas used in physical science. My objection is that this substitutes an external view of our employment of experiential concepts for the direct employment of the concepts themselves, and thus amounts to a denial of the reality of intrinsic experiential qualities. But phenomenological concepts have an authority of their own, which cannot be superseded by a theory of their application that does not employ them *in propria persona*: if we really want to talk about the facts of consciousness, we cannot substitute an external description of the application of phenomenological concepts for their actual use.

I believe we should begin from the natural idea of the objective facts of mental life—facts about how things are *for* conscious subjects—and ask whether a further development of this mentalistic conception is possible which will more readily permit the theoretical integration of mental phenomena with the straightforwardly physical conditions and processes to which they bear such an intimate relation. We have to start, in other words, from the data as we know them and as they are described by that special class of concepts which combine first- and third-person access in their conditions of application. We cannot start from a conceptual and observational repertoire which ignores the most interesting features of the phenomena we are trying to understand: that would be to ignore the data, which is an unscientific way of proceeding, to put it mildly.

The ambition of a truly scientific theory of consciousness should be to make transparent the relation between how things are for conscious subjects and how things are full stop, without reducing the former to some variety of the latter. The problem, though, is that if we try to imagine a scientific refinement of a resolutely mentalistic description of mental life, it is difficult to see how it will reach a point at which it can be fully integrated with a physical science like neurophysiology. The reason is that the objectivity of mental concepts depends not only on external observation and explanatory consistency but also on our capacity to share in a general way each other's point of view—something to which nothing in physical science corresponds. Physical science can aspire to depart farther and farther from dependence on our particular sensory or perceptual constitution, toward a conception that relies only on the explanatory resources of theoretical reason; the objectivity of mental concepts cannot abandon its reliance on the richer resources of our specific animal and human perspective (Davidson 1970, Nagel 1974, 1986).

There is a sense in which the progress of physical science depends on the development of a common point of view. However, this development involves moving progressively away from the natural viewpoint of human perception, toward a mathematical description of a world which is increasingly not just not perceptible, but not even perceptually imaginable. In any case, such a view has no special connection with the way things look or feel to particular organisms. But this is precisely what the description of conscious mental processes does have, which makes it singularly unsuitable for the kind of interlocking explanatory connection with a physical theory that would enable us to advance the project of a scientific understanding of consciousness beyond the discovery of external correspondences.

If one sees the problem in this way, the central question is whether it makes sense to look for a method of conceiving and describing the features of consciousness that both fits into a common theoretical structure with neurophysiological concepts and is true to their nature, rather than being a travesty or denial of it: more grandly, can we discover or create a common vantage point from which it would be possible to see how subjective experience and neurophysiology are internally connected? We would have to begin from the prescientific way of thinking about consciousness and hope that further developments could be guided partly by knowledge of the physical conditions which indicate how the features of consciousness are organized and what their important causal connections are. The question is how far this search for revised descriptions in terms that are more 'made for' physiological psychology—carved out so as to mesh with the physical concepts of the theory—will permit the retention of the features that make consciousness consciousness.

I believe a solution to the basic conceptual problem of non-interlocking systems of ideas is indispensable, but perhaps other kinds of progress can be made piecemeal. One cannot do everything at once. While I am not really in a position to judge, my inclination would be to start with mental phenomena that are not too 'cognitive', that lend themselves to measurement on some quantifiable scale and that already display evident orderly connections with physical variables, either in the body or outside it. The best cases would be those in which the physical variables are themselves interesting, i.e. are governed by relatively simple physical laws. Intensity and, to some extent, colour of light meet this condition, as do intensity and pitch of sound. Perhaps the perception of heat and cold, also, and maybe even the perception of pain that depends directly on a physical quantity like heat. Further, for all three of these types of sensation (auditory, visual and tactile), the relations in experiential space and in experiential time among sensory events provide promising targets for analysis. I am talking here about a *mental* relation, whose connection with physical space and time in the brain remains an open question, one which a psychophysical theory must address.

Most intentional mental states are completely out of reach of this kind of treatment, and I do not know how a scientific programme ought to proceed with them. For example, someone's thinking that the Democrats have very little chance of beating George Bush in the 1992 United States' presidential elections involves not just their brain but complicated relations between them and the rest of the world, such as their knowledge of the English language and of the American political system. Also, whatever one starts with, one must keep in mind that a major problem in any mentalistic theory will be how it conceives of the relation of composition of relatively unified experiences out of mental components. This applies with regard not only to simultaneous experiences from different senses, and complex experiences of a single sense like sight, but even to the analysis of experiences that seem simple into complex wholes—as may be true of the visual perception of shape. It seems inevitable that psychophysical explanation will apply first at the level of some kind of elements of experience; but if these elements come together in a single consciousness, they must also be components of a single point of view. Formation of a scientifically usable but still mentalistic version of this idea would be extremely difficult. The empirical study of the various deconnection syndromes may provide us with some guidance, but this will be indirect. For some of these matters, we can expect to learn about the present state of empirical research in the course of this symposium.

There is a sense in which I share the underlying motivation of the reductionists—to see how a unified theory of consciousness and the brain might be logically possible. But whereas they wish essentially to bring the mind within the domain of physical science, I believe that to be impossible; rather, the methods of scientific description, analysis and explanation have to be extended to include the mind. We are faced with the fact that brains are conscious and have points of view, and our available concepts provide no way of making this fact truly intelligible through the kinds of transparent internal relations among events and properties that a scientific theory can provide. Our mental and physical ideas are too far apart to permit this kind of unification: all they permit are opaque external relations. If a functionalist analysis of mental concepts were correct, this gap would be closed: mind and brain would occupy the same logical space, so to speak, and there would remain only the empirical question of how the brain makes it possible for human beings to operate as functional systems of the requisite type. But I believe functionalism is not a correct account of what consciousness is. Even if it is true that pain or colour vision plays a certain type of functional role in human life, that this role is played by pain or colour vision or any conscious state at all is a fact about us and not a tautology. Likewise the assertion that colour vision is a brain process is neither a tautology nor a statement about the brain process's functional role.

But I think the basic goal of functionalists and physicalists is right, even if the reductionist method of pursuing it is not. We should have in mind the ideal of an explanation of consciousness that shows it to be a necessary feature of certain biological systems—an explanation that allows us to see that such systems could not fail to be conscious. For the purpose of such strong theoretical understanding, merely extensional correspondences are not sufficient. We do not yet have the concepts in which such an explanation could be expressed, just as we did not have the concepts to express an explanation of magnetism before the discovery of electromagnetic fields. Such concepts can be developed only through the process of searching for a strong explanation. Unless we are driven by the demand for this form of understanding, we will not discover these concepts, because we will be satisfied with less—with mere descriptions, correlations and causal generalizations.

It may be objected that to take such a transparent form of explanation as a governing ideal—as what theories must strive toward because we believe it exists even if we have no idea how—is to set an unreasonable condition on science. Why is empirical descriptive adequacy not enough? Of course, we have nothing remotely resembling a *descriptively* adequate psychophysical theory—for either the psychological or the physical elements, let alone the correlation between them. Nevertheless, I believe that is not all we should be aiming for; we should be aiming beyond it toward something stronger, which it is reasonable to believe is there to be found, namely an account of how conscious states are generated by the brain which does not treat the relation as a brute fact. It is a reasonable article of scientific faith that at that level of generality there are no brute facts. Even the apparent impossibility (McGinn 1991) of discovering a transparent internal connection between the physical and the mental should give us hope: apparent impossibilities are a wonderful stimulus to the theoretical imagination.

I think it is inevitable that the pursuit of such an account will lead to an alteration of our conception of the physical world. Unless conscious points of view can be subjected to outright physical reduction, it will not be possible to understand how they necessarily arise in certain kinds of physical systems described only in the terms of contemporary physics and chemistry. In the long run, therefore, physiological psychology should expect cosmological results. This should not be surprising, since physical science has not heretofore tried to take on consciousness: when it does, the effort will transform it radically.

References

Davidson D 1970 Mental events. Republished in: Davidson D 1980 Essays on actions and events. Oxford University Press, Oxford, p 207–225

Dennett DC 1991 Consciousness explained. Little, Brown, Boston, MA

Lewis D 1966 An argument for the identity thesis. J Philos 63:17–25

Loar B 1990 Phenomenal states. In: Tomberlin JE (ed) Philosophical perspectives, vol 4: Action theory and philosophy of mind. Ridgeview Publishing, Atascadero, CA, p 81–108

McGinn C 1991 The problem of consciousness. Basil Blackwell, Oxford

Nagel T 1974 What is it like to be a bat? Philos Rev 83:435–451

Nagel T 1986 The view from nowhere. Oxford University Press, New York

Putnam H 1967 The nature of mental states. Republished in: Putnam H 1975 Philosophical papers, vol 2: Mind, language and reality. Cambridge University Press, Cambridge, p 429–440

Shoemaker S 1975 Functionalism and qualia. Republished in: Shoemaker S 1984 Identity, cause, and mind: philosophical papers. Cambridge University Press, Cambridge, p 184–205

Van Gulick R 1985 Physicalism and the subjectivity of the mental. Philos Top 13:51–70

DISCUSSION

Dennett: Tom, that is wonderfully clear. It does justice to the other side from your perspective—the understanding of the internal relations, which is the goal of objective scientific pursuit. You suggest that this goal cannot be attained in the case of human consciousness.

One thing you didn't acknowledge is that from my perspective this inexplicable residue looks like a rapidly shrinking domain, for which we can use your term, 'how things are for people'. These days, more and more facts that one would intuitively think of as facts about 'how things are for people' are being not only explained but predicted by the developments in science. Ramachandran (1987) came up with a brand new paradoxical motion illusion. He predicted this phenomenology from an understanding of the difference between the parvocellular and the magnocellular pathways. In his example, because the systems for detection motion and colour are distinct, when black dots are moved over a pattern where there is a yellow patch that is isoluminant with the background, the yellow patch paradoxically seems to move and stay in the same place at the same time. It is a very robust effect. Ramachandran predicted that this surprising effect would be there from his understanding of the functional separability of motion, location, colour and luminance. Because the theory said these systems were distinct in the brain, he predicted that they would be distinct phenomenologically, even though this was paradoxical. He turned out to be right.

So we are getting an internal understanding. I would say Ramachandran is rendering transparent a certain feature of 'how things are with people'. He is at the point where he can manipulate the phenomenology of subjects because he understands how the system works. You suggested that all that such work would ever give would be the observable physical surroundings of 'how things are with people'. But that seems to me to ignore the fact that those observable physical surroundings are in some sense what matters to people. If your science can tell you under exactly what conditions a subject will hate a certain stimulus or prefer one circumstance to another, or be unable to distinguish one circumstance from another, it seems to me that to say, 'but that just gives you the observable physical surroundings and circumstances of phenomenology' isn't a fair representation of the facts. As far as I can see, what's left to be inaccessible is pared down to something which one has to take on faith as making a difference even though it doesn't make any detectable difference. At that point, it seems to me, science would say, 'there's nothing left to explain'.

Nagel: Of course, many things about the physical surroundings are very important. It matters to me that I can make a headache go away by taking aspirin. It may even be that we could explain a great deal of what people do without referring to their conscious states. Still, if those conscious states exist, they are something that we should want to understand.

But data of the kind you cite, which allow us to predict and manipulate conscious states, don't yet provide us with the strong form of understanding of how conscious states arise from the brain. This is parallel to the situation in which, for example, a lot was known about the results and possibilities of certain kinds of chemical combinations before the development of the atomic theory. An important further step was made when we moved from the, often very systematic, knowledge about what would combine with what to yield what, to an understanding of what these substances and chemical reactions really were.

Dennett: But I am saying we are doing that: we are predicting entirely novel, never before seen on the planet, phenomenological effects, because we have the deep understanding (in a few simple cases) of the mechanics of them. This isn't simply putting together the phenomenological knowledge of the past, this is predicting new phenomenological effects. It is precisely analogous to creating new materials composed of novel organic molecules.

Marcel: Ramachandran doesn't actually make predictions on the basis of an understanding of the relationship between the brain states and the phenomenology. There is nothing in the theory that says anything about that relationship.

Humphrey: All Ramachandran would have predicted, if he had been prepared to spell it out, would have been that in certain circumstances people would *say* something specific—utter certain words.

Dennett: Say something, believing it—smiting their foreheads and saying 'it is paradoxical phenomenology'.

Humphrey: Tom Nagel wants to deny that people merely saying something is sufficient for access to their first-person phenomenology. Yet, while Tom claims there is a residue behind any behavioural data one could have, the only reason one could have for believing there is a residue is behaviour. Tom, you say that it's clear to you that babies, animals and so on are conscious. But why is it clear to you, unless it's that in certain circumstances, they *do* certain things which you associate with being conscious?

Nagel: I don't deny that behaviour is our evidence for other people's mental states. I deny only that functionalist analyses tell me what conscious states *are*. Facts about behaviour and circumstances and physiology provide us with evidence of consciousness, but there is a distinction in general between evidence and what it is evidence for. That's true of chemistry as well.

Humphrey: True of chemistry, true of immunology and so on. But when people come up with a *theory* of the immune system, surely it has to be a theory of the objective evidence for immunity.

Nagel: A theory of the immune system isn't a theory of the evidence for anything.

Humphrey: It is a theory of why the evidence is as it is.

Velmans: In Dennett's analysis, you could say that he is confounding what causes things with what things are like. You might, for instance, give a causal story of what makes people happy and still not know what happiness was. This would be true even if the neural causal antecedents of happiness were known. Neural causes and conscious effects are quite separate things. One could give a complete third-person account of stimulus conditions, brain processing and consequent behaviour, without specifying in any full sense how such things are experienced. Conscious effects can really be known only from a first-person point of view, and that is in no way reducible to a third-person functional story.

Lockwood: Can that be the right way to put it? It seems to me that both you, Max, in your defence of Tom Nagel, and Dan Dennett, in his criticism of Tom, were talking as though Tom's view was a dualist view, which it's not; Tom has described himself as a dual aspect theorist. Dan used this term 'surroundings', as though all the neurophysiological stuff was the 'surroundings' but the subjective impressions were something else. But that is not at all what is being suggested. A person who takes Tom's view will think that some of the things that are going on in the brain, some of the things that figure in Ramachandran's work and so on, actually *are* the subjective states. The sense in which there is a residue is not that there is an *ontological* residue—it's not that we think there are some extra events going on that are somehow invisible to the neurophysiologist. Rather, it's an *explanatory* residue. What remains unexplained, here, is why any of these brain processes should have a subjective aspect to them at all.

Gray: I think Mike has that right. I would like to make the same point in a slightly different way. Dan, you say we have a theory which is able to predict certain phenomena and then one can investigate whether those phenomena are correct. Compare the nature of that theory with the theory we have of electricity. There was a time when one could make predictions about what happened when you rubbed amber with velvet. But that was different from what happened once there was a theory of electromagnetism. The point about that theory is that it is a theory about electrons, and these are the very stuff of electricity—if the theory is correct, and there is a lot of evidence that it is. In contrast, for the kinds of experiments that Ramachandran has done, the theory is about brain systems; it's a theory about neurons and how they interact and how they in some way deal with physical information entering the retina. It is not a theory about the stuff of conscious experience in the way that electromagnetism is a theory about electrons.

Dennett: I am glad you raised that example, Jeffrey, because it lets me remind people of an old-fashioned use of the term 'phenomenology' which I would love to resurrect. Long before magnets or electricity were well understood, what scientists did with regard to those phenomena was what they called phenomenology. They tried to compile an explicit, detailed, objective, neutral catalogue of all the phenomena, everything that happened that made a detectable difference—that was what phenomenology was. You had phenomenology first, then you tried to get a theory out of it. I am proposing phenomenology of the mind—a neutral, objective description of every detectable difference that you can find.

Gray: As an endpoint, or as a way of gathering the data?

Dennett: That's the phenomenology; then you try to get a scientific account which, in the way Tom suggests, gives you the internal relations, it gives you the transparent explanation of why that's the phenomenology. Max Velmans said that I was proposing to give just the causes; I also propose to explain the effects. But when you have explained all the causes and all the effects that are detectable, I claim you have explained all the phenomenology. That's the way it is with electricity, that's the way it is with magnets, and I'm not yet convinced that that isn't the way it is with the mind.

Velmans: I was saying that conscious effects don't reduce to their antecedent neural causes. In principle, one might give a neural causal explanation of given conscious states, but how those states are experienced from a first-person point of view isn't part of the third-person causal story—so it can't be reduced to it.

Nagel: What do you mean by all the causes and all the effects? You mean the observable physical conditions and responses.

Marcel: No, he means what people say. In the Ramachandran experiments, the effects are the words of the subject, literally 'My God, it seemed to move'. Now, you would leave out 'My God', you would leave out 'it seemed', and be left with 'it moved'. But, I want to know whether those subjects are talking *about* anything. On Dennett's views, I don't know if they are talking *about anything.*

Williams: Tom, one question that has to be answered is why what you want is not a contradiction. To gain the transparent account, one would require something called 'the third-person view of the first-person view'. But what's going to count as a third-person view of the first-person view? It isn't enough to have the third-person view of everything that happens when there is a first-person view, it has to be a third-person view that *preserves* the first-person view. It is simply not clear that there could be such a thing as a third-person view that preserved the first-person view. If there could not be such a thing, what is the stopping point before saying that the requirement in transparent integration for consciousness into science is simply contradictory?

Nagel: The reason I think the problem is so difficult is that if we are limited to our present conceptual apparatus, its solution does seem to involve a contradiction. I think of this as a limitation in our present way of thinking about these things. For one thing, the facts of consciousness are not just first-personal, they are third-personal too, but the kind of third-personal that is inseparably connected with the possibility of immediate first-person access. What we should be looking for is not a third-person view of that peculiar, partly first-person material, but something that gets us out of the duality and allows us to think about facts of both of these kinds in a single form of understanding. Of course, just to say that isn't to get out of the contradiction.

Harnad: But what makes you optimistic, Tom? Do you have any inductive grounds for optimism? You specialize in giving *negative* analogies to suggest that precisely the pattern of conceptual revision that has worked so successfully in previous cases (e.g. matter, life) is doomed to fail in the special case of mind. I construe the example of electricity as falling under that same *dis*analogy. Some sort of unspecified new concept is clearly needed here, which you apparently think is possible, yet in the past you have given every reason for such a concept not being possible.

In your publications (Nagel 1974, 1986), you have said that in all previous cases, successful reconceptualization has involved replacing one subjective (first-person) view of an objective (third-person) phenomenon with another; that's what it is to have and understand a new empirical concept. That was how we came to see electricity as a flow of charge instead of as an elementary force, life as macrobiomolecular properties, etc. The *dis*analogy is that in the special case of mind we are trying to replace *subjectivity itself* with something other than subjectivity—appearances by something other than other appearances. There is no precedent for such a move in any of the other successful cases of scientific reconceptualization. Hence, each prior case seems to add inductive evidence *against* optimism in the special case of trying to reconceptualize mind as something physical or functional.

Velmans: I have a real problem with the notion that Tom Nagel's problem is a real problem. Psychology, as a matter of course (in my view), relates the third- and first-person perspectives continuously. Take a very simple perception experiment in which a subject is presented with a coloured spot on a screen and asked to report what he sees. The subject might say, 'I experience the colour red'. That is a first-person account. There is nothing to prevent a third-person explanation of the antecedent causes of that report, in terms of stimulus conditions, sense organ transduction, neural processing and so on. There is nothing to prevent one believing that the subject is actually experiencing a colour. One simply moves from a third-person account, which is in terms of physical energies, sense organ response and neural processing, to a first-person account of what the subject experiences. Of course, there are some interesting empirical questions about how third- and first-person accounts relate to each other; you might, for example, investigate the precise conditions in the brain which lead to a report or an experience of the colour red as opposed to the colour blue. But for explanatory purposes, this transition from third- to first-person accounts is a smooth one, and we do it all the time in psychology.

Marcel: It is not a smooth transition and that is one of the reasons I have problems with some of the things you seem to assume. You said brains necessarily give rise to experiences. Why do you think this? It seems to me there is a problem here, and we can approach it in three ways. First, we might try to treat it as a vehicle/content distinction. Second, we might treat it as a supervenience. In neither case do brains *necessarily* give rise to experience.

Thirdly, there is a problem of selfhood. Experiences are 'how it is for me'. Several phenomena seem to imply the necessity of selfhood for conscious experience, and therefore for the reality of selfhood. I don't believe that brains *per se* give rise to selves. I am something of a dualist on this, since I don't believe that brains do it, but rather that the level of causation is that of the social and cultural.

Nagel: That is not to be a dualist. My brain by itself can't generate the thought 'Bush will probably win the election in the fall'. That involves a great deal else besides what's going on in my brain. But this doesn't mean that my brain doesn't give rise to the basically biological core of sensation, appetite and so forth, which underlies the higher and more 'social' mental functions.

Marcel: My point is that if certain personal level aspects are necessarily involved —not in self-reflexive self-consciousness, but in the sensations themselves, i.e. that what they are is how things are for us—there is a problem there of a slightly different type. It is a type of problem that is not faced by other sciences.

Fenwick: The question of whether consciousness is totally dependent on the brain is a very important one. An example where consciousness seems to be totally independent of the brain is the near-death experience. In the near-death experience there is now evidence that information of the outside world can be experienced by a personal representation of the self in a way that doesn't seem to make use of the ordinary sense organs. This may seem unscientific, but I have listened to 500–600 accounts of people who have had this particular experience. In this experience, which often occurs after coronary thrombosis, the subject has the impression of leaving their body, travelling down corridors, away from the intensive care unit where their body is being rehabilitated, entering rooms and picking up information that could only have been picked up with their mind. The reductionist explanation suggests that this is either the falsification of memory, or it's to do with the generation of a different conceptual world. For example, the brain may re-run the spatial coordinates of self and put the self on the ceiling. Nevertheless, I think there is evidence that people can get information when out of their body in a way that doesn't use the physical eyes and ears of the body. If this is true, we have to think of mind in a different way, i.e. that the mind and body are separate. I suggest that it is still too early to have theories of an exact relationship between brain and mind. Dan Dennett tells us that mind is totally explicable by brain and that modern science can totally explain consciousness. I disagree. I'm not even sure that our basic understanding of the relationship of consciousness to the brain is, as yet, correct.

Gray: I cannot resist the opportunity to put into print my favourite experiment that I have never been able to do. I have often read descriptions of the near-death experience; it is the perfect subject for experimental test. You need a ward in which you could be reasonably certain that quite a large number of people will over a year or so be nearly at death's door. You have a rather high structure in the ward and written on the top, where nobody can see it, is a message, known only to the experimenter or, even better, kept in a sealed envelope in the Bank of England. When people say that they had felt they were hovering outside their body in this near-death state, one could ask them, 'What was the message?'

Fenwick: Jeffrey, that is in progress at this very minute!

References

Nagel T 1974 What is it like to be a bat? Philos Rev 83:435–451
Nagel T 1986 The view from nowhere. Oxford University Press, New York
Ramachandran VS 1987 Interaction between colour and motion in human vision. Nature 328:645–647

Functionalism and consciousness

Sydney Shoemaker

The Sage School of Philosophy, 218 Goldwin Smith Hall, Cornell University, Ithaca, NY 14853-3201, USA

Abstract. It is widely held that a mental state and the subject's introspective belief about it are always 'distinct existences' and only contingently connected. This suggests that for each sort of mental state there could be a creature that is introspectively 'blind' with respect to states of that sort, meaning that while it is capable of having such states, and of conceiving of itself as having them, it is totally without introspective access to its states of that sort. It is argued here that introspective blindness with respect to many sorts of mental states, in particular beliefs and sensory states, is not a possibility, because it is incompatible with requirements of rationality that are internal to the functional roles that are constitutive of these states. Introspective accessibility is essential to the functional roles of such mental states when the conceptual and cognitive resources of the subject of those states are sufficiently rich to make beliefs and thoughts about them a possibility. This is a version of the view that such states are necessarily self-intimating and is incompatible with the perceptual model of introspection favoured by some functionalists as well as by many non-functionalists.

1993 Experimental and theoretical studies of consciousness. Wiley, Chichester (Ciba Foundation Symposium 174) p 14–42

One way of formulating functionalism is by saying that mental states are defined, or constituted, by functional or causal roles. But not all of the causal role that a given mental state occupies in a given sort of creature will belong to its *defining* or *constitutive* functional role. In humans, wishing something were so has a tendency to generate the belief that the thing is so; but no one would suppose that no creature would count as a wisher or believer unless it had this tendency to engage in wishful thinking. This raises a question about the status of our conscious access to our own mental states. Everyone will agree that in humans part of the causal role of many of the mental states recognized by folk psychology is to produce introspective awarenesses of themselves, which for now I will equate with producing beliefs of a certain kind—beliefs that the subject is angry, in pain, desirous of a drink, or whatever. The question is whether this 'introspective link', as I will call it, is an essential feature of these causal roles, part of the defining or constitutive roles of the mental states in question, or

14

only an accidental feature of them, like the propensity to engage in wishful thinking.

The question may seem easy to answer. We ascribe many of these mental states to lower animals, about which it is at least very doubtful whether they have any capacity for introspective awareness, because it is very doubtful whether they have the concepts, of their own states and of themselves, that the introspective beliefs would require. Does this not show that the introspective link is not essential to such states? An analogy will help reveal why it does not. We have a notion of 'being in charge' which applies both to the man who is in charge of the butcher's shop at the local supermarket and to the man in charge of the sales division of General Motors. Obviously, what is involved in being in charge in the two cases is very different. To know what counts as being in charge in a particular case, you have to know more than the abstract definition of the notion; you also have to know the nature of the organization or institution in question. Likewise, in the case of a mental concept that is applicable to both humans and mice, in order to know what counts as having that state in a particular case, you have to know more than the abstract concept; you have to know something about the overall functional architecture of the creature in question. In any creature, we may suppose, perceptual experiences must play a role in the fixation of belief and the regulation of behaviour. If a creature, e.g. a mouse, is not capable of having higher-order thoughts, then in that creature playing this role cannot involve having higher-order thoughts. But it is compatible with this that in creatures that are capable of such thoughts, playing this role does involve having higher-order thoughts. So it might well be true in the case of humans, but not in the case of mice, that an essential feature of being in certain mental states is that the subject is aware, or apt under certain circumstances to become aware, that she is in them. Henceforth, when I discuss whether the introspective link is essential, I will be discussing whether it is essential in creatures cognitively and conceptually comparable with humans.

I think the view that the introspective link is not essential, i.e. does not belong to the defining or constitutive functional roles of folk psychological states, is widely held. Various sorts of considerations seem to lend it support. There is the evidence psychologists have gathered of the fallibility of many kinds of introspective reports (see Nisbett & Wilson 1977) and about such phenomena as 'blindsight' (see Weiskrantz 1987). There is the fruitfulness of research programmes in cognitive psychology which postulate psychological states and activities that are wholly inaccessible to consciousness. And there are philosophical considerations of the sort that figure in David Armstrong's 'distinct existences argument'—the argument that introspective beliefs, or introspective awarenesses, must be thought of as causal effects of the mental states that are objects of awareness, that causes and effects must be 'distinct existences', and that distinct existences, as Hume taught us, can be only contingently connected (see Armstrong 1963, 1968).

I shall speak of the view that the introspective link is only an accidental feature of the causal role of folk psychological mental states as the contingency thesis. I will now argue against a strong version of this thesis, according to which, for each kind of mental state it is possible for there to be a creature that is, as I will say, introspectively self-blind (for short, self-blind) with respect to states of that sort. Just as ordinary blindness is a perceptual rather than a cognitive deficiency, self-blindness is to be thought of as a quasi-perceptual rather than a cognitive deficiency. The self-blind creature will have the concept of the mental state in question, and will be able to entertain the thought that she has it, but will entirely lack the capacity to come to know introspectively that she has it or does not. If she does come to know this, it will be on the basis of 'third-person' evidence, e.g. information about her behaviour or physiological condition.

What an opponent of the contingency thesis should maintain is that the introspective link is implicit in features of the causal roles of folk psychological states that anyone (or at least any functionalist) would regard as essential to them. A notion that figures prominently in some versions of functionalism is that of rationality. The idea is that it is constitutive of certain kinds of mental states that their relations to inputs, outputs and other mental states is such as to bestow on the creature at least a minimal degree of rationality. For example, beliefs must at least tend to give rise to other beliefs to which they give evidential support, and to contribute to the production of behaviour likely to satisfy the creature's wants in circumstances in which the beliefs are true. And pains must at least tend to give rise to behaviour aimed at eliminating them or preventing their recurrence. To be the subject of such mental states, a self-blind creature would have to have the required degree of rationality. I shall argue that given that a creature has cognitive and conceptual capacities comparable with ours, its having the required degree of rationality involves its being disposed to behave in just the ways introspective access to its mental states should lead it to behave. To suppose that such a creature might nevertheless be self-blind is to suppose that introspective awareness is either epiphenomenal or, at best, just one of several ways of implementing the requirements of rationality. Anyone who holds this view will be hard pressed to find a satisfactory reason for thinking that *we* have introspective awareness of our mental states. A better view is that the contingency claim is false, and that introspective access supervenes on minimal rationality plus human cognitive and conceptual capacities.

I begin with an argument about belief that I have given elsewhere (see Shoemaker 1988, 1991). A rational agent who believes that P will be disposed to use the proposition that P as a premise in her reasonings. Moreover, she will know that for any proposition, if that proposition is true then, other things being equal, it is in anyone's interest to act on the assumption that it is true—for one is most likely to achieve one's aims if one acts on assumptions that are true. She will also know that to act on the assumption that something is true is to act as if one believes the thing; and she will know that if it is in one's interest to act in this way, it will be in one's interest to make manifest to others that one is so acting. This will increase the likelihood that other believers in the truth of the proposition will cooperate with her in endeavours whose success depends on the truth of the proposition, and it will tend to promote belief in that proposition within the community and so to promote the success of endeavours whose success depends both on the proposition being true and on its being believed to be true by participants in the endeavours. Knowing that it is in anyone's interest to act in these ways if a proposition is true, she will know that it is in her own interest so to act. So she can reason as follows: 'P is true. So it is in my interest to act as if I believed that P and, in normal circumstances, to act in ways that would make others believe that I believe that P. Since the circumstances are normal, I should so act.' Given that she is rational enough to act in conformity with the conclusions of her own practical reasoning, and to know what will make others believe that she believes something, such reasoning should lead her to behave in the ways characteristic of someone trying to manifest to others that she believes that P, including saying 'I believe that P'.

The reason for pointing out that such reasoning is available is not to suggest that it regularly goes on in us—obviously it does not—but rather to bring out that in order to explain the behaviour we take as showing that people have certain higher-order beliefs we do not need to attribute to them anything beyond what is needed for them to have first-order beliefs plus normal intelligence, rationality and conceptual capacity. The availability of the reasoning shows that the first-order states rationalize the behaviour. In supposing that a creature is rational, one is supposing that it is such that its being in certain states tends to result in effects, behaviour or other internal states, that are rationalized by those states. Sometimes this requires actually going through a process of reasoning in which one gets from one proposition to another by a series of steps, and where special reasoning skills are involved, but usually it does not. I see an apple and I reach for it. It is rational for me to do so, and this can be shown by presenting a piece of practical reasoning that is available to me, citing my desires and my beliefs about the nutritional and other properties of apples. But I need not actually go through any process of sequential reasoning in order for the beliefs and desires in question to explain and make rational my reaching for the apple. Similarly, the rational agent does not need to go through a process of sequential reasoning in order for her first-order belief that P, plus her other first-order beliefs and desires, to explain and rationalize the behaviour that manifests the second-order belief that she believes that P.

There are other considerations that support the claim that rationality requires introspective access to beliefs. One is that the appropriate revision of one's belief–desire system in the face of new experience would seem to require some sort of awareness of its contents (see McGinn 1982, Shoemaker 1988). But rather than pursue this, I want to move to the case of perceptual experiences.

Someone with normal perceptual access to things in the environment must at least be sensitive to the nature of her perceptual experiences, in the sense that the perceptual judgements she makes about things in the environment must be a function of her perceptual experiences, of how she is 'appeared to', together with her background beliefs, in particular her beliefs about perceptual conditions. This is not to say that her perceptual judgements are *inferred* from, among other things, the nature of the perceptual experiences. Normally, it is the having of the experience, not the belief that one has it, that issues in the perceptual judgement, and normally the beliefs about perceptual conditions that contribute to the judgement are only tacit. Still, the person must be sensitive to a vast number of combinations of experiences and beliefs about perceptual conditions. If she has an experience 'as of' red when looking at a wall and believes that the conditions are normal, she will judge that the wall is red; if she has that same experience and believes that the wall is illuminated by red light, she may judge that it is white. The question is whether a person could have the appropriate sensitivity to combinations of experiences and beliefs without having the capacity to be aware of the experiences.

The best we can do by way of conceiving of such a case is to suppose that our putative self-blind person is 'hard wired' to respond to various experience–belief combinations by making the appropriate perceptual judgements. Such a person would in some cases be in a position to infer that she was having a certain kind of experience—knowing what perceptual judgement she had made and knowing what her belief about perceptual conditions is, she would infer what her perceptual experience must be. But she would show her self-blindness by her inability to say what her visual experience is like, or how things appear to her, if she is deprived of information about perceptual conditions.

But I deny that this should count as a case of self-blindness, for I deny that the person, as described, has perceptual experiences of the sorts to which we have introspective access. By hypothesis, she has states that play part of the functional role of perceptual experiences. In combination with certain beliefs about perceptual conditions, these states give rise to the same perceptual judgements about the world that certain of our perceptual experiences give rise to when combined with those same beliefs. But this is not enough.

Beliefs about perceptual conditions are themselves often grounded on our perceptual experiences. Sometimes, thrown into an unfamiliar setting, we simultaneously reason to conclusions about what sorts of things we are perceiving and conclusions about what the perceptual conditions are. The beliefs that influence our judgements are not limited to beliefs about perceptual conditions. Any of one's beliefs about how perceptible things behave under various conditions, and about how the appearances of things change under various conditions, can play a role in determining one's perceptual judgements about how things are in one's vicinity. Think, for example, of how one might move from a belief that one is perceiving some ordinary object to the belief that one must be the victim of some holographic or drug-produced illusion; or how one might move from a suspicion that the latter is true to a firm belief that things are after all as they appear. In such cases, one is engaged in a certain kind of low-level theorizing. The data for the theorizing include facts about how one is appeared to, i.e. about the nature of one's experiences. So while perceptual judgements are often not inferred from facts about experiences, sometimes they are. Having normal perceptual access to things in one's environment requires having the capacity to engage in this sort of theorizing, and therefore requires having access to the facts about current experience that provide the data for it. In so far as the constitutive functional role of perceptual experiences is their role in providing perceptual access to the world, it requires, in creatures with cognitive and conceptual resources comparable with ours, their introspective accessibility.

If, as I have suggested, it is of the essence of many kinds of mental states and phenomena to reveal themselves to introspection, what sort of account can we give of the relation of these to the introspective awareness of them? Take the case of belief. A natural way of thinking is to say that the belief that P is one thing, the introspective belief that one believes that P is another, and that introspective awareness consists in the first giving rise to the second. Going with this is a way of thinking about how these mental states are realized in the brain. The belief that P is realized in one neural state, perhaps a highly distributed one, the belief that one believes that P is realized in another, and the brain is so wired that, under certain conditions, the first neural state gives rise to the second. This is what suggests that the existence of the belief should be logically independent of its being accessible to introspection, and that self-blindness with respect to belief ought to be a possibility. How are we to avoid this without denying, what seems obvious, that to believe something is not the same as to believe that one believes it?

When we speak of the realization, or implementation, of a mental state, we should distinguish between what I call the *core realization* of it and what I call the *total realization* of it. The core realization will be a state that comes and goes as the mental state comes and goes, and is such that, given relatively permanent features of the organism, it plays the 'causal role' associated with that mental state—it is caused by the standard causes of that state and causes its standard effects, usually in conjunction with other states. The total realization will be the core realization plus those relatively permanent features of the organism, of the way its brain is 'wired', which enable the core realization to play that causal role.

This suggests two ways in which a mental state and the belief that one has that mental state could be different and yet such that it is of the essence of the mental state that under certain conditions it gives rise to that belief. One possibility is that while the two states have different core realizations, and so different total realizations, their total realizations overlap in a certain way. Suppose that the core realization of pain in us is neural state N1, and that the core realization of the belief that one is in pain is neural state N2. While these are distinct states, it could be that the total realization of pain includes being such that under certain conditions N1 causes N2, and that the same thing is part of the total realization of the belief that one is in pain. If all the possible total realizations of a state and of the belief that one is in that state were related in this way, it would be of the essence of that state that under certain circumstances it tends to give rise to that belief; it might also be of the essence of that belief that in the absence of malfunctioning it is caused by that state. This would amount to the state's being self-intimating and the belief's being, if not infallible, at least highly authoritative.

This is not the only way in which we could get this result. Instead of the first-order state and the belief about it having different core realizations but overlapping total realizations, it might be that they have the same core realization and that the total realization of the first-order state is a proper part of the total realization of the first-person belief that one has it. I suggest this is how it might be when the two states are, respectively, the first-order belief that the sun is shining and the second-order belief that one believes that the sun is shining. My earlier discussion suggested that if one has a first-order belief *and* has a certain degree of rationality, intelligence and conceptual capacity (here including having the concept of belief and the concept of oneself), then automatically one has the corresponding second-order belief. If it is possible to have the first order-belief without having the second-order belief, this is because it is possible to have it without having that degree of rationality, intelligence and conceptual capacity. This can happen either because the conceptual resources of the creature are limited, as in the case of lower animals, or because the rationality of the creature is in some way impaired, as in cases where the states are unconscious in the Freudian sense. But according to this conception, all you have to add to the first-order belief in order to get the second-order belief is the appropriate degree of intelligence, etc. It is not that adding this pushes the creature into a new state (distinct from any it was in before), which is the core realization of believing that it has this belief. It is rather that adding this enables the core realization of the first-order belief to play a more encompassing causal role, one that makes it the core realization of the second-order belief as well as of the first-order belief.

If, as I have suggested, believing that one believes that P is just believing that P plus having a certain level of rationality, intelligence and so on, so that the first-order belief and the second-order belief have the same core realization, then it will be altogether wrong to think of the second-order belief as *caused* by the first-order belief it is about. Here the relation of an 'introspective' belief to the state of affairs it is about is altogether different from the relation of a perceptual belief to the state of affairs it is about. In the other sort of case, where the first-order mental state and the belief about it have different core realizations but overlapping total realizations, there is a sense in which the first-

order state can cause the belief about it; it can cause it in the sense that its core
realization causes the core realization of that belief. But this causal relationship
is altogether different from the sort that holds beween a perceived state of affairs
and the perceptual belief about it. Thought of as a relation between the mental
states, rather than one between their realizations, the relation is an internal one,
whose relata are not 'distinct existences'. Either way, our introspective access
to our own mental states differs markedly from our perceptual access to things
in our environment.

References

Armstrong DM 1963 Is introspective knowledge incorrigible? Philos Rev 72:417–432
Armstrong DM 1968 A materialist theory of the mind. Routledge, London
McGinn C 1982 The character of mind. Oxford University Press, Oxford
Nisbett R, Wilson TD 1977 Telling more than we can know: verbal reports on mental
    processes. Psychol Rev 84:231–259
Shoemaker S 1988 On knowing one's own mind. Philos Perspect 4:187–214
Shoemaker S 1991 Rationality and self-consciousness. In: Lehrer K, Sosa E (eds) The
    opened curtain, a US–Soviet philosophy summit. Westview Press, Boulder, CO,
    p 127–149
Weiskrantz L 1987 Neuropsychology and the nature of consciousness. In: Blakemore C,
    Greenfield S (eds) Mindwaves. Blackwell Publishers, Oxford, p 307–320

DISCUSSION

Gray: To me, a fundamental question is this: what do beliefs have to do with
our problems at all? Our problems are concerned with consciousness. If I walked
onto an escalator that, unknown to me, was not moving, I would demonstrate
very clearly by my stumbling that I believed that the escalator was moving, that
I believe escalators usually move, and that I believe that when I get onto a moving
escalator I have to make all sorts of postural adjustments. Although I would
be acting rationally and intelligently and doing all of those things that you have
just described, I wouldn't have the slightest conscious awareness in advance
of stepping on the escalator, that I was having any of these beliefs. If I train
a rat to turn left for food in a T-maze, then I repeat the trial but take the food
away, the rat's behaviour is entirely rational and demonstrates perfectly clearly
its belief that there is food on the left and not the right side of the T-maze.
I don't make any inferences about consciousness in that case. However, if I
accidentally catch its tail in the guillotine door and it jumps like crazy, I will
at once assume that it had the conscious experience of pain. So belief is not
part of the problem.

Shoemaker: I wasn't saying that beliefs are sufficient for consciousness, I
was saying that one case of consciousness is being conscious that you believe

something. Tom Nagel said earlier (this volume) that there are cases of consciousness that don't involve introspective consciousness, and I agree with that. Sometimes the consciousness is perceptual consciousness of states of affairs in the world. I was focusing, however, on the consciousness we have of our own mental states, including our beliefs which are just one special case. I was raising the question of what kind of connection there is between being in those states and having conscious access to them.

Gray: Let me give you another example, in which I was the subject and there seemed to me to be a very clear conscious experience, but my beliefs were totally ambiguous. I once had a cartilage removed from one knee and for some time I occasionally felt pain in the other knee in the daytime. For a long period after that, I had the following recurrent experience. I would wake up in the middle of the night believing (in your sense of 'believing', but for me dreaming, feeling or having the sensation) that I had pain in the remaining knee cartilage. The moment I woke up, the pain disappeared from my consciousness. I was never able to come to a clear belief as to whether I had been dreaming that I was in pain, without there being any real source of pain in my knee, or whether I really did have pain in my knee and, the moment I woke up, descending inhibition from the brain switched the pain off. So I had conscious experience and total ambiguity of beliefs about what it was. I think they are quite separate issues.

Shoemaker: I think the notion of a conscious experience is a very hazy notion; it is used to cover a number of different things. Sometimes when people talk about 'conscious experience' they mean a general term covering any kind of sensation, sometimes it's used for those states that occur in our consciousness of the environment, so it becomes more or less synonymous with 'perceptual states'. Sometimes it's used to mean experience of which the subject is conscious, which is something else yet again. We should not suppose that the term 'consciousness' is univocal, that it has one standard meaning.

Searle: Yes, but it's pretty clear what Jeffrey Gray is talking about. Of course, there are lots of different meanings of conscious experience, but the point he was making doesn't depend on the ambiguity of the notion of conscious experience.

Van Gulick: Part of what Sydney Shoemaker is proposing is an exploration of the relation between functionalism and consciousness. Functionalists have tried to see how much mileage you can get out of understanding consciousness in terms of higher-order intentionality, i.e. intentionality about other intentional states. Beliefs about beliefs or beliefs about other mental states (such as desires) would be one special case of this. But there might be lots of other higher-order intentional states that are much less properly characterized as beliefs.

Sydney, you talk about a personal level awareness, but isn't there a lot of room for non-personal level awareness that might actually play a more basic role in getting consciousness going? For example, part of what is salient about visual consciousness is that even if we are not being particularly reflective or introspective, we are still aware of what we are seeing. I look around this room and am immediately aware of what I'm seeing; I don't see it all, but I see a lot. Built into the visual system, not necessarily into the person but into this system, is a kind of information processing that involves a great degree of awareness on the part of the system of what it is that it's dealing with. I think this should count as non-personal level self-awareness. In learning, for example, you could ask: If we weren't aware of our beliefs, how could we update them on the basis of new evidence? But, does a person have to be aware of these beliefs? What about a dog? Can a dog update its beliefs? I assume it can, but to do so the dog need not have personal level awareness of its beliefs; there need only be some system in the dog that has some kind of implicit awareness, built in to how it processes new information. If during evolution the dog had not developed the ability to accommodate this new information, to understand the new information, to understand what it represents about the world, the dog wouldn't know how to make the required adjustments—but it does. It's not necessarily the dog at a personal level that has this higher-order awareness, it's more the dog at what Dan Dennett calls the sub-personal level, it's the system.

Shoemaker: I agree with that. But it's not clear that wherever there is awareness at a sub-personal level or wherever there is registration of information, processing of information and so on, there is consciousness. There could be sub-personal mechanisms that engage in a lot of such activity, but where we would not want to describe anything conscious going on at all.

Lockwood: Sydney, are you committed to the view that if you believe that you have a belief, that second-order belief must be a conscious belief?

Searle: There seems to be an infinite regress. Sydney, the way I understood your talk was you showed that if you had a belief, then normal rationality would automatically generate the belief that you have the belief. That leads to an infinite regress.

Shoemaker: If the issue is considered, then there is the second-order belief. If you don't consider whether you have the belief, then the second-order belief will be only tacit.

Searle: Then for every belief, if I am a rational agent, I have an infinite number of tacit second- and higher-order beliefs.

Wall: I think it can be resolved in an infinite *progress*. If you examine patients soon after an accident, 40% of them say, 'Doctor, you won't believe it, it doesn't hurt'.

Searle: That's a mind stopper! I assume the doctor does believe it!

There is a question about the connection between what Sydney said and consciousness. It isn't transparent to me that there *is* any connection. Sydney's view implies that for every belief we have, we must have an infinite number of beliefs. Sydney says we shouldn't worry, because we don't have to think about these infinite beliefs. But that seems to commit him to the view that his account has nothing to do with consciousness.

Marcel: The problems that arise within varieties of anosognosia are relevant to this, where the person has a neurological deficit, but they don't know they have it. There is the distancing from self. There is a nice example described by Bisiach & Geminiani (1991). The patient apparently has no sensation in their arm; when the doctor tests them, they have no sensation. Then, outside of the testing situation, but still unseen by the patient, the clinician drops something on the patient's arm. The patient may say, 'Careful doctor, you may hurt my fiancée's arm'. Which sort of belief are you talking about?

Shoemaker: It is clear that the person knows about something, but they don't have the appropriate first-person knowledge of it. It is like the example in Dickens' *Hard Times*. Mrs Gradgrind is dying and her daughter goes up to see her. The daughter goes into the room and says 'Mother, have you a pain?' Mrs Gradgrind replies: 'There is a pain, but I cannot be sure that *I* have it'.

Marcel: Sydney, I thought that for the first-order state (which I am going to take as sensation) to be phenomenal, in one view one had to have access. Clearly, it has phenomenal status.

Nagel: If you think somebody has hurt your fiancée, it's not like feeling a sensation.

Marcel: But the way that the person in this case knew about it was not purely informational.

Gray: There's a possible explanation of that sort of phenomenon which need not suppose that the person whose arm was touched had any sensation at all. It could be that the neural message which starts in the arm somehow gets hooked into language systems where the word 'hurt' surfaces without any other sensory experience attached. Confabulation based on the word 'hurt' could then do the rest.

Marcel: I do not understand how 'a neural message starting in the arm gets hooked into language systems'. The patient is describing a sensation. We do not have access to normal states, only to the contents of percepts and sensations.

Harnad: Tony, I'm inclined to accept your interpretation. But let's say that in situations where people say 'There's a pain and it's not mine, it's my neighbour's', what's really happening is that they are feeling a pain but some interpretative process is misinterpreting the pain. That's just evidence in favour of what I took to be Jeffrey Gray's point, namely that this kind of thing (misinterpreted pain) has nothing to do with the problem of consciousness.

Let me put it another way. Of course, misinterpreted pain has something to do with consciousness, but only in the sense that even the capacity to write science fiction or to understand art has something to do with consciousness. These are all different instances of the *particular contents* of consciousness. The basic problem of mind concerns how it is that any conscious content at all, any qualitative experience, any subjectivity, can exist (and in what it might consist, and how and why).

Consider a cockroach that can feel pain but lacks all higher-order interpretative capacity. You may pull off its legs, and if it could talk it would say 'hurting is happening'. Just a qualitative experience, no other beliefs, nothing. Yet even in this lowly example, one is already facing the *full-blown* problem of consciousness; you don't need to invoke the Ramachandran (1987) phenomena mentioned earlier; you don't need to invoke second-order beliefs. All you need is the fact that whatever it is the cockroach feels ('qualia', 'experiences', 'mental states', the content that we all know what it's like to be the subject of) does exist in the world! That's the real problem of consciousness. The rest is just the icing on the cake.

Marcel: But pains are not in the world!

Nagel: Sydney, could you expand a bit on how you think the kind of analysis that you offered helps to locate consciousness within a functionalist framework?

Shoemaker: I was assuming that there is some connection between consciousness and consciousness of. When we talk about conscious mental states, we should include cases where there is awareness of mental states, such that they are not subconscious or unconscious. I was concerned with the question of what the relationship is between being in mental states and there being consciousness of that sort. I don't want to say this is the only thing that can be covered by the term 'consciousness'. It seems to me there is some tendency for people to use the word 'conscious' such that it becomes almost synonymous with 'mental'—that is, anything that you might want to count as a mental phenomenon gets called conscious. I think we shouldn't do that, or we will no longer have a well-defined subject.

Nagel: I don't know that anybody would use the term consciousness that broadly. There is an enormous number of things that I know, most of which aren't conscious, and knowledge is clearly a mental condition.

Shoemaker: Let me return to the cockroach. It was assumed that if there is sensation going on in the cockroach, then there is consciousness and we have what the subject of this symposium is about. That seems to me to be using the word conscious too broadly. If the idea is that a cockroach has a certain low-level consciousness of the things in its environment, that is a use of the notion of consciousness that I understand. If you just say the cockroach has something we have decided to count as pain receptors and they are firing, then to speak of consciousness is stretching the term.

Lockwood: The question is: does the cockroach *feel* anything?

Nagel: If it feels pain, that is a conscious state.

Sydney, you said consciousness covers a lot of different things—perceptual awareness, sensation, awareness of one's own beliefs and so on. Is your suggestion that the functionalist approach to the subject should be to provide different analyses in functionalist terms—in terms of causal roles—of a number of things which have been to some extent illegitimately grouped together as a single phenomenon?

Shoemaker: I think so. But it's not that I think that these are distinct independent kinds of things. I think there is an important connection between experiences that are conscious in the sense that they are involved in one's perceptual consciousness of the world and states that are conscious in the sense that they are themselves the objects of introspective awareness. Part of the argument was that being conscious in the first of those senses entails at least being potentially conscious in the second of those senses.

Searle: There is a real problem that a lot of us have with functionalism. Let's say: the animal feels a pain. That is a plain fact, the animal has a sensation of pain. And that sensation has all of the subjective, touchy, feely features that Tom Nagel talks about. The problem with the functionalist analysis is that it tends to leave out those features. I don't see how you have got them back in.

Dennett: John, you have described what I view as the culprit intuition. Nick Humphrey asked, how do you know of these animals that they feel pain? How far down the evolutionary scale are you going to go? If you start with the conviction that this is a brute fact, that conviction conditions your understanding of what consciousness is in such a way as to render you impervious to theories of consciousness which suppose that this is actually a rather tendentious claim, that consciousness may trail off dramatically so that it just isn't a brute fact that a cockroach feels pain. We could look at the physiology of the cockroach and compare what happens when you pull off a cockroach's legs with what happens in a (normally understood to be) completely anaesthetized human being. Under normal operating procedures there are plenty of reflexes which are not touched by the anaesthesia. On that basis, we would say anaesthesia was not anaesthesia and that these people were feeling pain—unless they are given muscle relaxants they will keep clenching their muscles.

Searle: Let me state the point again. There are lots of marginal cases and there are lots of epistemic problems. Maybe we will never know what the cockroach pain feels like, maybe we will never know if the cockroach does feel a pain. There are lots of fuzzy areas, but there also are lots of areas that just aren't fuzzy at all. I have pains, my friends have pains, my dog has pains. If you want the epistemology of why I am so confident about this, I'll be happy to tell you in detail. But, basically, the epistemology is irrelevant. All we are interested in now is the fact of the pains. The problem with the functionalist analysis is that the essential feature of the pain gets left out of the analysis. It is no answer to that objection to say there are lots of fuzzy cases.

Gray: I suggest that we should distinguish between the terminology, which is one problem, but a problem which in the end we could probably resolve by committee, and the substantive problem. Sydney Shoemaker used the phrase 'low-level consciousness' for the presumed pain in the cockroach. He might use the same term for the dreamed pain that I described earlier. Certainly, my dreamed pain has the same force in the argument as does the presumed cockroach pain.

So we can agree that we could have terms for 'low-level awareness', or 'subconscious awareness'. But Stevan Harnad, John Searle and I are saying that the substantive problem is that there is *any form of conscious sensation at all* and the rest isn't a problem or, at any rate, it is a different problem.

Fenwick: I would like to take as an example different states of consciousness in patients with Alzheimer's disease. Before the onset of Alzheimer's disease, the patient certainly has beliefs, views, etc. The question is whether that state of consciousness is distinct from the state of consciousness that the patient has, as slowly the mind is whittled away by the Alzheimer process until there is left merely the bare perception of the moment. At that stage, I suggest, probably the patient with Alzheimer's disease has very little in the field of beliefs and views. I think the consciousness of the person with the intact mind is substantially different from the consciousness of the person who has had his mind whittled away.

Harnad: You think the Alzheimer patient isn't conscious?

Fenwick: No, I didn't say that. I said that I thought the quality of consciousness was different. I wonder if one could argue that it is different only in content or whether there is something else which is different about it.

Gray: If I understand Nick Humphrey correctly, he's agreeing that there are all sorts of higher-level states which depend upon the capacity for conscious sensation or conscious experience as a necessary ingredient. The reason we have a deep scientific problem lies in the understanding of the lowest level of sensation that might occur. The rest (including, for example, the different kinds of conscious experience in patients with Alzheimer's and in normal people) you can build up, once you understand the basics.

Van Gulick: When you say that all sorts of higher-order things depend on the capacity for conscious sensation, the functionalist asks an interesting question: is that just a fact about our particular biological lineage, or is that a general and universal fact about mentality? Namely, is it universally true that to get understanding and intelligence and awareness, in the sense of having something that really understands as opposed to merely seeming or behaving as if it understands, those capacities must depend on felt sensation? Or is that just a fact about our particular biological lineage where structures that arose with a kind of felt aspect became the basis for the development of higher cognitive structures? Could you get something with higher cognitive structures that has no feel to it at all?

Marcel: There are two reasons why I am not convinced of Jeffrey Gray's proposal that once we understand the basics we can build up the rest. I certainly think it is a basic problem, but there are several problems. We could just take a stipulative decision that by conscious we mean phenomenal. But it's not clear to me that phenomenal experience is separate from belief. Suppose I adopted the position that having experiences is a function of certain types of beliefs. Or suppose I adopted another position that transformed having sensations into beliefs. I can't be absolutely sure that phenomenal experience isn't a certain type of belief. I'm not sure you can bracket off all the other stuff and say that all you need is the basics. I used to take the position that it is sensation which allows all the other stuff on top. I'm not sure about that either now. Phenomenal experience may be a function of beliefs of a certain kind.

Van Gulick: I agree with John Searle that certain kinds of functionalist analysis do leave the phenomenal aspect out of experience. But it's quite another thing to say that that aspect cannot be captured in terms of some kind of better functional theory in the future. One thing one wants to do with functionalist theory is to try to draw a distinction between those functional roles which can be filled only by states that have phenomenal aspects, and those that could be filled by states without phenomenal aspects.

There is at present no well worked out theory of what roles can be filled only by states with phenomenal aspects and why, but it's quite another thing to say that you *can't* capture the phenomenal/non-phenomenal distinction in terms of functional role. Functional role put too coarsely or just in terms of relations to behaviour may be inadequate for the job. To find a better account, you might look at patients with brain damage, for example patients with blindsight or amnesics, and try to see what is preserved of responses, perceptions and cognition in the absence of phenomenal experience. That might give us a clue to what particular role is played in us by phenomenal experiences that have a feel or sensory aspect to them. If you can figure out those roles, you might be able to begin to understand what kind of things would be needed to play those roles and how those structures might be realized in something more basic, such as neural structures. Thus, you could try to carry your reductionist schemes forward. This is a programme for the future, it's not a theory that exists now.

Searle: The difficulty is this: the whole point of the functionalist analysis was reductive, it was an attempt to give a third-person account of what were apparently irreducibly first-person phenomena. The difficulty, however, is that precisely to the extent that the analysis succeeds, it seems to leave something out, namely the subjectivity of the phenomena. Then, to the extent that the analysis doesn't leave out the subjectivity, it ceases to be a functionalist analysis. So there is an intrinsic dilemma that the functionalist analysis faces. It's no help to say, 'Wait until next year because we are going to have a better functionalist analysis', because the problem is built into the attempt to do a reductive third-person analysis of what are intrinsically subjective first-person phenomena.

Van Gulick: A functionalist ought to be sceptical or at least suspicious about viewing the first-person/third-person distinction as dividing accounts of mind into two mutually exclusive categories. One would like to have a third-person account of what it is to have a subjective perspective, and then to analyse what it is to have a perspective in functional terms.

I don't agree with all of Dan Dennett's theory, but probably what Dan would want to say is, 'Look, we have lots of accounts of what it is to have a perspective and we can tell you a whole lot about it and about what is left over'. I think there is more left over than Dan does, but the goal of the functionalist ought to be to give an objective account of what it is to have a perspective. There is nothing self-contradictory about the notion of an objective account of a subjective perspective. We do this easily for the case of ordinary physical perspective. I have a perspective on the room, Dan has a perspective on the room; we can analyse that objectively. If we proceed to analysing the various aspects of the subjective perspective, such as one's conceptual perspective, is there something we can never capture? Perhaps there is, but there's nothing incompatible about a third-person account of a first-person point of view.

Searle: There is certainly nothing incompatible with the first-person facts about a description of perspective in third-person terms. The difficulty, however, remains. The difficulty is that the ontology of consciousness is a first-person ontology. The hard thing to swallow for functionalism is not the *epistemic* subjectivity of consciousness but its *ontological* subjectivity. It looks like the difficulty with functionalism is that it is resolutely set against accepting the first-person ontology.

Singer: I would like to give an example, which shows how a first-person experience must be assumed to play a functional role. My father suffered from Alzheimer's disease. One of the consequences of this was that at a certain point if he had to sit down in a chair, he would have to turn away from the chair in order to sit down. This is analogous to some of the difficulties that toddlers have in sitting down before they can sustain a mental image or representation of a chair. My father would be facing the chair, then we would try to turn him around to sit. He had apparently had some painful experiences where he had missed the chair earlier, and so he would resist. We would have to struggle with him to turn him around. He would ask, 'What are you trying to do to me?' We would reply, 'We want you to sit down in the chair'. We could say that from our standpoint, he is missing the memory capacity to reassure himself that one doesn't have to be looking at a chair to lower oneself properly into it. But he still had sufficient memory to say, 'Wait a minute, it's going to be painful, if I miss that chair and fall down'. His private first-person experience precluded in the disease his sustaining a mental picture of a chair and its spatial location, but he could still recall that if one missed the chair and fell down, it would hurt.

Harnad: There is a methodological problem that I think is going to arise over and over again at this conference, a form of self-delusion I have elsewhere dubbed 'getting lost in the hermeneutic hall of mirrors' (Harnad 1990, 1991). It again concerns the primacy of subjective content in putative physical or functional 'explanations' of consciousness. I will use an example which has not been proposed here yet, but which can stand in for all similar instances of this particular methodological pitfall, whatever your favourite candidate explanation of the mind might be.

Here is how everyone, inadvertently but invariably, cheats in a functionalist (or physicalist) theory of consciousness. You offer a purely functional story, but in interpreting it mentalistically you simply let the phenomenological 'flavour' slip in by the back door, without admitting or even realizing it. Once it's in, the rest of the story makes perfect functional sense and also agrees with our intuitions about consciousness. This is why I call such a construction a hermeneutic hall of mirrors: it is really just reflecting back what you projected onto it by interpreting it mentalistically in the first place, yet the effect is complete, coherent and convincing—as self-sufficient as a perpetual motion machine once you have assumed the little widget that keeps it going. You take a perfectly objective story and simply allow it, without explanation, to be interpreted as a subjective one: then it all makes sense and consciousness is duly explained.

This happens most commonly in computational models of cognitive states. In reality, all they amount to is a lot of strings of meaningless symbols that are systematically *interpreted* as 'the cat is on the mat', etc; but once you actually baptize them with that interpretation, the rest is simply self-corroborating (as long as the syntax will bear the weight of the systematic interpretation) and hence makes perfect functional sense. All the higher-order sentences, the sentences that are entailed by those sentences, etc, duly follow, and all of them 'mean' what they are supposed to mean, just as thoughts do. The only trouble is that, apart from hermeneutics, they're really just meaningless 'squiggles and squoggles' (as Searle 1980 would call them). The same is true of neurological and behavioural states that are interpretable as pain states. Abstain from hermeneutics and they are just inputs, nerve janglings and outputs.

Thus, all such cases just amount to self-fulfilling prophecy. When you read off the interpretation that you projected as vindication of the fact that you have explained a conscious state, you keep forgetting that it's all done with mirrors because the interpretation was smuggled in by you in the first place. That's what I think is happening whenever you propose a functional (or physical) account of mental states without facing the basic problem, which is: how are you going to justify the mentalistic interpretation other than by saying that, once made, it keeps confirming itself? Mind is not just a matter of interpretation; hence hermeneutics is begging the question rather than answering it.

Nagel: I would like one of you to say how you think a third-person theory of the operation of the first person can really be a theory about conscious states, without slipping in something which isn't a third-person analysis—which is just a straightforward phenomenological quality.

Van Gulick: Take the example of normal visual experience. There is a lot less detail in it than we sometimes assume. I still find plausible the old Kantian view that at least some aspect of our visual experiences forms a continuous manifold that is differentiated qualitatively by colours and other visual qualia. We want to know what functional role is played by that kind of representation versus other ways of representing information about one's spatial surround. And how might such a representation be realized by underlying structural features? You are not going to go right down to the neurons in one step, but you can draw a distinction between those processes driven by visual input that involve a phenomenal representation of that sort, and those that don't. Does blindsight involve that kind of phenomenal representation or doesn't it? You can begin to ask questions that look like they yield to some kind of functional analysis. Do they get down to the very basic feel of each of the sensory qualities or not? I don't know.

Nagel: Do they include an account of what it means to say that there is a sensory quality here? What is it about the functional account that implies that there is any sensory quality there at all? I admit that we are likely to discover that sensory qualities have certain functional roles, but to say that is to say something about the functional role of a certain kind of thing, and not what the thing itself is.

Dennett: It would be nice for the functional theory to be able to predict, on the basis of just third-person theory, when there is subjectivity, and to be able to explain why a water pitcher is not conscious but Tom Nagel is. Then we get to the problem cases; everybody admits there are going to be problem cases.

One of the problems (and this speaks to Steve Harnad's point about the hermeneutic hall of mirrors) is that it's not that the functionalists are playing a dirty trick, it's that everybody's intuitions are tricky and differ here, but you have to start somewhere.

Harnad: It's not a dirty trick, they are fooling themselves.

Dennett: Consider the phenomenon of people who are congenitally insensitive to pain. They are crippled. One reason they are crippled is that at night when they sleep, if they turn into an awkward and 'painful' position, they don't roll out of it automatically the way you and I do. They will sleep all night in a twisted position so their joints get damaged. Now, when in deep and dreamless sleep you roll over in such a way that your nociceptors fire rapidly and this causes you to roll out of that position until everything is hunky-dory again, is that an unconscious pain? Is that a sensation? I think people's intuitions differ. If that's an unconscious pain, then we have established something very important—there are unconscious pains. Now we have an interesting question: are cockroach pains conscious or unconscious?

Gray: But Dan, that's the point. If you had a successful functionalist theory, one would say to you: tell us from the theory which of those nociceptive sets of impulses produce conscious awareness, which do not, and why and how. Until a functionalist theory can do that, it can't make the distinction that you are trying to make between an unconscious set of nociceptive impulses and the conscious set that is felt as pain.

Dennett: You are setting a systematically impossible task to the functionalists. You are demanding that I tell you by my theory, but you have intuitions that you hold sacrosanct and if I tell you something that disagrees with your intuition, you will discount my theory.

Gray: No. On the contrary, I personally have no intuitions about the case you have given. Even if I did have intuitions, my and everybody else's intuitions would go the same way as did our intuitions about physical properties, if you had a theory that could demonstrate the correct way to have intuitions. That's what happens to intuitions; the theory has to be able to account only for the phenomena.

Velmans: I think there's another related issue that hasn't been touched on here. The whole argument, so far, from the functionalists' point of view, rests on the notion that there are different kinds of functional processes; some functional processes are accompanied by consciousness, some are not. No one would believe that there isn't a difference in brain terms between those two kinds of processes. Therefore, when consciousness arises in the brain, it is likely to be associated with distinct forms of neural functioning, which eventually a neurologist is going to be able to tell us about.

Now, it could be that the forms of neural functioning associated with consciousness are themselves producing all the functional differences observed in experimental, clinical or natural situations when consciousness is present (as opposed to when it is absent). So if we look at the brain from the outside, we can give a complete causal story of any functional differences in neural terms; we don't have to refer to the fact of individual experience. One could explain all the observed functional differences, purely in terms of differences in information flow or other forms of observed neural changes. That will get you home and dry from a functionalist point of view. But then you have to come back to John Searle's point and Robert Van Gulick's point that while some of these functional changes are occurring, this person is also saying that they feel something; it is the feeling that doesn't reduce to the brain story.

Van Gulick: I spoke of whether or not the process *involves* phenomenal representations. Admittedly, it's hard to draw the line as to what counts as a phenomenal representation. But however one draws that line, my suggestion was not that such representation is an accompaniment to an ongoing process, but that there are distinctively different processes involved when phenomenal representations participate in the processing versus when phenomenal representations are not part of what's being processed.

Velmans: I'm not denying that. I agree that when phenomenal representations appear there is a fundamentally different process going on. But if you are looking at somebody from the outside, from the third-person perspective, which is what the functionalist account does, you still just see brain processes. From a first-person perspective, of course, phenomenal representations are causally effective. One could give a completely first-person account of how one's experiences determine one's own behaviour, which did not refer to brain processes at all. It makes perfect sense, for example, to say that the way you react to an event depends on how you experience it. Alternatively, if you were not aware of some event, you might not react to it appropriately. It might also be possible, in principle, to determine the relationship between different perspectival accounts: for example, to determine how a causal story based on first-person phenomenal experiences relates to an account of the same causal sequence couched in third-person neural or information-processing terms. But you cannot conclude from this that phenomenal experiences *are nothing more* than brain processing. That would be to confound how things appear from a first-person perspective with how they appear from a third-person perspective (see Velmans 1991a,b).

Humphrey: As I understand it, the functionalist sees not brain processes, but logical operations. This is a very important distinction.

Jeffrey Gray threw down the challenge of providing a functionalist account of sensation. I think one needs to look in great detail at the phenomenology of sensation and ask: what is special about sensation? One needs to identify the peculiar sensory characteristics of, for example, a pain: its apparent privacy, its modality, its indexical properties, its present-tenseness. Take those characteristics, then apply a functionalist analysis to see what sort of operation would lead the subject of the centre of this logical operation to be in the subjective state he is in.

Velmans: You are no closer to the phenomenology with logical operations. The case I was making in terms of brain states described in functional terms applies in the same way to logical operations. A further consequence of your argument is that once a machine has the logical operations that you specify, it is necessarily conscious. But there is nothing about performing logical operations, as such, that would require us to believe in machine consciousness. Having hardware or logical operations sufficient for appropriate functioning does not entail having a first-person phenomenology.

Humphrey: You say there is nothing that would require us to believe the machine was conscious. But if Tom Nagel can say it is perfectly clear that animals or babies are conscious, then I think it should be equally clear that the machine is conscious. In fact, I think you might be more inclined to ascribe consciousness to a machine performing the right logical operations than to a cockroach.

Lockwood: With more knowledge about the physical correlates of conscious functioning, derived from neuropsychological studies, one could, in principle, have good inductive reasons for thinking that a cockroach—or even an appropriately constructed artifact—was conscious. But how far would that get us? When Dan Dennett was talking earlier, there was a very revealing slide. He started out by talking about *prediction* of conscious states and ended up by talking about *explanation*. It is perfectly possible to imagine neuropsychology progressing to the point where it could provide, with a high degree of confidence, very detailed specifications as to what, physically, had to be the case within some object for it to be conscious. But that couldn't conceivably solve the mind–body problem, as we currently understand it, simply because most of us in this room, regardless of our specific philosophical orientation, *already believe this to be a theoretical possibility*. That's because we believe in the supervenience of the mental on the physical. The point is that, even when we've acquired the ability to read off the phenomenology from the physiology, the correspondence will remain simply a brute fact, without some kind of radical conceptual shift in our thinking. The ability to tell, just by doing a physical scan, whether a cockroach was conscious or not, would solve no philosophical problems whatsoever, unless we could understand why the corresponding physical difference makes the phenomenological difference that it does—in this case, the biggest difference of all, that between having phenomenology and having none. Incidentally, I think the same goes for Nick Humphrey's (1992) hypothesis as to how the evolution of consciousness maps on to the physiological evolution. Even if one accepted that, one would still want to say, 'But why should those changes in the physiology have been associated with the emergence of consciousness, while others were not? Why did *they* make the crucial difference that they did?'

Gray: I think that's absolutely right. But, this is not to say that the functionalist analysis, or indeed the analysis of the brain processes that relate to particular conscious experiences, is a waste of time. On the contrary, it's by developing the functionalist analysis as far as it can go, by developing the understanding of the neurophysiology as far as it will go, that eventually we will be able to see what kind of theory can be made that would satisfy Michael Lockwood's demands, which seem to me to be the right demands.

Fenwick: But the major difficulty remains. How does one slip from the third-person observations of science into the first-person perspective of subjective experience? This is the real difficulty because the whole scientific theory, as I see it, is totally third-person. As such, it bears little interest to me coming at these things as an experiencer from a first-person perspective.

Dennett: That's the point of my awkwardly named heterophenomenological method. I claim that in the limit, what the third-person perspective gives you is a rationalized, defended best account from the third-person point of view of a particular subject's heterophenomenology. This is an account of what it is like to be that subject. I view that as the endpoint of this enterprise. But Jeffrey Gray says, even when you have reached that endpoint there is this further question: why should it be that this objective third-person scientific account, even if it does predict the phenomenology exactly, is true? At some point you have to start thinking that that's not an interesting question, because there is an explanation of why all the particulars are there.

Nagel: That is a very scientifically unambitious attitude. It is precisely when you have discovered an enormous amount of information about the relation between phenomena of type X and phenomena of type Y that the question arises: *why* is there this systematic relation?

Dennett: I think that gets explained. You would explain first which organisms have colour vision and which don't. Then you could explain what kind of colour vision each species has, and which preferences among colours they exhibit, and why and how you can distribute these effects and under which conditions. You would go on to explain under which conditions people will be rendered colour-blind and so forth. All of that would fit into a single framework where the internal relations, in your terms, are transparent. One can go on and predict that if we made a novel organism which had these features, it would have a certain phenomenology, never before seen on earth. If you concede that that very ambitious scientific project could succeed *in principle*, then you are left straining at a gnat.

Gray: Dan, are you really saying that if you carry your functionalist analysis through and you build the machine, or the computer simulation, that will accomplish all of those logical operations which you have worked out, that at that point you will say, 'Yes, I now know that this machine experiences the colour red'?

Dennett: Yes.

Nagel: The reason I'm confident that babies feel pain, isn't simply that they function in a certain way which could be simulated by a machine. It's based on the assumption of the biological uniformity of nature. Given the choice between the hypothesis that only adults or only humans feel pain while other biologically related creatures don't, and the hypothesis that there is much more continuity here, a general expectation of the uniformity of nature leads me to the belief that even cockroaches have sensation. But that is not to endorse the view that the phenomenology falls out of functional analogies alone. Sensation and consciousness are biological phenomena.

Marcel: How can you be so sure?

Libet: I want to address the contention that one can predict conscious phenomena from a knowledge of neuronal functions. I think it's a misleading and mistaken view. One can find out about the relationship between neuronal function and conscious experience only by first finding out what the conscious experience itself is in that relationship. In the example that Dan Dennett gave, Ramachandran (1987) could not have predicted any new subjective phenomenon if he had not already known something about the relationship between neuronal function and experiential colour vision. (I'm talking here about subjective experience of colour, not simply its detection.) So you could not predict anything about the conscious experience unless you knew the nature of the relationship in the first place from the knowledge of the conscious experience. Then, having established certain relationships, you might go on to infer the possibility of certain others. But you cannot start by looking at nerve cell functions and predict what a conscious experience is going to be.

Dennett: Don't you agree that at least you can do a lot of negative prediction? We can tell from neurophysiological evidence that certain animals do not have colour vision.

Libet: That behavioural evidence tells us only what electromagnetic wavelengths the animal can detect, not what its experiential colour vision may be. Stoerig & Cowey (1989) described this distinction in human patients with pathological loss of subjective colour vision. Your 'negative prediction' simply deals with the neurophysiological mechanisms that may be necessary for colour vision, but tells us nothing about the conditions sufficient to produce subjective colour vision.

Dennett: If they have phenomenology, it does not include colour.

Gray: There's no way that you could tell that from any neurophysiological evidence conceivable at the moment. You could not tell from the fact that certain insects don't have eyes and retinas like ours that they can't see. We know they can see through quite different kinds of retinal organization. We don't know what you necessarily have to have inside the head that will allow you to have colour vision. You can tell that only from behavioural data.

Dennett: I quite agree. But I am suggesting an informational analysis of just what's coming into the organism, what's available to the organism to work with. Let's take simple cases. It's pretty clear that a pen does not have colour vision, and that follows from 'physiological facts' about this pen and its circumstances. If you don't admit facts like that, if you think it's an open question whether or not a pen has colour vision, you end up in an extreme position.

Libet: There are certainly brain functions that are necessary to lead to the possibility of conscious experience, but that doesn't mean an organism with those functions has an awareness of the event. You can only tell that there is conscious experience by asking the human being or the animal, which we can't do, whether they have it. Possession of the minimal operations for colour vision does not mean that an animal experiences colour; colour vision as defined behaviourally means only that the animal can detect and respond to colours in a certain way.

Velmans: I have problems working out what's motivating functionalism. I don't see any problem, from the point of view of a scientific account of the world, in accepting that people have a first-person perspective as an 'objective' fact. That the first-person perspective relates in certain ways to conditions in the brain, whatever they might be, is another objective fact. That first-person phenomenology can't be reduced to anything that can be observed of the brain from the outside is a third objective fact.

Fenwick: The difficulty arises because all the time we collect third-person data and we have no first-person science. For example, we collect third-person observations of how people feel depressed, what their mental states are like. We can codify these observations, we can quantify them. But all these objective third-person data do not say anything about the first-person experience of depression. Much is said about the phenomenology of depression, but little about the subjective feeling of the experience.

Marcel: This gets back to Tom Nagel's belief that infants feel pain. First, what do you mean by pain and in what sense—what type of pain? Let me give two examples which relate to this and the difficulties that occur. For certain types of socially deprived animals (dogs), and possibly humans (autistic children), it is not clear that they have the same pain as us and what functional role it plays. Second, in different societies, what counts as pain is different. A situation functionally defined that will cause pain to the Chinese does not give Westerners pain (Kleinman 1986). Somatization differs between cultures and certain types of pain may depend on somatization.

Harnad: So what? What rides on this?

Marcel: Tom Nagel's intuitions about babies feeling pain. When he talks about sensations and functional abnormality, I want to know what type of biology he means. If he includes socially arranged beliefs as part of biology, that's fine. But suppose pains and other sensations do depend upon attitudes, beliefs, the realization or actualization of self. Tom's intuitions about sensations, including pain, being basic use a different sense of basic.

Harnad: The issue isn't whether or not Tom is right about his conjecture; the issue concerns a fact of the matter on the *supposition* that he was right.

Marcel: But what do you mean by a fact of the matter? When Peter Fenwick says that we psychologists are faced with first-person data, the 'fact of the matter' is not clear. When people say things to us, there is a real problem about what they are telling us about. It isn't necessarily the same thing as in you.

Harnad: May I introduce an intuition that lies behind this? I would like to ask Dan Dennett about the status—in that scientific Utopia when all the questions have been answered—of our 'zombie' intuitions: intuitions about possible creatures that could be behaviourally, functionally or neurally identical to us, interpretable exactly as if they had qualia, yet lacking them. These intuitions are not my favourites, but they do exist. I'd like to point out the significant but overlooked fact that we do *not* have 'quarkless zombie' intuitions in the case of modelling matter (physics) analogous to these 'qualeless zombie' intuitions that we have for modelling mind.

For the mind, at the end of the last scientific day, when there is a complete functional explanation of all the empirical data on the mind, I would still be able to ask what reason there is to believe that you haven't just modelled a zombie—a functional look-alike with no qualia. I could not raise the same question for quarks, despite the fact that quarks are just as unobservable as qualia. For if quarks do still figure in the Grand Unified Theory when physics reaches a Utopian state of completeness, we will *not* have intuitions that there could be an empirically indistinguishable zombie universe in which, although the theory posits that quarks exist, there are no quarks. Because quarks, like qualia, are objectively unobservable, that cannot be the reason for the difference in intuitions in the two cases. Unlike qualia, however, quarks would be functionally *necessary* to the predictive and explanatory power of the Utopian physical theory we are imagining—without positing them, the theory could not explain all the data. In our Utopian behavioural/cognitive theory, qualia will always be *optional* (as the hermeneutic hall of mirrors shows), because (assuming the theory would be a materialistic rather than a dualistic one) qualia could not play any independent causal or functional role of their own in it. Hence there will always be room for qualeless zombies. Moreover, whereas in Utopian physics we know that (by definition) the difference between a quarkful universe and a quarkless zombie universe would be one that did not make a difference, we know from our own first-person case that the difference between a qualeful universe and a qualeless zombie universe would be about the greatest difference we are capable of conceiving. There is, I think, something special about this, and I take it to be a mark of the mind–body problem.

Dennett: Consider a 'zagnet'. A zagnet is exactly like a magnet, it behaves exactly like a magnet, it passes every test from the subatomic to the submicroscopic level, but it's not really a magnet, its a zagnet. We don't take that seriously. So the challenge to me is to explain why we should have the intuition that there could be a zombie. A zombie for philosophical purposes is somebody who is indistinguishable by every physical test—no brain scan, no behavioural or neurophysiological or chemical test will tell a zombie who is not conscious from a real live conscious human being.

If you put the intuition as carefully as that, then I submit it is not so clear that this is a respectable intuition that there is such a thing as a zombie. To take the zombie intuition seriously, you have to suppose that there are real subjective differences in principle which make absolutely no other difference in the world at all, even to the subject. In other words, it follows that you right now do not know whether you are a zombie.

Searle: That's not the zombie hypothesis. The zombie hypothesis is that you might replace my brain with a different kind of substance which did not have the same causal powers as neurons to produce phenomenological states but had the same input/output functions as my neuronal system. Let's suppose you replace my brain with silicon chips in such a way that I can answer questions about where I was born and what it is like to be me. The only thing is that unlike neurons, the silicon chips are incapable of causing consciousness. They cause input/output functions—they take in input stimuli and produce output behaviour. The reason your zombie isn't a zombie is that we are forced to give up two intuitions and not one. The first intuition is that the same input/output function implies the same phenomenology. The second is that the same internal causal structure implies the same phenomenology. I accept the second of those intuitions. If you have exactly the same neuronal structure as me, then you have the same effects of neuronal structure as me. But if you have just the same input/output functions, it doesn't follow that you have the same phenomenological effects.

Dennett: That's very important, because I'm often accused of being a behaviourist, but my 'behaviour' includes everything that goes on in the brain too, at whatever level matters. I don't suppose that you think it matters right down to each molecule of neurotransmitter. Then, presumably, on your account there's plenty of room for variation in the structure of this surrogate brain without disturbing the consciousness.

Searle: It matters for what? There is the question of what matters for producing my input/output function, and there is the question of what matters for producing my subjective, qualitative, first-person states of consciousness. And those are not logically the same.

Dennett: They are curiously interrelated.

Searle: Of course, because the whole function of consciousness is to produce my behaviour.

Gray: Some of your behaviour.

Searle: Yes. But the existence of the consciousness is not the same as the existence of the behaviour. And, this is the crucial point, consciousness is not the same as a dispositional causal structure to produce the behaviour, because I could have a dispositional causal structure to produce that behaviour and not have that consciousness.

Van Gulick: But if you are a functionalist, you don't want to collapse into behaviourism. The rationale is to articulate some constraints on the inner route and the inner structure that generates behaviour, which differentiates among cases that might be behaviourally indistinguishable but very different internally. So the functionalist is looking for any number of those different intermediate levels of explanation and instantiation that may accommodate a wide range of different underlying physical structures but that are not defined by their behavioural input/output relations. If one is a functionalist, one should talk not just about what behaviour you get, but about *how* you get it and which ways of getting it would count as being conscious and which wouldn't.

Searle: But functionalism shares with behaviourism one crucial element, namely that the ontology is all third-person. We are supposed to be able to analyse consciousness in third-person 'objective' terms that make no reference to any inner, 'subjective' qualitative states. Instead of a big black box with a simple input/output function, you have a lot of little black boxes, each with its own input/output function. One of the things that's not supposed to be told in this story is a causal account of how the specific neurobiological phenomena produce consciousness.

Velmans: I have another problem with this that applies equally to physicalism of the kind supported by John Searle. Even if it were the case that the causal story included all the neural conditions for the production of consciousness, one could not conclude that consciousness just *is* a brain state or function. This reductionist argument amounts to saying that if neural conditions C1 to Cn cause a phenomenal experience P, then P must be the same type of thing as C1 to Cn. But this does not follow. For example, moving a wire through a magnetic field produces an electrical current in the wire, but this does not show the current in the wire to be just a type of movement of the wire through a magnetic field.

Williams: John, if the argument against functionalism is its reduction of consciousness to the third-person point of view, why on your view does it make all the difference whether the zombie hypothesis is put in terms of meat or non-meat?

Searle: It doesn't make any difference as such. The question was addressed to the specific version of the zombie hypothesis described by Dan Dennett, which is not the zombie hypothesis that matters. The one that matters concerns whether or not the inner structure—whatever it was made of—is supposed to be causally equivalent to the inner structure of a brain in one crucial respect, namely it is capable of producing subjective states of consciousness. The whole point of the zombie was that in the case of the zombie you have something which behaves exactly as if it were conscious at every level, but isn't conscious. But at every level means every *behavioural* third-person level.

Dennett: Every level in the brain.

Lockwood: The right level to focus on can be determined only by reference to the particular functionalist theory that is being proposed. After all, functionalism, as a philosophy, merely offers a very general prescription for constructing a substantive theory of the mind; it's not a substantive theory in its own right. If functionalism, as a philosophy, is correct, then it follows that some specific functionalist account of mental states and processes must also be correct. So suppose now that we are offered some specific functionalist theory. And let us imagine that an object were to satisfy all the conditions which, according to that theory, are necessary for a thing to be conscious, whilst physically differing from us, say, in the respects that this particular theory doesn't care about. In other words, the object is functionally equivalent to something that is uncontroversially conscious, at the level of description which the theory deems crucial, whilst differing from it at other levels. The point, then, is that we could always ask: 'How do we know that one of the things the theory doesn't care about, but which distinguishes you or me from the object being envisaged, is not, in reality, precisely what makes the difference between something being and not being conscious? Or between it having one sort of phenomenology and its having a quite different sort of phenomenology?' That, surely, is the proper role that 'zombies' play in the functionalist debate.

Humphrey: There's another thing which has been begged by Max Velmans' and John Searle's statement of the problem. They state that the brain structure *produces* consciousness, that there is a cause–effect relationship.

An alternative way of presenting the problem is to say that perhaps consciousness isn't a product—it isn't an output, it just *is*. Part of what I have tried to do with the analysis of sensations is to take a non-instrumental view of them: to say that sensations don't leave anything behind, they don't have any further effects, they just are. We need to get away from the instrumentalism of Dan Dennett's position, where anything that doesn't have some consequence is of no importance. 'Being conscious' is a *state of being* and doesn't necessarily leave anything behind.

Searle: I'm not sure I know what the details of your view are. I was worried about the view that Professor Shoemaker presented, which is a more familiar form of functionalism, in which the level of functional analysis is much higher than that of neurons. The whole point of this functional analysis is to allow that different physical systems could be functionally equivalent. For that reason, the analysis is never in terms of neurons but in terms of higher-level phenomena, such as beliefs and desires, and these are supposed to be analysable in terms of their causal relations.

Now, if one goes back a step and asks what motivates a functionalist theory of consciousness, the answer is that many people are worried about the subjective ontology of the mental. They find the intrinsic, subjective ontology of conscious mental states somehow ontologically intolerable. Note that nobody is a functionalist about, for example, hands. Nobody says that ontologically hands are problematic, so we have to resort to 'manual functionalism'. Hands are not defined in terms of their input/output grasping behaviour. Such a view would be crazy.

Dennett: No, but we are functionalists about hearts.

Searle: No, we are not. And that's why we call the functionally equivalent but artificial versions of hearts 'artificial hearts' and not 'real hearts'. But if, as I am suggesting, you ask why would we adopt a crazy view of beliefs and desires, which we would not think of doing for hands, the answer is that we are ontologically worried about the subjectivity of mental states. It is appalling to some people that nature should contain irreducibly subjective elements. But what I want to insist on is: *the fact is that nature does contain irreducibly subjective elements.* Once we accept the existence of and the irreducible subjectivity of the mental, then the motivation for functionalism is lost.

Dennett: I think in one regard you are being unfair to Sydney Shoemaker's functionalism. John, you are right that the point of functionalism is to get somewhere above the neuronal level to characterize what seem to be the crucial, constitutive levels—those that, when preserved, entail consciousness. John describes this higher level in terms of beliefs. The general tenor of scepticism here is that that can't be the right level, it's much too high. But I think that's an illusion which has to do with the fact that he's not being very specific about the contents of those beliefs. You have to recognize that any phenomenological distinction that you can make from the first-person point of view constitutes a difference in belief content. If you have every last one of those belief content distinctions captured in your functionalism, you have automatically captured every first-person-discernible content distinction in that person's phenomenology. What more could you want?

Shoemaker: Michael Lockwood asked why, if we have this creature that is functionally isomorphic with us, it couldn't lack mental states? At a certain point, the question comes down to what would we count as a creature with mental states. If we encountered a creature and we were satisfied that this was true of its functional organization, and we seemed to be able to carry on conversations with it, could we intelligibly suppose that it totally lacked mentality and consciousness? Here's where I reveal myself as a conceptual or analytic functionalist; it seems to me we wouldn't, and that's a manifestation of the concepts we have of mentality. We would be using our mental concepts as we learned to use them if we said of this creature, of course it has those mental states. If it passes all those tests and if its behaviour conforms externally and internally (as Dan Dennett says) to the functionalist description, then I think our concept is that it is an intelligent, sentient being.

References

Bisiach E, Geminiani G 1991 Anosognosia related to hemiplegia and hemianopia. In: Prigatano GP, Schacter DL (eds) Awareness of deficit after brain injury. Oxford University Press, New York, p 17–39
Harnad S 1990 Lost in the hermeneutic hall of mirrors. J Theor Exp Artif Intell 2:321–327
Harnad S 1991 Other bodies, other minds: a machine incarnation of an old philosophical problem. Minds Mach 1:43–54
Humphrey N 1992 A history of the mind. Chatto & Windus, London
Kleinman A 1986 Social origins of distress and disease. Yale University Press, New Haven, CT
Nagel T 1993 What is the mind–body problem? In: Experimental and theoretical studies of consciousness. Wiley, Chichester (Ciba Found Symp 174) p 1–13
Ramachandran VS 1987 Interaction between colour and motion in human vision. Nature 328:645–647
Searle JR 1980 Minds, brains and programs. Behav Brain Sci 3:417–457
Stoerig P, Cowey A 1989 Wavelength sensitivity in blindsight. Nature 342:916–918
Velmans M 1991a Is human information processing conscious? Behav Brain Sci 14:651–669
Velmans M 1991b Consciousness from a first-person perspective. Behav Brain Sci 14:702–726

Integrated cortical field model of consciousness

Marcel Kinsbourne

Center for Cognitive Studies, Tufts University, Medford, MA 02155, USA

Abstract. The idea that there is a localized module or limited capacity mechanism in the brain that subserves consciousness is wrong. Awareness is a product of the activity of widely distributed neuronal assemblies that represent diverse aspects of experience. Central to a representation's entry into consciousness is its integration into the currently dominant pattern of central neuronal activity (dominant focus). A representation anywhere in the forebrain could on one occasion enter consciousness and on another remain outside it, depending on whether it is, perhaps by temporal coherence of discharge of cell assemblies, integrated into the dominant focus. There is no privileged locus or 'internal eye' for the benefit of which input is elaborated and toward which information must be transported. When a perceptual decision is made there need be no re-enactment ('filling in') of the appearance in question. Nor is there a 'finish line', the crossing of which determines the perceived sequence of events. Neuropsychological syndromes that involve unawareness of a perceptual domain illustrate the explanatory value of this integrated cortical field model of consciousness. Awareness cannot be conceptualized as separate from the neural activity of which it is the subjective concomitant. Being aware is what it is like to have a particular pattern of neuronal activity. To regard consciousness as arising from brain activity by some esoteric transformation is misconceived.

1993 Experimental and theoretical studies of consciousness. Wiley, Chichester (Ciba Foundation Symposium 174) p 43–60

I shall discuss how the contents of awareness reflect the patterns of neuronal activity in the brain from which consciousness arises. I take as my premise a view that I call neurofunctional—that awareness is an irreducible property of the activity of functionally entrained neuronal assemblies and therefore is amenable to no further explanation. (Could multiple implementations of awareness be accomplished? Only if it proved possible to simulate in non-neuronal media the actual manner in which the neurons interact in the conscious individual; Dennett 1991.) The functional organization of the brain is therefore crucial for the study of consciousness.

Sensory input from the body's receptors and commands to the muscles all obviously 'come together' in the brain. Less obviously, some have supposed that they come together more precisely at some privileged spot in the brain. Because Descartes thought that this imagined locus was, in some mystifying manner, in communication with the soul, we call it the 'Cartesian theatre' (Dennett 1991, Dennett & Kinsbourne 1992). There, input is displayed in appropriately preprocessed fashion for the information of, and awaiting the decisions of, some ill-characterized 'observer'. Although Cartesian dualism has been rejected, it has left a legacy. This is the unscrutinized assumption that there is a point in the brain where represented input all comes together, which has seriously misdirected explanations both of the contents of awareness and of the structural and functional organization of the brain. It has led to the equating of the contents of awareness with those of a 'limited capacity mechanism' identified with focused attention and to the conception of the brain as a hierarchically organized communication system, ruled by an operating system to which corresponds the conscious mind (Johnson-Laird 1988). Intuition conspires with this mistake. The intuition of a unitary consciousness lends itself to the view that those representations in the brain which correspond to personal experience must be located 'in that part most deeply recessed from the outside world that is furthest from input and output' (Sherrington 1934). So a mitigated dualism, within the brain rather than between it and an incorporeal mind, survives. Yet intuitions must have been selected on account of their adaptive utility rather than any relation they might bear to objective reality. They are therefore disqualified from scientific argument.

Characterizations of what 'gets into consciousness' and why it gets there have overemphasized purposeful, intensely focused attention, and correspondingly have roughly equated awareness with such a state. 'Getting into consciousness' has been seen as a victory in competition for 'limited resources'. But, obviously, one is also fully conscious when attention is widely diffused, as across a landscape, and awareness also harbours moods and emotions. This diversity of contents has never plausibly been incorporated into a unitary model of the 'special' role that awareness might play in mental function. My alternative approach is to abandon the view that consciousness evolved for a specific adaptive purpose. I believe consciousness is instead a property of particular patterns of neuronal firing, activated by input, the diverse attributes of which are characterized in parallel by specialized processors scattered within the cortical neuropil and brainstem nuclei. Being conscious is what it is like to have neuronal circuitry in particular interactive functional states. Being in a particular state of mind is what it is like to have neuronal circuitry in a particular interactive functional state. What evolved by natural selection were the interactive functional neuronal states. I have suggested that these states offer the individual the opportunity to note (and subsequently recollect for further scrutiny) specific and unusual contexts of adaptively significant events (Kinsbourne 1988).

The distributed model of brain organization leads me to abandon the 'serial stage' notion of information flowing in ever more elaborated fashion 'downstream' as percepts become elaborated from the 'bottom-up' (Barlow 1972). Instead, once represented, any perceptual attribute, however elemental and 'upstream', is a candidate for inclusion in awareness. No further information need be transferred for awareness to be achieved, although local recombinations of the representations of different features may occur (Zeki & Shipp 1988). As for limited resources, these are nowhere to be found in the brain. The only resource limitation is inherent in the cerebral cortex itself (Kinsbourne 1981). Because this is a richly connected network, active cell assemblies in one area are a source of interfering cross-talk for cell assemblies elsewhere, one type of patterned discharge tending to generalize across wide areas of cortex, forming a dominant neuronal action pattern, or, adapting to consciousness a concept from Rusinov (1973), 'dominant focus'.

A 'box' for consciousness continues to be postulated (e.g. McGlynn & Schacter 1989). Kihlstrom (this volume) even dignifies this as the 'neuropsychological approach'. Yet known design characteristics of cerebral architecture do not encourage such a view. A hierarchical organization would result in what I have called the 'wasp-waist' brain. Information from multiple, more peripheral sources is cumulatively integrated 'downstream' until it is fit to be displayed on the screens of the Cartesian theatre (to the 'pontifical cell' of William James). No such convergences of neuronal projections have been discovered, and there is no area in the brain that receives inputs from all sensory sources. Instead, there are many projections to cortex in each modality and parallel streams of input relative to distinct sensory properties (Livingstone & Hubel 1987), which do not 'come together'. Corticocortical projections universally conduct in both directions, suggesting a role in facilitating 'binding' (see below). Indeed, when either hemisphere of the brain is temporarily anaesthetized by the intracarotid amobarbital (Wada) technique, the patient remains alert and responsive. Either hemisphere can sustain awareness; there is no point in either of them that is indispensable. Similarly, when the corpus callosum that connects the hemispheres is surgically split, each hemisphere can, under appropriate conditions, be shown to be individually responsive to question and command.

Functional measurements support the view that there is no consciousness centre. When subjects are given diverse tasks, metabolic studies reveal enhanced activity in the correspondingly specialized areas, but no additional and separate consciousness centre lights up. Indeed, convergence itself lacks cerebral metabolic support. When subjects make cross-modal comparisons the area for each modality exhibits activation, but no third area is revealed in which the cross-modal comparison might take place (Lassen & Roland 1983).

Abandoning the notion of a single awareness module, should one instead credit several scattered facilities with the special role of 'entering' information into awareness (Shallice 1978, Damasio 1989)—'weak Cartesian theatre'? This move sacrifices the benefits to intuition that made the centred model of awareness attractive in the first place, and yet, like the centred model, fails to address the lack of evidence for convergence to such points and the binding problem between them. Once one abandons a centred model, it seems more heuristically desirable to discard convergence completely, face the reality of parallel processing in the brain and attempt a model of a totally different kind.

Given that a representation of input is not formed in order to be shown to anyone or anything else, there is no reason to suppose that it need be mutliply replicated in serial fashion. I assume that any sensory attribute is represented only once in cortex. Whether or not it sends any information (its output) elsewhere, it interacts with other representations as a component of a self-organizing system. Consistent with this view, binding between representations of different sensory attributes occurs not by convergent integration but by temporal coherence of oscillation of the respective neuronal systems. In connectionistic terminology there is a settling process in a relaxation network. Such synchronization of the firing of widely separated cell groups has been repeatedly suggested and experimentally demonstrated (Gray & Singer 1989, Engel et al 1991). When extensive areas of cortex are recruited to the solution of a problem in focal attention, a 40 Hz rhythm in the electroencephalogram arises from wide areas of the cerebral convexity. My interpretation is that neuronal generators in a specialized area of cortex produce the appropriate patterned excitation and additional wide areas of cortex (each with its own specialization) double as a multipurpose computational space (Kinsbourne 1988). For example, verbal fluency depends on the integrity of the left frontal lobe, but involves a wide bilateral temporoparietal area in its execution, as indexed by increased metabolic activity (Parks et al 1988).

Which representations, then, contribute to awareness? None are specially designated for this purpose. Any one is capable of doing so, should it become entrained with the dominant neuronal action pattern in the cortex. The fact that a particular set of cell assemblies is entrained suffices to explain of what one is conscious. There is nothing further that is special about them. A representation is apt to become part of a dominant neuronal action pattern if sufficiently activated and not insulated from interaction by an inhibitory surround. Insulation I believe to occur if the activity has become automatic and therefore benefits from functional encapsulation (the only sense in which there are encapsulated 'Fodorian' modules in the brain). At any one time some representations are entrained, some are in the process of settling into the dominant neuronal action pattern, and others are losing their temporal coherence with it. Yet others are forming elsewhere in the brain. They will become candidates for awareness, if they gain enough activation.

How can we muster evidence for or against this model? No single 'critical' observation or experiment can confirm or discredit it. Many observations will have to be considered and their cumulative evidence for or against the concept taken into account. Here I will discuss some relevant data from a disorder of awareness.

It has often been pointed out that we are not conscious of the operation of our mental processes, but only of their outputs. These are the representations that are the substrates of further mental operations and some of them are the basis of conscious experience. How are these representations organized in the brain? Specifically, in partial impairments of consciousness should one envisage disconnection between intact preconscious representations and central conscious representations waiting in vain to be activated? Or are these impairments better understood as simply being due to underactivated representations?

The patient with left neglect has lost awareness of the left side of space and/or his body. He neither experiences input from that side nor initiates orientation or action toward it. In contrast to the patient with an anaesthesia or a paralysis, he is not aware of this selective disuse of information and action, and therefore does not attempt to compensate for it. In terms of the Cartesian theatre, screens that should depict information from the left are blank. But a more detailed analysis undermines such a conceptualization (Kinsbourne 1987).

Neglect, though of the left, is not of the left half of space. It is of the left side of things, or of the items towards the left in an array. There is a gradient of probability of detection of features from left to right, across individual stimuli, and across the whole visual field (Kinsbourne 1992). The patient may even react faster to features at the right end of things than do intact individuals (Ladavas et al 1990). The more severe the syndrome, the more biased to the right is attention and the more are right-sided features given excessive weight in perceptual decisions. Whole words are reported on the basis of a few letters that could have been the final letters of these words. Objects are reported as complete when only a right-sided segment is displayed. These and many other observations about neglect are best explained as follows: an opponent system for guiding the focus of attention in the lateral plane has become unbalanced. Each hemisphere houses a processor that drives attention to the opposite end of stimuli. The two opponent processors are in inhibitory interaction, and attention shifts along the lateral plane when the balance of activation changes. Presumably, because of inactivation of the opponent processor in the right hemisphere, which swings attention leftward, a disinhibited rightward-orienting facility swings to the right extreme of whatever is there to be observed (Kinsbourne 1970, 1977).

We are aware of an absence of information if we focus attention on the relevant sensory (or memorial) domain and find nothing there. With his attention perpetually focused right, the neglect patient is in no position to observe the absence of left-sided input. When appraising input, he must be achieving satisfactory matches between it and central representations, which, as Bisiach & Luzzatti (1978) demonstrated, are themselves incompletely expressed on the left. Because the central representations are themselves laterally incomplete, there is no mismatch with input and the resulting experience, veridical or not, seems normal to him.

It is hard to conceive of a centred mechanism that is variably denied input from projections dedicated to the left ends of things. It is more reasonable to think that awareness derives directly from representations, each hemisphere being responsible for maintaining the level of activation at the opposite end of the same representation. In neglect, the representations are underactivated at their left ends. When balanced activation is temporarily restored, neglect phenomenology, however extreme, normalizes.

Caloric stimulation is performed by irrigating one ear with water that is significantly hotter or colder than body temperature. This triggers ascending activation on the same or opposite side of the brain. Silberpfennig (1941) reported that during caloric stimulation (irrigation of the ear opposite to the lesion with cold water) normal perception is restored in neglect. This has been confirmed and extended, even to the extreme case of the patient disowning their left arm. Evidently, after non-specific stimulation, the damaged half brain regained its efficiency as an opponent processor in equilibrating representations across the lateral plane. Once the caloric effect has dissipated and neglect recurs, the patient does not recollect his brief experience of normality. Thus, when the representations are again distorted the patient can no longer represent the domain to which he had fleeting access, and therefore cannot evoke memories in that domain.

How might the speedy formation, aggregation and disintegration of neuronal assemblies be instantiated in the brain? In addition to the 'rigid' structural synapses that change rather slowly in synaptic weight, there are rapidly forming 'plastic' synapses (von der Malsburg 1973), mediated by the NMDA (*N*-methyl-D-aspartate) receptor complex (Cotman & Monaghan 1988), that can either persist and influence the synaptic weights, or dissipate rapidly without leaving any trace (Flohr 1991). Given that most of our experience is pertinent only to the immediate situation (e.g. optic flow as one navigates uneven terrain), a mechanism that does not clutter episodic memory seems adaptive.

What consequences for normal functioning would flow from a decentred brain? A few examples must suffice (see Dennett 1991 for extended discussion). If decisions about the environment are made, not at a single point but by numerous 'microtakings' distributed across the network, the relative timing of events becomes somewhat indefinite. The relative ordering of events occurring within a fraction of a second would not be an invariant function of the ordering of the physical stimuli with respect to some fixed central 'finish line', but would depend on the particular brain state, and even on the particular response called for. A decision indicated by a hand movement might not be the same as one made by a wink or the voice (Marcel 1993). Temporal anomalies in perception might occur, for instance as observed by Norman (1967).

Another consequence applies to the need for the brain to 'fill in' events that are inferred rather than directly observed, for example when the brain retrospectively determines that a change has occurred over time (as in the perception of apparent movement when stimuli appear in different locations in rapid succession). Having made this decision, the brain has no need subsequently to re-enact it (Dennett & Kinsbourne 1992). The same applies to the decision that a particular patterned input extends across a real or artificial blind spot (Ramachandran & Gregory 1991). Once the decision is made, that suffices for purposes of control of behaviour and any subsequent activation of pattern detectors is redundant. Indeed, when a second stimulus leads the brain to a conclusion such as that movement has occurred, or even that there was no first stimulus (metacontrast), it may remain moot whether there was in fact a fleeting experience of a single stimulus, superseded and obliterated by the movement or metacontrast mask, or whether the early stimulus never reached awareness in the first place. These and other instances are discussed more fully by Dennett & Kinsbourne (1992). When an input 'settles' into the dominant action pattern, it may never become clear *precisely* when during the settling the stimulus reached consciousness. For separate events, the unit of psychological time is coarser than the unit of physiological time.

From the perspective of this 'multiple drafts' model of ongoing awareness (Dennett & Kinsbourne 1992), the ostensibly unitary stream of consciousness is a product of memory, not direct experience. This high profile intuition is not veridical but a retrospective construct that applies particularly when the individual is in a remembering or a planning mode. It is composed (without filling in) of multiple discontinuous vacillating experiences that reflect converging, diverging and even concurrent streams of neural cell assembly activity representing multiple draft accounts of the experience of the moment— fiction of the unitary self.

Acknowledgements

These ideas benefited from fruitful discussions with Dan Dennett, Nick Humphrey and Ray Jackendoff.

References

Barlow HB 1972 Single units and sensation: a neuron doctrine for perceptual psychology. Perception 1:371–394
Bisiach E, Luzzatti C 1978 Unilateral neglect of representational space. Cortex 14:129–133
Cotman CW, Monaghan DT 1988 Excitatory aminoacid neurotransmission: NMDA receptors and Hebb type synaptic plasticity. Annu Rev Neurosci 11:61–80
Damasio AR 1989 Time-locked multiregional retroactivation: a systems-level proposal for the neural substrates of recall and recognition. Cognition 33:25–62
Dennett DC 1991 Consciousness explained. Little, Brown, Boston, MA
Dennett DC, Kinsbourne M 1992 Time and the observer. Behav Brain Sci 15:183–247

Engel AK, Konig IP, Singer W 1991 Direct physiological evidence for scene segmentation by temporal coding. Proc Natl Acad Sci USA 88:9136–9140

Flohr H 1991 Brain processes and phenomenal consciousness. Theory Psychol 1:245–262

Gray CM, Singer W 1989 Stimulus-specific neuronal oscillations in orientation columns of cat visual cortex. Proc Natl Acad Sci USA 86:1698–1702

Johnson-Laird PN 1988 The computer and the mind. Harvard University Press, Cambridge, MA

Kihlstrom JF 1993 The psychological unconscious and the self. In: Experimental and theoretical studies of consciousness. Wiley, Chichester (Ciba Found Symp 174) p 147–167

Kinsbourne M 1970 A model for the mechanism of unilateral neglect of space. Trans Am Neurol Assoc 95:143–145

Kinsbourne M 1977 Hemineglect and hemisphere rivalry. In: Weinstein EA, Friedland RP (eds) Hemi-attention and hemisphere specialization. Raven Press, New York (Adv Neurol 18) p 41–49

Kinsbourne M 1981 Single channel theory. In: Holding DH (ed) Human skills. Wiley, Chichester, p 65–90

Kinsbourne M 1987 Mechanism of unilateral neglect. In: Jeannerod M (ed) Neurophysio-logical and neuropsychological aspects of unilateral neglect. Elsevier, Amsterdam, p 69–86

Kinsbourne M 1988 Integrated field theory of consciousness. In: Marcel AJ, Bisiach E (eds) Consciousness in contemporary science. Clarendon Press, Oxford, p 239–256

Kinsbourne M 1992 Orientational model of unilateral neglect: evidence from attentional gradients within hemispace. In: Robertson I, Marshall JM (eds) Unilateral neglect: clinical and experimental studies. Erlbaum, Hillsdale, NJ, in press

Ladavas E, Petronio A, Umilta C 1990 The deployment of visual attention in the intact field of hemineglect patients. Cortex 26:307–317

Lassen NA, Roland PE 1983 Localization of cognitive function with cerebral blood flow. In: Kertesz A (ed) Localization in neuropsychology. Academic Press, New York p 141–152

Livingstone MS, Hubel DH 1987 Psychophysical evidence for separate channels for the perception of form, color, movement and depth. J Neurosci 7:346–368

Marcel A 1993 Slippage in the unity of consciousness. In: Experimental and theoretical studies of consciousness. Wiley, Chichester (Ciba Found Symp 174) p 168–186

McGlynn SM, Schacter DL 1989 Unawareness of deficits in neuropsychological syndromes. J Clin Exp Neuropsychol 11:143–205

Norman DA 1967 Temporal confusions and limited capacity processors. Acta Psychol 27:293–297

Parks RW, Loewenstein DA, Dodrill KL et al 1988 Cerebral metabolic effects of a verbal fluency test. J Clin Exp Neuropsychol 10:565–575

Ramachandran VS, Gregory RL 1991 Perceptual filling in of artificially induced scotomas in human vision. Nature 350:699–702

Rusinov VS 1973 The dominant focus. (Translated by B Haigh) New York Consultants' Bureau, New York

Shallice T 1978 The dominant action system: an information processing approach to consciousness. In: Pope KS, Singer JL (eds) The stream of consciousness. Plenum Publishing Corporation, New York, p 117–157

Sherrington CS 1934 The brain and its mechanism. Cambridge University Press, Cambridge

Silberpfennig J 1941 Contributions to the problem of eye movements. III. Disturbance of ocular movements with pseudohemianopsia in frontal tumors. Confin Neurol 4:1–13

von der Malsburg C 1977 Self-organization of orientation-sensitive cells in striate cortex. Kybernetik 14:85–199

Zeki S, Shipp S 1988 The functional logic of cortical connections. Nature 335:311–317

DISCUSSION

Fenwick: You said there is some oscillating mechanism which gathers things together when consciousness arises. I accept that's true. But what is the mechanism of consciousness arising?

Kinsbourne: It is not Cartesian, because we don't have a nodal point.

Fenwick: No, it is not moveable seats, as in the Cartesian theatre.

Kinsbourne: The seats are moveable, but there are no telephone wires between the seats.

Fenwick: I don't understand when you say there are no connections between brain areas: you don't have telephone wires but you did have oscillations.

Kinsbourne: Yes, there certainly have to be some interactions in the brain or we couldn't think. The question that you might then ask is, assuming that this kind of pattern is what it takes to be aware and that it determines what you are aware of, how does it do that? My answer is, the question is not coherent.

Shevrin: I don't know how critical it is to your whole argument, but you made a point in your paper that there is no evidence for information flow in the brain. Several colleagues and myself have reported a method demonstrating information flow from one part of the cortex to another, from P3 to P4, from Oz to P3 (Kushwaha et al 1992). This method is based on the Shannon–Weaver information theoretical approach (Attneave 1959). We were able to show information flow for both supraliminal and subliminal visual stimuli.

Kinsbourne: I was talking specifically about the cortex. There is obviously information flow from the periphery up the spinal cord, into the brainstem and into the cortex. Clearly, you can't respond before you have had the stimulus. There will be a time lag between activity at one point and activity at another point.

I believe that we need not assume that the representation is transmitted from point to point. The fact that something is represented itself is a sufficient reason for us to be aware of that item of information. That doesn't mean that the brain is not permitted to move information from point to point.

Shevrin: So there is information flow, but it's not critical with respect to your argument against some kind of gathering of information at a particular predestined point?

Kinsbourne: That is correct. Similarly, with respect to the issue of filling in: if there is no central observer, once something is represented, or once a decision is made, there's no need to go back and fill in all the squares that normally represent the appearances about which the decision was made. If the brain has decided there was apparent movement, it doesn't have to go back and re-enact a moving stimulus. The brain can but it doesn't need to, because there isn't this nodal point to re-enact for.

Gray: I am very sympathetic with what you said; I think it's probably right. However, I dispute that current techniques, such as PET scanning, are capable of addressing the issue—the temporal and spatial resolution are simply too gross at the moment. If there is information flow within those corticocortical connections, it occurs on a time scale that those techniques cannot detect.

Shevrin: I was referring to evoked potentials, which are perfectly capable of detecting information flow within milliseconds.

Gray: Evoked potentials certainly do better in that respect, but they don't give you, unless you are using multiple depth electrodes, enough spatial resolution. Functional magnetic resonance imaging may do the trick.

Shevrin: Spatial resolution is not necessary to determine the presence of information flow, but would help to identify its many sources.

Gray: The other point that I'm not clear about is the dominant focus. The concept goes back to Rusinov (1973); I think it's a lovely concept and it fits very well with your overall approach. You said that it's the total amount of neural activity which somehow constitutes the dominant focus at a particular time. But I swear that everybody's dominant focus (that is, conscious experience) is rapidly interrupted by a small pinprick, and I doubt that a small pinprick immediately takes over large chunks of brain, as shown, for example, in lighting up of a PET scan.

Wall: I want to challenge your general assumption that conscious perceptions reside in the cortex. Take pain, for example, which everybody has referred to this morning as a simple experience. There are six PET and SPECT scan studies on pain; the one thing they all agree on is that no specific area of cortex is always activated. So if we are going to talk about distributed things, we should include parts of the nervous system other than cortex.

Kinsbourne: That certainly has to be the case. We know that pain fibres don't project to cortex. But if a person suffers a sharp pain, is there any change in the cortical electrophysiology or metabolism?

Wall: Sure, but not one area which can be labelled as a pain area as distinct from all the related processes of arousal, alerting, attention, orienting and so on.

Kinsbourne: What is the change? What do you actually see, electrophysiologically or metabolically, when you record from cortex?

Wall: It depends on the circumstances. Only one group claims that the sensory cortex is activated at all; the other groups say that the sensory cortex is not involved or that its activity decreases. They see all sorts of bizarre structures— anterior cingulate and the hippocampus—lighting up, depending on the particular circumstances of the experiment. Cortex is involved, but cortex could just as well be the reference library rather than the unique site of the action. Traditionally, pain is located in the cortex, but when you look at the evidence, activity appears in variable areas of cortex and all over the place.

Gray: The argument doesn't change if the centre of activity is in the cortex or elsewhere in the brain. What Pat Wall says is extremely important, because it strongly suggests that whatever is critical to consciousness, if it is not distributed as Marcel Kinsbourne thinks, but localized, then it's not cortically localized.

But I would still like to know whether we can think of this dominant focus purely quantitatively. Even if you just look at subcortical structures, surely the painful stimulus which has this royal route to consciousness doesn't actually light up large chunks of any part of the brain, does it?

Wall: Curiously, one of the words that I haven't yet heard is attention.

Kinsbourne: One thing we are familiar with, is that if a novel or highly adaptively significant stimulus comes in, a stop system is activated. There is a, perhaps noradrenaline-mediated, signal to stop all unrelated ongoing activity. If that's the case, the signal could be stopping activity all over the place and our methods might not be able to show that it is. One would imagine that pain, even if it's not severe, would have some privileged way of stopping ongoing cognitive activity, because it has to be attended to as a matter of priority. I think it's a nice thing to consider. I don't think it really changes my argument.

Marcel: I would like to challenge your data. You want to get rid of certain aspects of Cartesian theatre. The way you do this is to talk about neglect, and the knowledge that one has neglect. You say it's no surprise that the patient does not know about it, because that's part of what they are neglecting. There are two points here. First, that version of anosognosia, i.e. unawareness of deficit, just won't do, if you are also going to deal with unawareness of other types of deficit, namely amnesic anosognosia, aphasic anosognosia or Anton's syndrome. Your characterization won't account for such cases, because those deficits can occur without anosognosia, and therefore the anosognosia cannot be part of the basic deficit.

More importantly, in many cases of neglect with anosognosia, it appears that there is a split consciousness. The patient both knows of his deficit and does not know. This seems to imply that one does need a second-order reflexive level of consciousness, because there is the deficit (a type, or lack, of experience) and simultaneous knowledge and lack of knowledge of the deficit.

Kinsbourne: Obviously, every statement can be refined but there isn't a simple, clear-cut dichotomy that either the patient knows about the handicap or they don't. Clearly, there are levels of awareness. I can still argue, as a first approximation, that whereas a strong representation will obtrude itself into awareness in a clear-cut fashion, a weaker representation might do so fluctuatingly, or at some intermediate level or in relation to only some parts of the brain. You know that whether one knows something depends on which part of the brain is being asked the question. In the wonderful Marcel/Dennett experiment, subjects can make one perceptual decision when answering with a finger and, simultaneously, a different decision when answering with their mouth. That observation is totally consistent with the kind of model I have presented.

Nagel: Could I just raise a question that relates to things Ben Libet is going to be talking about. Bartley (1958) described an experiment where when five flashes of light are presented they are perceived as individual flashes or a flicker.

However, when three flashes were presented, they were perceived as a continuous light. This seems to me to involve a failure to distinguish adequately between physical and phenomenological time. I think that distinction has to be accepted whatever one's view of the mind–body problem. When the five flashes are presented and the person reports a continuous flicker, not a steady flash followed by a flicker, you ask what actually happened in the original sequence. Isn't the answer that in phenomenological time, which is the time of the experience, there was a series of flickering lights? That may not be an event that is situated in a correlated physical time. In fact, the physical basis of a phenomenological temporal sequence may not be a temporally sequential process at all; it might even be a different kind of ordering which is produced by a physically temporal sequence of inputs. Why is there any problem about that?

Kinsbourne: This is exactly what we argue; we say there is no problem, and people yell at us. The question to ask is, if those first three flickers had stopped at that point, would they not have been seen as a steady light? There was a point in time when only the first three flickers had occurred, so did the person see them like that? If he did, why doesn't he report seeing that? One answer is that there was an Orwellian reconstruction of what happened, given better information later. Another answer may be that the process hadn't come to that level of fruition.

Nagel: You suggest there is no fact of the matter; I say there is a perfectly good fact of the matter.

Dennett: Which is it? There are apparently two possibilities. One is that in phenomenological time, first the subject was aware of a three-flicker steady-state as a steady-state; then the awareness of that was replaced in memory by a sense of five flickers. The other hypothesis is that *ab initio* in phenomenological time the subject was aware of five flickers. Those are manifestly two different hypotheses about phenomenological time: one is Orwellian, the other Stalinesque. We say there is no difference between them.

Nagel: Why Stalinesque?

Dennett: We say it's not that you can't tell, but that 'telling' would imply there was something that either was or wasn't going on somewhere in the brain which would make the difference between these two possibilities. At some point in physical time in the brain, the resolution of those first three flickers is accomplished, so that the complete stimulus becomes interpreted as five flickers. Suppose we can know to the microsecond when that resolution happens in the brain. That will not tell us whether it is a post-experiential Orwellian resolution which has replaced an earlier phenomenological experience with an Orwellian revision, or whether now that this resolution has happened it can enter into the phenomenological time series. We are saying the distinction in this context makes no difference. There are no grounds for making that distinction. It's not the verificationist point that we just can't tell and therefore it makes no difference—there is nothing to tell.

Libet: There is evidence that to become aware takes time. Consequently, one need not say that the subject is immediately aware of three flashes as a continuous light; they become aware after the flashes have happened. So if the three flashes are followed by further flashes and the subject has not yet become aware of the initial 'continuous' light, then obviously the content of the experience when it appears can be a modification of what happened. If you accept the experimental conclusion idea that there is a substantial delay in awareness of the signals, then there is no problem in accounting for retroactive alterations in the content of the experience when further signals are delivered.

Kinsbourne: But it doesn't follow that just because something else happened, the subject would necessarily not have been aware of the previous steady light?

Libet: Not necessarily, but the fact is that there is an alteration in the content of experience when further visual pulses are added to the first three. In order to account for this observed alteration, we can draw on conclusions from the evidence that delayed inputs to the cortex can retroactively modulate the subjective content of the experience elicited by the preceding inputs (e.g. Libet et al 1992). That easily leads to the proposal that the experience of the first three flashes has been modified by later flashes.

Kinsbourne: You could easily say either of two things, and that's one of them, the Orwellian. The other is the Stalinesque.

Harnad: I would like to mount a small defence of the Cartesian theatre. Let me make all the concessions that it costs me no pain to make: whether there is a narrow localization or whether there are distributed representations all over the brain doesn't bother me. I also know enough psychophysics to know that not only can points not be psychophysically located exactly in space, they can't be located exactly in time either if there is a lot of noise around temporal thresholds. So I will assume *a priori* that a conscious event has to be temporally distributed to some degree because you just don't have perfect psychophysical resolution. Granted all that, consider the following: we all have the experience sometimes when we are half asleep, and sometimes when we are awake, of a shudder. I want you to think of a *mental* shudder rather than a physical shudder; I want this to be an instantaneous event, an endogenous experience of a kind of shudder. Now, I would like to know what's wrong with a Cartesian theatrical view of *that*: there is a process in the brain, possibly distributed both in time and to a certain extent in space, that corresponds *exactly* to the moment when that shudder of mine occurred (within psychophysical limits)—no Stalinesque misperception and no Orwellian misremembering about it. What's wrong with the Cartesian theatre view of that?

Dennett: Let me try to answer that. Once you get down to that case, you have in effect very carefully removed all the conditions for creating the implications that are the problem with the Cartesian view. You have created this isolated and punctate conscious experience. Since there is no other conscious experience around, there is none that it has to be related to, in terms of before or after or simultaneous. It doesn't even seem to be before or after or simultaneous with anything. The fundamental problem of the Cartesian theatre model is that it supposes there is a place in the brain where the actual temporal relations of events occurring in that place represent the subjective temporal relations in the stream of consciousness.

Harnad: Yes, but temporal relations *between* things have to start with *things*. I am just starting with the simplest kind of thing. It has an absolute temporal locus.

Gray: There is a clock time.

Dennett: Within the limits of precision it has a clock time, fine. Suppose that some other conscious experience in you, when you shudder, has the same clock time. We are talking about physiologically measured clock time. I take it you would agree that nothing follows about whether you experience that other experience as simultaneous, before or after the experience that has the clock time of the shudder. It is quite consistent, as far as you are concerned, that two punctate events can have the same clock time, but be experienced as one happening considerably before the other. If you grant me that, when two events have the same clock time by your measurements, this says nothing about the subjective co-temporality of them, then fine. If you think that the fact that they happen at the same time by the way you measure them shows that they are experienced as simultaneous, then I still think you are guilty of the Cartesian theatre.

Harnad: I am trying to be guilty of the Cartesian theatre! Introducing a second experience is fine, but let's treat it properly. When I talk about the real clock time of the punctate shudder I mean when that shudder was *experienced*; I'm not talking about 'representation' because there isn't a real time when the shudder was externally presented to me; the shudder was simply an experience I had. I want to know when and where the brain process occurs when that real-time mental shudder occurs. When you are talking about two simultaneous endogenous events, again, for those to be simultaneous at some point in the same sense that the shudder was a punctate event at some point, you need another punctate event that happened literally at the same time as the shudder *experientially*—in other words, it was *experienced* at the same time as the shudder. I would say that, by definition, the brain substrate of that concurrent composite experience, the brain process that carried that experiential moment, had the same clock time too.

Dennett: Let's say, for no reason at all, the word 'cat' suddenly appears in your head. At the same clock time, the shudder happens.

Harnad: Experientially?

Dennett: If you say experientially, then I say that's consistent with—when we do the brain science—finding out that, in fact, the cat system was activated considerably before the shudder system was, but you interpreted them as simultaneous.

Nagel: Why do you put it that way, 'interpreted them as simultaneous'? Why don't you just say, Stevan had phenomenologically simultaneous experiences of the two? This doesn't involve interpreting anything going on in your brain, you just have these phenomenologically simultaneous experiences. That experience complex is produced by a temporally extended sequence of brain states. I see no problem in that at all. I don't see why it's incompatible with the Cartesian theatre view (not that I particularly want to defend the Cartesian theatre). Why couldn't a temporally extended physical time sequence of events produce a non-temporally extended event in phenomenological time?

Dennett: I think everybody would agree that nothing follows about the subjective timing of two stimuli. Let's say, one is auditory and arrives at the ear at time t; and exactly at time t the retina is irradiated in a certain way. We have two events which are co-temporaneous in ordinary objective time, but we don't yet know anything about how the subject will experience these. Later, we ask the subject, did you experience these as simultaneous? The answer is yes or no. We can repeat the experiment with different timings. Then, from the subjects, we get an account of the subjective time sequence—when they find things in sequence, when they can't tell A before B from A after B, and so on. I am claiming that the mistake of the Cartesian theory is to suppose that you should then try to map that time series back into the brain to try to find the place, in the brain, where events coming from the ear and events coming from the eye come together.

Harnad: That conflates several issues. You now have external stimuli, which produce complications: I spoke only of endogenous experiences. Then there is the big methodological problem about locating the temporally and spatially distributed event that corresponds to the actual time of the experience(s). Ben Libet tries to do this empirically, but Dan Dennett and I agree there is an uncertainty about locating that subjective time. I think this is a methodological handicap that we all suffer from, one there's no way to overcome (Harnad 1982, 1989). Other people, like Saul Sternberg (personal communication, see Harnad 1992) think it could be overcome in principle. Dan thinks it is a metaphysical fact that the reason you can't locate it is that there isn't a fact of the matter, whereas I think it's just a methodological problem.

Kihlstrom: The physical shudder that you experience half way between waking and sleeping is called myoclonic jerk. It is a physical consequence of the fact that the tendons and the muscles relax at different rates. When that happens, most people who experience this have an image: for me, it's falling off a motor cycle. The image occurs at exactly the same time as the shudder does—they are put together. However, there are experimental and anecdotal reasons in the literature on sleep to think that the mental image and the physical shudder do not occur at exactly the same time. Rather, the mental image is some kind of construction that's based on the physical shudder itself.

The evidence unfortunately is mostly anecdotal, but it's a good anecdote. In 1861, Maury reported having a whole dream about being in the French revolution and being taken prisoner by the revolutionaries and being walked up to the guillotine, and his head being put into the guillotine, and the guillotine coming down on the back of his neck. At that point he awoke to find that his headboard had fallen on the back of his head. So here is a whole dream that has been constructed retrospectively on the basis of a physical sensation.

Harnad: I agree with everything you said. The trouble is that you have chosen Dan's type of example, involving external stimuli and complex, composite experiences, which is exactly what I tried to avoid; that's why I said, think of an *endogenous punctate* shudder, and not the image story; and not myoclonic input that would be the cause of it. You are changing examples.

Dennett: I think that the analogy that we have used in reply to our critics (Dennett & Kinsbourne 1992) best illustrates why we say there's no fact of the matter in this. The British Empire signed the truce to end the war of 1812 on December 24th 1814. Fifteen days later the British general in New Orleans went into battle. This was also an official act of the British Empire. He had no idea that the British had already signed the truce. There is a problem here because these things are out of synchrony.

Suppose we know to the microsecond when every agent of the British Empire learned of the signing of the truce. We would find all these different times were spread out over several weeks. Now we ask ourselves: when did the British Empire learn of the truce? And we realize there is no fact of the matter of when the British Empire learned of the truce.

Harnad: But my shudder is one experience, mine! It's not a bunch of agents having a bunch of shudders. The Cartesian Empire has just one agent: me.

Dennett: That's exactly the point. Suppose we ask: when exactly do *you* become aware of some stimulus (e.g. the shudder)? In order to answer that question with precision, *you* would have to be located in some particular place in this whole system, because the shudder will start in one place then spread to some degree around various parts of your brain.

Suppose we know exactly where all that activity happens. Unless we can find some privileged place in the brain, and say that when the activity happens right there, that's the moment of consciousness, then we can't answer that question. There is no fact of the matter for the same boring reason that there is no fact of the matter of when the British Empire learned of the signing of the truce.

Libet: The British Empire as such has no subjective experience! Each individual in the Empire learns about the truce at his own time and place. The empire analogy does not deal with the significant facts of the matter.

Dennett: There are facts of the matter there. There is the fact of when the king learned, when the members of parliament learned and when the ambassador learned. Those are all facts of the matter; I concede every one of them. There is also a fact of the matter about when each and every part of the brain is activated by this event.

Humphrey: There was an emperor who said 'L'état c'est moi'. He spoke for the empire.

Dennett: If you hold *that* view of consciousness, you are supposing that *I* am located at some particular point in my brain; when the information reaches that point, I become aware of it.

Humphrey: Dennett and I wrote a paper about multiple personality disorder (Humphrey & Dennett 1989). We postulated something equivalent to a 'head of mind', like the 'head of state'. This *I* is the spokesman, this *I* has control of the language system and this *I* is the self that other people interact with.

Dennett: It is distributed around in the brain.

Marcel: You have just denied that the brain and the content should be put together, so why do you keep referring to distribution around the brain, when you are actually talking about these content questions?

Dennett: Because Steve Harnad insists that, at least under certain circumstances, we can precisely temporally locate subjective experiences. I concede that, depending on the experience, one can get more or less precise about when it happens, as one can with the British Empire. But nothing should be taken to follow from that about the relationship of that experience to other experiences. Using whatever standard measurement you use to establish that, you may discover that experiences A and B happened in the order AB, but as far as the whole system is concerned they happen in the order BA, so subjectively they happened in the order BA, although objectively they happened in the order AB.

Gray: I find this whole topic interesting but essentially a diversion. I'm very persuaded by the arguments that Dennett (1991) and Dennett & Kinsbourne (1992) have put forward for the multiple drafts theory. But in the end, I don't feel that it in any way strengthens the functionalists' approach to consciousness. It sets up a possible way of showing how the brain generates conscious experiences. But it doesn't address the issue of why the brain generates conscious experience or what the particular mechanism might be. It just says it does it in a distributive rather than a punctate manner: so what?

Dennett: Years ago I wrote a paper on pain (Dennett 1978), where as a little joke I said: suppose there is a theory of pain which says these are the causes of pain, these are the effects of pain. The trouble is, the chart doesn't have a little box right in the middle where the pain happens. In fact, if you look throughout the whole model, you ask, where's the pain happening? It is no good trying to put it in a little box somewhere; that's to make a big mistake. I am now generalizing that argument, saying that in general for consciousness it's a mistake to think there's a little box in the head where the consciousness happens.

Gray: What do you do? Do you ditch consciousness totally?

Dennett: No.

Gray: So you are still left with the problem.

Dennett: You are still left with a problem; it is a slightly different problem.

Searle: Because it is a big box rather than a little one.

References

Attneave F 1959 Applications of information theory to psychology. Holt, Rinehart & Winston, New York

Bartley SH 1958 Some factors influencing critical flicker frequency. J Psychol 46:107–115

Dennett DC 1978 Why you can't make a computer that feels pain. Synthese 38:415–456

Dennett DC 1991 Consciousness explained. Allen Lane, London

Dennett DC, Kinsbourne M 1992 Time and the observer: the where and when of consciousness in the brain. Behav Brain Sci 15:183–201

Harnad S 1982 Consciousness: an afterthought. Cognit Brain Theory 5:29–47

Harnad S 1989 Editorial commentary. Behav Brain Sci 12:183

Harnad S 1992 Editorial commentary. Behav Brain Sci 15:233–234

Humphrey N, Dennett D 1989 Speaking for our selves. Raritan 9:68–98

Kushwaha RK, Williams WJ, Shevrin H 1992 An information flow technique for category related evoked potential. IEEE (Inst Electr Electron Eng) Trans Biomed Eng 39:165–175

Libet B, Wright EW, Feinstein B, Pearl DK 1992 Retroactive enhancement of a skin sensation by a delayed cortical stimulus in man. Consci & Cognit 1:367–375

Maury LFA 1861 Le sommeil et les rêves. Didier et Cie, Paris

The problem of consciousness[1]

J. R. Searle

Department of Philosophy, University of California at Berkeley, Berkeley, CA 94720, USA

Abstract. This paper attempts to begin to answer four questions. (1) What is consciousness? (2) What is the relation of consciousness to the brain? (3) What are some of the features that an empirical theory of consciousness should try to explain? (4) What are some common mistakes to avoid?

1993 Experimental and theoretical studies of consciousness. Wiley, Chichester (Ciba Foundation Symposium 174) p 61–80

The most important scientific discovery of the present era will come when someone—or some group—discovers the answer to the following question: How exactly do neurobiological processes in the brain cause consciousness? This is the most important question facing us in the biological sciences, yet it is frequently evaded, and frequently misunderstood when not evaded. In order to clear the way for an understanding of this problem, I am going to begin to answer four questions: (1) What is consciousness? (2) What is the relation of consciousness to the brain? (3) What are some of the features that an empirical theory of consciousness should try to explain? (4) What are some common mistakes to avoid?

What is consciousness?

Like most words, 'consciousness' does not admit of a definition in terms of genus and differentia or necessary and sufficient conditions. Nonetheless, it is important to say exactly what we are talking about because the phenomenon of consciousness that we are interested in needs to be distinguished from certain other phenomena such as attention, knowledge and self-consciousness. By 'consciousness', I simply mean those subjective states of sentience or awareness that begin when one awakes in the morning from a dreamless sleep and continue throughout the day until one goes to sleep at night or falls into a coma, or dies, or otherwise becomes, as one would say, 'unconscious'.

---

[1]The theses advanced in this paper are presented in more detail and with more supporting argument in Searle JR (1992) *The Rediscovery of the Mind*, MIT Press.

Above all, consciousness is a biological phenomenon. We should think of consciousness as part of our ordinary biological history, along with digestion, growth, mitosis and meiosis. However, though consciousness is a biological phenomenon, it has some important features that other biological phenomena do not have. The most important of these is what I have called its 'subjectivity'. There is a sense in which each person's consciousness is private to that person, a sense in which he is related to his pains, tickles, itches, thoughts and feelings in a way that is quite unlike the way that others are related to those pains, tickles, itches, thoughts and feelings. This phenomenon can be described in various ways. It is sometimes described as that feature of consciousness by way of which there is something that it is like or something that it feels like to be in a certain conscious state. If somebody asks me what it feels like to give a lecture in front of a large audience, I can answer that question. But if somebody asks what it feels like to be a shingle or a stone, there is no answer to that question because shingles and stones are not conscious. The point is also put by saying that conscious states have a certain qualitative character; the states in question are sometimes described as 'qualia'.

In spite of its etymology, consciousness should not be confused with knowledge, it should not be confused with attention, and it should not be confused with self-consciousness. I will consider each of these confusions in turn.

Many states of consciousness have little or nothing to do with knowledge. Conscious states of undirected anxiety or nervousness, for example, have no essential connection with knowledge.

Consciousness should not be confused with attention. Within one's field of consciousness there are certain elements that are at the focus of one's attention and certain others that are at the periphery of consciousness. It is important to emphasize this distinction because 'to be conscious of' is sometimes used to mean 'to pay attention to'. But the sense of consciousness that we are discussing here allows for the possibility that there are many things on the periphery of one's consciousness—for example, a slight headache I now feel or the feeling of the shirt collar against my neck— which are not at the centre of one's attention. I will have more to say about the distinction between the centre and the periphery of consciousness later.

Finally, consciousness should not be confused with self-consciousness. There are indeed certain types of animals, such as humans, that are capable of extremely complicated forms of self-referential consciousness which would normally be described as self-consciousness. For example, I think conscious feelings of shame require that the agent be conscious of himself or herself. But seeing an object or hearing a sound, for example, does not require self-consciousness. And it is not generally the case that all conscious states are also self-conscious.

What are the relations between consciousness and the brain?

This question is the famous 'mind–body problem'. Though it has a long and sordid history in both philosophy and science, I think, in broad outline at least, it has a rather simple solution. Here it is: conscious states are caused by lower-level neurobiological processes in the brain and are themselves higher-level features of the brain. The key notions here are those of *cause* and *feature*. As far as we know anything about how the world works, variable rates of neuron firings in different neuronal architectures cause all the enormous variety of our conscious life. All the stimuli we receive from the external world are converted by the nervous system into one medium, namely, variable rates of neuron firings at synapses. And equally remarkably, these variable rates of neuron firings cause all of the colour and variety of our conscious life. The smell of the flower, the sound of the symphony, the thoughts of theorems in Euclidian geometry—all are caused by lower-level biological processes in the brain; and as far as we know, the crucial functional elements are neurons and synapses.

Of course, like any causal hypothesis this one is tentative. It might turn out that we have overestimated the importance of the neuron and the synapse. Perhaps the functional unit is a column or a whole array of neurons, but the crucial point I am trying to make now is that we are looking for causal relationships. The first step in the solution of the mind–body problem is: brain processes *cause* conscious processes.

This leaves us with the question, what is the ontology, what is the form of existence, of these conscious processes? More pointedly, does the claim that there is a causal relation between brain and consciousness commit us to a dualism of 'physical' things and 'mental' things? The answer is a definite no. Brain processes cause consciousness but the consciousness they cause is not some extra substance or entity. It is just a higher-level feature of the whole system. The two crucial relationships between consciousness and the brain, then, can be summarized as follows: lower-level neuronal processes in the brain cause consciousness and consciousness is simply a higher-level feature of the system that is made up of the lower-level neuronal elements.

There are many examples in nature where a higher-level feature of a system is caused by lower-level elements of that system even though the feature is a feature of the system made up of those elements. Think of the liquidity of water or the transparency of glass or the solidity of a table, for example. Of course, like all analogies these analogies are imperfect and inadequate in various ways. But the important thing that I am trying to get across is this: there is no metaphysical obstacle, no logical obstacle, to claiming that the relationship between brain and consciousness is one of causation and at the same time claiming that consciousness is just a feature of the brain. Lower-level elements of a system can cause higher-level features of that system, even though those features are features of a system made up of the lower-level elements. Notice, for example, that just as one cannot reach into a glass of water and pick out a molecule and say 'This one is wet', so one cannot point to a single synapse or neuron in the brain and say 'This one is thinking about my grandmother'. As far as we know anything about it, thoughts about grandmothers occur at a much higher level than that of the single neuron or synapse, just as liquidity occurs at a much higher level than that of single molecules.

Some features of consciousness

The next step in our discussion is to list some (not all) of the essential features of consciousness that an empirical theory of the brain should be able to explain.

Subjectivity

This is the most important feature. A theory of consciousness needs to explain how a set of neurobiological processes can cause a system to be in a subjective state of sentience or awareness. This phenomenon is unlike anything else in biology, and in a sense it is one of the most amazing features of nature. There are certain philosophical moods we sometimes get into when it seems absolutely astounding that any such thing could occur and it seems almost impossible that we would ever be able to explain it in purely neurobiological terms. Whenever we get in such moods, however, it is important to remind ourselves that similar mysteries have occurred before in science. From the point of view of Newtonian mechanics, electromagnetism seems amazing. From the point of view of inorganic chemistry, life seems amazing. But we know that electromagnetism and life occur and we now have means of explaining them. I am suggesting that we have to acknowledge subjectivity as a brute fact of nature and seek a neurobiological explanation for it.

Unity

It is important to recognize that in non-pathological forms of consciousness we never just have, for example, a pain in the elbow, a feeling of warmth, or an experience of seeing something red, we have them all occurring simultaneously as part of one unified conscious experience. Kant called this feature 'the transcendental unity of apperception'. Recently, in neurobiology it has been called 'the binding problem'. There are at least two aspects to this unity that require special mention. First, at any given instant all of our experiences are unified into a single conscious field. Second, the organization of our consciousness extends over more than simple instants. So, for example, if I begin speaking a sentence, I have to maintain in some sense at least an iconic memory of the beginning of the sentence so that I know what I am saying by the time I get to the end of the sentence.

Intentionality

'Intentionality' is the name that philosophers and psychologists give to that feature of many of our mental states by which they are directed at, or about, states of affairs in the world. If I have a belief or a desire or a fear, there must always be some content to my belief, desire or fear. It must be about something, even if the something it is about does not exist or is a hallucination. Even in cases when I am radically mistaken, there must be some mental content which purports to make reference to the world. Not all conscious states have intentionality in this sense. For example, there are states of anxiety or depression where one is not anxious or depressed about anything in particular but just is in a bad mood. That is not an intentional state. But if one is depressed about a forthcoming event, that is an intentional state because it is directed at something beyond itself.

There is a conceptual connection between consciousness and intentionality in the following respect. Though many, indeed most, of our intentional states at any given point are unconscious, nonetheless, in order for an unconscious intentional state to be genuinely an intentional state it must be accessible in principle to consciousness. It must be the sort of thing that could be conscious even if it, in fact, is blocked by repression, brain lesion, or sheer forgetfulness.

The distinction between the centre and the periphery of consciousness

At any given moment of non-pathological consciousness I have what might be called a field of consciousness. Within that field I normally pay attention to some things and not to others. So, for example, right now I am paying attention to the problem of describing consciousness but very little attention to the feeling of the shirt on my back or the tightness of my shoes. It is sometimes said that I am unconscious of these. But that is a mistake. The proof that they are a part of my conscious field is that I can at any moment shift my attention to them. But in order for me to shift my attention to them, there must be something there to which I was previously not paying attention to which I am now paying attention.

The Gestalt structure of conscious experience

Within the field of consciousness our experiences are characteristically structured in a way that goes beyond the structure of the actual stimulus. This was one of the most profound discoveries of the Gestalt psychologists. It is most obvious in the case of vision, but the phenomenon is quite general and extends beyond vision. For example, the sketchy lines drawn in Fig. 1 do not physically resemble a human face. If we actually saw someone on the street who looked like that, we would be inclined to call an ambulance. The disposition of the brain to

FIG. 1.   Sketchy lines perceived as a human face.

structure degenerate stimuli into certain structured forms is so powerful that
we will naturally tend to see this as a human face. Furthermore, not only do
we have our conscious experiences in certain structures, but we tend also to
have them as figures against backgrounds. Again, this is most obvious in the
case of vision. Thus, when I look at the figure I see it against the background
of the page. I see the page against the background of the table. I see the table
against the background of the floor, and I see the floor against the background
of the room, until we eventually reach the horizon of my visual consciousness.

The aspect of familiarity

It is a characteristic feature of non-pathological states of consciousness that
they come to us with what I will call the 'aspect of familiarity'. In order for
me to see the objects in front of me as, for example, houses, chairs, people,
tables, I have to have a prior possession of the categories of houses, chairs,
people, tables. But that means that I will assimilate my experiences into a set
of categories which are more or less familiar to me. When I am in an extremely
strange environment, in a jungle village, for example, and the houses, people
and foliage look very exotic to me, I still perceive that as a house, that as a
person, that as clothing, that as a tree or a bush. The aspect of familiarity is
thus a scalar phenomenon. There can be greater or lesser degrees of familiarity.
But it is important to see that non-pathological forms of consciousness come
to us under the aspect of familiarity. Again, one way to consider this is to look
at the pathological cases. In Capgras's syndrome, the patients are unable to
acknowledge familiar people in their environment as the people they actually
are. They think the spouse is not really their spouse but is an impostor, etc.
This is a case of a breakdown in one aspect of familiarity. In non-pathological
cases it is extremely difficult to break with the aspect of familiarity. Surrealist

painters try to do it. But even in the surrealist painting, the three-headed woman is still a woman, and the drooping watch is still a watch.

Mood

Part of every normal conscious experience is the mood that pervades the experience. It need not be a mood that has a particular name to it, like depression or elation; but there is always what one might call a flavour or tone to any normal set of conscious states. So, for example, at present I am not especially depressed and I am not especially ecstatic, nor, indeed, am I what one would call simply 'blah'. Nonetheless, there is a certain mood to my present experiences. Mood is probably more easily explainable in biochemical terms than several of the features I have mentioned. We may be able to control, for example, pathological forms of depression by mood-altering drugs.

Boundary conditions

All of my non-pathological states of consciousness come to me with a certain sense of what one might call their 'situatedness'. Though I am not thinking about it, and though it is not part of the field of my consciousness, I nonetheless know what year it is, what place I am in, what time of day it is, the season of the year it is, and usually even what month it is. All of these are the boundary conditions or the situatedness of non-pathological conscious states. Again, one can become aware of the pervasiveness of this phenomenon when it is absent. So, for example, as one gets older there is a certain feeling of vertigo that comes over one when one loses a sense of what time of year it is or what month it is. The point I am making now is that conscious states are situated and they are experienced as situated even though the details of the situation need not be part of the content of the conscious states.

Some common mistakes about consciousness

I would like to think that everything I have said so far is just a form of common sense. However, I have to report, from the battlefronts as it were, that the approach I am advocating to the study of consciousness is by no means universally accepted in cognitive science or even neurobiology. Indeed, until quite recently many workers in cognitive science and neurobiology regarded the study of consciousness as somehow out of bounds for their disciplines. They thought that it was beyond the reach of science to explain why warm things feel warm to us or why red things look red to us. I think, on the contrary, that it is precisely the task of neurobiology to explain these and other questions about consciousness. Why would anyone think otherwise? Well, there are complex historical reasons, going back at least to the 17th century, why people thought that consciousness was not part of the material world. A kind of residual dualism prevented people from treating consciousness as a biological phenomenon like any other. However, I am not now going to attempt to trace this history. Instead, I am going to point out some common mistakes that occur when people refuse to address consciousness on its own terms.

The characteristic mistake in the study of consciousness is to ignore its essential subjectivity and to try to treat it as if it were an objective third-person phenomenon. Instead of recognizing that consciousness is essentially a subjective, qualitative phenomenon, many people mistakenly suppose that its essence is that of a control mechanism or a certain kind of set of dispositions to behaviour or a computer program. The two most common mistakes about consciousness are to suppose that it can be analysed behaviouristically or computationally. The Turing test disposes us to make precisely these two mistakes, the mistake of behaviourism and the mistake of computationalism. It leads us to suppose that for a system to be conscious, it is both necessary and sufficient that it has the right computer program or set of programs with the right inputs and outputs. I think you have only to state this position clearly to enable you to see that it must be mistaken. A traditional objection to behaviourism was that behaviourism could not be right because a system could behave as if it were conscious without actually being conscious. There is no logical connection, no necessary connection between inner, subjective, qualitative mental states and external, publicly observable behaviour. Of course, in actual fact, conscious states characteristically cause behaviour. But the behaviour that they cause has to be distinguished from the states themselves. The same mistake is repeated by computational accounts of consciousness. Just as behaviour by itself is not sufficient for consciousness, so computational models of consciousness are not sufficient by themselves for consciousness. The computational model of consciousness stands to consciousness in the same way the computational model of anything stands to the domain being modelled. Nobody supposes that the computational model of rainstorms in London will leave us all wet. But they make the mistake of supposing that the computational model of consciousness is somehow conscious. It is the same mistake in both cases.

There is a simple demonstration that the computational model of consciousness is not sufficient for consciousness. I have given it many times before so I will not dwell on it here. Its point is simply this: *computation is defined syntactically*. It is defined in terms of the manipulation of symbols. But the syntax by itself can never be sufficient for the sort of contents that characteristically go with conscious thoughts. Just having zeros and ones by themselves is insufficient to guarantee mental content, conscious or unconscious. This argument is sometimes called 'the Chinese room argument' because I originally illustrated the point with the example of the person who goes through the computational steps for answering questions in Chinese but does not thereby acquire any understanding of Chinese (Searle 1980). The point of the parable is clear but it is usually neglected. *Syntax by itself is not sufficient for semantic content.* In all of the attacks on the Chinese room argument, I have never seen anyone come out baldly and say they think that syntax is sufficient for semantic content.

However, I now have to say that I was conceding too much in my earlier statements of this argument. I was conceding that the computational theory of the mind was at least false. But it now seems to me that it does not reach the level of falsity because it does not have a clear sense. Here is why.

The natural sciences describe features of reality that are intrinsic to the world as it exists independently of any observers. Thus, gravitational attraction, photosynthesis and electromagnetism are all subjects of the natural sciences because they describe intrinsic features of reality. But features such as being a bathtub, being a nice day for a picnic, being a five dollar bill or being a chair, are not subjects of the natural sciences because they are not intrinsic features of reality. All the phenomena I named—bathtubs, etc—are physical objects and as physical objects have features that are intrinsic to reality. But the feature of being a bathtub or a five dollar bill exists only relative to observers and users.

Absolutely essential, then, to understanding the nature of the natural sciences is the distinction between those features of reality that are intrinsic and those that are observer relative. Gravitational attraction is intrinsic. Being a five dollar bill is observer relative. Now, the really deep objection to computational theories of the mind can be stated quite clearly. Computation does not name an intrinsic feature of reality but is observer relative and this is because computation is defined in terms of symbol manipulation, but the notion of a 'symbol' is not a notion of physics or chemistry. Something is a symbol only if it is used, treated or regarded as a symbol. The Chinese room argument showed that semantics is not intrinsic to syntax. But what this argument shows is that syntax is not intrinsic to physics. There are no purely physical properties that zeros and ones or symbols in general have that determine that they are symbols. Something is a symbol only relative to some observer, user or agent who assigns a symbolic interpretation to it. So the question, 'Is consciousness a computer program?', lacks a clear sense. If it asks, 'Can you assign a computational interpretation to those brain processes which are characteristic of consciousness?', the answer is: you can assign a computational interpretation to anything. But if the question asks, 'Is consciousness intrinsically computational?', the answer is: nothing is intrinsically computational. Computation exists only relative to some agent or observer who imposes a computational interpretation on some phenomenon. This is an obvious point. I should have seen it ten years ago but I did not.

Reference

Searle JR 1980 Minds, brains, and programs. Behav Brain Sci 3:417–457

DISCUSSION

Harnad: It is lucky that you didn't spot that computation was merely observer relative ten years ago (Searle 1980), because if you had, a couple of other *true* things that you said would have become incoherent! For example, the idea that you could implement the same program as did the computer that passed the Turing test would become an arbitrary thing—there wouldn't be any interesting property that you shared with the computer, namely, the implementation of the same program.

Searle: I don't think that follows at all. The fact that computation is observer relative doesn't imply that computation is arbitrary. Consider another example: the notion of a bathtub is also observer relative but not just anything can be a bathtub. In order to function as a bathtub, an object has to have certain features. But all the same, the concept 'bathtub' is not a concept of theoretical physics. So it doesn't follow from the observer relativity of a concept of a bathtub that anything at all can be a bathtub.

The point I made ten years ago in the Chinese Room argument was this: take any computer program, say a program for understanding Chinese, and imagine that a conscious agent goes through the steps of the program. You will see that, for example, the conscious agent doesn't thereby acquire an understanding of Chinese. The point I'm making now is a separate point. Because computation is an observer relative notion, *computation is not discovered in a physical system*; rather a computation interpretation is *assigned to* the physical system. Just as the Chinese Room argument showed that semantics is not intrinsic to syntax, so this argument is designed to show that syntax is not intrinsic to physics. But it does not follow from this account that the notion of computation is arbitrary, that any system at all can be used as a computer. So observer relativity does not imply arbitrariness.

Harnad: Let me push this further. Let's focus on syntax, on whether we can talk about N different physical systems that all implement the same formal syntax. You may call that shared property observer relative; maybe that's not what I am challenging. But there *is* some property that those N systems all share, that is not shared by every other system. It is *that* property I (Harnad 1989) construed to be the real target of your Chinese room argument; that wasn't an incoherent target, fortunately, and hence your Chinese room argument had not been a refutation of an incoherent claim.

Searle: I think I should add a stronger comment than that. The supporters of strong artificial intelligence thought of programs as intrinsic to the computer system. The idea was that implementing the right program with the right inputs and outputs was constitutive of having cognition. That was the actual claim that was debated.

Gray: Let me challenge the statement (because it's obviously critical to what you are saying and I'm not sure whether it's true or not) that a syntactical system has to be observer relative. The series of bases that make up a string of DNA can be regarded as a syntactical system, in the very real sense that, depending upon that string, the RNA transcribed from it is translated into different proteins and all those go to make up an organism. That clearly is not observer relative; it has been developed as part of biological evolution. We don't have to put any interpretation upon the string of bases, although we now attempt to read it in the manner of modern genetics. The interpretation is there because of what the DNA sequence does.

At this point, one might answer, 'what that string of bases does is simply a matter of physics and chemistry'. Some years ago Polanyi & Prosch (1975) dealt with this issue, using an argument which shows that a string of DNA bases does indeed constitute a syntactical system. The laws of physics and chemistry not only don't determine the string of bases, but if they did fully determine the string, it would have no information capacity and natural selection would not be able to work on that sequence. What happens is that at each point in the chain, there are a number of alternative solutions in terms of the laws of physics and chemistry, and what particular base is then added to the sequence depends upon which particular base leads to a functionally surviving organism. At that point, the laws of physics and chemistry leave open a range of possibilities, providing an information capacity that is filled in by the genetics and, ultimately, Darwinian natural selection. I think that meets all the definitions of a syntactical system, and it is not observer relative.

Searle: I don't think that's quite going to work the way you stated it. I may have misunderstood, but the way I heard you say it is: there's a slack in what's determined by the physical realizations and therefore the system is intrinsically syntactical. I don't think you really want to argue that, and I'll tell you why. The notion of syntax here identifies an equivalence class. We could get the same syntax using some completely different medium—marbles or zeros and lines. You can do a computational simulation of the DNA sequence, which I assume is computationally adequate, since we know how the stuff works now, but the computational simulation doesn't produce babies.

The key notion is causation. The DNA molecule has a rather specific causal capacity to replicate itself—and that is not just syntax. Because you can have the same syntax in a totally different medium, marbles or computers, or marks on paper. The general point here is that anything can be given a syntactical characterization. We find this useful in the case of DNA, and we find it very useful to talk in intentionalistic vocabulary about DNA, but that doesn't tell us how it works as a physical system; it's still a physical system.

Dennett: In your talk, you posed the question: 'How exactly do neurobiological processes in the brain cause consciousness?' I don't see how anything could count as an answer to the question, given certain demands you put on it. Suppose we set out to answer the question, and we make the following initial assumption: not every detail of every microfeature of the neuronal activity of any particular brain is crucial for causing subjectivity, so we are going to see what the crucial ones are. When we look at our friends we see plenty of differences in their brains, and we suppose they all have subjectivity, so there's some scope for variation. We want to know which differences in neuronal behaviour matter and which don't. The only way I can conceive of doing this is by some version of J. S. Mill's method of differences. We try out different hypotheses. For example, maybe it matters that things happen on the left side of the brain rather than on the right side of the brain. We check that hypothesis and reject it because both left-handed and right-handed people are subjective. Other differences in brains we are not so sure about. Then suppose somebody puts forward the following bald hypothesis for testing: it doesn't matter really whether the brain is made of silicon or whether it's made of organic material, as long as the functional structure is preserved. We can test this by making large bits of silicon into functionally duplicating structures and see what happens.

Here the problem arises. I think you were saying, 'suppose the entity with the silicon brain passes all the behavioural tests and seems to have subjectivity, it will be just pseudo-subjectivity, it's not the real thing'. But now if you are prepared on this occasion to do that, what about us left-handers? Maybe my subjectivity is just pseudo-subjectivity, maybe the apparent subjectivity of females is just pseudo-subjectivity. The trouble with your posing the question this way is that you don't give us any way of actually testing my hypothesis, which is that silicon subjectivity is the only kind of subjectivity there is. You just say that's pseudo-subjectivity, and we know that at the outset. But if you know that, how do you know about these other cases?

Searle: To begin with, it does not seem to me that subjectivity is all that difficult, in principle, to investigate. Several people here make their living doing it. Pat Wall, among his other achievements, tries to figure out what the actual mechanisms are when people feel pain. When Tony Marcel deals with those unfortunate people with blindsight, he is talking about people who have different sorts of subjectivity from the kind that the rest of us have. So I think in real life it's not a metaphysical problem. There is an empirical problem: how do you study it in detail when you have a mechanism like the brain with 10^9 neurons all jammed in together, and almost any interesting method of studying it destroys the field you are studying? So you have to do PET (positron emission tomography) scans and computer-assisted tomography and a lot of ingenious empirical things, but there's no metaphysical problem.

So let's forget about real life and talk about this theoretical silicon brain. Let's say: my brain starts to deteriorate so that I'm going blind. I go to my brain-stabbers at the University of California Medical School and they are unable to do anything—Searle's brain is just degenerating in the visual cortex. In desperation, they insert silicon chips and wire them into my visual cortex. One possibility, not to be excluded on any *a priori* grounds whatever, is that miraculously my vision is restored—as a result of the insertion of the silicon chips, I can now see as well as I ever did. The silicon has exactly the same causal powers as the neurons that produce conscious experiences.

I don't believe it would ever happen this way, but it's not something you could exclude on philosophical grounds. My brain continues to deteriorate, they continue to replace my brain with silicon chips, and eventually, when I shake my head, I can hear the silicon rattling, but my mental life is completely unchanged. It turns out that silicon chips do absolutely everything that the neurons could do. That's a causal claim: it claims that the causal powers of a system of silicon chips are equivalent to the causal powers of the system of neurons. That is not excludable on any *a priori* grounds whatever. That's the optimistic version of the experiment, and I see no problem with that at all.

Dennett: Although *you* would have every reason to believe that silicon has the causal powers to produce subjectivity, I, by your own arguments, would have no reason to believe it at all.

Searle: No, I don't think that. For one thing we might replicate it with your brain.

Now let me give the pessimistic version of the same experiment. My brain is deteriorating, they plug in the silicon chips, everything seems to go pretty well, but there's one thing I discover. While my behaviour is indistinguishable from my normal behaviour, the area of my consciousness is shrinking. So they say to me, 'We are going to hold up a red object and we want you to tell us what you see'. I want to cry out, 'I can't see anything, I am absolutely blind', but I hear my voice say in a way that's totally out of my control, 'I see a red object'. On this thought experiment, the area of my conscious experience gradually shrinks to zero, I am phenomenologically dead, but the input/output functions are totally maintained by the silicon chips. If the first thought experiment makes any sense at all, that one does too.

Shoemaker: John, in the pessimistic version, you seem to imply that the conclusion is warranted that just after your consciousness fades out you have all the functional representation there without any mentality. Surely that's not warranted, because it's perfectly compatible with this that as you fade out somebody else is coming in.

Searle: That's another thought experiment. As you said, one could imagine an alternative locus of consciousness coming into me. The final possibility is that I maintain all of my mental life but no behavioural manifestations. People conclude I'm dead, they might as well pull out the plug. I want to scream out that I'm perfectly conscious. That's not science fiction, that's very close to the Guillain–Barré syndrome, where people are fully conscious but capable of exhibiting no behavioural manifestation for that.

So, altogether there are four different thought possibilities. First, the silicon chips are capable of producing both my conscious experience and my behaviour. Second, they produce my conscious experience without my behaviour. Third, they produce my behaviour without my conscious experience, and fourth, they produce my behaviour with a completely different set of conscious experiences. All of these illustrate the basic point: there is no necessary connection between consciousness and behaviour.

Van Gulick: John, your view that mental properties are caused by and realized in the brain is perfectly compatible with functionalism. (You would not describe yourself as a functionalist, but I will do so.) The functionalist view for the past 25 years has been that mental states are higher-order properties realized by underlying microstates. The functionalist is committed to there being a multiplicity of levels of explanation: some of them are very close to input/output logical construction; some of them are very close to the hardware; lots of them are in between. There are different levels of systematic explanation for any complex system, and the brain is perhaps the most complex there is. The way to proceed is by articulating structure at the conscious level, then trying to project it down to lower levels of organization. You won't get down to neurons in one jump, it may take many steps.

Can I just ask, what do you mean by neuron firings?

Searle: I was talking about action potentials at the synaptic connections and what goes on in the synaptic cleft.

Van Gulick: I think the term 'firing' is more apt for talking about depolarization of the axon, as opposed to what can go on in the dendritic arbour which is synaptic, but not firing.

Wall: I would like to return to your second question and consider pathological cases. Take the example of an aura preceding an epileptic attack. What the patient experiences, depending on the location of his epileptic focus, ranges from some very simple sensation like tingling in the fingers to an elaborate scene with music, people, and emotions. This all amounts to what you would identify as a conscious experience, with one exception: the patients know that it is not an hallucination. They know the scene does not exist in reality, but rather signifies that they are going to have a fit. But the experience is, as far as one can see, a perfect conscious experience with that one exception. I think that example is something very open for a neurobiological explanation, i.e. here is an otherwise normal person with a small area of their brain in an abnormal state and yet developing nine-tenths of a normal conscious experience.

Searle: Yes, those are fascinating cases. The ones I know best are in Dostoevsky, where he gives marvellous descriptions of what it felt like when he knew he was just on the verge of an epileptic fit.

Fenwick: There are occasional accounts in the literature of mystical experiences, so they are a general property of brain function. But is that all, or do we need a wider view of mind beyond the brain?

Marcel: Do you want to keep 'ownership' (of sensation) as a separate fact of consciousness, or is that going to go under subjectivity?

Searle: I'm a little puzzled by this. I can't make much sense of the philosophical discussions of the experience of the self, because people want the experience of the self to do a job it couldn't possibly do, namely guarantee personal identity or something like that. I do think there is a certain characteristic feel of what it feels like to be me. It doesn't carry any metaphysical baggage, because if you made a clone of me, he would have the same feel. Nothing follows from that feeling. There is this feeling of self-hood, but I don't know what you want that to do.

Marcel: There are two types of categories to consider. One is that certain sensations come with the feeling that they are *yours*. On the other hand, the content of my perception of the world is that it is 'out there': it feels mind independent, and not mine; I don't experience it as part of me. To me, those sorts of things don't easily fall under subjectivity, but they do seem to be interesting aspects of experience.

Searle: I don't know what to say about these pathological, or maybe not pathological, cases where people say they have their experiences occurring outside them. In my ontology, I have a sequence of experiences and they go on in my body. I don't have a third thing called the self. Part of those experiences are what I would call what it feels like to be me, or feel like an experience of self-hood. But nothing follows from that.

Marcel: In the first case, that's OK. I gave the second example because the content of most normal percepts is experienced as outside the body. Touch is really interesting, because there is a dual aspect to it. You can attend to what you are touching and then you have a percept of what is outside, or you can attend to your own self or body and then you have a sensation of an owned feeling or state of self. This is also possible with vision, but much harder to experience as part of self.

Nagel: I would like to discuss the satisfaction conditions for an explanation of how the brain produces consciousness. John, you are more content than I am to say it's obvious there is a necessary connection, but because we ourselves are conscious, we are not in a position to see both sides of the connection in such a way that we can see how it operates. While I agree that at the moment we don't see how to get ourselves into the position of finding consciousness deeply intelligible, I don't quite understand why you think that the fact that we ourselves are conscious is a permanent obstacle to attaining for that case the level of understanding we have about why water boils when it is heated.

Searle: That isn't quite the point. You are on record as maintaining that the mind–body problem poses a special, apparently metaphysical, difficulty which is not posed by other sorts of scientific explanation. The difficulty is this. In the case of why water boils when heated, if we understand the mechanisms fully, we can see why the water has to boil. Scientific explanation implies necessity, on your view. Now according to your view as I understand it, we can't get that kind of necessity for causal explanations of consciousness. Suppose Pat Wall and his colleagues had derived a complete neurobiological explanation for pain. Still, on your view, we wouldn't have an explanation of why this system has to be in pain, given all the causal conditions, in the way that we do have an understanding of why the system has to be boiling given all that we know about the kinetic theory of heat and so on.

My answer has three parts. First, I'm not sure that scientific explanation does have to have this kind of necessity, but let's concede that for the moment. Then the form of your argument is contraposition. Because scientific explanation implies necessity, no necessity implies no explanation. We can't have necessity for the mind–brain problem, so we can't have a scientific explanation. At this second stage of the argument, I made two points. One is, at most the argument would show that we can't grasp the necessity, but there might be a necessity even if we couldn't grasp it. Secondly, even if we couldn't grasp the necessity, that failure might be due to a peculiar asymmetry between this type of explanation and normal scientific explanations. Namely, in appreciating the necessity of a normal scientific explanation, our conscious thought processes grasp both sides of the necessary connection. But there might be an asymmetry where our conscious thought processes were themselves one of the terms of what has to be explained. Thus, if solidity could think, it might think: 'There will never be an explanation of solidity in terms of molecular behaviour, because there's no reason why I have to be solid, just because these molecules are wiggling around in that way'. If solidity thought that, it would be making a mistake. Because even if it couldn't appreciate the necessity, there is a necessity; its inability to appreciate the necessity has to do with the fact that it doesn't have an objective view of the situation.

Williams: What you seem to be leaving out is the fact that the small asymmetry to which you refer is the heart of the problem. While it remains there, and while we have as little insight into it as we do, your claim that the states of the brain cause the personal experience, that this is a necessary connection between them, is just bluff. We have no insight into what such a causal connection could be, at the level at which we actually understand this piece of nature. When people talk about the mind–body problem, they mean the difficulty (it may or may not be insoluble) of what it means to say that brain processes cause conscious states. So the alleged solution that they just do, isn't a solution, it's a statement of the problem.

Searle: I am struck by the fact that the neurobiologists who actually work on these problems don't sense any metaphysical gulf. If you read straightforward neurobiological accounts of how pain is caused, or you read accounts of how the visual system works, nobody ever says we will never be able to explain it because there's this huge metaphysical gulf.

Fenwick: That refers to how pain is caused, not how pain is sensed.

Searle: The notion of causation that is used is the standard notion of causation that's used in science, namely, as an answer to the question, 'how does it work?' If you deal with brain-stabbers on a daily basis, as I try to do in Berkeley, there is no metaphysical problem of what kind of causation is involved. We know that certain peripheral stimuli cause me to feel pain; we know they cause me to have certain visual experiences. I think the difficulties we have are not metaphysical logical differences, they are empirical difficulties—we don't know the details. If we had a complete science of the brain, if we really knew in detail how brain processes cause sensations of pain or visual experiences, then I think the traditional mind–body problem would simply disappear.

In response to Tom Nagel's specific point, at best it is epistemic. No serious philosophical gulf is raised by saying we can't grasp the fact of how the neuronal behaviour must cause us to be conscious. It doesn't follow from that that neuronal behaviour can't necessitate consciousness, and frankly, I just can't take it seriously that my point of view, that brain processses cause consciousness, is denied!

Nagel: I don't think that part of your point of view is denied. It is clear that brain processes cause sensations. It is only when you get to the 'how' that you get to the mind–body problem. I have a feeling that you think of the situation as our knowing that brain processes cause sensation in the way that people once knew that the germ cells cause the inherited characteristics of the organism— only they didn't know how it worked. I think there is a crucial difference there. Even before the beginnings of molecular biology, in some very broad sense we knew what the logical character of a filling-out of the explanation of heredity would be. We could form the conception of a chemical theory of how the instructions were all in there, without having any idea of the content of the theory. But, we don't have even that basic, outline idea of what an answer to the 'how' question would be like for consciousness. And you have offered an explanation of why we don't.

Where my disagreement with you lies, I think, is that I don't understand how this is a demystifying explanation of the apparent problem. I think that for the demystification to succeed, it would have to show that we could be confident that a necessary connection between these two domains existed, but for some reason that we could recognize, we could see that we wouldn't be able to work it out completely. I don't think that is accomplished merely by pointing out that we are ourselves conscious.

Searle: I think our great-grandparents had a discussion that was very much isomorphic with this about life. The standard argument was that one could not possibly explain life in these crude biochemical, mechanical terms. No biochemical explanation would ever be able to account for the élan vital.

I am maintaining two propositions. Number one: we know, as a matter of fact, that brain processes cause consciousness, and the sense of causation here is the most naive and pedestrian imaginable—brain processes make conscious events happen. Secondly, the consciousness in question is a higher-level feature of the system. That is a more problematical claim, but I'm prepared to argue for it in detail. But if you accept these two claims, there is no longer a meta-physical mind–body problem. In the most ordinary sense, brain processes cause consciousness, consciousness is a higher-level feature of the brain.

Now the hard work begins. How does the brain do it in detail? That's an empirical scientific question. If after we had a complete neurobiological answer to that question, some philosopher said, 'You haven't satisfied me', I do not think that we or the neurobiologists should be worried about that.

Gray: There's a third term in this set of contrasts. Tom Nagel described the term, then you refined it, John. You said it's not a metaphysical problem, and I agree. You said it is an empirical problem; but it is not an empirical problem in the sense that all we have to do is gather more data. It's a science-theory problem, as Tom said, in which at present we don't even know what the logic of the theory could look like. This is much more than an empirical problem. On the other hand, it isn't necessarily an insoluble science-theory problem. Nobody would have had the slightest idea of what Einstein's relativity theory would have looked like in advance. The logical structure of quantum mechanics is totally different from any logical structure that classical physics ever dealt with, yet we now have it.

Searle: I am using 'empirical' to contrast with 'metaphysical'; in that sense, 'empirical' issues include theoretical issues. The analogy between Newtonian and quantum mechanics is exactly the analogy I used in discussing the mind–body problem at the end of my book, *Intentionality* (Searle 1983). I said, when we come to understand the mind–body problem, the apparatus that we use may be as radically different from anything we now know as quantum mechanics is from Newtonian mechanics. Those are what I mean by empirical questions.

Williams: I agree with Jeffrey entirely: it is a case in which we haven't the foggiest idea what the theory would even look like. If that is so, isn't it fair to say that the question is metaphysical?

Humphrey: One reason we don't have the foggiest idea is that we are accepting this extraordinary language of brain processes 'causing' consciousness. John and Tom and others just take it for granted that this is the right way to describe it. John says this is the most commonsensical, naive view of it. But I don't think most ordinary people suppose that consciousness is an effect that follows from a brain process. If anything, they suppose consciousness just *is* a brain process. If someone dances a jig, you don't say the movements of their legs are causing the dance, the movements of the legs *are* the dance. What the brain processes perhaps cause is certain speech acts to be performed and so on, which we can interpret as evidence of consciousness. But the essential fact is that the original brain processes *are* conscious.

Searle: I think that consciousness is literally a feature of the brain, and hence literally conscious processes are brain processes. But an explanation of those phenomena has to explain how they work. Now, as far as we know anything about it, the story that everybody who works on this tells is a causal story. Neurobiologists talk about how certain stimuli of the nervous system go to the central nervous system, and how they then cause various other things to occur in the central nervous system, and how eventually the whole set of reactions cause the system to be conscious. It is possible that in the end, in a complete science of consciousness, we will have no use for the notion of causation. That I take as an empirical question. But right now, the story that biology tells is a causal story.

I read, just for fun, neurophysiology text books. I am struck by how different they are from the standard philosopher's model of science. There are almost no laws. Occasionally, they offer a law, but then they usually say it's false. The brain is described the way you would describe an internal combustion engine. It is a causal story from the beginning to end, and neuro-biologists are interested in how it works. The difference is that whereas the guys who describe the internal combustion engine know something about how it works, the guys who write neurophysiology text books for the most part don't know how the brain works. But that is a theoretical empirical ignorance, not a metaphysical impossibility.

Velmans: I think there are four types of causal story that you can tell about consciousness, brains and their interaction. The first story is based purely on how things look from a third-person perspective; it is couched entirely in the language of neurophysiology, brain processing and so on. The second causal story is purely a first-person perspective story, based on how causal sequences appear from a subject's point of view. For example, the causes of an experienced emotion might appear to be a previous thought, or some other prior experience. The third and fourth stories are mixed perspective explanations, which switch from a third-person perspective to a first-person perspective or vice versa. The cases that John Searle is talking about are cases of this kind. John, you say that the brain is capable of producing subjective states of consciousness. Expanded, this simply means that events which, from a third-person perspective, look like brain events produce effects which, from the first-person perspective of the owner of that brain, appear to be subjective experiences. Such switching is common in psychological investigations. For example, one might investigate the neural causal antecedents of a given form of pain from a third-person perspective, but to get any idea of how that pain feels (to complete the causal story) one has to switch to the subject's first-person point of view. Alternatively, one might be interested in how a person's experiences affect their body or brain (viewed from the outside)—involving a switch from a first- to a third-person perspective. For example, a person might report feeling embarrassed and an external observer might observe that this causes blood vessels in their cheeks to dilate (a blush). I think there is nothing wrong with any of these causal stories. All you have to realize is that sometimes you are describing events from a third-person perspective, sometimes from a first-person perspective, and sometimes you are switching from one perspective to another. It is all perfectly legitimate. What we need to find out is how these perspectives relate to each other in detail (see Velmans 1991a,b and this volume).

References

Harnad S 1989 Minds, machines and Searle. J Exp Theor Artif Intell 1:5–25

Polanyi M, Prosch H 1975 Meaning. University of Chicago Press, Chicago, IL

Searle JR 1980 Minds, brains and programs. Behav Brain Sci 3:417–457

Searle J 1983 Intentionality: an essay on the philosophy of mind. Cambridge University Press, Cambridge

Velmans M 1991a Is human information processing conscious? Behav Brain Sci 14:651–669

Velmans M 1991b Consciousness from a first-person perspective. Behav Brain Sci 14:702–726

Velmans M 1993 A reflexive science of consciousness. In: Experimental and theoretical studies of consciousness. Wiley, Chichester (Ciba Found Symp 174) p 81–99

A reflexive science of consciousness

Max Velmans

Department of Psychology, Goldsmiths' College, University of London, New Cross, London SE14 6NW, UK

Abstract. Classical theories of consciousness make it difficult to see how it can be a subject of scientific study. In contrast to physical events, it seems to be private, subjective and viewable only from a subject's first-person perspective. But much of psychology does investigate conscious experience, which suggests that classical theories must be wrong. An alternative, 'reflexive' model is proposed in which the external phenomenal world is viewed as *part of* consciousness rather than *apart from* it. Observed events are 'public' only in the sense of 'private experience shared'. Scientific observations are 'objective' only in the sense of 'intersubjective'. Observed phenomena are 'repeatable' only in that they are sufficiently similar to be taken for 'tokens' of the same event 'type'. This closes the gap between *physical* and *psychological* phenomena. Studies of consciousness face methodological difficulties. An experimenter E and a subject S may have 'symmetrical access' to events in the outside world in so far as they perceive those events (from a third-person perspective) using similar exteroceptive systems; but their access to the subject's body, brain and experience is 'asymmetrical' (E's third-person perspective versus S's first-person perspective). In so far as E and S each have partial access to such events, their perspectives are complementary. Systematic investigation of experience requires merely that experiences are potentially shareable, intersubjective and repeatable. In this the conditions for a science of consciousness are no different to those for a science of physics.

1993 Experimental and theoretical studies of consciousness. Wiley, Chichester (Ciba Foundation Symposium 174) p 81–99

I am always rather puzzled when people ask whether it is possible to have a science of consciousness, because much of psychology *is* a science of consciousness in spite of psychologists' frequent protestations to the contrary. Many of the papers at this symposium, for example, will elaborate on recent ways in which psychological and related brain sciences are proceeding with the study of conscious experience rather than agonizing over whether such a study is possible, and this has been true of experimental psychology since its inception in Wundt's laboratory in Leipzig in 1879. How could one study colour vision, perceptual illusions, emotions, dreams or imagery without making a systematic study of conscious experience, its relation to environmental input, to brain processing, and so on?

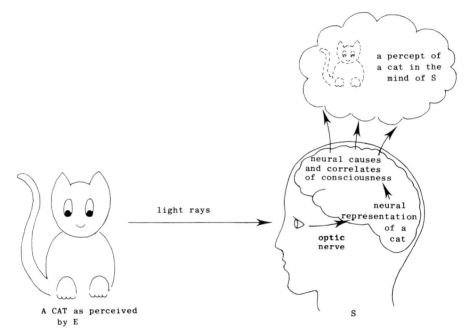

FIG. 1.   A dualist model of the causal sequence in visual perception. Light rays from
a cat (as perceived by an experimenter, E) impinge on the eye of a subject, S. Impulses
travelling up the optic nerve produce a neural representation of the cat within S's central
nervous system (CNS). CNS activity, in turn, has a causal influence on S's mind, resulting
in a percept of a cat. It is central to this model that the percept (of a cat) in the mind
of S is quite separate from both the neural representation (of a cat) in S's brain and
the cat (as perceived by E) out in the world. From Velmans (1990a).

So, why is it that in much philosophical, psychological and other scientific
writing, a scientific investigation of consciousness has been thought to be
difficult, if not impossible? The reason, I suggest, has to do with a deep-seated
confusion about how consciousness relates to the brain and physical world,
which permeates the entire dualist versus reductionist debate.

Consider the conventional model of perception shown in Fig. 1. Viewed from
the perspective of an external observer E, light rays travelling from the physical
object (the cat as perceived by E) stimulate the eye of the subject S, activating
his optic nerve, occipital lobes and associated regions of his brain. Neural
conditions sufficient for consciousness are formed and result in a conscious
experience (of a cat) in the mind of S. From E's perspective, the physical and
neurophysiological causes of S's experience are (in principle) observable, but
their perceptual effect (the experience itself) is not. E nevertheless infers that
S *has* an experience, for the reason that when E turns his gaze toward the cat
he has an experience of the cat himself.

It is clear from this simple model why consciousness is often thought to elude scientific study. From E's perspective, the cat is seen to be out in the world; it appears to be public, objective and observable from an external, third-person perspective. Consequently, a scientific study of cats presents no philosophical problems. By contrast, S's experiences seem to be private, subjective and viewable only from S's first-person perspective. If so, how can they form a database for science?

Dualists and reductionists have very different reactions to this problem. For dualists, S's experience is a non-material substance or entity, with no location or extension in space (represented as a 'cloud' in Fig. 1); consequently, dualists may accept that a study of consciousness is beyond natural science. Reductionists believe that S's experience will eventually be shown to be nothing more than a state or function of the brain (Fig. 2). If so, the study of consciousness may be safely left to neurophysiologists.

I do not intend to rehearse the advantages and disadvantages of these positions, as I do not believe the nature of consciousness can be understood in either dualist or reductionist terms. The intractability of the problems posed by consciousness arises not from irresolvable differences between dualism and reductionism, but from unfounded assumptions that they *share*. The models

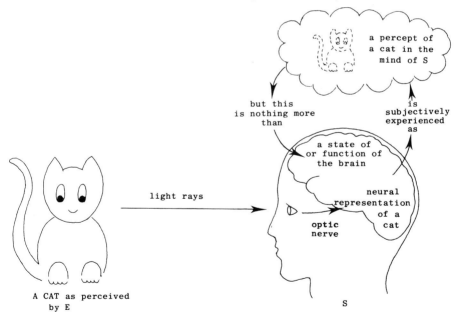

FIG. 2.   A reductionist model of the causal sequence in visual perception. As in Fig. 1, light rays from a cat impinge on the eye of a subject, S, leading to a neural representation of the cat within the CNS of S. This CNS activity is subjectively experienced as a percept of a cat (in the mind of S) but neurophysiological discoveries will show this subjective experience to be nothing more than a state or function of S's brain. From Velmans (1990a).

shown in Figs 1 and 2, for example, take it for granted that experiences are *separate* from the external physical world; in so far as experiences are thought to *be* anywhere, they are 'in the mind' or 'in the brain'. The physical world, on the other hand, is 'out there' beyond the body surface.

I have argued, by contrast, that the dualist and reductionist models need to be replaced by the reflexive model shown in Fig. 3 (Velmans 1990a, 1992a,b,c; see also commentaries by Gillett 1992, Rentoul 1992, Wetherick 1992). This differs only in the final step. As before, perception is initiated by some entity or event stimulating sense organs, afferent neurons and cortical projection areas, along with association areas, long-term memory traces and so on. As before, neural representations of the initiating event are eventually formed within the brain—in this case, neural representations of a cat. S also has an *experience* of a cat. But according to the reflexive model, there is no experience of a cat 'in S's mind' or 'in S's brain'. While S is gazing at the cat, his only experience of the cat is the *cat he sees out in the world*. If he were asked to *point* to his experience, he should point not to his brain but to the cat as perceived, out in space beyond the body surface. In this, S is no different from E. The cat as perceived by S is the same cat as perceived by E (albeit viewed from S's perspective rather than from E's perspective).

Thus, the reflexive model makes the conventional assumptions that representations of external events are formed within the subject's brain and that under appropriate conditions these are accompanied by experiences of the represented events. Unconventionally, it also suggests that the brain models the world by *reflexively projecting* experiences to the judged location of the events they represent. On this view, the world as experienced (the phenomenal world) is a representation, formed by sense organs and perceptual processes that have developed in the course of human evolution. Being *part of* consciousness, the phenomenal world cannot be thought of as *separate* from consciousness (contrary to Figs 1 and 2)[1]. This has profound consequences for whether the study of consciousness can be a science.

Note that if the phenomenal world is just a representation, it cannot be the 'thing-itself'. Physics and other sciences may represent the events we experience in a very different way; non-human animals exposed to the same events, but

---

[1]In the reflexive model, all experienced phenomena result from an interaction of an observer with an observed. In Fig. 3, light energy reflected from a given entity out in the world is processed by the perceptual apparatus of a subject, S, resulting in a cat as perceived (by S) out in the world. There is no *additional* percept *of* a cat in S's mind or brain. The phrases, 'a cat as perceived' and 'a percept of a cat' are *logically* distinct, but they do not refer to events which are *phenomenologically* distinct. In the interaction of the observer with the observed, the phrase 'a percept of a cat' focuses attention on the observer; the phrase 'a cat as perceived' focuses attention on the observed. But there is only *one* phenomenal cat (out in the world).

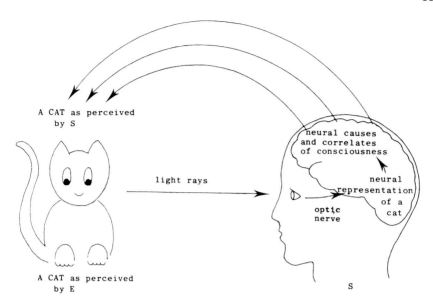

FIG. 3.   A reflexive model of the causal sequence in visual perception. As in Fig. 1,
light rays from a cat impinge on the eye of a subject, S, leading to a neural representation
of the cat within the CNS of S. Information within this neural representation is
incorporated within an 'experiential model' of the cat produced by the brain in the form
of a cat as perceived by S. This is 'projected' by the brain to the judged location of
the initiating stimulus, in the outside world. As in the dualist and reductionist models,
the neural representation of a cat in S's brain is separate from the cat (as perceived by
E) out in the world. Contrary to these models, however, S's percept of a cat and the
cat as perceived by S are the same. What S experiences is similar to what E experiences,
viz. a cat out in the world, but viewed from S's perspective rather than from E's
perspective. From Velmans (1990a).

equipped with different sensory and perceptual systems, are likely to inhabit
different phenomenal worlds.

Although this way of thinking about the world as experienced may seem odd
to those accustomed to thinking in either a dualist or reductionist way, it follows
a tradition in philosophy tracing back to Immanuel Kant, and the scientific
evidence for perceptual projection in visual, auditory and tactile sense modalities
is considerable (cf. Velmans 1990a). I do not have space to recount that evidence
here. For anyone who doubts that the phenomenal world *could* be a perceptual
projection, recent work with virtual realities may provide a quick, convincing
demonstration. Current virtual realities are crude; nevertheless, they give one
the impression of being surrounded by simple, virtual objects in a three-
dimensional virtual world through which one can move and with which one
can interact. This virtual world is entirely a perceptual construction based on
computer-generated images, fed to goggles, which are co-ordinated with body

movements and in some systems with tactile stimuli administered via gauntlets. This simulates the pattern of stimulation arriving at the senses that one might expect when interacting with entities and events in the actual world. In the reflexive model, the creation of such projected, virtual realities is easily explained—the computer-generated input stimuli simply tap into the same perceptual processes that construct the everyday phenomenal world. Natural light projection holograms provide another convincing demonstration. I own a fine hologram of the head of Sulis Minerva, goddess of the waters in the old Roman city of Bath. If the hologram is mounted in a box and one is not told that it is a hologram, it looks (from the front) just like the statue of a head in a box. But what one sees is just a three-dimensional *image* of a head in a box. In the reflexive model, this is again easily explained. The pattern of light reflected from the two-dimensional surface of the hologram resembles the pattern of light that would be reflected from a three-dimensional head located in the box. Accordingly, perceptual processes construe the reflecting surface to *be* a three-dimensional head and reflexively project an image of a head to its judged location, in the box. The image of a head out in space is the only image one experiences (there is no additional image of a head experienced to be in one's mind or brain). If the hologram were replaced by an actual head, perceptual processing would be the same.

   I shall now turn to the consequences of the reflexive model for a science of consciousness.

Public versus private events

As noted above, the *privacy* of conscious experience is often thought to place it beyond scientific investigation. Physical events, by contrast, are thought to be *public*. In the words of the philosopher Curt Ducasse:

   'In the case of the things called "physical", the patent characteristic common to and peculiar to them, which determined their being all denoted by one and the same name, was simply that all of them were, or were capable of being, *perceptually public*—the same tree, the same thunderclap, the same wind, the same dog, the same man, etc., can be perceived by every member of the human public suitably located in space and in time. To be material or physical, then, *basically* means to be, or to be capable of being, perceptually public.' (Ducasse 1960, p 85)

The reflexive model suggests a very different view. In this model, what we ordinarily refer to as the 'physical world' is simply the world as experienced around our bodies. This phenomenal world, being part of consciousness, is private to each human being. In the same way that you cannot experience *my* pain, you cannot experience *my* experience of a mountain. *All* experienced events are private, whether they be inner events (such as thoughts and dreams), events in the body, or events out in the world. In Fig. 3, the cat as perceived by E is private to E; the cat as perceived by S is private to S. Consequently, any description E or S gives of the cat is necessarily a description of their own private experience. At first glance, the consequences for science seem to be those spelled out by the father of operationalism, the physicist P. W. Bridgman, in 1936. In the final analysis, Bridgman concludes, 'science is only my private science'.

Yet, as Ducasse points out, there clearly is a sense in which some entities and events are also 'perceptually public'. The entity under observation in Fig. 3, for example, can be perceived to be a cat by both E and S, and by any other member of the public suitably located in space and time. But if each *phenomenal* cat is private, what is it about the cat that is 'perceptually public'?

Recall that in the reflexive model, objects as perceived represent 'things-themselves', but are not identical to them. The thing which is perceived by E and S to be a cat might be described in a very different way in physics. There may be something about a 'thing-itself' that is public in spite of the fact that each experience *of* it is private. When a thing is located beyond the body surface it is potentially accessible to the exteroceptors of any normally functioning human. Thus, *things-themselves* may be 'public' in the sense of being *publicly accessible*.

Further, to the extent that things are subject to similar perceptual processing in different human beings, it is reasonable to assume a degree of commonality in the *way* such things are experienced. While each experience remains private, it may be a private experience that others share. Consequently, *experienced things* (phenomenal objects and events) may be 'public' in the sense that they are *private experiences shared*.

Subjectivity and intersubjectivity

Once an essentially 'private' experience becomes 'public' in the sense that others have similar (private) experiences, there is also a transition from *subjectivity* to *intersubjectivity*. Each private experience is necessarily subjective in that it is always the experience of a *given* observer; once that experience is shared with another observer it becomes intersubjective. To the extent that an experience can be *generally* shared (by a community of observers), it can form part of the database of a communal science.

Intersubjectivity in this sense does not entail an *absence* of subjectivity, i.e. it does not entail the existence of some observer-free 'objectivity', even for observations and measurements in natural science. As Chalmers (1990) points out, science has developed many techniques for circumventing the idiosyncrasies of human perception, involving standardized procedures for translating data into meter readings, computer print-outs and so on. Consequently, anyone following the same procedures should get the same results. In this way, he claims, 'observations become objectified'. However, the repeatability of observations does not make them independent of an observer.

In the reflexive model, each observation results from an *interaction* of the observer with the observed; consequently, each observation is observer dependent and unique. If the conditions of observation are sufficiently standardized, the observation is repeatable, in which case intersubjectivity can be established by collective *agreement*. Different observers cannot have an *identical* experience; even if they observe the *same event* they each have their own, unique experience. Intersubjective agreement requires merely that their experiences are sufficiently similar to be taken for 'tokens' of the same 'type'. This applies particularly to scientific observations, where 'repeatability' requires intersubjective agreement amongst scientists observing similar events at *different* times and in *different* locations.

In sum, observed phenomena in natural science are (1) public only in the sense that they are 'private experiences shared'; (2) intersubjective rather than 'objective'; (3) repeatable only in the sense that they are sufficiently similar to be taken for 'tokens' of the same 'type'.

This re-analysis of the public, intersubjective, repeatable nature of physical phenomena applies equally to phenomena more usually thought of as 'conscious' or 'psychological', such as images and pains. For example, prolonged focusing on a red circle produces a green circle after-image. Each after-image is private, yet the phenomenon is public in the sense that anyone with normal vision focusing on the red circle under suitable conditions should have a similar experience, i.e. it is intersubjective and repeatable. Pain is often taken to be a paradigmatic case of a private, mental event within philosophy of mind. Nonetheless, the claim that aspirin diminishes certain forms of pain is publicly testable. If the claim is true, pain reduction should be a shared experience that is intersubjective and repeatable.

Within the reflexive model, such parallels between physical and psychological phenomena are to be expected for the reason that the entire phenomenal world is part of consciousness. The phenomena we call 'physical' are just a subset of the things we *experience*. Indeed, such phenomena can often be thought of as either 'physical' or 'psychological', *depending on the network of relationships under consideration*—a point made by the neutral monists Ernst Mach (1885), William James (1904) and Bertrand Russell (1948). As Mach puts it:

'The traditional gulf between physical and psychological research . . . exists only for the habitual stereotyped method of observation. A colour is a physical object so long as we consider its dependence upon its luminous source, upon other colours, upon heat, upon space, and so forth. Regarding, however, its dependence on the retina . . . it becomes a psychological object, a sensation. Not the subject, but the direction of our investigations is different in the two domains.'

In this situation, the traditional gulf between a *subjective first-person perspective* and an *external observer's third-person perspective* is equally narrow. Each experienced phenomenon results from an interaction of the observer with the observed. If the observer is interested in the nature of what is *observed* (for example, the nature of what is out in the world), he may be said to adopt a third-person perspective. If he is interested in the nature of his own *experience* (of the observed), he may be said to adopt a first-person perspective. But the observer's experience does not change as he changes perspective! All that changes is his focus of interest and, consequently, the relationships under consideration.

However, the study of conscious experience usually involves an interaction between at least *two* observers, an experimenter (E) and a subject (S). This raises several complications.

Symmetries and asymmetries of access

Consider, once again, the cat in Fig. 3. Suppose that E and S both focus on the cat and use similar (exteroceptive) perceptual systems and equipment to observe it. In this situation, we can define their access to the cat as being 'symmetrical'. But suppose E is an experimental psychologist and is interested not in the cat or in his own experience of the cat but in S's perceptual processing and consequent experience.

In a typical psychology experiment, S might be asked to attend to the cat (now thought of as the stimulus) while E shifts the focus of his attention to S, for example, to events taking place within S's body and brain, or to S's reports of what he experiences. From E's third-person perspective, the processes taking place within S's body and brain are, in principle, observable. S might *infer* the existence of such processes, but while he focuses on the cat he cannot *observe* them. Consequently, the access E and S have to S's perceptual processing is 'asymmetrical'. In this situation, the differences between E's third-person view of S and S's first-person view of himself are considerable. From E's point of view, this poses no problem as he has access to the information he needs.

In other situations, E and S *both* have access to events relating to S, although their access remains asymmetrical. S, for example, may have insight into the nature of his own psychological problems (via feelings and thoughts), which E might investigate by observing S's brain or behaviour. In medical diagnosis, S may have access to some malfunction via interoceptors, producing symptoms such as pain and discomfort, whereas E may rely on what can be detected from the outside, via his exteroceptors (eyes, ears and so on) supplemented by instrumentation. In these situations, neither the perspective of E nor that of S is automatically privileged. In so far as E and S each have partial access to the same condition, their perspectives are complementary (cf Velmans 1991a, section 9.3, Velmans 1991b, sections 8 and 9).

Access to S's experience is also asymmetrical, but in this case S has exclusive access to his experience whereas E can only infer its existence. From E's point of view, this does pose methodological problems, because information about S's experience can be obtained only indirectly, for example from S's verbal description or some other communicative response. This has not prevented a systematic investigation of experience, including quantification of experience (e.g. within psychophysics and psychometrics), although methodological solutions have often required considerable ingenuity (see Ericsson & Simon 1984, Finke & Shepard 1986, Libet 1985, Pope & Singer 1978)[2].

A non-reductionist science of consciousness

Reductionists retreat from a science of consciousness into a 'third-person perspectivism' which *denies* the legitimacy of S's experience, while simultaneously *asserting* the legitimacy of E's experience (of S). If the reflexive model is correct, this exclusive faith in E (at the expense of S) loses its foundation. S's consciousness is not some ephemeral 'cloud' that requires reduction to make it respectable for science, but his *entire* phenomenal world. This is *formed* by perceptual processing interacting with represented entities and events, but does not *reduce* to such processing. The phenomenal world of E is no different. Consequently, the experiences of S and E are equally legitimate.

From their respective vantage points, E and S have symmetrical access to some entities and events, and asymmetrical access to others. Whether E's third-person view of S or S's first-person view of himself is privileged depends entirely on what is being accessed and what requires explanation. One can err from either perspective.

E has access to S's brain states and behaviour, but S has access to his own experience. A complete psychology needs to draw on both forms of information; it also needs to investigate how information accessible to S relates to information accessible to E (cf. Velmans 1990b). If S's experiences are to form a database for science, they merely need to be potentially shareable, intersubjective and repeatable. In this respect, the conditions for a science of consciousness are no different from the conditions for a science of physics.

References

Bridgman PW 1936 The nature of physical theory. Princeton University Press, Princeton, NJ
Chalmers A 1990 Science and its fabrication. Open University Press, Buckingham, UK and University of Minnesota Press, Minneapolis, MN

---

[2]These references provide a small sample of methodological innovations; a comprehensive list would encompass much of experimental psychology. For some areas of experience, adequate methodologies still need to be developed, particularly where those experiences are difficult to quantify and control. Given the constraints on length, I focus only on the *general conditions for a science of consciousness* rather than on specific methodological problems and possible solutions.

Ducasse C 1960 In defence of dualism. In: Hook S (ed) Dimensions of mind. Collier Books, New York, p 85–89

Ericsson KA, Simon H 1984 Protocol analysis: verbal reports as data. MIT Press, Cambridge, MA

Finke RA, Shepard RN 1986 Visual functions of mental imagery. In: Boff KR, Kauffman L, Thomas JP (eds) Handbook of perception and human performance, vol 2: Cognitive processes and performance. Wiley, New York, p 37.1–37.55

Gillett G 1992 Consciousness, intentionality and internalism. Philos Psychol 5:173–180

James W 1904 Does 'consciousness' exist? Reprinted 1970 In: Vesey GNA (ed) Body and mind: readings in philosophy. Allen & Unwin, London, p 202–208

Libet B 1985 Unconscious cerebral initiative and the role of conscious will in the initiation of action. Behav Brain Sci 8:529–566

Mach E 1885 Contribution to the analysis of the sensations. Reprinted 1970 In: Vesey GNA (ed) Body and mind: readings in philosophy. Allen & Unwin, London, p 172–179

Pope KS, Singer JL 1978 The stream of consciousness. Plenum Press Publishing Corporation, New York

Rentoul R 1992 Consciousness, brain and the physical world: a reply to Velmans. Philos Psychol 5:163–166

Russell B 1948 Human knowledge: its scope and its limits. Allen & Unwin, London

Velmans M 1990a Consciousness, brain, and the physical world. Philos Psychol 3:77–99

Velmans M 1990b Is the mind conscious, functional, or both? Behav Brain Sci 13:629–630

Velmans M 1991a Is human information processing conscious? Behav Brain Sci 14:651–669

Velmans M 1991b Consciousness from a first-person perspective. Behav Brain Sci 14:702–726

Velmans M 1992a Synopsis of 'Consciousness, brain, and the physical world.' Philos Psychol 5:155–157

Velmans M 1992b The world as-perceived, the world as-described by physics, and the thing-itself: a reply to Rentoul and Wetherick. Philos Psychol 5:167–172

Velmans M 1992c Reply to Gillett. Philos Psychol 5:181–182

Wetherick N 1992 Velmans on 'Consciousness, brain and the physical world.' Philos Psychol 5:159–162

DISCUSSION

Marcel: When you used the term intersubjective, were you using it in the sense of conventional psychology, i.e. that there is a shared consciousness or that each person knows what the other is conscious of? It seems to me you are using it in an unconventional sense, whereby something is intersubjective merely because a lot of people see it. Normally, intersubjectivity is where each knows and there is a mutuality.

Velmans: But how do you establish that mutuality? I was saying, basically, your experience is subjective to you, my experience is subjective to me. By exchange of information, we establish our shared subjectivity, and thereby our intersubjectivity or mutuality.

Marcel: No. There are several approaches to intersubjectivity that do not rely on linguistic exchange, for example, those that appeal to Verstehen, to simulation, or to the idea of a 'virtual other'.

Nagel: Max, it seems to me that you are introducing an unnecessary puzzle in asking where is the head when you look at a hologram of a head. The head is the intentional object of my perceptual experience—what it is a perception *of*. Of course, the object of my experience is located in the box, but my visual experience of seeing a head in the box is in my head. Are you denying that?

Velmans: Yes. I would say that you are giving a characterization of your visual experience that misrepresents what you actually experience! You make a distinction between the intentional object of perceptual experience (the head as experienced), which you agree is out in the world, and your experience *of* a head, which you claim is in *your* head. But when you look at the hologram, you *don't* have an experience of the holographic head in your own head. The only visual experience you have is of a head in a box, out in the world.

Nagel: I don't say that I *experience* the visual experience of the head as being in my head. I just say it is *in fact* an event taking place in my brain. If we want to locate the mental event in space, its location is in my head. There is absolutely no incompatibility between that and locating the intentional object of that perceptual experience outside my head. These are really two completely different levels of description of the thing.

Velmans: I agree that 'a head as experienced' and 'an experience of a head' are two ways of describing the same thing. In the reflexive model, all observations involve an interaction of the observer with an observed. The phrase 'a head as experienced' focuses our attention on what is observed; the phrase 'an experience of a head' focuses our attention on the role of the observer. The two phrases are logically distinct, but they do not refer to events that are phenomenologically distinct. This is precisely my point. There is only one phenomenal head, and it is out there in the world.

That said, the reflexive model assumes exactly what other models assume about events taking place in the physical world and in the brain. So there are external physical events, representations of those events in the brain, influences of memory and consequent experiences. The whole story is the same. The only thing that is being challenged is the notion that *experiences* of events out in the world are in the head or brain. The only experience I have of the holographic head is the head I see out in the world. William James made the same commonsensical point, as did Kant, Russell, Whitehead and other theorists. The value of using a hologram of a head in a box to demonstrate this point is that we all know there really isn't a head in the box—it's only a three-dimensional image. So it's easier to get away from the notion that the experience of a head *can't* be out there in the world, because there is something already occupying its place—the object itself. But what applies to holograms applies in general. According to the reflexive model, perceptual processes in the brain reflexively project experiences to the judged locations of the events and entities those experiences represent.

Harnad: The *object* of the experience is out there, but the *experience* is inside, in the head. When one asks where the experience is, one is not asking about the locus of the object of the experience but about the locus of the experience. You seem to be conflating the two.

Gray: The reflexive argument seems to me to have an intuitive plausibility in vision. But what happens when I'm sitting with my eyes closed and listening to a string quartet on a gramophone? Where is the string quartet?

Velmans: The reflexive model calls a spade a spade for all phenomena. So if you are wearing earphones and you experience a symphony orchestra distributed in the space within your head, the reflexive model says the experience is within your head. The particular examples I was dealing with had to do with physical events out there in the world, because those are the ones that cause most of the problems.

Gray: You are telling me that in each case the experience is where it feels it is. But I'm asking about your reflexive model. In the reflexive model, you say there is a cat, there is the representation in the brain which is then reflexively projected back out to where the cat in fact is. How do you do that with the string quartet?

Velmans: What you are drawing attention to is that there are a number of natural subdivisions within the contents of consciousness, for example, events experienced to be out in the world, events experienced to be within the body or on its surface, and inner events without a clear experienced location. According to the reflexive model, the brain continuously attempts to produce a phenomenal representation of events, including a phenomenal representation of their location. So, when events originate in the world, the brain projects the corresponding events as experienced out in the world. An event that has its origin within the body, once processed by the brain, results in a bodily experience. Inner events such as thoughts and dreams relate to the processing of the brain itself; consequently, they are experienced to be in the head or to be without a clear location. So, if there really is an orchestra out there in space, you will normally hear the sounds out there in space. If you listen to the orchestra through earphones, you will usually hear the sounds inside your head. According to you, experiences are always inside the head. I agree that brain states are always inside the head, but this is not true of experiences. In the case of sound, this occurs only under special conditions.

'Inside the head locatedness' has been studied by Laws (1972). He investigated the acoustic differences between white noise presented through a speaker (perceived to be out in the world) or through earphones (perceived to be inside the head), using probe microphones placed at the entrance to the auditory canal. This revealed spectral differences produced largely by the pinnae of the ear being bypassed under one condition but not the other. He then devised an electrical equalizing circuit that would simulate the effects of the pinnae. When the equalizing circuit was switched into the earphone circuit, noise presented through earphones was experienced to be out in the world; when the circuit was switched out, the noise was experienced to be inside the head.

So all the reflexive model says is that the brain makes judgements about the location of events on the basis of the information it receives. Normally, in the case of sounds, information about location is provided by auditory cues, some of which are produced by spectral changes produced by the pinnae. If you produce those changes artificially, the brain judges the source of sound to be out in the world and projects the experienced sound to the judged location of the source. When pinnae effects are absent, the brain concludes that the source of sound cannot be beyond the pinnae, and 'inside the head locatedness' results.

Searle: There is a commonsense view that I think you may be denying; I'm not sure. Suppose I listen to a string quartet; I sit here and they are over there, and I listen to them play the music. Then I go home and I put on my earphones and listen to a tape of the same music. In both cases, there was an experience that occurred in my head. In both cases, there was an external cause of that experience. Are you denying that?

Velmans: I am saying there is a difference between those two situations. If there is an orchestra out there in space, you will hear the sounds out there in space. If you put the earphones on, you will hear the sounds inside your head. All the reflexive model says is, on the basis of the information that is arriving in the brain, the brain makes a decision about where the source of information is. Normally, the information about location is provided by auditory cues, some of which are produced by the modulation caused by the pinnae.

Libet: It seems to me that the reflexive model is simply a special case of what's going on all the time—subjective referral. If you stimulate the somatosensory cortex electrically, you don't feel anything in the brain or head at all, you feel it out in your hand or wherever the representation is of that cortical site. That applies to all sensibilities. There is referral away from the brain to the body parts; there is referral out into space, if the stimulus appears to be coming from there. The representations of the neuronal patterns of the brain are not isomorphic with what's coming in, so there is referral not only at a distance, but also in terms of the shape or configuration of the image, which is not identical with the neuronal representation at all.

Velmans: I agree.

Libet: So this is a general property of what's going on, it's not a special thing. On the other hand, to understand and explain subjective referral of neuronal representations is indeed a fundamental question on the mind–brain relationship.

Humphrey: There is an ambiguity which may be creeping in and suggesting this is more complicated than it is. When something happens to our bodies, when light arrives at our eyes or sound at our ears, we can represent that event at our body surface in two ways: either as a sensation, as a bodily event of some significance occurring at the boundary between ourselves and the environment, or as a perception, something happening in the external world.

These two can occur in parallel with each other, and to some extent can be dissociated. The same event may be sensed in one way and perceived in another.

Take the example of the remarkable experiments of Paul Bach-y-Rita (1972) on skin vision, in which he used mechanical stimulation on the skin of the back to represent the display from a television camera. In that situation, people can switch between perceiving a visual world of objects in space, public objects shared with other people, and feeling the tactile stimulus on their back as a private event. They have, in effect, a *visual* percept accompanied by a *tactile* sensation. You weren't distinguishing these two possibilities, i.e. that the same effect can be represented in these two ways, one of which is external, the other of which is located in one's own body.

Velmans: It's not a problem for the model at all. For a start that's a special case . . .

Humphrey: I don't think it's a special case.

Velmans: In the case of visual perception, for instance, there is no sense in which you can both experience an object out in the world and experience the retinal image.

For the tactile modality, a similar phenomenon to the one you mention was investigated by von Békésy (1967). He attached vibrators to both forearms of subjects and studied the effects of varying their frequency and phase relationships. When the phase relationships were arranged in a particular way, the two vibrators were experienced as producing a single vibration that seemed to jump from one forearm to the other. But if the stimulation continued for a few hours, it was experienced as a vibration out in the space between the limbs.

von Békésy's real purpose was to throw light on the nature of audition. In audition, the proximal stimulus is vibration of the eardrums, but what you actually hear is a sound out in space. You don't feel the vibration of the eardrums. In situations like those investigated by von Békésy and Bach-y-Rita, the brain is presented with a novel stimulus pattern and it attempts to assess its significance. That assessment may change over time, and as the interpretation of the stimulus changes so may the accompanying experience. Consequently, under some conditions the same stimulus can be experienced in more than one way, and one may also be aware of a transition between experiencing a stimulus one way or the other (a similar effect occurs with the Necker cube).

Wall: But to suggest that I can't experience the red after-image as a sensation belonging to me is just wrong. It moves when I move my eyes; an object in the real world does not. The crucial test of something being mine, which I can move around and manipulate, applies to the red after-image. Therefore, it's mine and it's not an object in the external world.

Velmans: I agree. I don't see why that's a problem for the reflexive model.

Wall: I like your introduction of virtual reality, but there's an important additional property of virtual reality machines. The subject experiencing such a machine has to move his head, move his hands, has to explore. The reason the hologram is better than the best photograph is that you can explore it and discover three dimensions in it. In those situations, where you are exploring the outside world, I understand your reflexive model. But when you explore memory traces inside your brain, you bring no new information from the outside world. Internal and external explorations are quite different phenomena.

Velmans: I agree with you, but again I'm not sure why this is a problem for the model. We experience an after-image differently from an actual object out there in the world, because the relationship of visual stimulation to events in the world is different, and the brain detects that difference. The fact that the retinal stimulation associated with an after-image moves as the eyes move gives the brain the information that the stimulation is associated with the eyes themselves rather than some stable object out in the world. The fact that our bodies move independently of the entities out in the world enables the brain to distinguish what's in the world from what is part of the body. The reflexive model assumes that different functional relationships detected by the brain are likely to result in different experiences. So that's not a problem for the model (see Velmans 1990, p 95).

Lockwood: Could you say more about how you think the kinds of considerations you offered actually provide a way forward in relation to the mind–body problem?

Velmans: One of the fundamental moves that the reflexive model makes relates to the very first question mind–body theories have to address: what consciousness is. When we are talking about consciousness or its contents we have to talk about all the contents, not just the ones traditionally associated with Cartesian dualism, such as images, thoughts and so on. In the reflexive model the contents of consciousness include the entire world as perceived. Once you accept that the entire phenomenal world is part of consciousness, you can no longer think of consciousness as being the insubstantial, non-extended substance proposed by Descartes. While some contents of consciousness (of interest to psychology) remain relatively ephemeral (images, dreams, thoughts), the physical world as experienced seems to be solid and extended in space. According to this way of thinking, inner experiences, body experiences and external objects and events as experienced are just subsets of the contents of consciousness. Consequently, the Cartesian separation of consciousness from what is not consciousness in terms of 'thinking substance' versus 'extended substance' breaks down.

At the same time, once you accept that the external phenomenal world is part of the contents of consciousness, reductionism loses its appeal. While it might be tempting to reduce some ghostly Cartesian consciousness to a state of the brain to make it respectable for science, to reduce the entire phenomenal world to a state of the brain is absurd. The reason is that states of the brain (of a subject) as observed by a neurophysiologist are just a part of the *neurophysiologist's phenomenal world*. Consequently, reductionism requires the neurophysiologist to deny the scientific status of the subject's experience while simultaneously taking for granted the scientific status of his own experience—a form of solipsism that philosophers of mind are usually concerned to avoid.

In the reflexive model, physical events as experienced are included within the contents of consciousness. Consequently, there is no unbridgeable mind–matter separation. This also has consequences for how one thinks about physics and the way physics relates to psychology. According to the model, physical science attempts to ascertain the deeper nature of the external phenomenal world, that is, the deeper nature of the external world that we *experience*. Strictly speaking, a 'phenomenon' isn't a 'phenomenon' *unless* it is observed or experienced (that is, unless it is part of the phenomenal world). Looked at in this way, physics investigates the deeper nature of what is experienced much as psychology does, although the relationships of interest in these disciplines differ.

The reflexive model just assumes that all observers have phenomenal worlds. If their focus of scientific interest is the nature of the external world that they experience, they are probably doing physics (or some other natural science); if their focus of interest is each other or themselves, they are probably doing psychology (or some related science). These differences of focus are accompanied by different methodological problems. For example, different observers may have similar (symmetrical) access to events out in the world. This is taken for granted in physics. But an external observer's access to events taking place within the body, brain and experience of a subject is likely to be different to that of the subject (asymmetrical access); in this situation, third-person perspective information may differ from first-person perspective information. It may then be necessary to examine the relative utility of first- and third-person information, and to gain a deeper understanding of how these perspectives relate to each other. But this presents no irresolvable *metaphysical* difficulties. So the reflexive model takes you right out of the dualist/reductionist debate.

Shevrin: There is one puzzle I have. Are you offering your reflexive model to explain, for example, intentionality and subjectivity, or do you define them as givens?

Velmans: If intentionality is construed just as something being 'about something', the reflexive model simply assumes that the contents of consciousness are representational. Representations, by definition, are representations of something. Therefore, consciousness is intentional because it is representational, but, for me, the property of being 'about something' isn't peculiar to consciousness. It seems perfectly reasonable to assume that unconscious representational states are also about something; they are constantly used by the brain to organize meaningful interaction with the world. Subjectivity, in the model, is assumed to be unavoidable. It follows from conscious experiences always being the experiences of a *given* observer with his/her unique vantage point on the world. In my paper, I argued that there is no such thing as observer-free objectivity, even for physics. We all have experiences, we share them in certain circumstances, we can agree about our experiences in certain circumstances, thereby establishing our intersubjectivity. It is not possible to be an observer without subjectivity. Nevertheless, there is a difference between intersubjectivity and what is *purely* a subjective experience.

Searle: There is a problem about this, and it's what I was trying to get at earlier. On the commonsense view, there is the world that exists totally independently of any observation whatever. If we all die, that world remains the same: Mount Everest still has snow on the summit and a hydrogen atom still has one electron. Are you denying that?

Velmans: No.

Searle: Now, if you accept that much, the next step is: sometimes when we experience that world, it impacts on our nervous system in such a way that the external independently existing world causes us to have in our heads conscious experiences of that world.

Velmans: I would say that such experiences are not phenomenally 'in our heads'; they are phenomenally distributed out in the space surrounding our bodies. But, I agree with the basic point you are making that there really is a world (a thing-itself) that such experiences represent.

Searle: There really is a world, it causes us to have experiences, those experiences are all in our heads, though of course they make reference to the world that is not in our heads.

Velmans: But the world is not normally experienced to be inside our heads!

Marcel: Max, there is some confusion here. First, will you accept the vehicle-content distinction? Are there vehicles out there? Part of the vehicles are out there in a causal chain. Let me give an example: I have a pain in my finger at the moment, my finger is on the table, is the pain on the table?

Velmans: No, the pain is in your finger.

Marcel: But my finger is on the table!

Velmans: I agree that your finger is on the table. And both your finger and the table are experienced to be out in the world—a case of perceptual projection. Suppose you pick up a pen and touch the paper on the table with the pen. Can you feel the tip of the pen touching the paper? If we don't think about it, our impression is that we *can* feel the tip of the pen touching the paper. That is another example of perceptual projection.

Marcel: That is irrelevant. The content of your experience may refer to what is in the world. But the experience itself is not in the world. The experience (as a vehicle) is in your head.

Dennett: Max, I can't understand your idea of the phenomenal world. I'm going to push you with an example. In the field of robot vision, they worry about such things as whether or not a 'mote' in the eye of the robot gets interpreted by the robot as something out in the world rather than something in the robot's visual system. All of the issues about illusion and subjectivity and objectivity have counterparts in this world. You can do an amazing amount of research in so-called robot vision, where all these issues come up again and again. In the sense in which you are talking about a phenomenal world, do these robots have a phenomenal world?

Velmans: My own assumption would be that they don't. I find it perfectly meaningful for people involved in building robotic representational systems to include information about the location of the events with which the robot is required to interact. One essential feature of location information would be: is an event located beyond the robot body surface or isn't it?

I would assume that the brain is doing a similar kind of calculation. The difference, I would argue, is that in the brain the processing doesn't stop there: there is not just calculation going on in the brain. There are, in addition, for reasons we don't fully understand, the conditions for having a phenomenal world. I would be quite happy to accept that robots and human bodies and brains might be functionally equivalent, in terms of their ability to interact with the world. But, while we clearly have a phenomenal world, I have doubts about the robot.

Dennett: Then I want to know why, as a psychologist, you worry about the phenomenal world and don't just pretend you are doing robotic vision. Every investigatable issue that comes up for you as a psychologist seems to have a parallel version in the land of robot vision.

Velmans: I would deny that. I would say that much of what's investigated in psychology is actually looking at the relationship between how bodies and brains function and how things are experienced. For instance, there is a difference between being able to discriminate between two colours and thereby being able to operate in a functionally appropriate way (say, having a moving device that is triggered to stop by the colour red and to move by the colour green) and actually having an experience of red or green. The whole study of colour vision, its neural antecedents, how different cultures label and categorize the colour spectrum in different ways and so on, takes it for granted that humans have a colour phenomenology and that one of the central points of interest is how the phenomenology depends on visual processing or is used in different ways in different cultures.

References

Bach-y-Rita P 1972 Brain mechanisms in sensory substitution. Academic Press, London
Laws P 1972 On the problem of distance hearing and the localization of auditory events inside the head. Dissertation, Technische Hochschule, Aachen, cited in Blauert J (ed) 1983 Spatial hearing: the psychophysics of human sound localization. MIT Press, Cambridge, MA
Velmans M 1990 Consciousness, brain, and the physical world. Philos Psychol 3:77–99
von Békésy G 1967 Sensory inhibition. Princeton University Press, Princeton, NJ

Experimental studies of ongoing conscious experience

Jerome L. Singer

Department of Psychology, Yale University, PO Box 11A, Yale Station, New Haven, CT 06520-7447, USA

Abstract. A research programme designed to find ways of applying a variety of methods in psychological science to studying the seemingly ephemeral phenomena of the human stream of consciousness and its manifestations in daydreams, interior monologues, imagery and related private experiences is described. Approaches include psychometric studies to establish normative information on daydreaming and experimental studies using signal-detection paradigms to capture the ongoing stream of thought. Recent experiments involve thought-sampling methods for identifying the determinants of the content of the stream of thought in adolescents or the ways in which self-beliefs and emotions are manifested in a group of cocaine and heroin abusers. Children's pretend play is studied as a possible forerunner of adult consciousness. It is proposed that the human condition involves a continuing tension between processing information generated from the physical and social milieu and the continuous operation of centrally generated material from long-term memory in the form of reminiscences, wishes, current concerns, expectancies and fantasies. This concept has implications for personality variation, affective arousal and adaptive behaviour.

1993 Experimental and theoretical studies of consciousness. Wiley, Chichester (Ciba Foundation Symposium 174) p 100–122

William James' (1890) introduction of the concept of a stream of consciousness, so stimulating to several generations of writers, from his own student Gertrude Stein to James Joyce, Virginia Woolf, William Faulkner and Saul Bellow, was largely ignored by psychologists for almost 60 years of the 20th century. More recently, however, as personality researchers and specialists in social cognition attempt to examine the major characteristics of the individual that account for beliefs about self or others and for attitudes that may govern overt behaviour, they find increasing renewed interest in introspection and reports of consciousness (Sabini & Silver 1981, Singer & Kolligian 1987). Brain researchers, students of artificial intelligence, psychophysiologists and investigators of the neural and autonomic concomitants of sleep are intrigued by the opportunity for studying personal 'scripts', ongoing images, fantasies and interior monologues (Ellmann & Antrobus 1991, Kreitler & Kreitler 1976, McGuire 1984, Schank & Abelson 1977, Singer & Bonanno 1990, Sperry 1976).

Although one must always keep in mind the limitations of using introspective reports for ascertaining causality sequences, the analyses of Natsoulas (1984), Baars (1987) and Singer & Bonanno (1990) all point to the rich range of information about beliefs and attitudes that emerges from introspective accounts, even from relatively less articulate subjects (Hurlburt 1990, Pekala 1991, Pope 1978).

In this paper, I shall focus on the study of ongoing consciousness through a variety of methods and experimental procedures. I propose we need such a basis for understanding at least one phase of the human condition, our 'private personality'. Experiences of interior monologue, mental glosses on one's social and physical surround, daydreams, fantasies, anticipations, recurring memories, all of which may interrupt or co-occur with our necessary processing of information, form a consensually agreed upon or physically measurable 'external world'. My personal strategy for 'navigating' the stream of consciousness over forty years of research has involved sets of convergent empirical methods with the hope that groups of new operations can yield reliable methods of measurement. These may lead to identification of the relevant phenomena and perhaps to formulation of theories and testable hypotheses about the determinants of ongoing sequences of thought and their implications for emotional reactions, information processing, the formation of interpersonal attitudes, beliefs about self and possibly even the roots of creativity, on the one hand, or to linkages to physical and mental health, on the other.

Psychometric approaches to the study of daydreams and ongoing consciousness

Rorschach inkblots

As a clinical psychologist, I began my effort to study imagination, daydreams and consciousness through some of the first empirical studies of correlates of responses to the Rorschach inkblots. Hermann Rorschach (1942) had proposed that persons who were inclined to 'see' human figures as associations to the blots, especially associations involving humans in action, were also more likely to show a rich fantasy life and engage in much daydreaming. Rorschach also reported that the persons who provided more of such human movement responses (the so-called M score) were more susceptible to inhibition in their movements or were more capable of controlling physical activity or behavioural motion. Research attention has focused chiefly upon linking the M response frequency to measures of fantasy, motor control, creativity, self-awareness and 'planfulness' (Moise et al 1988–1989, Singer & Brown 1977). Dozens of individual difference and factor-analytic studies consistently show that persons who give more M associations to inkblots (especially responses that are reasonably congruent with the blot shapes) are also more likely to tell rich and varied stories in response to thematic apperception test pictures, to score more highly on questionnaire measures of daydreaming frequency, and to provide more varied and cognitively complex free associations and person descriptions in other tests and in psychoanalytic sessions. They are also more likely to sit quietly in waiting rooms, to be able to slow down writing speed voluntarily, to resist laughing if so instructed when listening to a 'laughing' record, to show fewer impulsive responses in problem-solving tasks, to be more accurate in time estimates and to manifest less open aggression (Singer & Brown 1977). Clinically, percipients with a low M score respond better to support-expressive or direct therapies, whereas those scoring a higher M value do better in more psychoanalytic types of therapy where imaginative productivity and free associations are critical (Blatt 1990).

Questionnaires and self-report procedures

It soon occurred to me that more direct inquiries about people's daydreams and ongoing thought might provide useful normative data on the phenomena of private experience. Singer & Antrobus (1972) developed a series of 22 scales of 12 items, each designed to measure a wide range of patterns of self-reported inner experience and types of daydreams. This imaginal processes inventory (IPI) has been factor-analysed in several studies with subjects of all ages. An extensive new analysis of the IPI with a large sample of college students has led to a shortened version, the SIPI (Huba et al 1982, Segal et al 1980). From the varied uses of the IPI, some generalizations about the normative role of daydreams are possible.

Briefly, many studies indicate that most people report being aware of at least some daydreaming every day, and that their daydreams vary from obvious wishful thinking to elaborate and complex visions of frightening or guilty encounters. Cultural differences in frequency and patterning of daydreaming also emerge. Comprehensive factor analysis of the scales of the IPI indicates that the data yield three major factors that characterize ongoing thought: a positive–constructive daydreaming style, a guilty–dysphoric daydreaming style, and a poor attentional control pattern that is generally characterized by fleeting thoughts and an inability to focus on extended fantasy (Singer & Kolligian 1987, Singer & Bonanno 1990). Giambra (1977a,b) found evidence for factor patterns similar to those reported in our studies and tracked these across an extensive age range; in addition, he checked the test–retest reliability of daydreaming reports in response to this set of scales and found it to be surprisingly high.

Even with reliable and psychometrically well-constructed questionnaires, we are still left with the issue of whether individual respondents can really summarize accurately their ongoing experiences, the frequency of particular daydreams, etc. We must turn to other estimates of ongoing thought or other forms of self-report to ascertain the validity of the questionnaire responses. Reviewing such data, one finds that the self-reports of frequent or vivid daydreaming on questionnaires are correlated with:

(1) daydream-like thoughts obtained during signal-detection tasks, with imagery so vivid that the participants don't notice that a faint picture has been projected at the point they are fixating while imagining an object;

(2) with particular patterns of eye shifts during reflective thought;

(3) with particular emphasis on analogy usage when the structure of the language used in transcripts of regularly sampled thought reports is analysed;

(4) with particular forms of drug and alcohol use;

(5) with reported fantasies during sexual behaviour;

(6) with daily records of dreams recalled;

(7) with measures of hypnotic susceptibility;

(8) with measures of hallucinations of mental patients or flashbacks of traumatized war veterans, etc (Singer & Bonanno 1990).

The evidence from our own and related questionnaires suggests that the psychometric approach has considerable value in identifying individual stylistic variations in awareness of, and assignment of priorities to, processing centrally generated information.

More direct thought-sampling procedures

Laboratory studies of signal detection

My colleague John Antrobus and I developed a particular paradigm for attempting to estimate some parameters of ongoing thought. An approach that affords maximum 'control' over extraneous stimulation (at the cost of some artificiality or possibly reduced 'ecological validity') is the use of prolonged (45–60 minute) signal-detection sessions by participants seated in sound-proof, reduced-stimulation booths. Because the amount of external stimulation can be controlled, it remains to be determined to what extent individuals will shift their attention away from processing external cues (by which they earn money for accurate signal detection) toward the processing of material that is generated by the presumably ongoing activity of their own brains. Can we ascertain the conditions under which participants, even with high motivation for external signal processing, will show that they are experiencing task-unrelated images and thoughts (TUITs)?

Thus, if an individual detecting auditory signals is interrupted every 15 seconds and questioned about whether any stimulus-independent thoughts occurred, a 'Yes' response is scored as a TUIT. The participant and experimenter agree in advance on a common definition of what constitutes a task-unrelated thought, so that the experimenter has some reasonable assurance that reports conform to an established operational definition. A thought such as 'Is that tone more highly-pitched than the one before it?' is considered task-related and elicits a 'No' response. A thought such as 'I've got to pick up the car keys for my Saturday night date' is scored as a TUIT.

In this research paradigm, keeping the subjects in booths for a fairly long time and obtaining reports of the occurrence of task-unrelated thoughts after each 15 seconds of signal detection (with tones presented at rates of about one per second) have made it possible to accumulate extensive information on the frequency of occurrence of TUITs, as well as their relationship to the speed of signal presentation, the complexity of the task and other characteristics of the subjects' psychological states.

In addition to generalizations about the nature of cognitive processing (Singer 1988), the signal-detection model permits the study of individual differences. Antrobus et al (1967) showed that participants known by self-report to be frequent daydreamers were more likely as time went on to report TUITs than individuals who had said on a questionnaire that they were little given to daydreaming. Initially, the frequent daydreamers reported a considerable number of TUITs, but the same level of errors as the infrequent daydreamers. As time went on, however, the frequent daydreamers seemed to be preferring to respond to task-unrelated mentation: their error rate increased significantly, compared with the relatively stable rate of errors for the subjects who showed fewer TUITs.

Controlled studies of ongoing thought during signal detection afford a rich opportunity for investigating the determinants of the thought stream. The introduction of unusual or alarming information prior to entry into the detection booth (overhearing a broadcast of war news) can increase the frequency of TUITs, even though accuracy of detection may not be greatly affected (Antrobus et al 1966). Mardi Horowitz (1978) has demonstrated that intense emotional experiences prior to engaging in signal detection lead to increased ideation, as measured by thought sampling during the detection period. Such findings have suggested a basis for understanding clinical phenomena such as 'unbidden images' (Horowitz 1978) or 'peremptory ideation'.

Studies using auditory and visual signal detection or vigilance models with interruptions for reports have also shown that TUITs occur more than half of the time, even when subjects are achieving very high detection rates, when signals come as frequently as every 0.5 seconds or when the density (i.e. chords versus single tones) of signal information is increased. Indeed, there was evidence for parallel processing of the TUITs and the external signals. When external signals were visual, the visual content of TUITs was reduced relative to their verbal content and vice versa when the external signals were auditory. This suggests that our daydream processes in particular sensory imagery modalities (visual or auditory) use the same brain pathways as are needed for processing external cues. Studies of continuous talk in these laboratory settings point to the moderately arousing, vigilance-maintaining quality of ongoing thought and also to the dependence of such thought on physical posture, the social setting, etc. For example, when experimenters and participants are of the opposite sex there is a significant increase in TUIT reports during signal detections (Singer 1988, Singer & Bonanno 1990).

Thought sampling in more 'natural' circumstances

Some methods that sacrifice the rigid controls of the signal-detection booth for greater ecological relevance have been increasingly employed in the development of an approach to determining the characteristics and determinants of waking conscious thought. These involve (1) asking participants to talk out loud while in a controlled environment, with such verbalization being scored according to empirically or theoretically derived categories; (2) allowing the respondent to sit, recline, or stand quietly and interrupting them periodically for reports of thought or perceptual activity; or (3) requiring the person to signal by a button press whenever a new chain of thought begins, and then to report verbally in retrospect or to fill out a prepared rating form characterizing various possible features of ongoing thought.

Klinger (1990) has employed thought sampling in the ways described above to test a series of hypotheses about ongoing thought. He has made a useful distinction between 'operant' and 'respondent' thought processes. The former category includes thoughts that have a conscious instrumental property—the solution of a specific problem, analysis of a particular issue presently confronting one, examination of the implications of a specific situation in which one finds oneself at the moment. Operant thought is active and directed, and has the characteristics of what Freud called 'secondary-process' thinking. As Klinger (1978) has noted, it is volitional; it is checked against new information concerning its effectiveness in moving toward a solution or the consequences of a particular attempted solution; and there are continuing efforts to protect such a line of thought from drifting off target or from being distracted by external cues or by extraneous, irrelevant thought. Operant thought seems to involve a greater sense of mental and physical effort; it is a human capacity especially likely to suffer from fatigue or brain damage.

Respondent thought, in Klinger's terminology, involves all other thought processes. These are non-volitional in the sense of conscious direction of a sequence and most are relatively effortless. Most of what we consider daydreams are instances of respondent thought.

The use of thought sampling in a reasonably controlled environment also permits evaluation of a variety of conditions that may influence or characterize ongoing consciousness. One can score the participants' verbalizations on dimensions such as (1) organized, sequential thought versus degenerative, confused thought; (2) use of imagery, related episodes or event memory material versus logical, semantic structures; (3) reference to current concerns and unfulfilled intentions; (4) reminiscence of past events versus orientation toward the future; and (5) realistic versus improbable content. Two studies of my students may be cited here. Pope (1978) demonstrated that longer sequences of thought more remote from the participants' immediate circumstances were obtained when the respondents were reclining rather than walking freely and when they were alone rather than in company. Zachary (1983) evaluated the relative role of positive and negative emotional experiences just before a thought-sampling period. He found that intensity of experience rather than its emotional quality and, to a lesser extent, the relative ambiguity of the material, determined the frequency of recurrence in the thought stream.

Klinger's own research points to the relative importance of current concerns as determinants of the material that emerges in thought sampling. Current concerns are defined as those that occur between the time one becomes committed to pursuing a particular goal and when one either consummates or abandons this objective (Klinger 1990). Such concerns, as measured psychometrically, make up a useful operational definition of the Freudian wish in its early form as an unfulfilled intention or aspiration that is not necessarily libidinal or sexual (Holt 1976). They may range from unfulfilled intentions (e.g. to pick up a container of milk on the way home) to long-standing unresolved desires (e.g. to please a parent). One can evaluate current concerns before the thought-sampling sessions and estimate the relative importance of goals, the person's perception of the reality of goal achievement, and so on. Only after we have explored the range and influence of such current conscious concerns in sampling of the individual's thoughts, emotions and behavioural responses can we move to infer the influence of unconscious wishes or intentions.

In the 1980s there has been a considerable interest in thought-sampling studies outside the laboratory—research now involves accumulation of data over as long as two weeks, from participants who carry paging devices and report on their thoughts, emotions and current activities when signalled several times a day (Csikszentmihalyi & Larson 1984, Hurlburt 1990, Klinger 1990). The results suggest this method is feasible and suitable for hypothesis testing as well as for accumulating basic descriptive data (as in the Csikszentmihalyi & Larson study of teenagers).

In one such study, participants whose prior measured fantasies pointed to greater longing for closer association with others, reported more thoughts of other people and more positive emotional responses in social situations than did other participants, on the basis of a week-long accumulation of eight daily reports (McAdams & Constantian 1983). The relationship between similarly obtained frequent daily reports of thought and the same participants' scores on a daydreaming questionnaire, our IPI (Singer & Antrobus 1972), was evaluated by Hurlburt (1980). He reported significant correlations between the questionnaire scales of frequent daydreaming and acceptance of daydreaming and the accumulated daily reports of daydreaming, based on two days of dozens of interruptions.

The accumulation of thought samples has also proven useful in studies of clinical groups, such as bulimiacs or patients with panic disorder, where the time, locale and contingent circumstances associated with recurrent thoughts have yielded meaningful data (Singer & Bonanno 1990). I have found that samples of ongoing conscious thought of normal individuals include many of the metaphors or symbols that are also reported by them in recounting subsequent night dreams, i.e. the ongoing consciousness is already laying the groundwork for what seem to be the strange or creative settings of the night dream (Singer 1988).

Children's imaginative play as a forerunner of the thought stream

With Dorothy Singer, I have carried out a series of observational studies and experiments that involve recording the spontaneous play and language of preschool children, especially between the ages of 2½ and 5 years, when make-believe or pretend play is most prevalent (D. Singer & J. Singer 1990). In this work, we rely on pairs of trained observers who independently record samples of children's behaviour during 'free play' periods in the day care centre (or, occasionally, at home). These samples can be obtained on several occasions in a week and, in some studies, recurrently over a year. We must, of course, rely on the spontaneous verbalizations of the child in scoring the degree to which play introduces elements of fantasy and transcends the concrete description of objects or the child's motor actions. One can then look at variables such as affective responses, cooperation with others, leadership and aggression, and also examine the kinds of language forms used.

A detailed review of findings from this approach would take us far afield, but one can assert that, as Jean Piaget (1962) suggested, symbolic play emerging by the third year is a key factor in leading towards more advanced cognitive processes. Yet contrary to Piaget, make-believe does not fade once concrete operational thought appears. It never goes away and seems to be a welcome, if concealed, feature of middle childhood. As we have tried to show (D. Singer & J. Singer 1990), pretending and make-believe either as private experiences of daydreaming or in the form of adult play, e.g. carnival dressing-up, persist throughout life.

Task-unrelated images and thoughts during eleven days of signal detection

With John Antrobus, I studied a group of participants who returned to the laboratory on eleven consecutive days for a one-hour session of detecting auditory signals at a frequency of one per second. They were interrupted every 15 seconds and pressed buttons indicating if they had experienced (1) No TUIT;

(2) a TUIT that involved a perceptual response, e.g. to an extraneous noise, physical discomfort or other sensory-derived reaction not specific to the listening to and discriminating of the auditory signals, the task for which they were paid; (3) a TUIT that involved specific thoughts about the experimental situation, e.g. 'How much longer?'; (4) a TUIT that involved experimentally remote responses, e.g. 'I'm picturing myself canoeing with Sadie this weekend'. The participants had been accustomed, before the experiment, to common definitions and we asked them, during training, to verbalize actual thoughts. They were in relatively sound- and light-proof booths and wore earphones through which the signals (randomly presented high or low pure tones, one class of which was the one demanding a button press) were presented.

Fig. 1 shows the average findings for the group across eleven days of one-hour sessions of reports every 15 seconds. The subjects sustained an overall accuracy, as in most of our studies, of 80 to 100%. The percentage of reports other than 'No', that is, the task-unrelated thoughts, remains steady across eleven days at 52–58%. On the first few days, either the perceptual or experiment-related responses represent as much as 40% of the TUITs. By the second or third session most of the TUITs are quite remote from the immediate experience of the signal-detection booth. The participants have accustomed themselves to the setting and, while merrily continuing to process signals, almost all of their reported TUITs represent memories, wishes, fantasies or other thoughts far removed from the immediate setting.

We might conclude that even in an environment that makes a continuing demand on us for external signal detection, our brain may be continually active in generating information from long-term memory. We seem to orient ourselves to new settings, then our brain's channel capacity soon allows us to perform accurately our main task of environmental attention while also becoming aware of our centrally generated, long-term memory stimuli.

Determinants of the content of ongoing thought

For a more natural thought-sampling procedure, we set up a hierarchy of possible conditions that might lead to recurrence of material from an experimental situation during later thoughts sampled after experimental intervention from a group of adolescents (Klos & Singer 1981). The thought reports were rated by trained judges for their similarity to the particular experimental scenarios experienced by our subjects. The judges were provided with samples of all the different possible experimental scenarios, but were ignorant of the actual experimental conditions. We could then estimate the probability that the exposure of a participant to a particular experimental condition matched up with its recurrences in the person's later stream of thought.

It was proposed that even for first-year college students, parental involvements were likely to prove especially provocative of further thought. We chose to

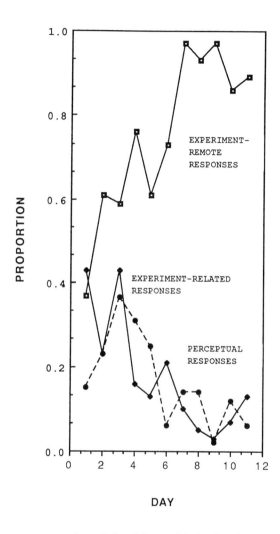

FIG. 1.   The average proportion of the different kinds of task-unrelated images and thoughts (TUITs) in the total TUITs reported during a 45 minute signal-detection period on each of eleven days of participation by five subjects. All types of TUITs reported during each session made up, on average, 55% of the responses obtained after each 15 second period of detecting signals; thus about 45% of the time subjects answered 'No' to the query 'Were your thoughts unrelated to those specifically about detection of the signals?' Perceptual or experiment-related TUITs drop off sharply as the participants gain more experience in the experimental situation and experimentally remote TUITs become more prominent.

evaluate the relative recurrence in later thought of (1) generally resolved versus unresolved situations (the old Zeigarnik effect); (2) a mutual non-conflictive parental interaction; (3) a confrontation with a parent that involved a collaborative stance by the adult; and (4) a comparable confrontation in which the parent's attitude was clearly coercive. It was proposed that exposure (through a simulated interaction) to each of these conditions would yield differences in the later recurrence of simulation-relevant thoughts in the participants' consciousness.

More specifically, we predicted that unresolved situations would have a greater impact on later thought than resolved situations, that conflict situations would recur more in later thought than non-conflictive simulated interactions with a parent, and that the confrontation with a coercive parent would cause more later thought than one with a collaborative parent. Finally, we proposed that a history of long-standing stress with one's actual parents would amplify all of these conflict effects. Our experimenters and judges were unfamiliar with participants' scores on the long-standing parent stress measure. In summary, we predicted that while an unresolved, non-conflictive situation might recur more often in later thoughts than a resolved, non-conflictive simulation, more powerful effects on recurrence would emerge for the parent conflict situations and especially for those with a coercive parent, particularly if the subject had a history of parental stress.

The data provided clear support for the major hypotheses. The frequency of thoughts' recurrences occurred in the predicted order (Fig. 2). The effects were clearly amplified by a history of long-standing interpersonal stress with a parent. The 'pure incompletion effect' was a modest one, observed mainly in the non-conflictive situation. It was overridden by the increasing coerciveness of the imaginary conflict situations. Of special interest is the fact that, once exposed to a simulated parental conflict, young people with a history of stress reflected this brief, artificial incident in as many as 50% of their later sampled thoughts. If we tentatively generalize from these results, the thought world of adolescents who have had long-standing parental difficulties may be a most unpleasant domain, since many conflictive chance encounters or even film or television plots may lead to a considerable degree of associative thought recurrence. The implications of a method of this kind (combined with estimates of personality variables or of other current concerns) for studying various groups (e.g. patients after surgery) are intriguing.

Self-belief discrepancies in cocaine abusers

In some studies recently completed with S. Kelly Avants and Arthur Margolin, we sought to test hypotheses derived from the work of Tory Higgins on the linkage between self-belief discrepancies and specific affective states. Higgins (1987) had proposed that we all formulate, consciously or otherwise, a series

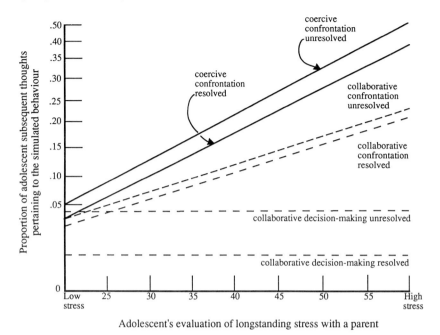

FIG. 2. Adolescent stress and simulated parental confrontation. Adolescents' thoughts during a 20 minute post-experimental period were rated by judges as bearing a clear similarity to the scenarios of the simulated (1) resolved or unresolved, (2) collaborative or confrontational, or (3) coercive or collaborative conflict situations that subjects had undergone earlier. The abscissa reflects previously obtained measures of the subjects' degree of reported stress with their actual parents. Thus, while unresolved simulations recur in later thought more than resolved ones, and confrontational or conflictual episodes more than collaborative decision-making simulations, the simulated coercive parental conflict is much more likely to recur in later thought. All the conflictual effect recurrences are greatly affected by the degree of individuals' experience of long-standing stress with parents. From Klos & Singer (1981), reproduced with permission of the American Psychological Association.

of beliefs about ourselves in various manifestations. These can be about our Actual Self, our Ideal Self, our Ought Self (what we think our parents might have wanted us to be), or other representations such as Past, Future or Dreaded Self. The Actual Self, as reported by a participant's listing of traits or tendencies, reflects how one describes one's self as accurately as possible. One's Ideal Self represents the aspirations one holds for the best one might be, e.g. 'star athlete, popular, deeply respected . . .' The Ought Self might reflect more early family or social group expectations, e.g. 'scholarly, obedient, religious . . .' A Dreaded Self might yield terms like 'sexually impotent, unmarriageable, friendless . . .'.

Higgins had shown that individuals found to have large measured discrepancies between Actual Self and Ideal Self were also likely to suffer from depression or sadness, while those with discrepancies between Actual Self and Ought Self were more likely to experience agitation, anxiety and fear. Indeed, experimental priming of Actual–Ideal or Actual–Ought Self discrepancies generated sadness or agitated emotional reactions, respectively. Discrepancy scores, which could be calculated by counting non-recurring trait words listed for Actual Self, Ideal Self or Ought Self, proved predictive in differentiating depressed (Actual–Ideal) versus socially fearful (Actual–Ought) clinical groups.

We hypothesized, on the premise that cocaine abusers may be self-medicating a depressive mood by using an 'up-lifting' drug, that this class of abusers should show more evidence of an Actual Self–Ideal Self discrepancy than either a group of heroin users or a non-abusing control group. Our results clearly support this hypothesis (Fig. 3). We also obtained thought samples of the participants and we could show how cravings for cocaine emerged along with reports of greater Actual–Ideal discrepancies on a day-to-day basis. We then asked these patients to keep logs of their moods and of their thoughts of self (as 'Addict', 'Ideal', 'Craving', etc), while a cognitive–behavioural therapy intervention sought to help them identify and practise more adaptive self-representations. Follow-up thought samples revealed correlations between each of: less craving, fewer Actual–Ideal discrepancies, more positive Future Selves and physiologically measured abstinence.

We have extended the self-belief discrepancy study to a large sample of normal individuals. We have measured many personality variables, clinical attitudes such as depression, and various manifestations of Self (Actual, Ideal, Ought, Dreaded, Past, Future). Our participants are involved in experiments that seek

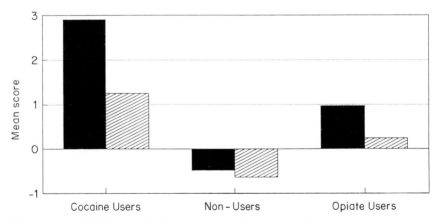

FIG. 3. Actual Self–Ideal Self and Actual Self–Ought Self discrepancies for cocaine users, opiate users and non-users. A high score (arbitrary units) indicates that subjects' descriptions of their Actual Self are considerably different from the way they describe either their Ideal Self or their Ought Self (for definitions, see text). ■ , Actual–Ideal; ▨ , Actual–Ought.

to prime particular self-discrepancies to determine whether these will increase recurrent thoughts about these concerns. The subjects carry paging devices for a week, which signal them randomly eight times a day so they can report on mood, specific thoughts and contingent events. We hope by this method to ascertain to what extent the conscious thoughts of the respondents show consistency with personality measures and cross-sectionally measured self-schemata, as well as reflecting priming of particular self-belief discrepancies.

A cognitive–affective perspective

I should like to close by summarizing my conclusions from years of applying these methods to the study of ongoing thought. I propose that human beings are best regarded as creatures who are biologically endowed with the necessary capacities and motivated from birth to explore their environments and to move gradually toward labelling and assigning meaning to their experiences. The human information-processing systems are closely tied to the separate, differentiated affective system, so that we are aroused, frightened, angered or depressed by sudden or persistent incongruity between our expectancies (plans, goals or wishes) and the information presented in a given situation. Likewise, we are moved to laughter and joy when incongruities are resolved, or to interest and to exploration when the novelty we confront is at a moderate level rather than an extreme one (Mandler 1984, Singer 1974, 1984, Tomkins 1962). If there is an overarching human motive from this perspective, it is to assign meaning, to make sense of the world. The theorizing and empirical research of the Kreitlers highlights the heuristic value of such an approach for the study of personality (Kreitler & Kreitler 1976).

If we are indeed 'wired' to make sense of our environment, to select, to identify, to label, to encode and to schematize new stimulation, what are the sources of this information? For human beings (as far as we can tell), the stimuli derive either from the 'objective' world, the consensually measurable physical and social stimuli in our milieu, or from the 'subjective' or private world of our memories and ongoing mental processes (Cartwright 1981, Pope & Singer 1978). At any given moment, a human being must assign a priority to responding either to those stimuli that come from external sources (sounds, light patterns, smells, touches or tastes) or to those that appear to be 'internal' (the recollections, associations, images, interior monologues, wishful fantasies or ruminative worries that characterize consciousness). Bodily sensations or signals of pain or malfunction from our organ systems represent a kind of intermediary source of stimulation, although such experiences often appear to us to have an 'objective' quality, despite their inherent embedment within our physical selves. We must generally give greater weight in our instantaneous assignments of priority to externally derived stimuli, or else we are likely to be hit by cars or to bump into poles. But human environments are characterized by sufficient redundancy, and our motor skills and cognitive plans for specific situations generally are so overlearned and well differentiated, that we have ample opportunity to engage in elaborate memories, plans or fantasies, even while driving a car or participating in a business meeting.

Our human condition is such that we are forever in the situation of deciding how much attention to give to self-generated thought and how much to information from the external social or physical environment. This dilemma represents, I believe, a way of formulating the introversion–extroversion dimension of human experience. It may be seen as one manifestation of, or perhaps even as the prototype for, the major existential dilemma of the human being—the persisting dialectical struggle between autonomy and association (Singer & Bonanno 1990). Under the umbrella of the overarching motive for meaning, we humans are always seeking, on the one hand, to feel loved, admired or respected, to feel close to an individual or a group, and, on the other, to sustain a sense of autonomy and individuality, of self-direction, privacy in thought or uniqueness in competence and skill. Although the individual stream of consciousness may be seen as the human's last bastion of privacy and sense of uniqueness, our studies of ongoing consciousness suggest that a great majority of our thoughts are about affiliation and attachment to others!

Acknowledgement

Some of the recent research described herein was supported by a grant from the John D. and Catherine T. MacArthur Foundation to the Program on Conscious and Unconscious Mental Processes, University of California, San Francisco School of Medicine.

References

Antrobus JS, Singer JL, Greenberg S 1966 Studies in the stream of consciousness: experimental enhancement and suppression of spontaneous cognitive processes. Percept Mot Skills 23:399–417
Antrobus JS, Coleman R, Singer JL 1967 Signal detection performance by subjects differing in predisposition to daydreaming. J Consult Psychol 31:487–491
Baars BJ 1987 A cognitive theory of consciousness. Cambridge University Press, Cambridge
Blatt S 1990 Interpersonal relatedness and self definition: two personality configurations and their implications for psychopathology and psychotherapy. In: Singer JL (ed) Repression and dissociation. University of Chicago Press, Chicago, IL, p 299–335
Cartwright RD 1981 The contribution of research on memory and dreaming to a twenty-four-hour model of cognitive behaviour. In: Fishbein W (ed) Sleep, dreams, and memory. (Adv Sleep Res Ser, vol 6) Luce, Manchester, MA
Csikszentmihalyi M, Larson R 1984 Being adolescent. Basic Books, New York
Ellman S, Antrobus JS 1991 The mind in sleep, 2nd edn. Wiley, New York
Giambra LM 1977a Adult male daydreaming across the life span: a replication, further analyses, and tentative norms based upon retrospective reports. Int J Aging Hum Dev 8:197–228

Giambra LM 1977b Daydreaming about the past: the time setting of spontaneous thought intrusions. The Gerontologist 17:35–38
Higgins ET 1987 Self-discrepancy: a theory relating self and affect. Psychol Rev 94:319–340
Holt RR 1976 Drive or wish? A reconsideration of the psychoanalytic theory of motivation. In: Gill MM, Holzman PS (eds) Psychology versus metapsychology: psychoanalytic essays in memory of George S. Klein. (Psychol Issues Monogr 36, vol 9) International University Press, New York, p 158–197
Horowitz MJ 1970 Image formation and cognition. Appleton Century Crofts, New York
Huba GJ, Singer JL, Aneschensel CS, Antrobus JS 1982 The short imaginal processes inventory. Research Psychologists Press, Port Huron, MI
Hurlburt RT 1980 Validation and correlation of thought sampling with retrospective measures. Cognit Ther Res 4:235–238
Hurlburt RT 1990 Sampling normal and schizophrenic inner experience. Plenum Publishing Corporation, New York
James W 1890 The principles of psychology, 2 vols. Republished 1952. Dover Press, New York
Klinger E 1978 Modes of normal conscious flow. In: Pope KS, Singer JL (eds) The stream of consciousness. Plenum Publishing Corporation, New York, p 225–258
Klinger E 1990 Daydreaming. Tarcher, Los Angeles, CA
Klos DS, Singer JL 1981 Determinants of the adolescent's ongoing thought following simulated parental confrontations. J Pers Soc Psychol 41:975–987
Kreitler H, Kreitler S 1976 Cognitive orientation and behavior. Springer-Verlag, New York
Mandler G 1984 Mind and body. Norton, New York
McAdams D, Constantian CA 1983 Intimacy and affiliation motives in daily living: an experience sampling analysis. J Pers Soc Psychol 4:851–861
McGuire WJ 1984 Search for the self: going beyond self-esteem and the reactive self. In: Zucker RZ, Aranoff J, Rabin AI (eds) Personality and the prediction of behavior. Academic Press, New York, p 73–120
Moise F, Yinon Y, Rabinowitz A 1988–1989 Rorschach inkblot movement response as a function of motor activity or inhibition. Imagin Cognit Person 8:39–48
Natsoulas T 1984 The subjective organization of personal consciousness: a concept of conscious personality. J Mind Behav 5:311–336
Pekala R 1991 Quantifying consciousness. Plenum Publishing Corporation, New York
Piaget J 1962 Play, dreams, and imitation. Norton, New York
Pope KS 1978 How gender, solitude and posture influence the stream of consciousness. In: Pope KS, Singer JL (eds) The stream of consciousness. Plenum Publishing Corporation, New York, p 259–289
Pope KS, Singer JL 1978 Regulation of the stream of consciousness: toward a theory of ongoing thought. In: Schwartz GE, Shapiro D (eds) Consciousness and self-regulation. Plenum Publishing Corporation, New York, vol 2:101–135
Rorschach H 1942 Psychodiagnostics. Grune & Stratton, New York
Sabini J, Silver M 1981 Introspection and causal accounts. J Person Soc Psychol 40:171–179
Schank RC, Abelson RP 1977 Scripts, plans, goals, and understanding: an inquiry into human knowledge structures. Erlbaum, Hillsdale, NJ
Segal B, Huba G, Singer JL 1980 Drugs, daydreaming and personality. Erlbaum, Hillsdale, NJ
Singer DG, Singer JL 1990 The house of make-believe: children's play and the developing imagination. Harvard University Press, Cambridge, MA
Singer JL 1974 Imagery and daydream methods in psychotherapy and behavior modification. Academic Press, New York

Singer JL 1984 The human personality. Harcourt Brace Jovanovich, New York

Singer JL 1988 Sampling ongoing consciousness and emotional experience: implications for health. In: Horowitz MJ (ed) Psychodynamics and cognition. University of Chicago Press, Chicago, IL, p 297–346

Singer JL, Antrobus JS 1972 Daydreaming, imaginal processes, and personality: a normative study. In: Sheehan P (ed) The function and nature of imagery. Academic Press, New York, p 175–202

Singer JL, Bonanno GA 1990 Personality and private experience: individual variations in consciousness and in attention to subjective phenomena. In: Pervin L (ed) Handbook of personality: theory and research. Guilford Press, New York, p 419–444

Singer JL, Brown SL 1977 The experience-type: some behavioural correlates and theoretical implications. In: Rickers-Orsiankina MA (ed) Rorschach psychology. Krieger, Huntington, NY, p 325–374

Singer JL, Kolligian J Jr 1987 Personality: developments in the study of private experience. Annu Rev Psychol 38:533–574

Sperry R 1976 A unifying approach to mind and brain: ten year perspective. In: Corner A, Swab DF (eds) Perspectives in brain research. Elsevier Science Publishers, Amsterdam

Tomkins SS 1962 Affect, imagery, consciousness. Springer-Verlag, New York

Zachary R 1983 Cognitive and affective determinants of ongoing thought. PhD thesis, Yale University, New Haven, CT

DISCUSSION

Kihlstrom: Jerry, can you talk a little about people's awareness of where these TUITS come from and where they go? For example, you might think that a task-unrelated thought could come from some unconscious source, or it might reflect some kind of day residue. To what extent are people able to reflect on the origins of the things that pass through their mind? Do they surprise them? If they did, you might think the thoughts were coming from some place that's unknown. Or can the subjects relate the thoughts to a particular event or circumstance?

Another point is that because these things flit through the person's mind, they can't be very deeply processed, which suggests that they would not be well remembered later on. You collect people's TUITs on-line, in the course of doing the tasks. Have you ever tested their memory for them later on?

Singer: We haven't tested the memory in a formal study. I believe that a huge percentage of our TUITs are simply forgotten, because of interference effects from the environment and social situation. If you did a little introspection, you might be able to retrieve a few of the TUITs you experienced while I was talking. But there are so many of them, that's the point we have tended to neglect. There are so many random thought processes that we tend to forget a great deal. People in these experiments and in other thought-sampling experiments that we have done are surprised at how much of the time they do spend daydreaming.

There is a kind of meta-attitude that people develop. Some people are particularly attentive to their memories and fleeting thoughts or associations. Because I study this all the time, I'm extremely self-conscious about it. As I'm giving a talk, I can catch myself having a fantasy right at that moment, and I would be able to narrate it to you if I had enough time. This is because I'm on the look out for these thoughts; most people are not. One of the differences between introverts and extroverts might be that introverts are the kinds of people who are aware of their TUITs a lot of the time, they really think they are worth something. Of course, writers like James Joyce and Saul Bellow are acutely sensitive to their association flow.

Carr: In your work on the visual signal-detection tasks, you are trying to measure ongoing rates of spontaneous thought. You have shown that when people are supposedly doing a signal-detection task, spontaneous unrelated thoughts occur. You have found some factors that influence the rate at which different sorts of thoughts arise, as if there were some spontaneous activity in these mechanisms that was sensitive to factors that would normally be expected to influence the rate of such activity, even though the person is not at the time overtly engaged in a task that requires this kind of activity. Spontaneous thoughts appear to depend on information processing mechanisms that exist and may even continue to operate independently of current task activity. What are those mechanisms like? An hypothesis can be found in the work of Dan Wegner.

Wegner has done his so-called 'White bear' experiments. He gets people to sit and describe their environment. In advance, he tells them, 'Don't ever think about a white bear. But if you should happen to think about one, raise your hand'. He records the number of 'illicit' white bear thoughts during this period. Then he allows the subject to continue with the description task afterwards, and says, 'Now you can think about a white bear any time you want, and if you do tell me.' Wegner finds that while people are fairly successful at suppressing white bear thoughts during the first part of the task, they do occasionally have them, even though they are told not to. But in the second part, there is a gigantic rebound effect—they think about white bears all the time.

Why is this story relevant? There have been various attempts to replicate the white bear phenomenon, including a failed one by Rose Zacks at Michigan State University (personal communication). If the phenomenon is real, it suggests that whatever mechanisms support endogenous generation of thoughts, they are sensitive to opponent-process rebound effects. These may be the same as similar, better understood opponent-process mechanisms in sensory perception, such as colour vision. This suggests, in turn, that the mechanisms involved in consciousness have properties that are shared with other physiologically well understood mechanisms and operate in similar kinds of ways. Do you agree with that kind of notion?

Singer: I would agree with the general notion; I'm not sure that I completely accept the specific interpretations of the white bear experiment. (For a full discussion of issues related to Wegner's work and also some of our own earlier studies of mental control of conscious thought suppression, see Wegner & Pennebaker 1993, Antrobus et al 1964, Singer & Antrobus 1965, Bonanno & Singer 1993.) We did similar experiments many years before Wegner. We were interested particularly in what happens if you ask someone to imagine certain kinds of scenes, and how this is reflected in their eye movements. We made electrophysiological studies of the eye movements during those conditions. We used instructions such as: 'Imagine you have a secret wish that's very important. You allow that wish to come true mentally and imagine it as vividly as possible.' We found that under those circumstances a person's eyes tend to become relatively fixed. It is as if one wants to blot out extraneous stimulation and just focus on a private image of some kind.

Then we said, 'Now suppose we can read your mind and you want to suppress this image'. Under those conditions we found a great deal of eye movement, even if the eyes were covered. We did not at that point think of rebound, so we didn't test for that effect specifically. Our whole effort was to try to show what you said in your second point, that these processes are part of the general cognitive system. They are in no sense something peculiar or independent. The same processes that support external perception seem to operate for imaginal thought.

Carr: Do you think that that line of work and the conclusion you have drawn speak in any profound way to the mind–body issues that have been discussed here? For example, it seems quite consistent with John Searle's straightforward idea that conscious processes arise naturally from the ordinary operation of the nervous system.

Singer: I would say yes. Personally, I'm having great trouble sorting out my position on the various views. I accept the principle of Dr Searle's that all consciousness emerges from brain processes. At the same time, I want to stress that I do not feel such a position is incompatible with one aspect of Dr Velmans' position, namely that all our experience is, from the start, representational. I believe that we approach each new information processing situation using schemata from previous experience and then reshape the new combined schemata through our subsequent ongoing conscious thoughts about the material, thus reconstructing and reshaping memories.

Fenwick: I have a general question which relates to responsibility. More and more, psychiatrists are called into court to give their views as to whether people are responsible for their behaviour. Our knowledge of brain function has been significantly enhanced by the use of modern techniques, such as structural imaging by magnetic resonance imaging or functional imaging by positron emission tomography, and by our increasing knowledge of brain chemistry. For example, we know that 5HT is related to impulsivity and aggression. Is a person to be held morally responsible for behaviour, however reprehensible, caused by low levels of 5HT? The more we understand about disorders of brain function, the more the question of personal responsibility seems to recede under the onslaught of reductionist science.

Now your studies have shown that if you put people into a boring situation, their intrusive thoughts start blocking out the signals they have to detect. Air-traffic controllers, for example, may miss a moving radar image as an intrusive thought interferes with cognition. Are they *responsible* for not seeing these signal blips, if the very mechanisms that they use to detect them let them down?

Another example is patients with epilepsy, who may have abnormal brain discharges which are very quick—less than 250 ms. But during that time the patient's cognition is disturbed in a major way. It has been shown in Holland, using a special car that senses the position of the car on the road, that if one of these discharges occurs, the car may deviate from the centre of the carriageway. If an accident was caused in that split second, could the person be held responsible, when it was abnormal activity in their brain (of which they had no knowledge) that caused the accident to occur? If consciousness is merely a brain function, does 'moral responsibility' have any meaning? My question is, what effect is your research having on our understanding of human responsibility?

Singer: I think we simply have to accept as a natural human process that the brain is constantly active and generating all kinds of alternative stimuli. Intellectuals like ourselves are particularly prone to this: we walk along the street thinking through some complex problem, and we are likely to bump into a pole or walk past our apartment door and then can't understand why our key won't open the next apartment door. I think part of our responsibility as adult human beings is to make some determination in particular situations as to how much priority we can give to long-term memory derived stimulation, which confronts us almost all the time, and how much we can give to the necessities of an immediate milieu. I would not be terribly sympathetic to the notion that even though we are confronted with the persistent dilemma of having to sort out our priorities, that is, whether to go on with mental reflection or to pay attention to the traffic, we bear no responsibility for an accident. I would say that part of being adult and a responsible human being is that we assign the priorities in relation to the social demands of the situation. A feature of human responsibility, even for the epileptic, is to recognize our characteristic styles and adjust to situations.

Van Gulick: Peter Fenwick said that in the signal-detection task, the subjects' thoughts intruded and interfered with their detection ability. I thought they were still very good at the task.

Singer: Yes. It is impressive that we have much more channel space than we often realize. When we greatly increase the information load on the subjects, there is certainly a reduction in the number of TUITs, but note that the 55% occurrence of TUITs corresponds with about a 90% detection rate. Even when we increase the frequency of TUITs by presenting upsetting information before the test, we still get good detection rates.

Carr: You showed modality-specific interference.

Singer: Yes. When auditory signals are being processed, the TUITs are more likely to involve visual memories or fantasies, and when visual signals are being presented the TUITs are more likely to involve verbal thought or inferior monologue. We also find interesting individual preference styles. There are people who just process their TUITs and don't care about the money.

Shevrin: There is an interesting dichotomy reflected in the discussion, namely that agency seems implicitly to be assigned solely to consciousness, while the brain is regarded as an automatically operating mechanism lacking agency. I think it's worth considering that agency is also present in unconscious operations. Or, brain operations unaccompanied by consciousness do not exclude agency. Therefore, one can raise the issue of responsibility for unconscious acts for the more conventional acts based on conscious volitions, although the former may be more difficult to determine. I think Ben Libet's work on the neurophysiological, pre-conscious origins of voluntary acts speaks to this issue as well. The implicit dichotomy between consciousness and agency, on the one hand, and unconscious and brain mechanisms, raises a serious question.

Gray: That must be right, but it addresses the wrong issue. Peter Fenwick made it clear that he was talking, not about a natural science concept, but about a socio-legal concept. The issue was how, as a society, we need to think about responsibility and the conditions under which one is to be treated as an agent.

Marcel: People vary in the extent to which they can control unwanted thoughts. In clinical depression and under certain anxiety situations, it's very hard to exclude unwanted thoughts. One of the only methods that works (and that is hardly at all) is to use a suppression task like articulatory suppression. Intrusive thoughts do impair hugely what you might think of as 'automatic' perceptual processes.

There are studies addressing this on people driving in traffic. The perceptual–motor linkage of braking due to the expanding visual flow field when you are approaching a truck in front has been thought to be quite automatic. But, it turns out that intrusive thoughts impair this. This is important and it relates to when you talk about responsibility. Forget about brain responsibility, it's just a practical question at a psychological level.

Singer: One of the characteristics of depressive thought is its somewhat contentless structure, or its repetitive structure of self-demeaning statements (Williams & Dritschel 1988).

To come to your point about driving, we have done experiments where we put someone in front of a screen across which stripes are moving, and they are encouraged to engage in different kinds of thought. The movement of stripes on the screen produces what's called the optokinetic nystagmus reflex (continuous following movements by the eyes). We measure the movement of the eyes electrophysiologically when they are tracking these stripes. If the subject engages in very vivid fantasy, the eye tracking activity drops drastically. So we are capable, when preoccupied with elaborate thought processes usually of a visual nature, of blocking out the optokinetic nystagmus effects (Singer et al 1971).

Marcel: I was concerned about essentially our own ability to control the source of content. In states of depression, and certainly in anxiety, people sometimes can't control their dominant action patterns.

Velmans: That stresses the point made by Howard Shevrin that the locus of control is actually unconscious. It's a little like asking: who is in control when you are speaking? How much conscious control do you have over the words that are produced? In normal conversation, I am usually conscious of what I'm going to say only once I've said it. Who is in control of the next thought that comes into my mind? Whatever the locus, whatever the mechanism is, it's all in the unconscious processing (see Velmans 1991a).

Libet: When the subjects are having daydreams and doing the signal detection, are they aware of the signal? When they report having had a daydream in a certain period, do you ask whether they remember seeing or hearing a signal?

Singer: We haven't asked them that in the form you suggest. We know that they got the signal right because their button presses indicate recognition that the tone presented was the targeted one. We have also obtained verbal reports in some studies which indicate conscious thought specifically about the signals, e.g. 'Was that tone louder than the last one?' We do have systematic evidence of parallel, as well as sequential, processing of tones and TUITs (Antrobus et al 1970).

Libet: I think that they might not be aware of the signal, even though still detecting it and responding correctly.

Singer: You can drive quite safely, depending on the road conditions, while engaged in very elaborate thought processes or in conversation with someone else. In fact, we found in one study that talking to oneself may keep one awake and moderately alert during a prolonged signal-detection session (Antrobus & Singer 1964).

Gray: A boring methodological point: on 50% of occasions, the subject reports having a task-unrelated thought. That is the frequency I would have expected. Nonetheless, it is an estimate that one wants to be sure is correct. It seemed to me that the method of the first experiment could include an artifact. You sampled the TUITs every 15 seconds. If that was every fixed 15 seconds, could there have been a conditioning element, either classical or instrumental, involved in the method? So subjects would be expecting to be asked every 15 seconds whether they were having a task-unrelated thought. That would almost certainly influence the likelihood that one was or was not having such a thought.

Singer: That's certainly possible. We have also conducted studies changing the time intervals. There is still a high rate of TUITs. If there is a random interruption rate, the number of TUITs is reduced substantially, so there is an element of anticipation involved. In daily life, I propose that we also anticipate situations that will allow us time to attend to our thoughts.

Harnad: Is there any evidence for cyclicity?

Singer: Kripke & Sonnenschein (1978) reported a study which seemed to suggest some support for that. We have never studied it.

References

Antrobus JS, Singer JL 1964 Visual signal detection as a function of rates of stimulus presentation and sequential variability of simultaneous speech. J Exp Psychol 68:603–610

Antrobus JS, Antrobus JS, Singer JL 1964 Eye movements accompanying daydreaming, visual imagery and thought suppression. J Abnorm Soc Psychol 69:244–252

Antrobus JS, Singer JL, Goldstein S, Fortgang M 1970 Mindwandering and cognitive structure. Trans N Y Acad Sci 31:242–252

Bonanno G, Singer JL 1993 Controlling one's stream of thought through perceptual and reflective processing. In: Wegner D, Pennebaker J (eds) Handbook of mental control. Prentice Hall, Englewood Cliffs, NJ, p 149–170

Kripke DF, Sonnenschein D 1978 A biological rhythm in waking fantasy. In: Pope KS, Singer JL (eds) The stream of consciousness. Plenum Publishing Corporation, New York, p 321–332

Singer JL, Antrobus JS 1965 Eye movements during fantasies. Arch Gen Psychiatry 12:71–76

Singer JL, Greenberg S, Antrobus JS 1971 Looking with the mind's eye: experimental studies of ocular motility during daydreaming and mental arithmetic. Trans N Y Acad Sci 33:694–709

Velmans M 1991a Is human information processing conscious? Behav Brain Sci 14:651–669

Wegner D, Pennebaker J (eds) 1993 Handbook of mental control. Prentice Hall, Englewood Cliffs, NJ

Williams JMG, Dritschel BH 1988 Emotional disturbance and specificity of autobiographical memory. Cognit Emotion 2:221–234

The neural time factor in conscious and unconscious events

Benjamin Libet

Department of Physiology, University of California at San Francisco, School of Medicine, San Francisco, CA 94143-0444, USA

Abstract. Our earlier evidence had indicated that a substantial duration of appropriate cerebral activity (up to about 0.5 s) is required for the production of a conscious sensory experience; this means the sensory world is experienced delayed with respect to real time. Subjective timing of the experience can be retroactively referred to the time of the earliest signal arriving at the cortex. Our 'time-on' theory states that the transition from an unconscious to a conscious mental function is determined, at least in part, by an increase in the duration of appropriate neural activities. Our experimental finding that conscious intention to act appears only after a delay of about 350 ms from the onset of specific cerebral activity that precedes a voluntary act provided indirect evidence for the theory. In a direct experimental test a signal (stimulus to somatosensory thalamus) was correctly detected in a forced-choice test even when the stimulus duration was too short to produce any awareness of the signal; to go from correct detection with no awareness to detection with awareness required an additional 400 ms of the repetitive identical neural volleys ascending to sensory cortex. 'Time-on' theory has important implications for a variety of unconscious–conscious interactions.

1993 Experimental and theoretical studies of consciousness. Wiley, Chichester (Ciba Foundation Symposium 174) p 123–146

Philosophical theories and analyses of the relationship between conscious mind and neural activities in the brain have been important in examining ways of looking at this relationship (e.g. Nagel 1979). Any theory that purports to specify how the mind and brain are actually interrelated should be testable by observations, whether experimental or descriptive. The proposal by Descartes, that the mind is located in the pineal body, was testable; unfortunately, he did not or could not test what happens upon destruction of the pineal. Our own approach has been to frame questions in terms of neuronal functions that may mediate the production of and the transition between conscious and unconscious events, and to investigate these experimentally by simultaneously observing and manipulating cerebral neuronal functions on the one hand and introspective reports of subjective experiences on the other (Libet et al 1964, Libet 1966, 1973).

The conscious experiences studied were either simple somatosensory ones ('raw feels') or conscious intentions/wishes to initiate (or block) a simple voluntary action (sudden flexion of a wrist). These psychologically simple events minimized potential complications from emotional or other impacts on the validity of introspective reports, they were amenable to experimental tests of their reliability, and areas of cerebral cortex involved in their mediation were available for electrophysiological study with intracranial and extracranial electrodes in awake human subjects.

Is conscious experience produced by all kinds of cerebral neuronal events?

Some have argued or speculated that this is the case. Our direct evidence gives a flatly negative answer to this question. We must distinguish between activities that may be necessary and those that are sufficient for conscious events. For example, the reticular formation in the brainstem and thalamus is clearly necessary; lesions in this system can abolish all evidence of conscious functions. But it does not follow that conscious experience is produced or 'resides' there; cessation of the heart beat also quickly abolishes conscious experience, but there is clear evidence that the heart is not where conscious experience arises.

A peripheral sensory stimulus normally elicits a large electrophysiological 'primary evoked response' of primary sensory (cerebral) cortex, beginning about 20 ms after a stimulus and lasting about 50–100 ms. This primary evoked potential can be elicited without the normally accompanying, later event-related potentials when (a) the skin stimulus is below the threshold for sensory awareness, or (b) a single stimulus pulse is applied to the somatosensory pathway in the brain where it produces no sensation at all, as seen in Fig. 1 (Libet et al 1967). In these conditions, a substantial activation of large numbers of cortical neurons occurs without producing any reportable awareness. Similarly, large electrophysiological responses of cerebral cortex can be recorded adjacent to a cortical stimulus site (the so-called 'direct cortical response'). We found such large responses both with cortical stimuli below the intensity that could produce any sensation and when stimulus pulses that were at supraliminal intensity for sensation were not repeated for a sufficient time (up to 0.5 s) (Libet et al 1967, Libet 1973). We could abolish the direct cortical responses by local application of the inhibitory transmitter γ-aminobutyric acid (GABA) with no demonstrable effect on the conscious sensory responses to stimuli at the sensory cortex or at the skin. This demonstrated that the neuronal activities represented by direct cortical responses were neither necessary nor sufficient for conscious responses.

Are there neuronal events that can uniquely mediate the distinction between conscious and unconscious mental events?

An answer to this question appeared to be a more achievable goal than specification of all the neuronal functions that are necessary and sufficient for

AER s

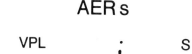

FIG. 1.   Cortical evoked potentials versus conscious sensory responses. Evoked potentials of somatosensory cortex were recorded subdurally in response to thalamic or skin stimulus pulses in the same subject. Each tracing represents the average of 250 responses at 1.8/s; total trace length is 125 ms. VPL: stimuli in ventral-posterolateral nucleus of thalamus. The subject reported not feeling any of these stimuli, even though a large primary evoked potential was elicited by pulses of current at six times liminal I for VPL electrode (liminal I being the minimum peak current to elicit sensation when delivering a train of pulses with duration >0.5 s, at 60 pulses per second in this case). S: stimuli at skin. With pulses at twice liminal I, subject reported feeling every stimulus pulse, although the primary evoked potential was smaller than that with the VPL stimuli. Skin stimuli are followed by later components of evoked potentials out to >0.5 s (not shown here) which are not elicited by VPL stimuli. From Libet et al (1967).

producing a conscious event. We, therefore, began our studies with this approach (Libet et al 1964, Libet 1966).

Stimulus durations up to 0.5 s are required in the cerebral sensory system. Stimulating somatosensory cortex with pulse trains, at the liminal intensity needed to produce any sensation, we found that train durations of about 500 ms were necessary to elicit any reportable conscious sensation. Stimuli below either that intensity or train duration produced no sensation at all (Libet et al 1964; see also Libet et al 1979, 1991). Similar requirements held for stimuli in the subcortical ascending sensory pathway, e.g. in ventrobasal thalamus or medial lemniscus. But a single stimulus pulse near liminal intensity was sufficient when applied to the peripheral nerve pathway, at the skin or on the dorsal column of the spinal cord (Libet et al 1967, Libet 1973).

Must a single pulse stimulus to the skin also induce prolonged neural responses of cerebral cortex in order to elicit a conscious sensation?   The answer to this had to be more indirect, but at least three lines of evidence have been convincingly affirmative on it. These will be only listed here without all the experimental details.
  (i) Skin stimuli that were too weak to evoke the appropriate later components of event-related potentials at the cerebral cortex but could still evoke a primary response did not elicit any conscious sensation, as mentioned above. Pharmacological agents (e.g. atropine or general anaesthetics) that depress these late components also depress or abolish conscious sensory responses.

(ii) The sensation induced by a single stimulus pulse to the skin can be retroactively enhanced by a stimulus train applied to somatosensory cortex, even when the cortical stimulus begins 400 ms or more after the skin pulse (Libet 1978, Libet et al 1992). This indicates that the content of a sensory experience can be altered while the experience is 'developing' during a roughly 500 ms period before it appears.

(iii) Reaction times to a peripheral stimulus were found to jump discontinuously, from about 250 ms up to more than 600–700 ms, when subjects were asked deliberately to lengthen their reaction time by the smallest possible amount (Jensen 1979). This surprising result can be explained by assuming one must first become aware of the stimulus signal in order to delay one's response deliberately; if up to 500 ms is required to develop that awareness, then the reaction time cannot be deliberately increased by lesser amounts.

Neural delay and subjective timing.   A neural delay, of up to about 500 ms before a conscious sensory event can appear, would mean that we do not experience the sensory world in real time. But the subjective timing of an event need not be identical with the actual time of the neural production and appearance of the experience. We demonstrated that there is normally a subjective referral of the experiential event backwards in time to the time of the primary evoked potential; the latter begins in the somatosensory cortex about 10–20 ms after a skin stimulus (Libet et al 1979). The subjective time of the experience is thereby antedated in a way that 'corrects' for its neural distortion from 'real' time (see Fig. 2).

Is there a general timing principle applicable to all awareness? That is, is awareness of any event, whether induced by a sensory stimulus or originating endogenously as a mental operation in the brain, subject to similar neural delays of up to 500 ms before it can appear? We tested one non-sensory, endogenous event, by studying the time of appearance of the *conscious* intention to perform a voluntary act.

Conscious intention relative to brain initiation of a voluntary act.   Evidence of the onset of cerebral processes that specifically precede a voluntary act is obtainable by a scalp recording of the 'readiness potential'. This potential, a slow negative wave, had been found by Kornhuber & Deecke (1965) to precede each 'self-paced' movement by 800 ms or more. We subsequently established that a readiness potential began about 550 ms before even a spontaneous endogenous voluntary act unhampered by any restrictions on when to act or by any 'pre-planning' of when to act (Libet et al 1982). Using a 'clock-time' method for obtaining the subject's reports of when he/she was first aware of any intention or wish to act, we showed that the readiness potential began about 350 ms before the appearance of the conscious intention to act (Libet et al 1983a)

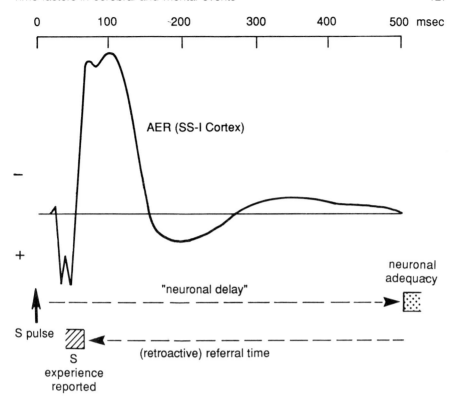

FIG. 2.   Diagram of hypothesis for subjective referral of sensory experience backward
in time. The average evoked response (AER) recorded at somatosensory (SS-I) cortex
was evoked by pulses just suprathreshold for sensation (at about 1/s, 256 averaged
responses) delivered to skin of contralateral hand. Below the AER, the first line shows
the approximate delay in achieving the state of neuronal adequacy that appears (on the
basis of other evidence) to be necessary for eliciting the sensory experience. The lower
line shows the postulated retroactive referral of the subjective timing of the experience,
from the time of neuronal adequacy backward to some time associated with the primary
surface-positive component of the evoked potential. The primary component of the AER
is relatively highly localized to an area on the contralateral postcentral gyrus in these
awake human subjects. The secondary or later components, especially those following
the surface-negative component after the initial 100 to 150 ms of the AER, are more
widely distributed over the cortex and more variable in form, even when recorded
subdurally (see, for example, Libet et al 1975). This diagram is not meant to indicate
that the state of neuronal adequacy for eliciting conscious sensation is restricted to neurons
in primary SS-I cortex of postcentral gyrus; on the other hand, the primary component
or 'timing signal' for retroactive referral of the sensory experience is a function more
strictly of this SS-I cortical area. (The later components of the AER shown here are
small compared to what could be obtained if the stimulus repetition rate were lower
than 1/s and if the subjects had been asked to perform some discriminatory task related
to the stimuli, as seen for example in Desmedt & Robertson 1977). From Libet et al
(1979), by permission of *Brain*.

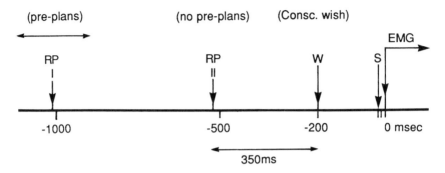

FIG. 3. Diagram of sequence of events, cerebral and subjective, that precede a fully self-initiated voluntary act. Relative to 0 time, detected in the electromyogram (EMG) of the suddenly activated muscle, the readiness potential (RP) (an indicator of related cerebral neuronal activities) begins first, at about − 1050 ms when some pre-planning is reported (RP I) or about − 550 ms with spontaneous acts lacking immediate pre-planning (RP II). Subjective awareness of the wish to move (W) appears at about − 200 ms, some 350 ms after onset even of RP II but well before the act (EMG). Subjective timings reported for awareness of the randomly delivered S (skin) stimulus average about − 50 ms relative to actual delivery time.

(see Fig. 3). This indicated (i) that development of the *awareness* of intention to move required a substantial period of cerebral activity and (ii) that initiation of a voluntary act is developed unconsciously by the brain. It is important to note that conscious intention does appear about 150–200 ms before the act, and that during this interval the subject can block or veto the consummation of the volitional process (Libet et al 1983b). The implications of these findings for the question of free will are discussed below (see Libet 1985).

'Time-on' theory for mediation of the transition between conscious and unconscious mental events

Many, if not most, mental functions or events proceed without any reportable awareness, i.e. unconsciously or non-consciously. These apparently include cognitive detection of sensory signals and appropriate behavioural responses to them, for example in the blindsight phenomenon (Weiskrantz 1986) and in word primings (see Holender1986), and in the cerebral initiation of a voluntary act (Libet 1985). There is descriptive evidence for unconscious processing of even complex functions, as in problem-solving or intuitive and creative thinking. On the other hand, the simplest kinds of mental functions can be accompanied by awareness/subjective experience, like the awareness of a localized tap on the skin or of a few photons of light on the retina, etc. It is not, then, simply the complexity or creativeness of a mental function that imparts to it the quality of subjective awareness of what is going on. The cerebral code for the distinction between the appearance or absence of awareness in any mental operation would seem to require a mediating neuronal mechanism uniquely related to awareness *per se*, rather than to complexity, etc. In view of our finding of a substantial temporal requirement for the production of even a threshold sensory awareness, I have proposed a 'time-on' theory that provides one potentially controlling factor for the neural distinction between conscious and unconscious mental events.

The theory states (i) that certain appropriate but short-lasting neuronal activities may mediate unconscious mental events and (ii) that these mental events may acquire awareness, i.e. become conscious, only if those neuronal activities persist for an adequate time (up to about 500 ms, depending on the conditions of intensity, etc). That is, it is the duration ('time-on') of neuronal activities that may control the transition between conscious and unconscious events. Part (ii) was already experimentally supported, but a direct test of both parts (i) and (ii), for the case of unconscious versus conscious detection of a sensory signal, has been carried out (Libet et al 1991).

Experimental test of theory

Our earlier evidence had shown that a stimulus in the ventrobasal thalamus, in the cerebral somatosensory pathway, had to last up to 500 ms to produce a sensory experience (Libet et al 1967, Libet 1973). For the present test the duration of stimulus pulse trains in the thalamic nucleus was varied between 0 and 750 ms at random in different trials. In each trial the subject was asked to make a forced choice as to which of two lighted intervals 'contained' the stimulus, even if he/she felt nothing, and also to indicate his/her level of awareness of any sensation elicited by the stimulus. Because the stimulus was delivered randomly in either of the two intervals, correct answers above the pure chance rate of 50% would indicate a degree of detection, accompanied by either sensory awareness or by no awareness (i.e. the choice being a pure guess). The study was made possible by the availability of suitable human subjects in whom stimulating electrodes had been chronically implanted in the somatosensory (ventrobasal) thalamus for therapeutic control of intractable pain. Each brief stimulus pulse of a train at 72/s was at the same liminal intensity in all trials of a given series of train durations. Therefore, each pulse excited essentially the same nerve fibres and delivered the same amount of ascending sensory input to the cortex; only the number of such inputs varied among different trials in a series.

Results of the study are summarized for all subjects in Table 1. Statistical analysis clearly showed (i) that detection (correct > 50%) occurred with stimulus durations too brief to elicit any sensory awareness (150 ms or less), and (ii) that to move from correct detection with no awareness to correct detection with minimal awareness (i.e. only to add awareness to a correct answer) required an

TABLE 1 Forced-choice responses versus awareness level

Awareness level	Number of pulses 0		1–10		11–19		19–37		39–55		1–55	
	No. of trials	% correct	No. of trials	% correct	No. of trials	% correct	No. of trials	% correct	No. of trials	% correct	No. of trials	% correct
Level 3	169	53	1050	57	773	75	270	67	144	85	2237	66
Level 2	23	39	208	68	296	88	204	89	167	99	875	85
Level 1	3		32	66	92	96	186	98	283	99	593	97
Overall	195	51	1290	59	1161	80	660	84	594	96	3705	

Trials are grouped according to the awareness level reported by subjects in each trial. Horizontal line of data for Level 3 includes all trials (at stimulus pulse trains indicated) in which subject reported feeling no sensation and just guessing the correct choice. Level 2 indicates trials in which subject reported being uncertain about a sensation, or 'something more than nothing'. Level 1 indicates some sensation felt, even if slight. In each trial, the subject had to choose which of two lighted intervals contained the stimulus (delivered to ventrobasal thalamus); a 50% correct response is expected on pure chance. The 66% correct figure for all trials with Level 3 awareness indicates a probability of 32 ± 2% for an otherwise incorrect response to be reported correctly, even though subjects reported feeling nothing. From Libet et al (1991).

additional 385 ms of train duration. Thus, the transition between psychological detection of a sensory signal without awareness and the detection with awareness can be controlled simply by the duration of the repetition of similar ascending activations of sensory cortex. The requirement of long trains for awareness statistically confirmed our previous findings when we stimulated either sensory thalamus or sensory cortex.

How would the minimum duration of neuronal activity lead to a conscious experience?

There appear to be at least two general options: (i) The repetition of appropriate neuronal activities for up to 0.5 s finally elicits some specific neuronal event that 'signifies' or is accompanied by a conscious event. (ii) The substantial minimum duration of neuronal repetition could itself constitute the 'code' for the appearance of an accompanying conscious event. The required neuronal activities in either option could be localized in some specific site in the brain (an unattractive possibility that implies a specific location for conscious awareness) or they could be more globally distributed in the brain.

The possibility that the generation of a conscious event in the first option is mediated by an integrative mechanism sensitive simply to intensity and duration of the neuronal activities does not agree with available evidence: (i) when stimuli to the ventrobasal thalamus or to somatosensory cortex (postcentral gyrus) were just below the liminal intensity (for eliciting sensory experience with long stimulus durations of more than one second), then no conscious sensation was elicited even with durations of 5 s or longer (Libet et al 1964, Libet 1973). Such 'subliminal' intensities are not below threshold for eliciting neuronal responses; substantial electrophysiological responses of large populations of neurons are recordable with each such 'subliminal' stimulus pulse. Were simple integration of intensity and duration the controlling mechanism, a sufficiently long train duration of stimulus pulses would be expected to become effective for awareness. (ii) At a liminal intensity which becomes effective with an average 0.5 s of train duration, the neuronal responses recordable electrically at the cortex exhibit no progressive alteration during the train and no unique event at the end of the 0.5 s train (Libet 1973, 1982). Obviously, not all the possible neuronal activities were recordable, but this evidence offers no support for a progressive integrative factor. (iii) The minimum train duration that can elicit awareness, when the intensity is raised as high as possible, has not been firmly established, although it would appear to be in the order of 100 ms. However, it was empirically quite definite that a single stimulus pulse localized to the medial lemniscus could not elicit any conscious sensation no matter how strong (Libet et al 1967); this was true even when the intensity of the single pulse was 20–40 times the strength of the liminal I (liminal I is the minimum peak current to elicit sensation when delivering a train of pulses with duration >0.5 s). Although the intensity of stimulus may not necessarily correlate linearly with the number of axons excited, the effectiveness of 10 pulses (at 20/s) at liminal I contrasted with the ineffectiveness of a single pulse at 40 times this liminal I, argues against a simple integrative mechanism. However, it must be admitted that a 'leaky integrator' may still be compatible with this evidence (a suggestion made by Francis Crick, personal communication).

Mildly supportive of the second option is the fact that no specific or unique neuronal event has thus far been found in recordings of 'direct cortical responses' to stimulation of the cortex (Libet 1973) or in event-related potentials (e.g. Libet et al 1975). Admittedly, many possibilities of an undetected neuronal event remain. The decision between the two options remains open, pending further experimental investigations.

Implications for interactions between conscious and unconscious mental events

Cerebral representation. If the transition from an unconscious to a conscious mental function could be dependent simply on a suitable increase in duration of certain neural activities, then both kinds of mental functions could be represented by activity in the same cerebral areas. Such a view would be in accord with the fact that the constituents and processes involved in both functions are basically similar, except for the awareness quality, and with the general view that both types of functions are probably mediated by broadly distributed neural activity. Separate cerebral sites for conscious versus unconscious functions would not be necessary, although this possibility is not excluded.

All-or-nothing character of awareness. If the transition to and production of awareness of a mental event occur relatively sharply, at the time a minimum duration of neuronal activities is achieved, this suggests that an awareness appears in an all-or-nothing manner (Libet 1966). That is, awareness of an event would not appear at the onset of an appropriate series of neural activities and develop gradually. Conscious experience of events, whether initiated exogenously or endogenously, would have a unitary discontinuous quality. This would be opposed to the continuous 'stream of consciousness' nature postulated by William James and assumed in many present theories of the nature of consciousness; it is, however, in accord with a postulate of unitary nature for mental events adopted by Eccles (1990) as part of his theory for mind–brain interaction.

Filter function. It is generally accepted that most sensory inputs do not achieve conscious awareness, even though they may lead to meaningful cerebral responses and can, in suitable circumstances (of attention, etc), successfully elicit conscious sensation. The 'time-on' requirement could provide the basis for screening inputs from awareness, if the only inputs that elicit awareness are those that induce the minimum duration of appropriate activities. Such a requirement could prevent conscious awareness from becoming cluttered and permit awareness to be focused on one or a few events or issues at a time.

Delayed experience versus quick behavioural responses. Meaningful behavioural responses to a sensory signal, requiring cognitive and conative processing, can be made within as little as 100–200 ms. Such responses have been measured quantitatively in reaction time tests and are apparent in many kinds of anecdotal observations, from everyday occurrences (as in driving an automobile) to activities in sports (as when a baseball batsman must hit a ball coming at him in a tortuous path at 90 miles per hour). If actual conscious experience of the signal is neurally delayed by hundreds of milliseconds, it follows that these quick behavioural responses are performed unconsciously, with no awareness of the precipitating signal, and that one may (or may not) become conscious of the signal only after the action. Direct experimental support of this was obtained by Taylor & McCloskey (1990), who showed that the reaction time for a visual signal was the same whether the subject reported awareness of the signal or was completely unaware of it owing to the use of a delayed masking stimulus.

Subjective timing of neurally delayed experience. Although the experience or awareness of an event appears only after a substantial delay, there would ordinarily be a subjective antedating of its timing back to the initial fast response of the cortex, as discussed above (see Libet et al 1979). For example, a competitive runner may start within 100 ms of the starting gun firing, before he is consciously aware of the shot, but would later report having heard the shot before starting.

There is another facet to this issue: for a group of different stimuli, applied synchronously but differing in location, intensity and modality, there will almost certainly be varying neural delays at the cortex in the times these different experiences appear. This could lead to a subjective temporal jitter for the group of sensations. However, if each of these asynchronously appearing experiences is subjectively antedated to its initial fast cortical response, they would be subjectively timed as being synchronous, without subjective jitter; the differences among their initial fast cortical responses are approximately 10 ms and too small for subjective separation in time.

Unconscious mental operations proceed speedily. If there is virtually no minimum 'time-on' requirement for unconscious (or non-conscious) mental processes in general, then these could proceed quickly, in contrast to conscious events. This feature is obviously advantageous, not only for fast meaningful reactions to sensory signals but also for the more general operations of complex, intuitive and creative mental processes, many of which are deemed to proceed unconsciously. Conscious evaluation would be expected, according to the theory, to be much slower.

Opportunity for modulation of a conscious experience.   It is well known that the *content* of the introspectively reportable experience of an event may be modified considerably in relation to the content of the actual signal, whether this be an emotionally laden sensory image or endogenous mental event (which may even be fully repressed, in Freud's terms). For a modulating action by the brain to affect the eventual reportable experience, some delay between the initiating event and the appearance of the conscious experience of it seems essential. The 'time-on' theory provides a basis for the appropriate delays. We have some direct experimental evidence for such modulatory actions on the awareness of a simple sensory signal from the skin: an appropriate cortical stimulus begun 400 ms or more after the skin pulse could either inhibit or enhance the sensory experience (Libet et al 1972, 1992, Libet 1978, 1982).

'Time-on theory', conscious control and free will.   The experimental evidence indicates that a voluntary act is initiated in the brain unconsciously, before the appearance of the conscious intention. The question then arises, what role, if any, does the conscious process itself have in volitional actions? (In this, we are considering only the processes immediately involved in the performance of a voluntary movement. The issue of conscious planning of how, whether and when to act is a separate one.) Clearly, free will or free choice of whether 'to act now' could not be the initiating agent, contrary to one widely held view.

We must distinguish the initiation of a process leading to a voluntary action from control of the outcome of that process. The experimental results showed that a conscious wish to act appeared at about − 200 ms, i.e. before the motor act, even though it followed the onset of the cerebral process (readiness potential) by about 350 ms (see Fig. 3). This provides a period during which the conscious function could potentially determine whether the volitional process will go on to completion. That could come about by a conscious choice either to promote the culmination of the process in action (whether passively or by a conscious 'trigger'), or to prevent the progress to action by a conscious blockade or veto. The potential for such conscious veto power, within the last 100–200 ms before an anticipated action, was experimentally demonstrated by us (Libet et al 1983b). It is also in accord with common subjective experiences, that one can veto or stop oneself from performing an act after a conscious urge to perform it has appeared (even when the latter is sudden and spontaneous).

Even if we assume that one can extrapolate these results to volitional acts generally, they do not exclude a possible role for free will. However, the potential role of free will would be constrained; free will would no longer be an initiator of the voluntary act, but only a controller of the outcome of the volitional process, after the individual becomes aware of an intention or wish to act.

In a general sense, free will could only select from among the brain activities that are a part of a given individual's constitution.

If we generalize the 'time-on' theory to apply to all mental functions, a serious potential difficulty arises if the theory should also apply to the initiation of the *conscious control* of a volitional outcome. If the conscious control function itself is initiated by unconscious cerebral processes, one might argue there is no role at all for conscious free will, even as a controlling agent. However, conscious control of an event is not the same as becoming aware of the volitional intent. Control implies the imposing of a change, in this case after the appearance of the conscious awareness of the wish to act. In this sense, conscious control may not necessarily require the same neural 'time-on' feature that may precede the appearance of awareness *per se*. There is presently no specific experimental test of the possibility that conscious control requires a specific unconscious cerebral process to produce it. Given the difference between a control and an awareness phenomenon, an absence of the requirement for conscious control would not be in conflict with a general 'time-on' theory for awareness. Thus, a potential role for free will would remain viable in the conscious control, though not in the initiation, of a voluntary act.

Summary of conclusions

Conscious experience or awareness of sensory or volitional events appears to depend on a unique set of neuronal activities; a controlling factor in this is a substantial 'time-on' or duration for these activities. The sensory world is experienced with a delay with respect to real time, but a subjective antedating mechanism 'corrects' this distortion.

Unconscious mental operations or events, including complex cognitive and creative functions, could be mediated by brief neuronal activities and thus proceed rapidly. The transition from an unconscious function to one with awareness may be controlled simply by the duration of neuronal activity.

Voluntary acts may be initiated in the brain unconsciously, before any awareness of conscious intention to act, but conscious control of whether the motor act actually occurs remains possible.

Acknowledgements

I am indebted to the many cooperative patients and to my splendid chief research colleagues (Bertram Feinstein, Elwood W. Wright, W. Watson Alberts, Curtis A. Gleason, David Morledge and Dennis K. Pearl) for making the experimental studies possible. The most recent study (Libet et al 1991) was supported by USPHS grant NS-24298.

References

Desmedt JE, Robertson D 1977 Differential enhancement of early and late components of cerebral somatosensory evoked potentials during forced-pace cognitive tasks in man. J Physiol 271:761–782

Eccles JC 1990 A unitary hypothesis of mind–brain interaction in the cerebral cortex. Proc R Soc Lond Ser B Biol Sci 240:433–451

Holender D 1986 Semantic activation without conscious identification in dichotic listening, parafoveal vision, and visual masking: a survey and appraisal. Behav Brain Sci 9:1–66

Jensen AR 1979 ''g'': outmoded theory or unconquered frontier. Creat Sci & Technol 2:16–29

Kornhuber H, Deecke L 1965 Hirnpotentialanderungen bei Willkurbewegungen und passiven Bewegungen des Menschen: Bereitschaftspotential und reafferente Potentiale. Pfluegers Arch Gesamte Physiol Menschen Tiere 284:1–17

Libet B 1966 Brain stimulation and the threshold of conscious experience. In: Eccles JC (ed) Brain and conscious experience. Springer-Verlag, Berlin, p 165–181

Libet B 1973 Electrical stimulation of cortex in human subjects, and conscious sensory aspects. In: Iggo A (ed) Handbook of sensory physiology, vol 2: Somatosensory system. Springer-Verlag, New York, p 743–790

Libet B 1978 Neuronal vs. subjective timing for a conscious sensory experience. In: Buser PA, Rougeul-Buser A (eds) Cerebral correlates of conscious experience. Elsevier Science Publishers, Amsterdam, p 69–82

Libet B 1982 Brain stimulation in the study of neuronal functions for conscious sensory experience. Hum Neurobiol 1:235–242

Libet B 1985 Unconscious cerebral initiative and the role of conscious will in voluntary action. Behav Brain Sci 8:529–566

Libet B, Alberts WW, Wright EW, Delattre L, Levin G, Feinstein B 1964 Production of threshold levels of conscious sensation by electrical stimulation of human somatosensory cortex. J Neurophysiol (Bethesda) 27:546–578

Libet B, Alberts WW, Wright EW Feinstein B 1967 Responses of human somatosensory cortex to stimuli below threshold for conscious sensation. Science (Wash DC) 158:1597–1600

Libet B, Alberts WW, Wright EW, Feinstein B 1972 Cortical and thalamic activation in conscious sensory experience. In: Somjen GG (ed) Neurophysiology studied in man. Excerpta Medica, Amsterdam, p 157–168

Libet B, Alberts WW, Wright EW, Lewis M, Feinstein B 1975 Cortical representation of evoked potentials relative to conscious sensory responses and of somatosensory qualities—in man. In: Kornhuber HH (ed) The somatosensory system. Thieme Verlag, Stuttgart, p 291–308

Libet B, Wright EW Jr, Feinstein B, Pearl DK 1979 Subjective referral of the timing for a conscious sensory experience: a functional role for the somatosensory specific projection system in man. Brain 102:191–222

Libet B, Wright EW, Gleason CA 1982 Readiness-potentials preceding unrestricted 'spontaneous' vs. pre-planned voluntary acts. Electroencephalogr Clin Neurophysiol 54:322–335

Libet B, Gleason CA, Wright EW, Pearl DK 1983a Time of conscious intention to act in relation to onset of cerebral activities (readiness-potential); the unconscious initiation of a freely voluntary act. Brain 106:623–642

Libet B, Wright EW Jr, Gleason CA 1983b Preparation- or intention-to-act, in relation to pre-event potentials recorded at the vertex. Electroencephalogr Clin Neurophysiol 56:367–372

Libet B, Pearl DK, Morledge DE, Gleason CA, Hosobuchi Y, Barbaro NM 1991 Control
    of the transition from sensory detection to sensory awareness in man by the duration
    of a thalamic stimulus. The cerebral time-on factor. Brain 114:1731–1757
Libet B, Wright EW, Feinstein B, Pearl DK 1992 Retroactive enhancement of a skin
    sensation by a delayed cortical stimulus in man. Consci & Cognit 1:367–375
Nagel T 1979 Mortal questions. Cambridge University Press, Cambridge
Taylor JL, McCloskey DI 1990 Triggering of pre-programmed movements as reactions
    to masked stimuli. J Neurophysiol (Bethesda) 63:439–446
Weiskrantz L 1986 Blindsight: a case study and implications. Clarendon Press, Oxford

DISCUSSION

Searle: I have a factual question about the readiness potential. You confidently ascribe mental reality to the readiness potential prior to the wish. You said it was an unconscious mental phenomenon.

Libet: I said there is an initial period of cerebral activity during which the volitional process is unconscious.

Searle: Of course, at the level of the neuronal firings, the cerebral activity is all unconscious. I thought you were saying that in addition to the conscious wish, and in addition to the patterns of neuron firing, there is something else, namely the unconscious mental event.

Libet: I'm calling it that in the sense that the developing voluntary intention to act may be regarded as a mental event.

Searle: But there's no mental reality to the formation of a readiness potential—at least the way I heard you describe it.

Dennett: Its occurrence predicts the voluntary motion.

Van Gulick: I am concerned that what you are studying isn't a very good paradigm of typical voluntary motion. In one experiment, people are asked to pick a time to move their finger. They move it any time they want, it's spontaneous, but it doesn't strike me as a very good model of a voluntary action. You say there is no pre-planning, but, typically, when I make a decision, say, to interrupt the conversation and follow up on John's remark, there is a lot of consciousness that preceded the choice of my beginning to speak—a lot of conscious pre-planning.

Searle: Ben, are you not attributing any mental reality beyond the straight neurophysiological processes?

Libet: Only to the extent that people talk about unconscious mental processes in general. But, these unconscious cerebral activities can resemble the conscious processes in their cognitive, conative, problem-solving functions, so it may be appropriate to regard this as mental as much as a conscious function is, but without the awareness feature.

Searle: But generally people don't know what they are talking about!

Wall: I would like to challenge one of Ben Libet's assumptions. Ben, you assume that there is the great timekeeper somewhere in your head, who is dependent on cortical activity. When the cortical activity is sufficient, he presses his dodgy stopwatch which jumps back 500 ms. My simple question is, why put that timekeeper in the cortex? Why not somewhere else?

Gray: Why put the sensation in the cortex? The other implicit assumption in this is that when you stimulate the cortex, and presumably when you stimulate the medial lemniscus or the thalamus, that is where the sensation is elaborated. We don't know enough about the necessary and sufficient conditions of brain happenings for sensation to occur for us to assume that your stimulation is necessarily instantly doing the right things, rather than requiring a long period of reverberation to recruit other necessary machinery.

Libet: I was not committed to any location of the sensory experience. I was simply providing conditions that could control the neural time required to develop the experience and the subjective timing of it. The spatial extent of brain loci in these processes is not yet being specified.

Wall: But you are dependent on cortex providing the start time around which all other events are ordered in time.

Libet: I think the sensory cortical primary evoked potential is a necessary condition for the referral in time. That doesn't mean the referral is carried out there.

Gray: But that evoked potential itself reflects inputs into the cortex from all sorts of places that we don't properly understand.

Libet: The *primary* evoked potential is a very straightforward response to the fast specific projection pathway, via medial lemniscus to ventrobasal thalamus to somatosensory cortex. The primary evoked potential does not involve a response to other diffuse inputs, although the later evoked components do.

Wall: I would like to refer to two experimental facts which suggest that the cortex is not the primary site for detecting the nature and timing of a sensory stimulus (Wall 1970). When the thoracic cord in rats is cut to leave only the dorsal columns intact, the sensory input to the cortex is limited to only the dorsal column–medial lemniscus system. Distal stimuli evoke a large cortical evoked potential, which is normal in size, shape and duration, but the forward part of the animal shows no sign of reaction to the stimulus. This shows that the animal cannot utilize the presence of cortical responses unless other systems are active at the same time. Secondly, animals and humans react to single stimuli in the periphery and in sensory transmission systems but, as Dr Libet shows, it is necessary to stimulate cortex repeatedly before any sensation is provoked.

Libet: I can't explain the first set of results, except to say that it seems to indicate that evoked potential processes are not sufficient for the rat to react. Perhaps the diffuse ascending projections cut in that experiment are the necessary feature for the rat to react at all.

Let me add one experiment we did do that relates to the loss of specific projection inputs. We had one subject with a one-sided stroke that had completely and permanently blocked out the specific sensations for the hand and arm. The other side was normal. We compared the subjective timing of the two hands. We gave a skin stimulus to each hand and asked the subject about their relative timings. She reported the stimulus to the good hand as coming before that to the bad hand when they were stimulated together. We had to delay the stimulus to the good hand by about 400 ms before she said both stimuli occurred together. So in this case, the interference with the primary projection pathway produced a later, delayed subjective timing, which supports what I am talking about.

Kinsbourne: You make the assumption that after a stimulus has lasted half a second, awareness happens suddenly, but you don't know that. It could be that after that half second there is an indeterminate period, then the awareness follows. Given that, your theory about projecting back in time, may or may not be correct. It may be that it takes quite a while after the end of the half second for the artificial input to be appreciated, so that actually the relationship between that and the natural input is a normal one, and you don't need to assume the referral backward in time.

Libet: You are postulating that there is an extra delay for the experience to appear after the end of a 0.5 s cortical stimulus, and that there is no such extra delay for appearance of the skin-induced experience (after its neural delay of 0.5 s). That would be an *ad hoc* distinction based simply on your argument that the cortical stimulus is 'artificial'. But there is no experimental evidence to support your distinction and there is not even any theoretical basis for speculating that there is an extra delay only after the end of the adequate cortical stimulus.

In fact, there is experimental evidence against your suggestion (Libet et al 1979, Table 3A). When delivery of a peripheral single-pulse stimulus was delayed (from the onset of the cortical stimulus train) by more than the minimum cortical duration, subjects tended to report the cortically induced sensory experience as appearing before the peripherally induced one. This agrees with there being no extra delay for the experience to appear after the end of an adequate cortical stimulus. Furthermore, if one stimulates in the ventrobasal thalamus, which is on the direct pathway to the somatosensory cortex from the skin, one finds exactly the same stimulus time requirement as at the cortex.

Dennett: Ben, you are saying there is a neuronal delay, and the actual onset of consciousness begins at one time but is referred back to the time of the primary evoked potential. You interpret this period as a 'rising to threshold' for consciousness.

Libet: Not a 'rising to threshold'. The period of neuronal delay is regarded as being due to a minimum time of neuronal activities required to produce the reportable conscious experience, without specifying the mechanism that operates during that period of activity.

Dennett: Here's another interpretation of the data, which eliminates the problem of referral. The conscious experience happens at the time of the primary evoked potential. The later time you measure is the end of the Orwellian 'archive preparation' time; the duration is the length of time a memory trace has to be 'cured' before it is sufficiently in memory so that it can drive a later retrospective verbal response. That's the Orwellian account of this. Then we could say that the consciousness happened at the earlier time, but when conscious events happen they are wiped out of memory, unless there is a 500 ms curing time, which is what it takes to drive that conscious event into memory. Then the conscious event actually occurs in the brain at the moment it seems to occur. I would like to know what evidence you have that favours the theory which says that consciousness itself doesn't begin until the later time, and then it has a referral back in time.

Libet: The evidence for subjective referral backwards in time makes your proposal (that the conscious response appears almost immediately but producing the reportable memory of it requires the neural delay of 0.5 s) almost untenable. The crucial test of the referral hypothesis lay in the experiment with stimulating electrodes in the medial lemniscus (the fast cerebral pathway for somatosensory signals to thalamus and then on to cortex). Each pulse in the medial lemniscus puts a primary evoked response on the sensory cortex, just as a stimulus at the skin does. But, in contrast to the skin, the medial lemniscus has the same stimulus time requirement as does sensory cortex—you have to stimulate at the liminal intensity for 0.5 s before any sensation can be reported.

So, each stimulus pulse in medial lemniscus evokes a fast primary response by somatosensory cortex, but, in the experiment described here, it was empirically established that the stimulus train of pulses in medial lemniscus had to persist for at least 200 ms to elicit any reportable conscious sensation. When the skin stimulus pulse was delivered 200 ms after onset of the medial lemniscus stimulus, the subject reported that the lemniscus-induced sensation appeared before the skin-induced sensation, in contrast to the order reported for a similar cortical stimulus (Libet et al 1979). So, even though the medial lemniscus stimulus could not have produced the reportable experience for up to 500 ms (depending on stimulus intensity), the subject timed the experience as if there were no delay relative to a skin-induced one. That result leads to the conclusion that the subjective timing of the medial lemniscus-induced sensation was subjectively antedated to match the subjective timing of the skin-induced sensation.

Nagel: How do you rule out the possibility that even a 300 ms stimulus produces an experience which never fixes in memory, so it's never reported? That is Dan's question.

Libet: To rule out conclusively every possible explanation for an observation is often not feasible experimentally: the proposal for a fixation of memory is like this. Because we commonly reject hypotheses that lack supporting evidence, the more significant question here is: what is the evidence to support Dennett's proposal? The answer is, none, as far as I know. On the contrary, there are experimental reasons to regard that theory as improbable.

Firstly, there are the inferences from the evidence I have just cited on backward referral. To account for the observation that subjective timings are similar for the single-pulse skin stimulus and the 200 ms train of medial lemniscus stimuli, your proposal would have to assume that the time for memory fixation is the same in both cases. Each of these sensory experiences would then become reportable only after 200 ms following the initial signal. But how would that explain the observation that a cortically induced sensation is subjectively timed to appear about 200 ms after the skin-induced sensation (or after 500 ms, if the stimulus intensity is weaker)? Dennett & Kinsbourne's (1992) proposal requires them to postulate that there is an *extra* delay for the appearance of the cortically induced experience, an extra delay that has to be equal to the duration of the cortical stimulus! Aside from the *ad hoc* nature of that speculation, there is the experimental evidence against it, that I mentioned in reply to Marcel Kinsbourne's comment.

Secondly, although development of a very short-term memory of an experience is required for reportability some seconds after the stimulus, the process for producing that memory need not reside in the specific neural activity involved in producing the experience. Our recent demonstration (Libet et al 1991) that very brief thalamic stimuli can be detected without generating awareness provides evidence against the proposal of Dennett and Kinsbourne. Because our subjects made their forced-choice responses after the same post-stimulus period of some seconds, whether or not they were aware of the stimulus, the same short-term memory of the signal was obviously produced, even by cortical stimuli of 100 ms or less. So, contrary to Dennett's proposal, the 200 to 500 ms of neural activity in question is not necessary for the production of a short-term memory of the signal, unless one adds the further *ad hoc* speculation that the memory process for a reportable conscious response has a fixation time much longer than the memory process for exhibiting a later detection without reportable awareness.

All in all, the kind of additional *ad hoc* tailoring of assumptions that seem to be required to make the Dennett explanation workable is what we normally reject from serious scientific consideration.

Harnad: If Dan Dennett's interpretation were valid, this wouldn't be evidence against it.

I would like to ask Dan what this thing is that happens and then vanishes without a trace. You do not seem to be saying merely that it vanishes without a trace after it happens if it fails to be consolidated, but that even at the instant when 'it' allegedly happens, it somehow has no conscious manifestation! But then why would you call 'it' a conscious experience at all?

Dennett: Remember, the game I'm playing right now is competing the Orwellian view against the Stalinesque. Our claim is that this is a false contrast.

Gray: If it's false, why do you ask him the question?

Dennett: Because Ben Libet thinks that he can prove the Stalinesque version. I'm saying that everything Ben says to show that the Stalinesque version is true, could equally well be cited to support the Orwellian view. Stevan, by your own account, when people respond very swiftly—if somebody is asked to tap a button as soon as they see a red light—they wait until they are conscious of the red light and then they press the button. If you use that as a test of consciousness, you have to put the consciousness back significantly earlier, because it doesn't take the subject 500 ms to become conscious of the red light in order to initiate the button press.

Harnad: That just stipulates that to get a reaction at all you must first be aware of the stimulus. This need not be true: you could react first and be(come) conscious of it afterwards (Harnad 1982).

Rossetti: Several experiments have demonstrated that motor reaction time to a visual stimulus may be shorter than the time to conscious awareness of the same stimulus (e.g. Castiello et al 1991). Have you tried to reproduce your experiment with the subject giving a motor response instead of a verbal one to the cortical stimulation?

Libet: I didn't do that, precisely because a vocal response could appear before awareness. There is another experiment that's more directly related to the issue of when the subject becomes aware of the signal. A subject is given a skin pulse, for example (this has also been done with a visual stimulus), then given a train of cortical pulses starting up to 0.5 s after the skin pulse. The delayed cortical stimulus can mask the sensation induced by the skin stimulus. The argument in Orwellian terms would be that you have wiped out the memory. But a second masking stimulus can wipe out the sensation elicited by the first masking stimulus, and awareness of the original skin stimulus reappears. If the memory was wiped out in the first case, how could the experience reappear?

Dennett: The Orwellian theory admits from the outset that the memory erasure isn't complete: after all, in a forced-choice guess test, you would see that subjects did better than chance at guessing whether the first stimulus had occurred.

Libet: The issue of the memory and the Orwellian approach started with the difference between the cortical stimulus taking half a second and the skin stimulus being experienced immediately (as if there were no delay). There is an *ad hoc* assumption that the cortical stimulus involves something different, i.e. abnormal or artificial, compared to the skin stimulus. Let's eliminate that possibility and compare a cortical stimulus with a medial lemniscus stimulus; both of these stimuli are 'abnormal'. They both need the same duration of repetition to elicit any sensory experience, but the subjective timing is completely different. The sensation induced by the medial lemniscus stimulus is timed subjectively as starting right at the beginning of that stimulus; the sensation induced by the cortical stimulus is subjectively timed as though it appears at the end of that stimulus train. We have here excluded any assumptions about the difference between the natural skin stimulus and the cortex, so where is the difference based on the Orwellian memory?

Dennett: Direct stimulation of the cortex and of the medial lemniscus are both very strange and unusual cerebral events. One wonders what assumptions underlie your supposition that the direct application of electrical stimulation to the cortex produces an event which is anything like a normal event. You are saying that it is *ad hoc* for me to distinguish these two. It seems to me that it's *ad hoc* for you to suppose that they are the same.

Libet: But I'm saying, compare stimulation of the medial lemniscus with stimulation of the cortex—they both need the same duration of activation, and they are both, in your sense, strange and unusual cerebral events. But their subjective timing is strikingly different.

Dennett: Well, one of them has a primary evoked potential, the other doesn't.

Libet: Exactly; that's the difference.

Shevrin: According to Dennett, in the Orwellian view there is misremembering and in the Stalinesque view there is misperceiving, and there's no way we can tell the difference. However, the existence of revised memories and misperceptions doesn't rule out the possibility of empirically distinguishing between the Orwellian and Stalinesque views. For example, if the memory is revised, the original memory should not be available, only the revised version, as argued by Loftus et al (1985).

Dennett: Why can't they both be available under different circumstances?

Shevrin: Well, what do you mean by revision then?

Dennett: Another draft just becomes more available.

Shevrin: You have offered the analogy of working at the wordprocessor. Once you change the text, there is a new draft and the earlier draft is no longer available. If the earlier draft is available, if traces of it are left, that sounds Stalinesque to me, not Orwellian. It is not simply misremembering. If you have the original trace, and a revised trace, and a re-revised trace, then you have three different drafts available. Therefore, there is a canonical version, in the sense that the original memory is more correct than its revisions, which is exactly what you denied at first.

Marcel: It's not canonical.

Shevrin: Take your example of the jogger (Dennett & Kinsbourne 1992). The jogger runs by without glasses, and then you have a draft of the jogger running by without the glasses that leaves a trace of itself. Then it gets mixed up with the memory of another jogger who wears glasses, and then you have a revised memory of the first jogger as having glasses. It seemed to me that you were saying that once that happens, the original version of the jogger without the glasses is no longer available. There is now a new revised text. But what you are saying now is that the earlier draft left a trace of itself and is thus available to influence future perceptions. That sounds Stalinesque.

If it is correct that under certain conditions one can recover the original trace, then one can distinguish between the Orwellian (original trace unavailable) and the Stalinesque (original trace available).

Marcel: We can apply this to both visual masking and eye-witness testimony. In the latter, you can recover the original memory under certain conditions. Take Ben Libet's example of the unmasking of a masked stimulus. Every time there is a new stimulus it masks the mask—you actually revise the draft. You can go on doing that for quite a long time. But that is exactly what Dan Dennett would like. I don't like this, but I think it's right—you do keep on revising it. But it doesn't mean you have destroyed the original, because it can be recovered.

Nagel: I don't understand the need for these elaborate alternative views. They all seem to arise from the desire to find something in real physical time corresponding to phenomenological temporal relations. There is no reason there should be a temporal physical representation of subjective time at all. Why do you need all these revisions?

Dennett: If what you say is right, and I think it is, then it is a criticism of Ben Libet, because he is saying he can time the onset of consciousness to a moment that is a lot less than somewhere within 500 ms. You are saying there is no issue in a 500 ms window; Ben is saying there is.

Harnad: There is either an equivocation or a misunderstanding here. This seems to be very similar to the error of not distinguishing the timing of an experience from the timing of the object of that experience. Your point is valid but it's not exactly what's under discussion here. Howard Shevrin's point is equally valid because he's talking about something different. When Howard says the original draft continues to exist, he is speaking of it as a candidate for an ongoing *conscious* experience, not as a record that is registered or shared but not experienced.

The real issue is: when did X happen? If X really happened at draft one, then there *was* a conscious experience. If it didn't happen, there wasn't one.

Nagel: So you think there has to be a precise answer in physical time to the question: when did my conscious wish to move my finger occur? I don't see why that event has to have a precise temporal location.

Gray: What do you mean by 'precise'?

Nagel: Well, it certainly occurred within a one minute interval.

Gray: So you permit sequencing. Is the issue simply a question of the precision with which one can speak about and time the occurrence of conscious events, or is it that in some way the whole concept of time doesn't apply to conscious events?

Nagel: They can be physically located in a rough way. They have to be, because they do have certain physical causes and physical effects. But they also have, internally, a precise subjective temporal structure which doesn't have to mirror anything in the temporal character of their physical basis. For example, in the case of the subjective simultaneity in the 'will' experiment between the perception of the clock hands reaching a certain point and the experience of deciding to press the button—that is a precise phenomenological simultaneity. It doesn't have to correspond to any precise physical clock time at all, including the time when the clock handle objectively hits the top. It's just something that happened in the mind at roughly that time.

Velmans: One consequence of what you are saying is that it's not legitimate to study the fine detail of the way temporal relationships are experienced. That can't be right. For instance, it's perfectly proper to study the precise physical conditions under which people report two events as being phenomenally simultaneous rather than consecutive. The fact that there may not be just one set of physical conditions which will produce phenomenal simultaneity or an experienced, temporal difference doesn't mean it is not important to explore how different sets of physical relationships or neural encodings of them are translated into different experiences. So all these debates are important.

Harnad: I think I have a way to re-state the point about timing. Suppose the *content* of the event we are trying to time is: 'This *seems* to be occurring at time *t*'. Let that be the experience we are talking about, the instant of the seeming-to-occur-at-time-*t*. But what we are really interested in is the true clock time (possible *t*) of the moment of that *seeming*, and not the time *t* that was merely its *content*. When Ben Libet is looking for the exact moment the experience of willing a movement occurred, he too is looking for the clock time of the *seeming*, not the clock time figuring in its content.

Velmans: I have quite a different problem with Dan Dennett's argument, which has to do with his use of the term 'memory'. Normally, when we speak of people remembering or forgetting, we take it for granted that they have already had an experience which they can either report or not at some later time. According to Dan, Ben Libet's findings can be explained in terms of an Orwellian loss of memory that takes place in the initial few hundred milliseconds after stimuli are projected to the brain. In other words, Dan assumes that temporal sequence is initially experienced one way, but when contradictory temporal information about the same stimulus arrives, the initial experience is forgotten and replaced by an updated experience. However, according to most psychological theories, stimuli arriving at the cortex may be coded and identified within the first few hundred milliseconds, but unless they are attended to they do not enter short-term memory. So consciousness of a stimulus and subsequent remembering or forgetting follow an initial period of preconscious processing. No doubt, stimuli are represented in the central nervous system within the first few hundred milliseconds and it may be that those representations can be overwritten by following representations. But to call that 'forgetting' (with the implication that what is forgotten has already been experienced), seems wrong.

I am also worried about the unfalsifiability of Dan's suggestion. Let's imagine a standard procedure in psychophysics—establishing a visual stimulus threshold.

You gradually turn up the intensity of a stimulus and at a certain point the subject says that he can see it. It is standard procedure to assume that the subject's report is accurate. Then you gradually lower the intensity again until the subject says he can't see it. Again, it is standard to accept the subject's report as accurate. But, according to Dan, inability to report the stimulus might have resulted from rapid forgetting, and he could extend that claim to any reports that subjects make about not having experienced something. So, in spite of any claims subjects make to the contrary, Dan could maintain his position. That makes his position unfalsifiable.

References

Castiello U, Paulignan Y, Jeannerod M 1991 Temporal dissociation between motor responses and subjective awareness. A study in normal subjects. Brain 114:2639–2655

Dennett DC, Kinsbourne M 1992 Time and the observer: the where and when of consciousness in the brain. Behav Brain Sci 15:183–201

Harnad S 1982 Consciousness: an afterthought. Cognit Brain Theory 5:29–47

Libet B, Wright EW Jr, Feinstein B, Pearl DK 1979 Subjective referral of the timing for a conscious sensory experience: a functional role for the somatosensory specific projection system in man. Brain 102:191–222

Libet B, Pearle DK, Morledge DE, Gleason CA, Hosobuchi Y, Barbaro NM 1991 Control of the transition from sensory detection to sensory awareness in man by the duration of a thalamic stimulus. The cerebral time-on factor. Brain 114:1731–1757

Loftus EF, Schooler JW, Wagenaar WA 1985 The fate of memory: comment on McCloskey and Zaragoza. J Exp Psychol Gen 114:375–380

Wall PD 1970 The sensory and motor role of impulses travelling in the dorsal columns toward the sensory cortex. Brain 93:505–524

The psychological unconscious and the self

John F. Kihlstrom

The Amnesia & Cognition Unit, Department of Psychology, University of Arizona, Tucson, AZ 85721, USA

Abstract. Documentation of implicit expressions of memory in head-injured, mentally ill and normal individuals has offered a new perspective on the problem of unconscious influence on conscious experience, thought and action. The phenomenon of implicit memory is described and used as a basis to develop an analogous concept of implicit perception. In both cases the person shows the effects of current or past events, even though these events are not accessible to phenomenal awareness. There is collateral evidence for the emotional unconscious: emotional states can serve as evidence of implicit perception or memory, and there is evidence of desynchrony between the subjective experience of emotion, which can be identified with consciousness, and the effects of emotional responses on physiology and overt behaviour. Theoretical approaches to the psychological unconscious include a connectionist approach, which affords a limited role for conscious processing in mental life; a neuropsychological aproach, involving the disconnection of a module serving consciousness from the rest of the cognitive system; and a psychological approach, which emphasizes the central role in conscious awareness of mental representations of the self as the agent or experiencer of events.

1993 Experimental and theoretical studies of consciousness. Wiley, Chichester (Ciba Foundation Symposium 174) p 147–167

The doctrine of mentalism holds that mental states stand in relation to action as do causes to effects. That is to say, as Kant noted in his *Critique of Pure Reason*, that what we do is determined by knowledge, feeling and desire. Throughout most of the history of scientific psychology, most analyses of mental life have focused on conscious mental states. On the other hand, there has always been a substantial body of clinical and experimental evidence that our experiences, thoughts and actions are affected by mental structures and processes that lie outside of phenomenal awareness and voluntary control.

The cognitive and emotional unconscious

We may take a familiar example from cognitive neuropsychology: patients suffering bilateral damage to the medial temporal lobes, including the hippocampus, show a gross anterograde amnesia, meaning that they are unable to remember even very recent events. Nevertheless, careful examination shows that they have preserved some sort of memory for these events. Thus, if they have studied a list of words incuding the item *ELASTIC*, they will fail to recall or recognize these items after a short period of distraction. However, if they are presented with three-letter stems, like *ELA---*, and asked to complete them with the first word that comes to mind, they are more likely to produce *ELASTIC* than, for example, *ELATED*. This advantage for studied over non-studied items is known as a priming effect. The typical outcome of such studies is that the magnitude of priming is approximately the same in amnesic patients as it is in intact subjects who show normal memory for the study list (for reviews, see Schacter 1987, Shimamura 1986). Interesting priming effects are preserved in the functional amnesias of dissociative disorders, as well as in the organic brain syndromes (Kihlstrom et al 1992a, Schacter & Kihlstrom 1989). In my laboratory, similar findings have been obtained in subjects with post-hypnotic amnesia (Kihlstrom 1980) and in surgical patients who have undergone general anaesthesia (Kihlstrom et al 1990); interestingly, there is as yet no evidence for implicit memory for sleep learning (Wood et al 1992).

Such results illustrate the distinction between two expressions of episodic memory, explicit and implicit (Eich 1984, Jacoby & Dallas 1981, Schacter 1987, 1992). *Explicit memory* refers to the person's conscious recollection of some past event, as commonly reflected in recall, recognition, or any other task that refers to some time in the past and asks the subject to describe what he or she did, or experienced, at the time. By contrast, *implicit memory* refers to any effect on experience, thought or action—priming effects or savings in relearning or other indications of transfer—that is attributable to some past event; these tasks made no reference to any particular past event, but memory for such an event is implicit in the subject's enhanced performance. A wide variety of experiments indicate that explicit and implicit memory are dissociable in at least two senses: (1) implicit memory can be spared even when explicit memory is grossly impaired; and (2) many experimental manipulations have differential effects on explicit and implicit memory.

Recently, my students and I have introduced the concept of *implicit perception*, analogous to implicit memory (Kihlstrom et al 1992b). The obvious example is the phenomenon of 'subliminal' perception, where a degraded stimulus (i.e. too weak, exposed too briefly, or obscured by metacontrast or a mask) cannot be consciously detected, but nevertheless influences performance on some task. More dramatic examples are found in the case of 'blindsight' following damage to the striate cortex, in the functional blindness, deafness and tactile anaesthesia observed in the conversion disorders, and in analogous phenomena produced by hypnotic suggestion. *Explicit perception* refers to the person's conscious awareness of an event in the current (or immediately past) environment, as reflected in the individual's ability to detect signals, identify objects or describe the form, colour, distance or movement of stimuli. *Implicit perception* refers to a change in experience, thought or action that is attributable to a current event, independent of the person's conscious awareness of that event; again, perception is implicit in task performance. Our hypothesis is that explicit and implicit perception are dissociable, in much the same way as explicit and implicit memory are.

The explicit/implicit distinction can be extended to other domains. For example, several investigators have been concerned with *implicit learning*, in which subjects acquire complex rules and categories through experience, without being able to articulate the rules or category definitions themselves (Reber 1989, Lewicki 1986). Similarly, it appears that subjects can distinguish between soluble and insoluble problems, without being aware of the solution itself—a phenomenon that may be relevant to the experience of intuition in creative problem-solving (Bowers 1984). Taken together, these studies exemplify the *cognitive unconscious* (Rozin 1976, Kihlstrom 1987), in which perception, memory, learning and thinking influence ongoing experience, thought and action outside of phenomenal awareness.

Similar considerations support the notion of an *emotional unconscious* (Kihlstrom et al, unpublished 1993). Freud held that our behaviour is influenced by unconscious affects and drives, but this phenomenon can be understood without all the encumbrances of psychoanalytic theory. For example, the multiple-systems theory of emotion holds that emotional responses have three components—subjective, behavioural and physiological—that are only imperfectly coupled (Lang 1968). This leaves open the possibility of desynchrony (Rachman & Hodgson 1974), in which, for example, the subjective feeling of fear disappears, but the emotional and physiological correlates of fear persist. For example, Weinberger et al (1979) identified a group of individuals as 'repressors' (low scores on anxiety but high scores on social desirability) who deny distress but respond behaviourally and physiologically in a manner resembling highly anxious individuals. This particular form of desynchrony is an example of the dissociation between two expressions of emotion: explicit (reflecting the conscious awareness of an emotion, feeling state or mood) and implicit (referring to changes in experience, thought or behaviour that are attributable to an emotional response).

Another aspect of the emotional unconscious may be observed when a person experiences an emotional response, but is unaware of the event that precipitated that response (e.g. Johnson et al 1985, Kunst-Wilson & Zajonc 1980). In this case, emotion serves as an index of implicit perception or memory. This is what the English poet Thomas Brown had in mind when, freely translating Martial, he stated 'I do not love you, Dr. Fell, but why I cannot tell'. It is also what Breuer and Freud meant when they concluded in their *Studies of Hysteria* that 'hysterics suffer from reminiscences'. In their view, hysterical symptoms were implicit expressions of memory for past traumatic experiences—memories that were denied conscious access by virtue of repression, but which return to consciousness in disguised form.

Unconscious, preconscious, subconscious

One of the attractions of psychoanalytic theory was that it afforded a way of conceptualizing the nature of unconscious mental life. But now, 100 years later, other sorts of models are available. Traditional information-processing theory has generally accepted a distinction between automatic and controlled cognitive processes (e.g. Logan 1988, Shiffrin 1988). Automatic processes are executed inevitably under appropriate stimulus conditions, without requiring any intent or deliberation on the part of the subject. For example, individuals can decode written or spoken language without trying to do so; in fact, they cannot consciously prevent such a thing from happening. In the present context, the most interesting property of automatic processes is that we can have no conscious access to their operations. To continue the example, even very young children speak and listen fluently without consciously referring to the rules of grammar.

Alternative theoretical approaches to cognition also make room for unconscious processes. It has been proposed that some aspects of information processing are modular in nature (Fodor 1983, Jackendoff 1987). In theory, cognitive modules are isolated from other aspects of mental function: other modules have access to their products, but not to their internal processes. The same restriction applies to conscious awareness. A rather different perspective has been offered by parallel distributed processing approaches to cognition (e.g. McClelland & Rumelhart 1981, Rumelhart et al 1986), in which information is represented by a stable pattern of activation across a large number of task-specific processing units. By virtue of massive parallelism, both the number of processing units and the speed with which they operate exceed the span of conscious awareness. Only when the system relaxes to steady state, or when processing is slowed by virtue of stimulus ambiguity, does the representation become accessible to phenomenal awareness.

Automaticity, modularity and connectionism are based on rather different assumptions about the mind, but all assume that there is a vast repertoire of skills, rules, strategies and other processes that guide experience, thought and action outside of conscious awareness. The operation of procedural knowledge (Anderson 1983, Winograd 1975) may be described as *unconscious processing* in the strict sense of the term, because it is denied to introspective phenomenal awareness in principle, under any circumstances—it cannot be known directly, but only by inference. At the same time, it should be clear that the psychological unconscious should not be restricted to procedural knowledge. In implicit perception, it is the stimulus itself, not just the processes that analyse it, that is denied to conscious awareness; in implicit memory, it is the event itself, not just the processes that encode and retrieve it, that is denied to conscious recollection. Obviously, some other categories are needed to represent completely the scope of unconscious processing.

Following Freud, we can identify as cases of *preconscious processing* those instances (e.g. subliminal perception, the amnesic syndrome) where the mental representation of an object or event has been degraded by experimental or subject conditions. For example, a stimulus may be presented at an intensity that is too weak, or for a duration that is too short, to permit conscious perception; or brain damage or experimental conditions may so impoverish encoding that the memory trace is inaccessible to conscious retrieval. But there are other instances, as in hypnosis or the dissociative and conversion disorders, where the event is in no sense degraded, but the event is denied conscious representation none the less. Following William James and Morton Prince, we can refer to these cases in terms of *subconscious processing*. In either case, it is clear that unconscious procedural knowledge can act on declarative knowledge that is not itself accessible to phenomenal awareness.

The distinction between preconscious and subconscious processing is important, because it addresses the question of restrictions on non-conscious processing. In many examples of implicit perception and memory, the extent of unconscious influence is severely limited. Greenwald (1992) (see also Kihlstrom et al 1992c) has concluded that there is good evidence for the preconscious processing of physical features of stimuli, and some evidence for simple semantic analyses, but no convincing evidence for the processing of complex meanings. Similarly, implicit memory in the organic amnesic syndrome appears to be largely supported by a perceptual representation system that retains information about the physical properties, but not the semantic features, of events (Schacter 1992, Tulving & Schacter 1990). Unconscious processing is not always analytically limited: for example, the priming observed in post-hypnotic amnesia (Kihlstrom 1980) clearly relies on the processing of semantic relationships.

Most likely, the scope of non-conscious processing depends on the precise manner in which the mental representations in question are rendered inaccessible to conscious awareness. When the stimulus is degraded (as in subliminal perception) or brain damage prevents optimal encoding (as in the organic amnesic syndrome), preconscious processing may be restricted to simple analyses, of the sort that can be performed by automatic or modular processes. We would not expect much beyond perception-based repetition priming during surgical anaesthesia, for example. Of course, to the extent that complex mental processes can become automatized through practice, the scope of preconscious processing may be expandable to some degree. Thus, if subjects have allowed certain complex judgements to become routine, these may be performed even on subliminal stimuli—especially if they are presented near the subjective rather than the objective threshold. But when conscious awareness is disrupted by a dissociative process, as in hypnosis, or the dissociative and conversion disorders, rather more complicated forms of analysis appear to be possible.

Consciousness and the self

Although many issues remain to be resolved, experimental and clinical demonstrations of unconscious influence are now common. Theoretical developments have lagged somewhat farther behind. Traditional information-processing theories identify the unconscious with preattentive or automatic processing, or states of partial activation. Parallel distributed processing models seem to suggest that virtually all information processing is unconscious. Schacter (1990) has proposed a neuropsychological model, in which a cognitive module mediating conscious awareness can be disconnected from modules mediating perception, memory and the like. However, as noted earlier, not all instances of unconscious processing involve degraded stimuli or automatic, preconscious processing, and there are disruptions of consciousness that do not involve brain damage.

A psychological model that stays close to phenomenal experience suggests that consciousness is mediated by a particular knowledge structure, the *self* or the person's mental representation of him- or herself (Kihlstrom 1992). According to this view, the 'self structure' resides in working memory, where it routinely makes contact with mental representations of the local and global environment, the individual's current processing goals, and other knowledge structures activated by perception, memory and thought. This connection to the self, which identifies the self as the agent or experiencer of some represented event, appears to be the key to consciousness. After all, as William James noted, consciousness is a consciousness *of something*, but it is also *personal*: consciousness comes when we take possession of our thoughts, feelings and desires, and ac¹·nowledge them as our own.

Interestingly, both Ernst Claparede (1950) (discussing Korsakoff's syndrome) and Pierre Janet (1907) (in his treatises on hysteria) noted the absence of the self in cases of unconscious influence. Following their lead, we may propose that when a link is made between the mental representation of self and the mental representation of some object or event, then the percept, memory or thought enters into consciousness; when this link fails to be made, it does not. Nevertheless, unconscious percepts and memories, images, feelings and the like can still influence ongoing experience, thought and action—perhaps by serving as sources of activation which spreads to other knowledge structures and activates them.

The situation can be portrayed in an associative-network model of memory operating according to a principle of spreading activation, much like ACT* (Anderson 1983). Knowledge is represented by nodes standing for concepts, and by associative links for the relations between them. Fig. 1 shows the three basic

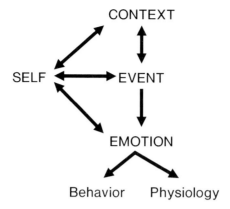

FIG. 1.   Schematic representation of an event linked to co-activated mental representations of self and episodic context, and giving rise to an emotional state.

elements in the mental representation of a particular event (whether constructed in perception or reconstructed from memory): an *event node*, representing a raw description of the event; a *context node*, representing the spatiotemporal context in which the event occurred; and the *self node*, representing the self as the agent or experiencer of the event. These nodes are each linked to many other nodes in the memory network, to which activation can spread. For example, if the event concerns a doctor, activation may spread to associated concepts like *nurse* or *hospital*; or the connotative meaning of the event may give rise to an emotional state, with behavioural and physiological consequences.

Now, imagine that for some reason the link to the self does not get made. Perhaps the stimulus is so degraded that it does not get represented in working memory or perhaps the person is anaesthetized for surgery. Alternatively, the link may get made at the time of perception, but it may not be stored in permanent memory: hippocampal damage may prevent the consolidation of such an association, or the formation of the association may require a certain degree of elaborative processing at the time of encoding. Or, the link may be stored in permanent memory, but inaccessible at the time of retrieval. Perhaps the spread of activation down the associative pathway is inhibited by some sort of dissociative process; or, as may occur in cases of genuine multiple personality, there may be two or more self-concepts simultaneously resident in memory, but the one that is active at the moment is not linked to the knowledge in question. In any of these cases, the person is not going to be conscious of the event in question. Nevertheless, the event node may serve as a source of activation that spreads to other nodes, producing the phenomena of priming that exemplify the cognitive unconscious. Or, the emotional state generated by the event may have behavioural and somatic effects, producing the phenomena of desynchrony that exemplify the emotional unconscious.

The general framework set out here certainly requires elaboration and experimental testing; developments would be facilitated by implementation in an operating computer simulation. That is on the agenda for the future. For the present, we may be content with three conclusions. First: there is now plenty of clinical and experimental evidence for the influence of unconscious perception and memory on the person's experience, thought and action. This evidence is not confined to a single paradigm, but is derived from a number of different methods, ranging from subliminal perception to hypnosis, from neuropsychology to multiple personality, each shedding unique light on the problem. Second: the psychological unconscious, as we now understand it, is quite different from the dynamic unconscious envisioned by classical psychoanalysis. We can honour Freud's insights about unconscious influences, at the same time as we free ourselves from the confines of his theory. Third: the operations of the psychological unconscious are not curious anomalies, but are central features of mental life that can be accommodated within the framework of contemporary cognitive theory. The role of the self in conscious experience provides a basis for uniting the two cultures of modern psychology: cognitive neuropsychology on the one hand, and personality and social psychology on the other.

Acknowledgements

I thank Terrence Barnhardt, Lawrence Couture, Jennifer Dorfman, Martha Glisky, Elizabeth Glisky, Lori Marchese, Sheila Mulvaney, Robin Pennington, Michael Polster, Victor Shames, Susan Valdesseri and Michael Valdesseri for their comments. The point of view represented here is based on research supported by grant # MH-35856 from the National Institute of Mental Health.

References

Anderson JR 1983 The architecture of cognition. Harvard University Press, Cambridge, MA

Bowers KS 1984 On being unconsciously influenced and informed. In: Bowers KS, Meichenbaum D (eds) The unconscious reconsidered. Wiley, New York, p 227–272

Claparede E 1950 Recognition and me-ness. In: Rapaport D (ed) Organization and pathology of thought. Columbia University Press, New York, p 58–75 (Original work published 1911)

Eich E 1984 Memory for unattended events: remembering with and without awareness. Mem Cognit 12:105–111

Fodor J 1983 The modularity of mind: an essay on faculty psychology. MIT Press, Cambridge, MA

Greenwald AG 1992 New look 3: a paradigm shift reclaims the unconscious. Am Psychol 47:766–779

Jackendoff R 1987 Consciousness and the computational mind. MIT Press, Cambridge, MA

Jacoby LL, Dallas M 1981 On the relationship between autobiographical memory and perceptual learning. J Exp Psychol Gen 110:306–340

Janet P 1907 The major symptoms of hysteria. Macmillan, New York

Johnson MK, Kim JK, Risse G 1985 Do alcoholic Korsakoff's syndrome patients acquire affective reactions? J Exp Psychol Learn Mem Cognit 11:22–36

Kihlstrom JF 1980 Posthypnotic amnesia for recently learned material: interactions with 'episodic' and 'semantic' memory. Cognit Psychol 12:227–251

Kihlstrom JF 1987 The cognitive unconscious. Science (Wash DC) 237:1445–1452

Kihlstrom JF, Klein SB 1992 The self as a knowledge structure. In: Wyer RS, Srull TK (eds) Handbook of social cognition, 2nd edn. Erlbaum, Hillsdale, NJ, in press

Kihlstrom JF, Schacter DL, Cork RC, Hurt CA, Behr SE 1990 Implicit and explicit memory following surgical anesthesia. Psychol Sci 1:303–306

Kihlstrom JF, Tataryn DJ, Hoyt IP 1992a Dissociative disorders. In: Sutker PB, Adams HE (eds) Comprehensive handbook of psychopathology, 2nd edn. Plenum Press, New York, p 203–234

Kihlstrom JF, Barnhardt TR, Tataryn DJ 1992b Implicit perception. In: Bornstein R, Pittman TS (eds) Perception without awareness. Guilford Press, New York, p 17–54

Kihlstrom JF, Barnhardt TR, Tataryn DJ 1992c The psychological unconscious: found, lost, and regained. Am Psychol 47:788–791

Kunst-Wilson WR, Zajonc RB 1980 Affective discrimination of stimuli that cannot be recognized. Science (Wash DC) 207:557–558

Lang PJ 1968 Fear reduction and fear behavior: problems in treating a construct. In: Shilen JM (ed) Research in psychotherapy. Am Psychol 3:90–102

Lewicki P 1986 Nonconscious social information processing. Academic Press, New York

Logan GD 1988 Towards an instance theory of automatization. Psychol Rev 95:492–527

McClelland JL, Rumelhart DE 1981 An interactive activation model of context effects in letter perception. I. An account of basic findings. Psychol Rev 88:375–407

Rachman S, Hodgson SI 1974 Synchrony and desynchrony in fear and avoidance. Behav Res Ther 12:311–318

Reber AS 1989 Implicit learning and tacit knowledge. J Exp Psychol Gen 118:219–235

Rozin P 1976 The evolution of intelligence and access to the cognitive unconscious. In: Sprague JM, Epstein AN (eds) Prog Psychobiol Physiol Psychol 6:245–280

Rumelhart DE, McClelland JL, and the PDP Research Group 1986 Parallel distributed processing—explorations in the microstructures of cognition, vol 1: Foundations. MIT Press, Cambridge, MA

Schacter DL 1987 Implicit memory: history and current status. J Exp Psychol Learn Mem Cognit 13:501–518

Schacter DL 1990 Toward a cognitive neuropsychology of awareness: implicit knowledge and anosognosia. J Clin Exp Neuropsychol 12:155–178

Schacter DL 1992 Understanding implicit memory: a cognitive neuroscience approach. Am Psychol 47:559–569

Schacter DL, Kihlstrom JF 1989 Functional amnesia. In: Boller F, Grafman J (eds) Handbook of neuropsychology. Elsevier Science Publishers, Amsterdam, vol 3: 209–231

Shiffrin RM 1988 Attention. In: Atkinson RC, Herrnstein RJ, Lindzey G, Luce RD (eds) Stevens' handbook of experimental psychology, vol 2: Learning and cognition, 2nd edn. Wiley, New York, p 739–812

Shimamura AP 1986 Priming effects in amnesia: evidence for a dissociable memory function. Q J Exp Psychol A Hum Exp Psychol 38:619–644

Tulving E, Schacter DL 1990 Priming and human memory systems. Science (Wash DC) 247:301–305

Weinberger DA, Schwartz GE, Davidson RJ 1979 Low-anxious, high-anxious, and repressive coping styles: psychometric patterns and behavioral and physiological responses to stress. J Abnorm Psychol 88:369–380

Winograd T 1975 Frame representations and the declarative–procedural controversy. In: Bobrow D, Collins A (eds) Representations and understanding. Academic Press, New York, p 185–210

Wood JM, Bootzin RR, Kihlstrom JF, Schacter DL 1992 Implicit and explicit memory for verbal information presented during sleep. Psychol Sci 3:236–239

DISCUSSION

Searle: In what I take to be the main thesis of your paper, the claim is that there are these unconscious mental events. The emphasis has to be on 'mental'. I want to describe two different hypotheses; you tell me why you should prefer one rather than the other.

One hypothesis is: there are all sorts of things that have an impact on the nervous system, and leave effects on the nervous system, that don't come into consciousness. Nonetheless, they affect subsequent conscious thoughts, feelings and behaviour. That's the hypothesis I think is right. For example, when I am sound asleep, my memories exist in my brain in forms that are capable of causing conscious memory experiences, even though there is nothing mental occurring at that time while I am asleep.

The second hypothesis is that in addition to the level of neurophysiological description and all of the effects on it and of it, there is an unconscious mental level. Freud actually said that all mental states are in themselves unconscious and that what we call consciousness is like perception. You go into the attic where all your unconscious things are and you shine the light of perception on these things—that's what bringing a mental state to consciousness is.

I thought all the evidence you gave supported the first of those views. Then at the very end it seemed to me you blew a trumpet in favour of the second.

Kihlstrom: I certainly wouldn't want to be remembered as having blown a trumpet in favour of anything psychoanalytic.

I do want to insist that these things are mental in a sense that they are representations of experience. They are constructed through perception or reconstructed through memory or whatever, and simply have an impact on the person's ongoing experience without themselves being conscious. I don't think this is the same as playing with somebody's neurotransmitter system, which would not be mental in that sense. These are representations. I think the best evidence for the representational status is the fact that you can get conscious access to them under some conditions. The whole beauty of hypnosis and hysteria, and the reason I'm interested in hypnosis and hysteria, is that we can cancel the amnesia suggestion and the person remembers the word list perfectly well. Similarly, when a person recovers from a fugue state, the person remembers his or her past perfectly well. You have to give those things the status of mental representations; they are not merely neurotransmitters hanging around in the brain matter.

Searle: If you ask what fact about the actual state, at the time that it's unconscious, makes it mental, the answer you gave was (I think the correct answer) a dispositional answer. That is, there are certain circumstances in which you are capable of bringing that state to consciousness. Take a very unproblematic case: I believe, even when sound asleep, that George Bush is President of the United States. There is no little sentence in my head that I'm thinking quietly about; the only fact about me when I'm asleep is that I have neurophysiological structures that are capable of bringing that belief to consciousness. Those are two different views and they are not equivalent. The evidence supports the weaker view, namely, attributions of unconscious states are attributions of a dispositional capacity of neurophysiological structures to cause conscious states. So the opposition that you make between a genuine mental state and these neurophysiological phenomena is a false opposition. There are neurophysiological structures in the brain capable of producing conscious thoughts and behaviour. It is perfectly reasonable to call those structures unconscious, even unconscious thoughts and beliefs. The mistake is to suppose that somehow the evidence you have given supports a Freudian style . . . .

Kihlstrom: Never, in my entire career, have I said that this evidence supports a Freudian view!

Searle: Then leave out Freud! On your view, is there supposed to be an ontological realm of unconscious mental states that have all their mental aspects in addition to the neurology?

Kihlstrom: One of the reasons I was interested in doing those experiments was that it brought to light an interesting divergence between how some philosophers—not necessarily you— and some psychologists define things as mental. I think it's a very big mistake to identify the mental with the conscious; it is psychologically not correct. Here you have percepts and memories and emotions that have, by any behavioural standards, psychological reality, even though the person is not consciously aware of them. That is a very striking empirical fact from psychology that people ought to pay attention to.

Marcel: John, if you don't support Freud, I have heard you support Pierre Janet. It is not that these priming effects are unconscious or mental, but that there is a split consciousness. The mere fact that x facilitates a subsequent y does not mean that x is mental. This is the case for priming. It's like the fact that when I do press-ups, I get better at doing press-ups. There is nothing mental about that. I want to know what criteria you have that these priming effects are mental. Secondly, the evidence you use to show the priming effects are mental is that people can perfectly well recall them under certain circumstances. If they can be recalled, they must have been conscious. Their non-consciousness is purely a split in consciousness.

Kihlstrom: There is an important vocabulary problem here. This is one William James talks about in the *Principles*: he offers 10 disproofs of the idea that there is an unconscious. Then in the very next paragraph, he says, 'nevertheless, there is this thing we have to give a name to, maybe it's co-conscious, maybe it's sub-conscious'. When I use the term unconscious, I'm using it in the broad, historically valid, psychological sense of not accessible to conscious awareness.

Williams: Can I make a distinction, which we ought to be able to make at this point in the proceedings? There is one question, which you and John Searle are discussing—the question of whether there are psychological or mental processes which are not consciously registered. Personally, I agree with you, and disagree with Searle, in thinking that there are such processes. This seems to be a separate issue from the existence of something called 'the unconscious', which is invoked in psychoanalytical theory.

Kihlstrom: I never used that term, except to define a domain of inquiry.

Williams: One reason for separating the questions is that in Freud's doctrine about the unconscious, there is a necessary conceptual link between the idea of the unconscious and the idea of repression: things are in the unconscious for reasons that are connected with motivation of various kinds. Whether we should think of the mind in such terms seems to me a separate question from the one that's under discussion in your paper.

Kihlstrom: I view unconscious as an adjective, not a noun. Unconscious and conscious are qualities of mental life.

Shevrin: I would like to address John Searle's question because I think it's critical, at least from my point of view as a psychoanalyst, and because the question bears on my empirical efforts to explore this question. Is the unconscious simply to be considered dispositional, such that we know about it only by its influence on consciousness? Or is the unconscious to be considered another 'realm' of unconscious mental life, having the ability, for example, to influence complex and meaningful actions in a way that bypasses consciousness? One could cite clinical evidence that actions (behaviours in the strict sense) can be influenced by events, which the person is not aware of at the time but which are active at the time, and not simply dispositional. Compulsions, phobias, enactments of post-hypnotic suggestion and sleep-walking are examples.

There is an analogy that captures the difference, and I think the difference is important. I went to the theatre yesterday: the stage was set and the actors were on stage. There is a great deal of unseen stage machinery which makes that possible. The stage machinery is the dispositional elements, what you see lit up in front of you is consciousness. In the Freudian notion of the unconscious, there are two stages, or there can be three or four stages: there is the lit stage and, alongside, there is another stage that is in darkness, on which things are happening, interacting with and influencing what is occurring on the lit stage. Actors from the lit stage disappear onto the unlit stage and what goes on there influences the action on the lit stage, although we can only infer from events on the lit stage what might be happening on the unlit stage.

I would like to cite some empirical evidence to support this Freudian view of the unconscious. With evoked potentials, you can detect the activity of the brain when an individual is not conscious of a subliminal stimulus. When certain words of particular importance to an individual's unconscious conflict, as determined by psychoanalysts, are presented tachistoscopically, the brain responds differently when they are subliminal to when they are supraliminal. A discriminant analysis revealed that the brain responses to the words related to the unconscious conflict are better categorized as going together when they are subliminal than when they are presented supraliminally. The reverse relationship is found for brain responses to words selected to reflect the patient's conscious experience of a particular symptom believed to be caused by the unconscious conflict (Shevrin et al 1992). What is instantiated by the evoked potentials is an act of categorization which is psychological in nature. The process is ongoing and active; it isn't simply dispositional, nor is it in any way reflected in consciousness. I would like to submit that as evidence in favour of the Freudian unconscious as a set of mental operations rather than as a set of dispositions.

Dennett: John Searle talks about events being mental if they have the disposition to become conscious, if the person is in a state with content such that that very content can become conscious. He overlooks another possibility: the feature of these events that I would cite as a basis for calling them mental is that they are content specific. They are the result of a categorization process; there is a difference between the state of 'ocean' and the state of 'tower', if those are your primes. The fact that one of them is 'ocean' is not necessarily tied to the fact that that's the content of that unconscious brain process. The content may not be able to be made conscious, but it may be able to influence something else that becomes conscious, by being semantically related to it.

Searle: That's a dispositional analysis.

Lockwood: John, if one asks: 'Is this an unconscious mental state or is it just a neurophysiological state that has the power to produce certain actions and conscious states under appropriate circumstances?', it's easy to persuade oneself that there isn't a real issue here at all. But it seems to me there may be a real issue, if one looks instead at the *dynamics* of what is being proposed here. Suppose that our best psychological theory says that there are states which are not directly accessible to consciousness but which give rise to behaviour and conscious thoughts and feelings, and evolve over time, in ways that can be most naturally and straight-forwardly explained by using essentially the same (folk-psychological) language and categories that we customarily employ at the conscious level. Then, it seems to me that one is thereby giving substantive content to the supposition that these states are, in some sense, genuinely mental. (Of course, speaking as a materialist, this doesn't prevent them being neurophysiological as well.)

Marcel: But surely the data go against the notion that they are semantic. If you look at the literature on priming effects, people like John Williams have shown you don't get unconscious *semantic* priming effects. There are associative priming effects, but they are not semantic, and that's a crucial distinction.

Gray: For the purpose of this argument, associative priming can do exactly what Dan was trying to do with semantic priming.

Marcel: No. It's not representation. This depends on your criterion for the mental. I understood John Kihlstrom to say the criterion was one of representation. If the priming is purely associative, then I don't see why there is anything necessarily representational about it. And if so, it's not mental.

Dennett: How do you distinguish pure association from the semantic priming effects?

Marcel: One examines whether there is a difference in effectiveness of priming between stimuli that are associated but do not co-refer and stimuli that co-refer but are not associates. It appears that you get automatic priming for associates when the prime is unconscious, but not for pairs of stimuli linked only by their meaning.

Humphrey: I want to get back to John Kihlstrom's interesting remarks about the self and its relation to unconscious processes. His ideas are quite well supported by some of the data from patients with blindsight, particularly the evidence of the difference between human beings and animals. I worked many years ago with monkeys who had had the striate cortex removed: they retained extraordinarily sophisticated visual capacity, much better than anything which has yet been discovered in human beings with lesions of the striate cortex. One way of thinking about this is that the monkey has an advantage in that it doesn't have a particularly highly developed concept of self. Hence, the monkey's non-sensory visual percepts are nothing like so surprising to the monkey as to the human. For a human to have a percept which isn't *his own* percept (related to himself) is very odd indeed. So human patients retreat into saying, 'I don't know what's going on' and denying their ability to see at all. For the monkey, I suspect perceptual information doesn't create the same sort of existential paradox, therefore the monkey is much more ready to use it.

Interestingly, for one particular monkey I worked with for a long time, there were conditions under which she became unable to see again—if she was frightened or she was in pain. It was as though anything which drew attention to her self undermined her ability to use unconscious percepts.

Dennett: For people who haven't seen the film of this monkey, Helen, it is important to stress how amazing she is. Nick and I showed a film of this monkey to a group of primate experts. We said when we started the film: 'There is something wrong with this monkey, what is it?' Nobody guessed that she was blind; her behaviour was absolutely consistent with her having perfectly good vision. The only thing they noticed was when there was a bit of sticky tape on the floor she kept trying to pick it up, and failing.

Gray: Dan, doesn't your allegiance to the Turing test therefore make you say she isn't blind?

Dennett: Manifestly, she isn't blind.

Kihlstrom: The reason she's not manifestly blind is that her circumstances are such that she's able to capitalize fully on implicit perception.

Marcel: Nobody has ever asked a cortically blind monkey whether it can see, though Alan Cowey has proposed a way of doing it.

There are two different points to be made. First, in all human cases studied, the patients are blind only within a circumscribed area, maximally a half-field. So they can see in their preserved field. Second, neither do they have no experience of stimuli in their blind field, nor do they have percepts that are not experienced as their own. They often experience stimuli presented to the blind field, but the experiences are not 'visual'; the patients say they are 'felt'.

Harnad: There is a good example in spatial location. I have read that patients with blindsight can localize objects (say, on the left or right) because they feel some sort of inclination or urge to orient towards them.

Marcel: Sorry, that is not the case. There has never been a problem with location. No blindsight patient has ever been described who had a scotoma that went over the body midline.

Harnad: It doesn't have to be over the midline; their sensation is an inclination to turn in the direction of the object.

Marcel: Turning in the direction is not the issue; it's often a question of what shape the stimulus is.

Shevrin: The interesting findings about implicit perception and implicit memory that John Kihlstrom described raise a question in my mind. In a psychological sense, why does it work? Why are we able to retrieve information in consciousness in one way and not in the other? If the information is available, why does it take some kind of indirect means, like free associations or word stems, for the unconscious to be retrieved?

Kihlstrom: I worry a little about the use of the word 'retrieval'. I'm not sure that information is ever retrieved in the usual sense. Consider, for example, an amnesic patient who hears the word 'water' and then produces the word water as opposed to 'watch' on a stem-completion test. That patient never retrieves the memory in the same way that an analytic patient is supposed to retrieve a repressed childhood recollection. They never say, 'Oh yes, I remember, it was water'.

Shevrin: That's not what we rely on psychoanalytically: that happens in very rare instances. As I have described (Shevrin 1992), it is necessary to distinguish the content, or information, from the vehicle through which the content becomes conscious. The vehicle may be a perception, thought, memory, image, etc. What most often happens in psychoanalysis is that a particular content, belonging to a childhood event, will emerge as an image or in a dream, not necessarily as an explicit memory. There are many examples in psychoanalytical work in which a patient will forget in one session entirely about some events described with much feeling in the preceding session, yet the psychoanalyst will detect clear evidence of the content in the patient's various associations. In short, the analyst is relying on the patient's implicit memories.

Kihlstrom: And interpreting them in some ways in the same way as the experimenter does. This idea of retrieval has a kind of intentionality to it that just seems wrong for what seems to be a passive operation of an associative network.

Shevrin: So what's your explanation?

Kihlstrom: I think the simple-minded answer is, implicit perception works by spreading activation.

Shevrin: But why isn't spreading activation helpful in explicit consciousness?

Kihlstrom: We have talked about first-person and third-person analyses of consciousness, we have forgotten the second person. Suppose I asked you, 'Howard, what are you aware of right now?'. In an associative network theory of memory all this information is supposed to get unpacked. The query: what do you see now? is supposed to light up little nodes in the associative network. One of them corresponds to 'you', which is the self node; others correspond to the things you are seeing right now. But if there is no connection, if there is no link between the self node and the node that's stimulated by what you are seeing, you can't answer that question. That's how you programme it in Anderson's ACT* computer simulation (Anderson 1983). You create a self-structure to which all percepts and memories running through working memory will be related. If the association is preserved, you are able to report; if it is not preserved, you are not.

Gray: The issue of what are non-conscious mental operations is very important. There is at least one way—I think the right way—in which we haven't yet talked about it. We are basically concerned with the scientific and conceptual issues of what is consciousness, what is the mental and so on. Among those issues is the question, what level of analysis should we work at? John Searle's point, certainly in his writings as I have understood them, is that you need only two levels of analysis: the level of analysis of the neurophysiologist, neuroanatomist, neurochemist and so on, and the level of fully conscious mental states. I have disputed that (Gray 1987) and I would like to summarize the argument in relation to something which is nicely neutral with respect to all of these issues about Freud and psychoanalysis (which can obscure the main focus of what I take this conference to be about).

The dispute in print has been about language processes. John Searle says there are brain events going on and out comes language, but it is a category mistake to talk about the brain as doing phonetics, syntax and semantics. These are clearly mental operations—nobody could deny that syntax and semantics are something different than simply neurophysiological processes. So the dispute has been: is it right to treat the brain processes that lead to spoken language as themselves having a level of analysis that is beyond the neurophysiological? My argument is as follows.

Clearly, anything that is going on in the brain to produce syntax or semantics is part of neurophysiology; there are nerve cells doing all the things that nerve cells have to do. Then, however, one must ask: why are the nerve cells doing those things and not others? The answer to that question is *not* in terms of neurophysiology, it is in terms of constraints that are required for communication between individuals, because that's what speech is about. The constraints on speech between individuals include a level of syntax, because without syntax you don't have the informational combinatorial capacities that you need for language, and a level of semantics, because without that you don't have shared referents. Neither the semantic nor the syntactic properties that are necessary are properties of neurophysiological events; they are properties of the communication system. Therefore to analyse them you need the level of analysis of mental operations. In that sense, there is unconscious mental processing—syntactical and semantic properties are mental, clearly, and they are unconscious because we haven't the slightest idea of how the syntax or semantics is working as we talk.

Searle: I didn't actually disagree with anything you just said. Maybe I'm not making myself clear or maybe I haven't understood what you said. My view is as follows. It's clear that we will have to have different levels of description of what is going on in the brain, and some of those levels of description are at a much higher level than that of standard neurophysiological text books. But, at the same time, some of the higher levels are not at the level of consciousness. For example, in order to describe the brain's unconscious capacity to form relative clauses, we need to talk at a much higher level than the level of neuron firings. There has to be a much higher level of description than that.

I am asking what facts correspond to these claims. What's the mode of existence of the phenomena that we are describing here? I have said the only facts that I have ever seen anybody be able to identify are facts involving neurophysiology, described at these different levels, and facts about consciousness. I can't find any other mental facts. This point comes out especially strongly when we examine rule-governed behaviour. It's clear that we do follow rules; it's clear that sometimes we follow rules unconsciously. However, since Chomsky, it has become fashionable to attribute rules and rule following behaviour to people, where the rules aren't even the kind of thing that could ever be the content of a conscious mental state. On Chomsky's view, it isn't that the child doesn't happen to think 'move alpha'; it couldn't think 'move alpha', because the expression 'move alpha' is just the linguists' way of describing the rule. The rule itself isn't the kind of thing that you could ever follow consciously. Against this view, I want to say that it is not a rule, rather, there is a pattern of behaviour that is produced by neurophysiological structures, where the structures have neurophysiological but not mental reality.

Kihlstrom: On those grounds, I think the kinds of things I'm talking about here satisfy your criterion of the mental. If the stimulus were not masked or were a little stronger or the person didn't have so much hippocampal damage, what had been presented would be perfectly perceptible or perfectly memorable.

Harnad: It seems to me that if (according to the best current empirical theory in linguistics) 'move alpha' is a useful, predictive, explanatory descriptor of a process going on in one's head and playing a role in generating one's linguistic capacity, then it surely does not matter whether it is 'mental' (i.e. conscious or potentially conscious) or not. 'Move alpha' could be a correct 'higher-level description of neural activity' either way.

Searle: It matters to Chomsky.

Williams: The point was made earlier that consciousness seems to be either all or nothing. The classical argument for unconscious perceptions, which was given by Leibniz, goes against that claim. You can be woken up by a bell. Leibniz's view was that if you were woken up by a bell, you were woken up by *hearing* a bell and you gradually became conscious of hearing a bell. This seems an absolutely commonsensical description of the situation; it has three consequences. It implies that there is such a thing as hearing when you are not conscious that you are hearing. Second, it implies there are degrees of consciousness. Third, it implies there can be an unconscious mental activity which is not analysable into disposition.

Marcel: You are right. The evidence psychologically is against what Ben Libet said. He said, the production of a conscious experience has a unitary, all or nothing character. That is not the case.

Singer: I think if there is a thrust to the work that I have been doing, it is that people do much more preparation at a conscious level for all kinds of subsequent acts than they realize. We overlearn all kinds of mental associations, social connections, potential situations and so on, in much the same way that we overlearn the movements required to ride a bicycle. A great deal of the time we are preparing ourselves for sets of, for example, speech patterns. While it can be said that we don't pay attention to our speech, that it seems to come out without thought, this may be because the material to be spoken was often rehearsed extensively beforehand. I have often prepared, mentally, things I might say in certain circumstances. There is a tremendous amount of research on the advantages of mental practice. Imagery practice for atheletes, for example, shows that there are advantages, in addition to physical practice, of mental practice. This is not inconsistent with what John Kihlstrom has been saying. It could be argued that it helps us understand why certain things seem to operate automatically without subsequent specific recollection of their initial practice or rehearsal.

Searle: I don't take my position to be inconsistent with John Kihlstrom's. Secondly, I'm really not overwhelmed by the Leibnizian argument. What's the factual difference between saying, 'There is an unconscious hearing of the bell and eventually because the guy is hearing it unconsciously he wakes up' and saying 'There is a stimulation of the guy's nervous system which eventually reaches the threshold of consciousness and he wakes up'? I can't hear any factual difference.

Let me give you another example, closer to real life. Many of us suffer from back pains; sometimes the pain wakes you up. How should one describe that? It seems to me there are two different descriptions. One is this: 'I have an unconscious pain. It keeps going all night long and sometimes it gets so bad that it wakes me up'. A second description is this: 'I have this stimulation of my sciatic nerve, and eventually it reaches the threshold of consciousness, at which point I wake up'. I can't hear anything that's added (that isn't a source of confusion) by saying, in addition to the neurophysiology, there is this extra mysterious thing, the unconscious pain.

Van Gulick: I would like to tie together a few pieces of the discussion. Yesterday, our focus was on subjectivity. Today we have been focusing on a variety of issues to do with the conscious/unconscious distinction. John Searle has been arguing that there is no way to make sense of unconscious mental states, except as dispositions that give rise to conscious mental states. Dan Dennett, John Kihlstrom and some others have proposed that representational characteristics can be present in unconscious states that cannot be brought to consciousness. I think that's one of the strong arguments for the existence of non-dispositional unconscious states. One of the two traditional marks of the mental is the intentional or representational. There are many patterns that John Searle is willing to acknowledge at higher levels of neural organization that he wants to keep as non-mental, but it's very hard to see how you can possibly capture the relevant patterns without describing them in representational or intentional or semantic terms.

On the other hand, there's also the other traditional mark of the mental: the qualitative or subjective. There are reasons, like the one Sydney Shoemaker gave, for thinking that there are lots of qualitative states that may be mental in the qualitative sense but are unconscious in the sense that they cannot be referred to self and they cannot be reported. A good example is the work of Stoerig & Cowey (1990) on apparent chromatic sensitivity in patients with blindsight who report themselves as being blind and not having any experiences, and yet can show very good colour discrimination.

Marcel: They show wavelength discrimination, not colour discrimination.

Gray: I have been feeling glimmerings of a possible consensus, or at least a hypothesis which would integrate a number of things that people have been saying from very different angles. Like many other things in this field, I suspect it goes back to something Larry Weiskrantz (1986) wrote.

You get into a lot of traps, if you think of consciousness as being primarily about stimulus detection and response execution. Max Velmans (1991) wrote a very good paper, in which he went systematically through all the things that consciousness is supposed to be about in terms of stimulus detection and response execution; he showed that consciousness was always too slow, it came too late. The obvious reply is to say consciousness is not to do with stimulus detection or response execution at all, because those things happen unconsciously. (And I would continue to say that they happen unconsciously through *mental* processes.) Therefore, what consciousness is doing is something to do with monitoring after the event. The key word probably is monitoring, and I think that's the word Larry Weiskrantz used—monitoring and predicting what's about to happen next; looking to see whether the world matches the prediction and detecting mismatch. All of those things take some time after the actual stimulus input. In the kind of experiment Ben Libet described (this volume), detection of the stimulus, i.e. the first bit of neuronal processing, goes all the way up to the sensory cortex. Consciousness comes in after that and is then used to generate further processes which are concerned with monitoring whether what has just come in is what ought to have come in and seeing what it predicts about what next ought to come in. All that, I take to be part of what's occurring in the Kinsbourne–Dennett view of multiple drafts (Dennett 1991, Dennett & Kinsbourne 1992). The multiple draft theory is about trying to get the best handle on what is going on and what ought to be going on next. So there is plenty of time for the editing, and some of that may be the time that was described in Ben Libet's cortical stimulus experiments. Some of these ideas I will try to develop in my paper tomorrow (Gray, this volume). I feel that if we stop thinking about consciousness as to do with stimulus detection and action, we might get somewhere.

Humphrey: Jeffrey, what has a stab of pain got to do with this kind of cognitive monitoring?

Gray: I was expecting that question, because it's precisely the one I have been asking myself for a number of years. I think the answer might be that a system which is concerned with predicting what ought to happen next and keeping, as it were, the whole ship steering along the right course, is a system which must also have a very important interrupt mechanism for times when what comes in is not according to plan. The pain itself we know occurs after the response—it is too late to organize the removal of the finger from the hotplate. So I think even pain can be fitted in; it occurs after the event, and it is telling you that the action pattern you have been carrying out is the wrong action pattern, you had better review that.

Marcel: There is no point in trying to stipulate what consciousness is. People here are referring often to different things, which may be related or may not be. Some people are referring to sensation, phenomenal aspects, some may be referring to intentionality, some to reflexivity, some to reportability. I would prefer that we didn't use the word consciousness, but referred to which of those we are talking about. Otherwise, there is a systematic confusion and ambiguity.

Gray: Some of us still believe that consciousness matters, that the distinction between neurophysiological processes that don't have consciousness tacked on and those that do, matters.

Marcel: But which do you mean by the word consciousness?

Kihlstrom: I think it would be a disaster if we identified consciousness with reportability. People can be conscious of things they can't report. If you mean reportable *in principle*, perhaps we can agree.

References

Anderson JR 1983 The architecture of cognition. Harvard University Press, Cambridge, MA (Cognit Sci Ser 5)

Dennett DC 1991 Consciousness explained. Allen Lane, London

Dennett DC, Kinsbourne M 1992 Time and the observer: the where and when of consciousness in the brain. Behav Brain Sci 15:183–201

Gray JA 1987 The mind–brain identity theory as a scientific hypothesis: a second look. In: Blakemore C, Greenfield S (eds) Mindwaves. Blackwell Publishers, Oxford, p 461–483

Gray JA 1993 Consciousness, schizophrenia and scientific theory. In: Experimental and theoretical studies of consciousness. Wiley, Chichester (Ciba Found Symp 174) p 263–281

Libet B 1993 The neural time factor in conscious and unconscious events. In: Experimental and theoretical studies of consciousness. Wiley, Chichester (Ciba Found Symp 174) p 123–146

Shevrin H 1992 Subliminal perception, memory, and consciousness: cognitive and dynamic perspectives. In: Bornstein RF, Pittman TS (eds) Perception without awareness: cognitive, clinical and social perspectives. Guilford Press, New York, p 123–144

Shevrin H, Williams WJ, Marshall RE, Hertel RK, Bond JA, Brakel LA 1992 Event-related potential indicators of the dynamic unconscious. Consci & Cognit 1:340–366

Stoerig P, Cowey A 1990 Wavelength sensitivity in blindsight. Nature 342:916–918

Velmans M 1991 Is human information processing conscious? Behav Brain Sci 14:651–726

Weiskrantz L 1986 Blindsight: a case study and implications. Oxford University Press, Oxford

Slippage in the unity of consciousness

Anthony J. Marcel

Medical Research Council, Applied Psychology Unit, 15 Chaucer Road, Cambridge CB2 2EF, UK

Abstract. Many psychological studies assume a unity of consciousness. Doubt is cast on this assumption (a) by psychophysical studies in normal subjects and those with blindsight showing the simultaneous dissociation of different modes of report of a sensation, and (b) by clinical studies of anosognosic patients showing dissociations of awareness of their own states. These and other phenomena are interpreted to imply two kinds of division of consciousness: the separation of phenomenal experience from reflexive consciousness and the non-unity of reflexive consciousness. Reflexive consciousness is taken to be necessary for report and is associated with the self as the subject of experience and agent of report. Reflexive consciousness is operative only when we attend to our own states. When we are involved in the world reflexivity intervenes less and our consciousness is more unified.

1993 Experimental and theoretical studies of consciousness. Wiley, Chichester (Ciba Foundation Symposium 174) p 168–186

The meaning of 'the unity of consciousness' depends on the way the term 'consciousness' is used. Within psychology the term consciousness is used variously to refer to (a) phenomenal experience, that which has qualitative properties or qualia; (b) thoughts or ideas that we are aware of having; (c) reflexive consciousness, i.e. second-order direct knowledge of (a) or (b). (When consciousness is used to refer to a general state, e.g. in anaesthesia, it usually refers to the probability of (a) or (b).) One sense of the unity of consciousness is the possible integrality of these referents (as opposed to their separability). Another sense is the oneness of a sensation (or quale). Finally, linked to this, there is the sense of the unity of reflexive consciousness, that there is a single subject of experience and action. Either there is or there is not a particular sensation at a particular moment for an individual. The importance of these notions of unity can be elucidated by examining how they manifest themselves in empirical psychology.

To what do perceptual speech acts refer?

Much empirical psychology is concerned with experience and sensations (our conscious phenomenology), although it is often not acknowledged as such (see

Marcel 1983, 1988). This is explicit in the distinction between classical and modern psychophysics. Statements such as 'I saw a light' are usually taken to be *reports— reports that refer to phenomenal experience*; whereas in the case of forced-choice discrimination, responses are not assumed to be reports or necessarily to reflect phenomenal experience or sensations. In recent research the contrast between the content of voluntary reports and greater accuracy in what the subject considers to be guesses is taken to reflect the difference between conscious and non-conscious representations. This distinction is used as a criterion in establishing non-conscious perception in normal people (Cheesman & Merikle 1985) and in establishing non-conscious perception and memory in neurological cases of cortical blindness and memory (Weiskrantz 1988). Thus, in both central visual masking with normal people and in blindsight the individual may report that they see nothing, but when enjoined to guess accuracy is significantly above chance.

An important feature of experimental procedures is that non-verbal responses are usually treated tacitly as conventionalized functional equivalents to perceptual speech acts of report. Thus pressing a button may be treated as another way of saying, 'The two lights seem equally bright to me *now*' or 'I feel that *this* word was on the list I heard yesterday' (Dennett 1982). Such actions are conventionalized because an experimenter asks the subject to respond in that way and the subject complies. They are short-hand communicative gestures.

Consider the assumptions that underlie such common experimental procedures. (1) That responses treated by subject and experimenter as referring to experience do indeed refer to experience. (2) That different ways of responding really are functionally equivalent as conventionalized descriptive speech acts. (3) That phenomenal experience is unitary. The second assumption can be re-expressed: since responses which are reports or descriptions are temporally and logically posterior to what they describe, they cannot influence what they describe. In the case of an experience, an additional argument for the supposed equivalence of different forms of subjective report and for their inability to affect the original experience is the very supposition that the experience is unitary. The experience is supposed to be unitary in two (linked) senses: first, the 'quale' is supposed to be single and indivisible (irrespective of its physical composition or the subject's analytical attitude); second, the subject of experience, namely the reporter responsible for the action, is supposed to be unitary. These assumptions seem so sensible that experimenters almost never make them explicit. However, some recent experiments and certain clinical phenomena call these assumptions into question.

Experiments on the non-equivalence of modes of report

The experiments

The genesis of the present experiments was a study by Zihl and von Cramon (1980). They asked three hemianopic subjects with blindsight to indicate those occasions when they 'felt' that a light was present following an auditory signal, by blinking, by pressing a button and by saying 'yes'. (It is important to realize that it is not the case that individuals with blindsight have *no* conscious experience of stationary visual stimuli. It is not, according to them, *visual* experience.) Discriminative sensitivity was greater in the blink than the button press and least in the speech response. The following experiments were carried out in an attempt to replicate and illuminate this dramatic dissociation.

The first two experiments were carried out on G.Y., a 27-year-old subject with a dense right hemianopia since he was eight years old, who has served in many studies of blindsight. The first experiment required G.Y. to respond in three ways on each trial to detection of a bright light subtending 2° of visual angle in his blind field, illuminated for 200 ms. There were 10 blocks of 40 trials. On each trial there was an auditory click, then, randomly on 50% of trials, the light was illuminated.

The instructions were: 'When you *'feel'* that a light has come on, (a) blink your right eye, (b) press the button beneath your right forefinger, (c) say 'yes'. Do not guess unless you have to.' There were no instructions for speed.

The results are shown in Table 1. The data are given in terms of percent Hits (correct positive responses) and False Positives (incorrect positive responses), with median latencies. There are two main points.

(1) None of the latencies are of a 'reflex' nature. Indeed, they are considerably longer than the usual median of simple go / no go latencies, suggesting intendedness. (The improvement over blocks of trials without feedback and any possible transfer of learning between response types in this and the subsequent experiments do not mitigate those aspects of the data focused on here.)

(2) The most important point is that on identical trials the subject's different detection reports dissociated. He often said 'yes' with his eye but not with his finger and the same for finger versus voice, but sometimes showed the reverse pattern. On several occasions, he was asked if he remembered the instructions and he did so correctly. He did not realize that there was a paradoxical discrepancy.

Is this discrepancy due to (a) the modality/type of response, or (b) the order/time delay of the response? If G.Y. treated the responses as independent decisions, then, since he spontaneously tended to perform them in a certain order, time delay might be relevant. The second experiment was carried out to investigate these factors, to examine the effect of performing only one response at a time, and to contrast a 'feel' condition with a 'guess' condition.

In this experiment G.Y. was confronted with the same visual situation but each response was tested separately. Firstly, baseline performance was established for each response with two blocks of 40 trials for blink, finger and vocal response, with the following instructions: 'Respond as soon as you have an impression of whether a light came on. Try not to delay too long'. After this,

TABLE 1   G.Y.'s detection performance with simultaneous use of three response types

Type of response		Percent hits: Percent false positives[a]	
		Blocks 1 + 2	Blocks 9 + 10
Blink		60 : 45	85 : 22.5
	Latency (ms)	287	301
Button press		55 : 42.5	70 : 27.5
	Latency (ms)	365	369
Verbal		50 : 42.5	57.5 : 45
	Latency (s)	2–6	2–7

[a]Percent hits, the percent of trials on which the light illuminated that a 'Yes' response was given. Percent false positives, the percent of trials on which there was no light that a 'Yes' response was given.

in the main test, for each type of response there were three conditions, each of eight blocks of 40 trials.

(1) Respond as fast as possible being as accurate as possible.
(2) Respond only when a second auditory click occurs: 2 second delay.
(3) Respond only when a second auditory click occurs: 8 second delay.

After all the nine conditions had been run, two extra blocks of trials were run for each condition of response type and delay. In these, G.Y. was instructed to *guess* whether a light had come on, irrespective of any conscious sensation, and was told that lights occurred on about 50% of trials.

The results are shown in Table 2. There is an effect of response delay on all response types. In addition, there is still an effect of response type. Even when vocal responses are being made as fast as other responses and are at their 'best', they are still less 'accurate' than other responses. Most importantly, in the 'guessing' conditions, performance was better than in each corresponding 'report' condition. Furthermore, there was now almost no difference between response types, even though they had not reached a ceiling. The differences in performance between response types cannot be due only to differences in criterion or confidence, because what varies is the difference between rates of correct detection and incorrect detection responses.

To see whether these phenomena are restricted to subjects with blindsight, the third experiment attempted to replicate Experiment 2 with 10 normally sighted subjects. Viewing conditions were essentially the same as for G.Y., but with normal subjects one cannot use exactly the same stimuli as for blindsight subjects. Therefore, for each subject a first procedure involved the determination of a threshold luminance increment for the target. A range of luminance increments was used with three response categories: 'Definitely seen', 'Guess yes', 'Not seen'. The eventual stimulus value was set at the intensity yielding 50% 'Guess yes' responses (which produced 25–30% 'Definitely seen' responses). The procedure in the main experiment was exactly the same as that for Experiment 2 on G.Y. The instructions were the same except that instead

TABLE 2   G.Y.'s report and guessing performance with response type and delay tested separately

| Type of response | Percent hits: Percent false positives[a] | | | |
	Pre-test	Blocks 1 + 2	Blocks 7 + 8	Guessing (Blocks 9 + 10)
Blink				
Pre-test (RT = 264 ms)	70 : 40			
Speeded (RT = 227, 218 ms)		67.5 : 40	85 : 20	87.5 : 20
IS = 2 s		60 : 40	85 : 27.5	85 : 15
IS = 8 s		60 : 45	72.5 : 25	80 : 15
Finger				
Pre-test (RT = 391 ms)	60 : 40			
Speeded (RT = 340, 346 ms)		62.5 : 37.5	70 : 35	80 : 20
IS = 2 s		47.5 : 52.5	75 : 40	90 : 20
IS = 8 s		55 : 52.5	60 : 42.5	80 : 15
Verbal				
Pre-test (RT = 947 ms)	50 : 42.5			
Speeded (RT = 623, 644 ms)		62.5 : 50	60 : 45	77.5 : 15
IS = 2 s		42.5 : 45	55 : 45	80 : 25
IS = 8 s		40 : 37.5	50 : 42.5	75 : 20

RT, reaction time. The two values are the two means of medians for Blocks 1 + 2 and for Blocks 7 + 8. IS, the delay between the trial-offset signal and the imperative signal, i.e. the signal to respond. [a]Percent hits and percent false positives as for Table 1.

of 'have an impression of whether the light came on' the phrase used was 'have an impression as to whether you saw the light'. Again, two final blocks of trials with guessing instructions were given.

Because all subjects except one showed the same pattern of data, the results for these nine subjects are shown together in Table 3, in the same manner as for Experiment 2. These normal subjects almost exactly reproduce the results obtained with G.Y. For the 'report of sensation' conditions, there are separate effects of response type and delay. For the 'guessing' conditions there is still a small effect of delay, but again almost no effect of response type, with accuracy increasing for all response types without reaching a ceiling.

After finishing, each subject was given the same task as G.Y. in Experiment 1, i.e. all three responses were required on each trial. In this condition the normal subjects differed from G.Y. in that none of them showed a dissociation between response types, except for a small criterion bias on the vocal response. However, in this condition subjects were not required to make speeded responses. The literature indicates that speeded responses do produce a dissociation (Cumming 1972). Therefore a fourth experiment was run, where ten different normal subjects were required to report a conscious sensation of the light 'as fast as possible but as accurately as possible', using all three responses on each trial. Again

TABLE 3 **Normal subjects' report and guessing performance with response type and delay tested separately (Group results)**

| | Percent hits: Percent false positives[a] | | | |
| | | | | Guessing |
Type of response	Pre-test	Blocks 1 + 2	Blocks 7 + 8	(Blocks 9 + 10)
Blink				
Pre-test	55 : 42.5			
Speeded (RT[b] = 317, 311)		60 : 42.5	77.5 : 35	85 : 20
IS = 2 s		57.5 : 40	67.5 : 32.5	85 : 15
IS = 8 s		52.5 : 37.5	52.5 : 27.5	70 : 12.5
Finger				
Pre-test	45 : 40			
Speeded (RT = 581, 575)		57.5 : 40	65 : 32.5	80 : 25
IS = 2 s		55 : 40	67.5 : 35	85 : 22.5
IS = 8 s		52.5 : 42.5	55 : 37.5	80 : 20
Verbal				
Pre-test	42.5 : 40			
Speeded (RT = 905, 830)		50 : 45	55 : 42.5	80 : 20
IS = 2 s		40 : 37.5	45 : 37.5	75 : 20
IS = 8 s		37.5 : 35	35 : 32.5	67.5 : 12.5

[a]Percent hits and percent false positives as for Table 1.
[b]RT, IS, as for Table 2.

after eight blocks, two blocks of guessing trials with all three responses together were used. The results are shown in Table 4. Now results similar to G.Y. in Experiment 1 were obtained. Subjects showed a simultaneous dissociation (on the same trial giving a 'Yes' response with one type of response but not with another) in 'report' trials, but almost none in 'guessing' trials.

Interpretations

The main phenomenon in this set of experiments is that the detectability of a light depends on the response used. Subjects on the same trial report with their finger that they see a light and report orally that they do not, or the reverse. They do not seem to have forgotten the instructions, since the same overall detection rates are obtained when each response type is tested separately. One interpretation of these data is that the responses are not actually reports of an experience, even though subjects think they are, but are just responses to non-phenomenal information reflecting differential causal links between perceptual representations and different action systems. However, there are several reasons to discount this interpretation. First, the spontaneous latencies are too long for 'reflexes' and the differences remain when long response delays are imposed.

TABLE 4   Normal subjects' report and guessing performance with simultaneous speeded use of three response types

	Percent hits: Percent false positives[a]		
Type of response	Blocks 1 + 2	Blocks 7 + 8	Guessing (Blocks 9 + 10)
Blink	65 : 37.5	77.5 : 30	87.5 :20
Finger	62.5 : 42.5	67.5 : 32.5	82.5 : 20
Verbal	55 : 42.5	57.5 : 40	80 : 25

[a]Percent hits and percent false positives as for Table 1.

Second, when asked, subjects insisted that their responses were 'reports'; usually, if people deny awareness of some stimulus, they are quite unwilling to make voluntary responses based on such non-conscious representations (see Marcel 1988, for discussion). Third, the most compelling reason to treat the main results as reflecting reports of experience is the difference when subjects were instructed to guess. Without exception, the results showed better discrimination, the response type effect was almost eliminated and the pattern of response delay effects was altered. Such data are exactly what lead in both clinical and normal research to the distinction between conscious and non-conscious perception.

If the subjects' behaviour does reflect reports of an experience, it would appear that an experience is not independent of report, but depends on how and when it is reported. This hypothesis has two variants, both of which may obtain. The first is that *the nature of an intended response influences the experience*. This idea is supported by the finding of Joanette et al (1986) that awareness of a stimulus in patients with neglect depends on which hand is intended for the response. The results of Bisiach et al (1985) suggest that the nature of the response used to report a visual experience can alter the memory of the experience in as little as two seconds. I have supportive preliminary data on normal subjects where a post-trial signal informs the subject which type of response to use. However, in Experiments 1 and 4 all three responses were required on a trial, which casts doubt on this hypothesis as a complete or satisfactory account. This leads to the second variant of the hypothesis in question, namely that *different ways of reporting have differential access to an experience*. Whether or not this requires non-unitary representations of a single experience, it certainly calls into question the existence of a unitary reflexive consciousness or a unitary subject of experience responsible for report.

It is worth noting a parallel to Experiments 1 and 4 obtained by Cumming (1972). On each trial, letters were shown briefly and laterally masked. Subjects had to detect the presence of a specified target letter by pressing a key. When responding with no time pressure, subjects failed to detect the target letter when it was present but severely masked. However, when urged to respond fast, subjects 'tended to respond to the presence of a target letter with a fast press of the 'target-present' key, and then, a moment later, to verbally apologise for having made an error'.

In discussing such cases of dissociation of different types of report of a supposedly single experience, Allport (1988), in an ironical vein, raises the issue of which of them should be taken as the more valid measure of consciousness. But if we use the criterion of a difference in accuracy between trials when the subjects are instructed to report and those when they are instructed to guess (Cheesman & Merikle 1985, Weiskrantz 1988, Marcel 1983), then *all* of the 'report' responses used in the experiments discussed here reflect consciousness. Note that Allport's question presupposes a single unitary consciousness. If we abandon this assumption, the results under 'report' instructions reflect separate non-unitary consciousnesses. But if this is so, we have to say either that the phenomenal experience of the target light is multiply represented or that separate reflexive consciousnesses (associated with different responses) have differential access to a single experience. The latter seems more parsimonious, though it implies not only a distinction between phenomenal and non-phenomenal representations (those of our states to which we can and cannot have access), but also a separation of phenomenal experience or sensation from reflexive consciousness and divisions in the latter. The apparent conflict in the present experiments and those of Cumming disappears if we assume that it is under precisely such conditions that the target sensation is differentially available to divisions of reflexive consciousness. It need not be assumed that divided reflexive consciousness is the normal state of affairs. But it is worth considering that it is psychologically possible and obtains in 'limit' situations (e.g. speeded responding under masking) and in various clinical conditions in which dissociative phenomena occur. Alternatively, it is possible that such splits in consciousness are always present but that in 'normal' situations they are not obvious because the contents of different divisions of consciousness agree or cohere.

Dissociative phenomena in anosognosia

Certain clinical neurological deficits of a primary nature and our (secondary) awareness of such deficits may have important implications for (1) the separation of types or levels of consciousness, and (2) dissociative states within a level of reflexive consciousness. These are reflected by two types of dissociation.

Different levels of consciousness

It is now acknowledged that there are several types of neurologically acquired impairment where in one form the deficit is total but in another superficially similar form the patients seem to lack consciousness associated with the specific function, but the information associated with the function is processed non-consciously. Examples of this are blindsight, amnesia, prosopagnosia, neglect and extinction, associative agnosia and Wernicke's aphasia (for reviews see Marcel 1988, Weiskrantz 1988, Milner & Rugg 1992). In these cases, the patients seem unaware of the intact function but are sensorily aware of their deficit. Indeed, the deficits seem to consist in specific unawarenesses. Thus the blindsight patient insists that he does not see in his blind field.

On the other hand, there are many cases, especially in the acute phase following neurological trauma, where there is one of the above specific deficits, either with or without preservation of non-conscious function, but where the patient is unaware of the deficit. This is termed anosognosia (see Prigatano & Schacter 1991, for recent reviews). It is unlikely that anosognosia is a necessary part of the deficit itself, since in most cases the anosognosia disappears but the primary deficit remains, and the primary deficit can occur without anosognosia (Bisiach & Geminiani 1991).

The separate occurrence of cortical blindness *without* non-conscious vision, cortical blindness *with* non-conscious vision (blindsight) and anosognosia for either of the first two suggests something both about what is lacking in blindsight and what is lacking in anosognosia. Whatever is lacking in blindsight, it is this lack which leads one to believe one is blind; without access to this lack, one does not know that one is blind. Indeed, how do normal people know that they see (or remember or understand language or recognize someone)? It is not purely by observing that they do not bump into obstacles; it is because they have visual experience. It is tempting to suppose that there are aspects of the contents of phenomenal experience that are specific to different modalities of experience and different functions. If normal people know that they see because they experience visual phenomenology, the cortically blind patient knows that he does *not* see because he experiences the lack of such visual qualia (especially by contrast with intact areas of visual field).

If the above is acceptable, then the person who does not know that they have become blind must have impaired access to their lack of visual (or other specific) qualia or sensations. But this type of second-order knowledge itself seems to be of an experiential nature. Thus we seem to be led, on this analysis, to postulate a division between (i) *phenomenal content or experience specific to functions or modalities* and (ii) *representation of such content at the level of reflexive consciousness* or *access to such content by reflexive consciousness*.

Dissociations within reflexive consciousness

As Bisiach & Geminiani (1991) point out, there can often be a double dissociation *within* the level of knowledge reflected by anosognosia. On the one hand, a patient may verbally admit or complain of his hemiplegia (unilateral paralysis), while trying to act as if he were normal. Two real examples are a man bemoaning his paralysis but trying to get out of bed and walk, and a woman who had wept when describing her paralysis asking for her knitting less than 20 seconds later. On the other hand, there are many hemiplegic patients who in conversation seem unaware of their deficit and resolutely deny any deficit, and yet lie still in bed and never attempt to initiate voluntary activities requiring coordinated use of limbs on both sides. Bisiach points out that this double dissociation cannot be conceptualized in verbal/non-verbal terms, because the apparent knowledge and lack of knowledge can occur either way round.

In current work by Richard Tegner and myself on anosognosic hemiplegic patients, we have observed the above and other dissociations. The patient is asked to rate his/her current abilities on a range of uni- and bimanual and uni- and bipedal activities (e.g. tying a knot, clapping) and is also asked how well the questioner could perform each activity 'if I (the questioner) were in your (the patient's) current condition'. A number of patients rate their own ability as perfect but then say that the questioner would be quite unable to perform the task if he/she were in the patient's condition 'because you would need both hands/feet'! It would seem that the patient's access to their state depends on the personal stance taken (first-person versus third-person). This observation echoes that made by Kinsbourne & Warrington (1963), where a patient with anosognosia for his jargon aphasia was satisfied with his own impaired speech when a recording was played back but rejected the identical utterances as unintelligible when hearing a recording by another speaker. Another observation we have made is that if we ask the patient in a normal manner what is wrong with them, or directly ask about movement or sensation in their left arm or leg, they will deny that anything is wrong. However, if we lean close and ask in a confiding manner and in an almost childish voice 'Does your arm ever not do what you want it to?' or 'Is your arm ever naughty?', the patient will often confidingly reply in the affirmative.

It should be pointed out that such patients do not have a general thought disorder or confusion, because their lack of knowledge or contradictions is restricted to their deficit. Indeed, a patient with a hemiplegia and a hemianopia may be anosognosic, or exhibit contradictory knowledge, only with respect to his hemiplegia. Secondly, the anosognosia for hemiplegia in such patients is not just a face-saving denial that the patient is fully aware of, nor is the lack of knowledge entirely due to motivation. Neither of these seems likely, since vestibular stimulation (irrigation of the canals of the outer ear) of hemiplegic patients with a unilateral neglect and anosognosia produces a temporary remission of the neglect and anosognosia (Cappa et al 1987). However vestibular stimulation works (e.g. by attentional biasing), it is unlikely in a simple manner to affect confusion, face-saving or psychodynamics.

What then do the two types of dissociation mentioned here suggest? First, it seems that we can separate sensations from a reflexive acquaintance with those sensations. With this conceptual division it would not be self-contradictory to talk of a non-conscious pain (Nelkin 1989). Second, it seems that we can simultaneously both be aware of a sensory state and be unaware of it, i.e. our reflexive consciousness can be non-unitary. For a sensation to be able to be reported, it has to be accessible to reflexive consciousness. If different ways of reporting are differentially at the disposal of separate divisions of reflexive consciousness, it would be possible to report the presence of a sensation and simultaneously report its absence, as in the experiments described above. It would appear that different divisions of reflexive consciousness (with and without access to specific sensory information) can dominate in the control of behaviour or communication at any one time. Thus the awareness of our states and capacities can be dominated by a simultaneous unawareness of such states, or vice versa. Bisiach's and our own observations suggest that the dominant division is a matter of personal stance and emotional state.

Dissociative states and the self

The separation of reflexive consciousness from phenomenal sensations and the non-unity of the former, with unequal access to any single sensation or experience, seem unparsimonious. Yet dissociative phenomena are suggestive of such a view. In hypnotic analgesia, subjects orally rate a given painful stimulus as much less painful than they have done before hypnosis. However, if they have a pen they may simultaneously spontaneously write a pain rating that is as high as before hypnosis (Hilgard 1977). Hilgard and others have reported other such 'hidden observer' phenomena. For example, if a hypnotically deaf or analgesic subject who seems oblivious of the sensation in question is asked 'does any part of you know about the pain/sound?', they may answer 'I know, but she does not'! In current research on patients under general anaesthesia in short gynaecological operations, where no paralysing agent is used and continuous ventilation is not required, the patients can sometimes be engaged in conversation. Much the same phenomenon as in hypnosis is occasionally observed concerning dissociative knowledge of pain (personal communication and joint observation with John Evans). Such observations must obviously be treated with extreme caution, but we should be prepared to take them seriously.

What is here termed reflexive consciousness has a very close connection with selfhood (see Kihlstrom, this volume). What is reportable is *my* experience. Indeed, ownership is just as much a necessary feature of autobiographical episodic memories as it is of sensations. Amnesia may be seen as a loss of adherence of memories to the self. In fugue states, the accessible memories are those of the then-dominant and now-dominant self. But whatever the structure of self, there is no reason that there should not be more than one self in a single body or brain. Usually they may have much the same experiences, or cohere, or even be singular. But, if not, then what is reported by different 'selves' may be at odds. This can be seen in multiple personality disorder (Humphrey & Dennett 1989) and in post-traumatic stress disorder (Langer 1991). When demands are made to respond quickly or when stimuli are brief, experiences may adhere differentially or be differentially accessible to coexisting self-structures. In anosognosia something similar may occur, which would account for the effects of 'personal stance' and mood noted above. It is likely that although there is coexistence, one self-structure dominates at any one time. It would follow that the anosognosic patient, the normal subject in the experiments reported and the multiple personality could appreciate that there is a contradiction in their behaviour (if pointed out to them) but could not experience the contradiction directly. Indeed, the assumption of unity of consciousness is difficult to shake off precisely because we can logically never directly experience more than one consciousness or self. The dominance of one reflexive consciousness as subject and agent is also a reason that dissociations such as those in the experiments reported are not usually observed even by others, because they are not usually behaviourally manifest.

Finally, one should consider states where there is no non-unity of consciousness. Such states are those which do not involve reflexive consciousness. Phenomenologists such as Merleau-Ponty (1962) and psychologists such as Duval & Wicklund (1972) have pointed to the difference between a non-reflexive mode, where attention is focused on the world or task, and a reflexive mode, where attention is focused on oneself. The latter is characteristic of experimental situations, pathology and 'extreme' states such as fatigue, illness and intense emotions. When we attend fully to the outside and are totally involved in an activity our reflexive consciousness is non-operative. This is when we have 'perceptions' rather than 'sensations', when we do not experience pains, itches, fatigue, when self as a segregated intentional object of experience disappears, and with it our reflexivity.

Acknowledgements

I should like to acknowledge Petra Stoerig who originally brought Zihl & von Cramon's work to my attention, and Robert Hess who helped set up the experiments. I am also grateful for discussion with Dan Dennett, Marcel Kinsbourne, Edoardo Bisiach and Jay McClelland.

References

Allport A 1988 What concept of consciousness? In: Marcel AJ, Bisiach E (eds) Consciousness in contemporary science. Oxford University Press, Oxford, p 159–182

Bisiach E, Geminiani G 1991 Anosognosia related to hemiplegia and hemianopia. In: Prigatano GP, Schacter DL (eds) Awareness of deficit after brain injury. Oxford University Press, Oxford, p 7–39

Bisiach E, Berti A, Vallar G 1985 Analogical and logical disorders underlying unilateral neglect of space. In: Posner MI, Marin OSM (eds) Attention and performance XI. Mechanisms of attention. Erlbaum, Hillsdale, NJ, p 239–249

Cappa S, Sterzi R, Vallar G, Bisiach E 1987 Remission of hemineglect and anosognosia during vestibular stimulation. Neuropsychologia 25:775–782

Cheesman J, Merikle PM 1985 Word recognition and consciousness. In: Besner D, Waller TG, MacKinnon GE (eds) Reading research: advances in theory and practice. Academic Press, New York, vol 5:311–352

Cumming GD 1972 Visual perception and metacontrast at rapid input rates. DPhil thesis, Oxford University, UK

Dennett D 1982 How to study human consciousness empirically: or, nothing comes to mind. Synthèse 53:159–180

Duval S, Wicklund RA 1972 A theory of objective self-awareness. Academic Press, New York

Hilgard ER 1977 Divided consciousness: multiple controls in human thought and action. Wiley, New York

Humphrey N, Dennett DC 1989 Speaking for our selves: an assessment of multiple personality disorder. Raritan 9:68–98

Joanette Y, Brouchon M, Gauthier L, Samson M 1986 Pointing with left vs right hand in left visual field neglect. Neuropsychologia 24:391–396

Kihlstrom JF 1993 The psychological unconscious and the self. In: Experimental and theoretical studies of consciousness. Wiley, Chichester (Ciba Found Symp) p 147–167

Kinsbourne M, Warrington EK 1963 Jargonaphasia. Neuropsychologia 1:27–37

Langer LL 1991 Holocaust testimonies: the ruins of memory. Yale University Press, New Haven, CT

Marcel AJ 1983 Conscious and unconscious perception: an approach to the relations between phenomenal experience and perceptual processes. Cognit Psychol 15:238–300

Marcel AJ 1988 Phenomenal experience and functionalism. In: Marcel AJ, Bisiach E (eds) Consciousness in contemporary science. Oxford University Press, Oxford, p 121–158

Merleau-Ponty M 1962 Phenomenology of perception. Humanities Press, New York

Milner AD, Rugg MD 1992 The neuropsychology of consciousness. Academic Press, London

Nelkin N 1989 Unconscious sensations. Philos Psychol 2:129–141

Prigatano GP, Schacter DL (eds) 1991 Awareness of deficit after brain injury. Oxford University Press, Oxford

Weiskrantz L 1988 Some contributions of neuropsychology of vision and memory to the problem of consciousness. In: Marcel AJ, Bisiach E (eds) Consciousness in contemporary science. Oxford University Press, Oxford, p 183–199

Zihl J, von Cramon D 1980 Registration of light stimuli in the cortically blind hemifield and its effect on localization. Behav Brain Res 1:287–298

DISCUSSION

Humphrey: With your anosognosic hemiplegic patients, take a patient who had one paralysed arm. You ask them, 'If *I* had my arm paralysed, could I shuffle a pack of cards?' and they reply that of course you wouldn't be able to. What if you ask them, 'If *you* had one arm paralysed, how would you shuffle the cards?'

Marcel: We have done this with normal people and with these patients. We say, 'If your arm was paralysed, how well would you be able to do the task?'

Both groups give a zero rating. But as far as the patients are concerned, their arm isn't paralysed.

Humphrey: Although they have just acknowledged that it was?

Marcel: No, they haven't acknowledged that it is. You said, '*If* your arm was paralysed, how well would you be able to do it?' If you ask them why they are in hospital, they say, 'I fell over', or one girl said, 'I have such a terrible cough'.

Wall: And this is not a confused patient?

Marcel: No. To say they were confused, you would have to have evidence that they were confused about things other than their deficit. The only thing they seem not to know about is their deficit and those circumscribed activities. If you talk about activities not associated with their deficit, they do know about other capacities of theirs. And if one did not remember one's stroke or was not aware of one's hemiplegia, one would attribute one's presence in hospital to another cause: that is hardly confusion.

Kinsbourne: Elizabeth Warrington and I published two patients with jargon aphasia (Kinsbourne & Warrington 1963). This is an aphasia in which the person speaks in a rapid fluent stream of partly unintelligible verbiage, but acts as if his speech output were quite normal.

We had two patients with strokes that affected the left hemisphere. We made a tape-recording of each man's speech. This was replayed either in its original form or re-recorded in somebody else's voice—same garbage, different voice—to the patient. When the patient heard his own output in somebody else's voice, he expressed disgust and said, 'I can't understand this guy'. When he heard the same message in his own voice he said, 'Very very good'. So it is more than the patient being unaware of the deficit.

Marcel: It might be better to say that there is another factor which modulates the awareness of the deficit. For example, if it is my deficit, I am unaware of it; but if it is someone else's, I am aware of it. This brings in the issue of selfhood and ownership, which also seems relevant to the effects of using a child-like and confiding manner on avowal of the deficit.

Traditionally, people who study cognition really like to leave affect (emotion) and conation (will) out. I think it may not be possible to do so anymore.

With regard to the effect of the questioner's emotional tone, what role is it playing? Is it that the knowledge of the deficit is in a form accessible only to a regressed self? Or should we apply another classic model to anosognosia? This is that if the input from the external world is cut off in some domain, then other internally generated, 'primary process' material takes the place of such input. This is one account of hallucinations and could well be applied to the sensory confabulations one gets in anosognosia, as well as to the role of the emotional state in determining what knowledge is accessible.

Shevrin: Are the disorders described by Tony Marcel intrinsic to the disorder themselves, or are they pathological consequences due, in part at least, to other factors? The childish talk that apparently elicits more information than adult enquiry might be accounted for by the fact that when people are traumatized they are often emotionally in a more regressive, child-like state.

The other example concerned the ability of the person to respond sensibly when asked hypothetically, if the examiner had the disorder, would he be able to perform normally. I would need to ask whether there were some personality predisposition in this person that inclined them to projection—the tendency to disallow something in oneself and to ascribe it to someone else.

These are answerable questions: the extent to which the particular disorder is a function of the actual loss itself, and to what extent it draws upon other causes that are broader and predispositional in nature.

Harnad: Tony, what is the time course of these anosognosias? Do the patients go from complete dissociation to verbal dissociation?

Marcel: I'm not sure what you mean by 'complete' and 'verbal' dissociation. But in neglect with anosognosia for hemiplegia, all the dissociative phenomena seem to go together. For example, when patients are given vestibular stimulation (irrigation of external canal of the contralateral ear with iced water), all their symptoms show a temporary remission, then all the symptoms seem to return together.

Kihlstrom: It's important to remember that there are at least two different varieties of anosognosia. One occurs in the case of hemianopsia or hemiplegia. The anosognosia occurs in essentially the acute stage of the illness, and it can't be attributed to anything like gross confusion. But many demented patients also become anosognosic and that's a different thing entirely: these people are anosognosic because their dementia has got to such a point that they don't know what end is up.

Marcel: What I am discussing is different from anosognosia in dementia; the people I am reporting are non-dementing stroke patients in the acute stage or with a 'prolonged acute' stage. One of our control groups is normal people, who are also not entirely accurate or sure about their own mental and physical abilities.

Singer: Tony, concerning the experiment with normal individuals, could one say that the subjects find it easier to just blink or provide some non-verbal sign of awareness, when responding to a complicated visual or mixed modality image? They may lack the verbal skills appropriate to the response.

Marcel: The non-verbal response doesn't always show an advantage. Similarly, the ocular response is not always superior to that with the finger. The subjects don't have a complex visual image; they look at a fixation point on a blank field and the stimulus is an increase in illumination 10° to the right of the fixation point.

Singer: But the experience they are having is still not the sort of thing that we ordinarily verbalize about. We value poets because they can represent in words the images that we cannot communicate. So the verbal description is somewhat handicapped.

Marcel: What do you mean by not ordinarily verbalize? Do you mean that doctors shouldn't rely on verbal reports of patients' symptoms?

Singer: Sometimes, there are experiences that can't easily be formulated in words because of limitations in vocabulary.

Marcel: All the subjects have to do is indicate, verbally or otherwise, whether they are experiencing, or guessing whether there was, a difference in light intensity. These subjects have undergone lengthy psychophysical threshold determination and training procedures.

Singer: Then what is your explanation of the difference?

Marcel: My explanation of the difference is exactly what I put in my paper; I actually think Dan Dennett and Marcel Kinsbourne have something to say about this. I think there is no unity of consciousness where sensation is concerned, i.e. where one is attending to oneself. We know from a lot of experiments in psychology that, for example, if one is preparing to respond, the mode of the prepared action influences the experience. But suppose it is not that. Suppose different internal reporters have differential access to a sensation. Suppose there is not just one reporter. I don't say that's the end of the story. I think that when you are attending to the world, there *is* a single reporter. But in the mode of attending to your own sensations, there may well be a lack of unity of the reporter, i.e. of consciousness.

Kinsbourne: Are these trials go/no go or discriminative?

Marcel: It's go/no go. But it's not a reaction time experiment.

Kinsbourne: They might just have forgotten to make one of those movements at certain times.

Marcel: But we can ask them to stop at any point and ask them what are their instructions. They repeat the instructions accurately.

Kinsbourne: That's not enough.

Marcel: Because each response type shows the same hit:false positive rate when tested separately as when they are tested together, forgetting cannot be the explanation.

Van Gulick: Tony, there are two different things going on in your data. One is the difference between the three sets of responses and the increasing accuracy as you go towards the verbal response.

Marcel: No, there is *less* accurate discriminability with the verbal response. Let's take the two second delay (Tables 2 and 3). The subject is not allowed to respond until after a second signal two seconds later. The discrimination rates for the different report modes on the last blocks of trials are highest for blink, next for finger and lowest for oral.

Psychologists never usually compare different types of response. They assume that they are equivalent as acts of report. When comparisons are made, especially with speeded responses, you often find disparate results.

Van Gulick: Tony, what is the difference in the just guess condition? How does that condition, which you suggest involves the absence of any expression by the conscious self about whether or not it saw the target, lead to a higher frequency of accurate reports? Why does the link between the stimulus and the verbal have an easier access that seems to allow a more accurate connection in the guess condition?

Marcel: When you tell subjects to guess, their performance improves, almost to a ceiling (of nearly 100% accuracy). The biggest increase is for the verbal response. Why are they able to respond more accurately when they guess? You could say, they are not bothering to tell you anything about their experiences or sensation, they are just letting a non-conscious representation have an effect on their action. Why *it* should be able to be more accurate in telling you which response to give is an interesting point. Nobody has answered this. Perhaps it is because the intervention of reflexive consciousness creates 'noise'.

Kihlstrom: There are possibly two different classes of answers. One is the Weiskrantz (1986) answer, that there are two visual systems and they have different characteristics. One visual system is tapped by the signal-detection question: what do you see out there? The other visual system is tapped by the question: what do you think is out there, or what do you guess is out there? Those visual systems have different d' (hits:false positives) values associated with them.

The vertical differences that you know are very puzzling and very interesting; the horizontal differences are also very interesting and they are ubiquitous in the signal-detection literature. That difference between detecting and guessing is exactly the distinction that Terry Barnhardt, Doug Tataryn and I are trying to make between explicit and implicit perception (Kihlstrom et al 1992). When people are asked to detect, they are asked what they see. When they are asked to guess, they are asked to speculate about what's out there. It is no longer a detection test or even a visual test.

We see this kind of effect in hypnotic blindness and hypnotic anaesthesia. Remember the Kunst-Wilson & Zajonc (1980) experiment, where the subjects were not able to discriminate in a memory test between polygons that were shown and polygons that weren't. But if the subject had simply shifted his or her criterion and said, 'I'm going to recognize each of the polygons I like', then recognition would have gone way above chance. Barbara Sackitt (1972) has wonderful psychophysical data on this. She did essentially my variant of the Kunst-Wilson & Zajonc experiment with vision. She came down to a point where she just allowed herself to guess, and her d' goes way up, as opposed to when she is really trying to detect the targets. The interesting point is: what's the first thing we are taught in signal-detection theory? That the value of d' is independent of response criterion. This is not true.

Shevrin: I am unconvinced. Why is it that when the person is asked to say what they see, the response is less accurate?

Fenwick: What happens if you use a different stimulus? Do you get the best results when you use a visual stimulus and a visual output?

Marcel: I have started to use a tactile stimulus and the order of response mode sensitivity seems to be reversed.

Fenwick: So the most marked effects occur when the stimulus and response systems are most closely linked.

Velmans: It's not surprising that one's ability to blink to a light flash is going to be simpler in some way than one's ability to make verbal reports, because there may be some pre-existing link between blinking and a visual stimulus. If one's ability to press a button in response to a tactile stimulus is also better than one's ability to make a verbal response, it may be because the manual response system is similarly associated with a tactile form of input stimulus.

I have no problem with the notion that if you push the human information-processing system to its limits, then you can find all sorts of interesting ways in which to create dissociations. But, the general point that Tony Marcel wants to make is that if you can demonstrate dissociations in these extreme conditions, that shows something profound about a non-unitary self under normal conditions or about the dissociation of these systems in normal experience.

Marcel: I didn't say that.

Velmans: Let me say what I thought you said and then you can show me where I'm wrong. I agree that it's really interesting that you can get different reports from different reporting systems about the same stimulus, provided you really push the system to its limits. However, in normal situations it may be that such dissociations don't occur. Although sometimes dissociations occur, the self and the systems that report experience normally operate in an integrated way, just as they seem to do.

Marcel: I am not pushing them to the limits. These are confident judgements. I told the subjects to respond only when the signal was clear. There are cases where I am not pushing them on reaction time at all.

Secondly, when you ask: what do I assume about the normal? I don't know what 'normal' means. I said there are different ways in which attention can be allocated. I'm saying you can't argue that there is a logical necessity on this point. You can't argue there is always a unity.

Van Gulick: Max Velmans' explanation wouldn't explain why the difference in response virtually disappears when you go to the guess condition.

Marcel: Exactly!

Humphrey: Tony asked us to accept that these are all speech acts. Suppose he had looked at pupil response. In that case, the pupil would have contracted every time the light intensity increased and there would have been no false positives. Why shouldn't the pupil response also count as a speech act, if it can be interpreted by somebody else?

Marcel: Because the experimenter and the subject have to agree that the subject is going to respond in the given way. The subject would not have blinked had I not asked them to. A pupillary response to light intensity is not normally under voluntary control.

Humphrey: I'm suggesting that by block 12 of the trials, it is no longer a speech act, in that sense.

Marcel: If it was no longer a speech act in that sense, why is there still the difference between the report and the guessing conditions? Furthermore, the subjects are quite able to withhold their responses until the imperative signal, when this is delayed by two or eight seconds.

References

Kihlstrom JF, Barnhardt TR, Tataryn DJ 1992 Implicit perception. In: Bornstein R, Pittman TS (eds) Perception without awareness. Guilford Press, New York p 17–54
Kinsbourne M, Warrington EK 1963 Jargonaphasia. Neuropsychologia 1:27–37
Kunst-Wilson WR, Zajonc RB 1980 Affective discrimination of stimuli that cannot be recognized. Science (Wash DC) 207:557–558
Sackitt B 1972 Counting every quantum. J Physiol 223:131–150
Weiskrantz L 1986 Blindsight: a case study and implications. Oxford University Press, Oxford

Pain and the placebo response

P. D. Wall

Department of Anatomy & Developmental Biology, University College London, Gower Street, London WC1E 6BT, UK

Abstract. The placebo response is a powerful widespread phenomenon which relieves many conditions including pain. It depends on the patient's belief or expectation that the therapy is effective. It is an unpopular topic because it is confused with quackery or seen as an expensive artifact or taken to challenge the rationale of a therapy or to mock the reality of the senses. In order to avoid taking the subject seriously, myths are invented claiming that placebos work only on hysterics or hallucinators or that they are the equivalent of doing nothing or that they act only on the mental results of pain and not on the pain itself. These myths are dismissed. A model of the brain is presented in which preconscious decisions are made as to appropriate behaviour. Pain is perceived only after a decision has been made that it is appropriate to the biological needs of the individual.

1993 Experimental and theoretical studies of consciousness. Wiley, Chichester (Ciba Foundation Symposium 174) p 187–216

The word placebo has been used since the 18th century as a term for mock medicine. Its origin and meaning are usually given as a simple translation from the Latin as 'I will please'. I find that a highly improbable use of Latin by educated men of the time who would actually have said 'Placebit', 'It will please'. It seems to me much more likely that the word alludes to Psalm 116:9 'Placebo Domino in regione vivorum', which appears in the King James Bible as 'I will walk before the Lord in the land of the living'. This line beginning with Placebo is the first line of the vespers for the dead. Priests and friars pestered the populace for money to sing vespers for the dead. Placebo could have been the derisory word for these unpopular and expensive prayers, just as the words hocus pocus come from the first line of the Communion, 'Hoc est corpus', 'This is the body (of Christ)'. This is surely the way in which Geoffrey Chaucer (1340) used the word placebo when he writes, 'Flatterers are the devil's chatterlaines for ever singing placebo', as does Francis Bacon (1625) 'Instead of giving Free Counsell sing him song of placebo'. This adds a more subtle meaning to the word where the sycophant tells the listener what he expects and wants to hear, rather than the truth. That remains a placebo.

This topic needs no excuse because it is full of surprise, power and paradox. However, there are three reasons why it is relevant to introduce the facts of the phenomenon to philosophers as well as to brain scientists. First, one notices a tendency for philosophers to use pain as a basic starting point for consideration of sensation and perception, because they think it can be presented as a simple phenomenon with obvious cause and inevitable effect and with a neural mechanism linking the two with confidence. The placebo should disenchant them of that and substitute intrigue. Second, theory is often challenged by experimenters with examples of subtle tricks played on conscious experience by our inability to cope with threshold ambiguous situations. Too often, neurological cases presented as educational material are so rare that I have never seen such a case or, if I have, I have a quite different interpretation from the experts. The placebo response is very common and rugged and operates in the presence of massive causes and effects. Finally, I wish to propose experiments which may emerge as much from philosophical clarity as from the testing of traditional hypotheses.

I will not attempt a precise definition of the placebo or of its effect. Those who require them can wade their way through the first 163 turgid pages of an otherwise lively book edited by White et al (1985). The reason for this agonized search for an acceptable definition is that most definitions threaten to breach the general obsession with a clear separation of mental from bodily sites of action. This search goes beyond the pleasures of academic, pedantic, talmudic need for acceptable precision. Legal regulations governing the introduction of a new pharmaceutical compound require the company to demonstrate that the novel molecule has a specific therapeutic action which is more powerful than the company's and doctor's and patient's belief that the novel molecule has a specific therapeutic action. A satisfactory answer is worth millions of pounds. It takes the question out of the philosophers' conundrum-riddled tutorial onto the floor of the stock exchange. It demands a precise dissection of the 'true' truth from the generally accepted, even universally accepted, 'believed' truth. Whatever the definition, it has nothing to do with the existence of a rationale for the statement. The question applies equally to the herbalist who states, 'The experience of the ages allows me to assure you that infusion of foxgloves helps dropsy', as to the pharmaceutical company which states, 'MK-801 helps strokes because excitotoxic amine-elicited calcium ion entry depends on NMDA channels which are antagonized by MK-801'. For what follows, I need go no further than Burton in 1628 in *The Anatomy of Melancholy*, 'There is no virtue in some (folk remedies) but a strong conceit and opinion alone which forceth a motion of the humours, spirits and blood which takes away the cause of the malady from the parts affected' and 'An empiric oftentimes, or a silly chirugeon, doth more strange cures than a rational physician because the patient puts more confidence in him.'

Two examples of the placebo effect

I wish here to give only two contemporary examples of the effect of strong opinions from the legion of placebo effects. Surgery is rarely the subject of a placebo test, in spite of an admonition by Finneson (1969) in his book on surgery for pain: 'Surgery has the most potent placebo effect that can be exercised in medicine'. In the 1950s, it became a common practice to ligate the internal mammary arteries as a treatment for angina pectoris. Angina is a painful condition attributed to an inadequate blood supply of muscle in the heart wall. The rationale for the operation was that if the internal mammary arteries were ligated, the blood in these arteries would find alternative routes by sprouting new channels through nearby heart muscle, thereby improving the circulation in the heart. This relatively simple operation was carried out in large numbers of patients to the satisfaction of many. However, the rationale came under suspicion when pathologists were unable to detect any of the supposed new blood vessels in the heart. Therefore, two groups of surgeons and cardiologists (Cobb et al 1959, Dimond et al 1958) decided to test the rationale by carrying out sham operations to incise the skin and expose the arteries in some patients while proceeding with the full ligation in others. The patients and their physicians did not know who had the true operation and who had the sham. The majority of both groups of patients showed great improvement in the amount of reported pain, in their walking distance, in their consumption of vasodilating drugs and some in the shape of their electrocardiogram. The improvement in both groups was maintained over six months of observation. (No such trial would be permitted today for ethical reasons, although these tests were carried out for the ethical reasons of the day at Harvard and the University of Pennsylvania.) The interest here is not only the evident power of the belief that therapeutic surgery had been completed but that improvement was sustained for at least six months, in spite of the general belief that placebos have a brief and fading action.

The second example is the work of Hashish et al (1988) who examined the effect of ultrasound therapy, which others had found to be the equal of steroids in reducing pain and jaw tightness (trismus) and swelling after extraction of wisdom teeth. To determine the effective level of ultrasound, they set intensity at different levels in a manner which was unknown to the patient and the therapist. When the machine was set to produce no ultrasound, there was a marked beneficial effect, even superior to the results of the normally used intensities. Naturally disturbed by the apparently bizarre finding, the experimenters wondered if the therapeutic effect was produced by the massage of the injured area coincident with the application of the ultrasound. They therefore trained patients to massage themselves with the inactive ultrasound head with the same movements used by the professionals. This was completely ineffective. Evidently, the therapeutic phenomenon required an impressive machine and someone in a white coat to transmit the effect, even though the emission of ultrasound was not required. I introduce this particular example, chosen from many, because the placebo therapy not only reduced the pain report but also improved the ability to open the mouth and reduced the swelling.

The reduction of pain will suprise those people who consider pain as a reliable and inevitable sensation associated with tissue damage. However, there are others who would categorize pain as a mental perception and therefore as subject to error and manipulation. These two attitudes are practical examples of the Cartesian dualistic divide, where sensation is the consequence of the working of a body mechanism while perception is a mental process. There are others who will argue that this division between body and mind is a historical artifact produced by a muddle of academic, religious, introspective argument. Whichever attitude is taken, surprise should remain that the placebo also affected the contraction of jaw muscles normally attributed to a reflex action in the flexion reflex category which loops through the medulla. Furthermore, the placebo affected the swelling, which is a classical component of the local inflammation triggered by local damage.

Four reasons for the discomfort provoked by the topic

Quackery

From the 18th century, the word placebo became attached to quackery. As a rational medicine developed, placebo could be used as a word to hammer Burton's 'empirics and silly chirugeons'. Beyond this, even the rational physicians were not above the use of a placebo as a form of deception, either for diagnostic purposes or to get rid of unwanted or unprofitable patients. This, in turn, provoked the ethical and practical discussion of whether the doctor–patient relationship would survive the discovery by patients that doctors used deception on occasions. This debate on the role of truth-telling and paternalism in the clinic continues (Rawlinson 1985) with discussion of such phrases as 'the benevolent lie'. The ethical problem extends to clinical trials. If it is the doctors' duty to do their therapeutic best, how can they suggest that the patient should submit to a comparison of one therapy which the physician believes to be powerful versus another they believe to be less effective? 'Informed consent' by the patient does not solve this ethical question, it merely recruits the patient to join in the doctor's dilemma. As awe and trust by the patient for the paternal doctor fade, so does the frequency of informed consent and of the placebo response. In 1807 Thomas Jefferson wrote 'One of the most successful physicians I have ever known has assured me that he used more bread pills, drops of coloured water and powders of hickory ashes than of all other medicines put together. . . I consider this a pious fraud'.

A tiresome and expensive artifact

A considerable fraction of the huge cost of clinical trials for a new drug resides in the legal requirement for a placebo trial. When a new idea has been developed by a clever research team, one has sympathy when their enthusiasm has to be contained while trials are in progress which have an apparently obvious outcome to the enthusiasts. Not only is the expensive delay assigned to the fault of a meddling bureaucracy, but the existence of a fraction of patients who show placebo responses is considered to be of no intellectual interest but simply an intrusion in the search for true mechanisms.

One attractive short cut is to compare the new therapy with an established one without a placebo stage in a cross-over trial. This does not address the possibility that both therapies are placebos. The cross-over option is particularly favoured in those therapies such as surgery or psychotherapy where there is no legal requirement for placebo trials. Often an alternative therapy is not available or is so well known to the patients that it would be impossible to recruit volunteers to a placebo trial. An example is a massive study of long-term consequences of headache and backache after epidural anaesthesia during labour (MacArthur et al 1992) where the authors call for a randomized study to confirm their results. It is obvious that there is no alternative therapy which would be comparable in the mind of a patient with epidural anaesthesia. Furthermore, there is a myriad of cultural, educational, social and medical reasons for a mother accepting or rejecting the offer to be assigned at random to one or another therapy, one of which was epidural anaesthesia. Given the ethical and practical problems in assessing the apparently straightforward question of long-term consequences of an epidural anaesthetic, it is not surprising that the majority of non-pharmaceutical therapies have never been tested or have been tested in very inadequate ways (Koes et al 1991, 1992). For example, in a large-scale survey of thousands of amputees with pain, Sherman et al (1980) identified 40 different forms of therapy but only 15% of the patients were relieved. In a search of the literature, no rigorous trials are reported to justify any of the 40 therapies for this condition. In two surveys of tests for the effectiveness of manipulation, osteopathy and chiropracty for pain, the great majority were shown to be inadequate, while the acceptable trials produced contradictory answers (Koes et al 1991, 1992).

A question of logic

The very mention of a placebo trial is likely to be taken as a hostile questioning of the logic on which a therapy is based. To request an investigation of the placebo component which is an inevitable part of any therapy is to invite anger. Anger confuses the question of whether something should work with the question of whether it does work. Too bad.

The reality of the senses

Everyone assesses their own sanity by cross-checking their sensation with objective reality. On the rare occasions where there is a mismatch, special names are applied—hallucination, illusion, delusion, madness, drunkeness, etc. For anyone, there is a simple intuitive sense apparent on reading Descartes (1644): 'If for example fire comes near the foot, the minute particles of this fire, which you know move at great velocity have the powers to set in motion the spot of skin of the foot which they touch, and by this means pulling on the delicate thread which is attached to the spot of the skin, they open up at the same instant the pore against which the delicate thread ends just as by pulling on one end of a rope one makes to strike at the same instant a bell which hangs at the other end'. It seems so reasonable that we should possess sensory mechanisms which represent the state of the world as reliably as the tolling of the bell represents action at the end of its rope. It seems equally reasonable that we should possess a separate entity, the mind, which can decide whether to ignore the bell or write a poem about it. Even a philosopher like Bertrand Russell who questioned Cartesian dualism still required a reliable sensory apparatus that generated sensation as the closest representation of events the machinery would permit. Sensation for him was generated by a continuous uncensored flow of information. If this flow was faulty or variable, then even a great cognitive brain would necessarily be faulty. If the sensory apparatus was censored or corruptible, then sense could become nonsense and reality an individual construct of a particular mind. We have many reasons and facts which lead us to reject that conclusion. We trust our senses, the five senses of Aristotle. Pain appears to us as the sensation provoked by injury. A broken leg provokes an appropriate sensation and location of pain. Placebos in no way affect the leg and its fracture but modify the sensation of pain and its perception. No wonder the topic provokes a sense of discomfort.

Diversions generated to avoid a consideration of the nature of placebo responses

When doctors who are not involved in a therapy under trial learn that it turns out to be a placebo, they howl with laughter. When you are the subject in a trial and discover that you have reacted to a placebo, as I have, you feel a fool. When you are the proponent or inventor of a therapy, whether based on contemporary rationale or old-fashioned faith, you are resentful of the need for placebo testing. If the test reveals a substantial placebo component in the response, diversions are created to eliminate consideration of the placebo effect. These add to the four general reasons for discomfort with the effect.

The placebo differentiates between organic and mental disease

This is the most dangerous and cruel attitude which has been used by physicians and surgeons when they detect placebo responses. An example is shown in the reaction of the profession to the true or sham operation on the internal mammary artery described above (Cobb et al 1959, Dimond et al 1958). Amsterdam et al

(1969) describe patients with angina in whom there appears to be an adequate circulation in the coronary arteries. It is then immediately assumed, without evidence, that these are the patients who would respond to a placebo while those with true cardiac ischaemia could not. This idea had already been suggested by psychiatrists using the phrase 'somatic hallucination' (Farrer 1964). Clearly, this approaches the diagnosis of hysteria (Merskey 1989), although in hysteria, the somatization fails to imitate any known organic disease so that the alert diagnostician can differentiate hysteria from the condition it mimics. Here we have the proposal that some patients mimic an organic disease so precisely that a diagnostic test, the placebo, is needed to separate the two classes. The proposal is very attractive to those who seek an absolute separation of organic from functional disease and who believe that every true pain is precisely causally related to an observable organic lesion. The proposal is dangerous nonsense if one considers the hundreds of papers, of which 986 are reviewed in Turner et al (1980), where placebo responses are described in patients suffering pain appropriate to a diagnosed overt organic lesion, such as postoperative pain or cancer.

I will simply relate two illustrative anecdotes. A patient with classical causalgia following a near miss on his sciatic nerve by a bullet had responded to a saline injection interspersed in a regular series of morphine injections. A very senior orthopaedic surgeon concluded that there was therefore nothing wrong with the man, by which he meant there could be no causative lesion in this surgeon's territory of interest, i.e. peripheral nerves and bones, and therefore this was a mental condition as proven by the placebo response. The patient's pain and the vascular signs disappeared with a sympathectomy of the leg, a procedure of which the patient had no knowledge or expectation. This patient's pain was caused by a peripheral nerve lesion and cured by a peripheral lesion. The second anecdote is related by Professor Collins who became head of neurosurgery at Yale. In a forward hospital in Korea, while operating on a series of casualty admissions, he began to suffer severe abdominal pain which was obviously acute appendicitis. Faced with extreme emergency casualties, he ordered the theatre sister to give him an injection of morphine. His pain subsided and he completed the surgery, after which he himself became a patient and his inflamed appendix was removed. Returning to duty after his recovery, he was leafing through the operating room report book when he came across the sister's entry, 'Major Collins ordered a 15 mg morphine injection so that he could continue operating but, since he appeared distressed, I thought it best to give him an intramuscular injection of saline'.

The placebo is the equivalent of no therapy

This is clearly not true. The placebo has a positive effect. If cancer patients receive narcotics at regular intervals, the secret substitution of a single saline injection in the series of morphine injections results in the relief of pain and other signs and symptoms in the majority of patients. Furthermore, the time course of relief imitates that produced by the administration of the narcotic. The saline injection is not the same as missing an injection, since the placebo produced a decrease of pain while missing an injection would be followed by an increase of pain.

The positive effect of the patients' belief that some therapy is in progress makes it extremely difficult to investigate the natural history of a disease which is not influenced by some form of medical intervention. On rare occasions, it is practically and ethically possible to disguise therapy so that the patient does not know that anything is happening. For example, it may be possible to secrete a drug in orange juice which is routinely provided or a drug may be clandestinely injected into a long intravenous drip line out of sight of the patient. Such elaborate plots have been used, but are obviously limited in most practical trials and raise difficult ethical problems. One scheme to discover the natural history of a disease is simply to leave a group of patients on the waiting list, while treating other groups with true or placebo therapies. There are obvious limits, depending on the society and culture, which determine how long a patient will patiently remain waiting. The richer and/or more aggressive patients or those who are in particular misery remove themselves from the waiting list and go to another doctor, thereby tilting the nature of the remaining list of patients.

A common tactic to obtain the natural history is to study retrospectively the course of the disease in patients before the therapy under study was available. This method is so full of problems that many journals now refuse to publish such studies. We can observe an accumulation of the problems of drug testing if we consider how to test a new therapy for AIDS (acquired immune deficiency syndrome). It is generally believed that the demographic focus of AIDS in the United States has shifted from gay whites to poor blacks. We can see the precise figures for such a move in a very different country in the careful figures from a very wary South African government department (Department of National Health and Population Development 1992). Until 1988, the great majority of cases of AIDS occurred in gay white men. From 1989 to 1992, the number of new cases of AIDS in white men declined. During that period there was a steady large increase in equal numbers of black men and women. Over the entire period from 1982 to the present, only eight cases of AIDS have been diagnosed in white women, four of whom had received infected blood transfusions. Clearly, the distribution is changing so rapidly that a retrospective control would be useless. Therefore let us consider the problem of how to test a new AIDS therapy. We must remember that before a trial started, the media publicity would have informed the public that a remedy had been discovered. Who in these circumstances would volunteer to take part in a placebo-controlled trial? The answer is that a small number of honest and poor people would take the 50 : 50 chance that they would get the new drug at no cost. The rest would buy, beg, borrow or steal for the drug. This would leave the control group as an odd minority. Even they may not be reliable, because some members of just such a control group in New York have been found, by blood testing, to be buying the drug under trial on the black market. We need new and subtle methods to measure the three quite separate factors—natural history, placebo response and specific response (Finkel 1985).

A fixed fraction of patients respond to placebos

This myth is widely stated in papers and textbooks, with the figure of 33% being commonly quoted. The idea is to label a fraction of the population as mentally peculiar. Where these sources quote the origin of the myth, they refer to Beecher (1955) who gives the figure of 35.2%. However, this figure is an average of Beecher's own eleven studies, each of which varied widely from the average. Double-blind studies show the fraction of placebo responders varying from close to 0% (Tyler 1946) to near 100% (Liberman 1964), depending on the circumstances of the trial. Clinical pains are associated with a larger number of placebo responders than experimental pains (Beecher 1959). The subtlety of the conditions has commercial as well as theoretical interest. Capsules containing coloured beads are more effective than coloured tablets, which are superior to white tablets with corners, which are better than round white tablets (Buchaleq & Coffield 1982). Beyond this, intramuscular saline injections are superior to any tablet but inferior to intravenous injections. Tablets taken from a bottle labelled with a well-known brand name are superior to the same tablets taken from a bottle with a typed label. My favourite is a doctor who always handled placebo tablets with forceps, assuring the patient that they were too powerful to be touched by hand. More seriously, I will discuss the conversion of experimental subjects to placebo responders (Voudouris et al 1989, 1990). There is no fixed fraction of the population that responds to placebos.

Placebo responders have a special mentality

This proposal is an extension of the fixed-fraction myth. It proposes that there are groups in the population with distorted mental processes which lead them to confuse true therapies with placebos. For those who cannot imagine that a normal person would ever make such a mistake, the idea is attractive. It was first proposed by Beecher (1968) and promptly dropped. With the rise of personality psychology, there were any number of pejorative mental tendencies which could be detected in the population by the analysis of the answers to questionnaires. Some of these seemed attractive labels to hang on those who responded to placebos to differentiate them from the normal subject who would never make such a silly mistake. These labels include suggestible, hypnotisable, neurotic, extrovert, introvert, acquiescent, willing to please and unsophisticated.

For anyone who rates high on masochism in a personality questionnaire, I suggest they wade their way through the 36 papers on the topic in Turner et al (1980) and the many more in White et al (1985). Most papers report no correlations with personality type and the rest are contradictory.

Pain is a multidimensional experience and the placebo affects only a part

Beecher (1959) made an intuitive introspective commonsense division of one's personal reaction to pain as having two separable dimensions: one deals with intensity and the other with reaction. This is reminiscent of Cartesian sensation followed by perception. Melzack & Casey (1968) even assigned different parts of the brain to create these two dimensions, which gave a new respectability to this ancient idea. Melzack & Torgerson (1971) then analysed the way in which people used words about pain and derived three dimensions: sensory, affective and evaluative. From this, the widely used McGill Pain Questionnaire evolved. By now, four dimensions have been isolated (Holroyd et al 1992). Gracely et al (1978) and Gracely (1979) examined the placebo response to discover if all dimensions of pain were equally involved. They used volunteer experimental normal subjects who received gradually rising electrical shocks to the teeth. The subjects were asked to rate separately the intensity of the pain and the unpleasantness of the pain, i.e. Cartesian sensation and perception, or Beecher's intensity and reaction, or Melzack's sensation and affect. The subjects were then given a saline injection with the assurance that they were receiving a powerful analgesic. The intensity of the pain was completely unaffected, while at low shock levels the unpleasantness was markedly reduced but at higher intensities was unaffected. This important experiment would seem to bring us back to the most classical position: sensation as a body mechanism is unaffected by a placebo at any stimulus level. Minor unpleasantness as a mental perception is affected by the mental suggestion implicit in the presence of a placebo. When the stimulus intensity rises, the appropriate unpleasantness perception regains its proper place, in spite of implied suggestion from the placebo. These clear experiments would seem to remove the mystery from the placebo and to return the entire subject to classical dualism. Gracely et al (1978) went on to show that diazepam, a tranquillizer, could produce exactly the same effect.

Up to this point one could say that the experiments support a particular version of Cartesian dualism in which there is a reliable sensory apparatus unaffected by these manipulations and that sensation is observed by a mental apparatus which assigns unpleasantness to the pure sensation and which is subject to suggestion and to tranquillizers. However, Gracely et al (1979) went on to investigate the effect of fentanyl, a narcotic, on the same type of pain and the result is summarized in the title 'Fentanyl reduces the intensity but not the unpleasantness of painful tooth sensations'. This abolishes the idea that a reliable sensory apparatus feeds a dependent mental apparatus which assigns unpleasantness. The three experiments taken together suggest that there are two separate dimensions, intensity and unpleasantness, which can be manipulated independently. We should now ask if the placebo result, i.e. intensity is unaffected but low level unpleasantness is affected, can be taken as a general statement about analgesic placebos. The first prediction would be that placebos would work on minor pains but not on severe pain, but that is precisely the opposite of Beecher's observations (1955) and of those of Lasagna et al (1954). The second prediction is that patients responding to a placebo would report the pain intensity unchanged while the unpleasantness was relieved, but patients with migraine or postoperative pain or cancer report relief of both aspects. Even in experimental situations, both threshold and intensity are affected by placebos (Voudouris et al 1989, 1990). My conclusion is that the identification of distinct categories of pain experience is a valid and useful aspect of pain study but that the placebo effect can change these dimensions separately or together, depending on the circumstances of suggestion, expectation and instruction.

The placebo response is produced by endogenous narcotics

The publication of this statement by Levine et al in 1978 had an enormous and lasting impact. It gave the placebo instant respectability in 20th century terms and partially liberated it from those doubts and denials I have listed above. The logic of this reasoning for the admission of the placebo to polite society is zero. If a newspaper headline read: 'Scientists discover the origin of music and poetry' followed by an article showing that music could not be performed when curare prevented the effect of acetyl choline released from motor axons, one would not be overwhelmed by the insight into the nature of music and poetry. Similarly, it is not clear what insight into the overall placebo phenomenon is provided by showing that some link in the machinery involves endorphins.

In addition, there are several problems with the original experiment which reported that high doses of naloxone, an opiate antagonist, abolished the placebo reduction of pain following wisdom tooth extraction. There are three reasons the experiment is complex and difficult. First, the pain did not have a steady baseline but was naturally rising and falling during the period of observation. Second, while naloxone by itself has no effect when there is no pain (El Sobky et al 1979), in the presence of pain, naloxone by itself exaggerates the pain, depending on the dose (Levine et al 1979). Third, some subjects were excluded from the analysis for reasons which are questionable. This difficult experiment has not been repeated, but Mikic & Binkert reported at the 2nd World Congress on Pain in Montreal in 1978 that they were unable to show an influence of naloxone on the placebo effect on pain caused by cold. Gracely et al (1982) also examined the effects of naloxone and placebos on the pain of tooth extraction and concluded that the naloxone effect was independent of the placebo effect. The careful studies of Grevert et al (1983) have been quoted as supporting

Levine et al (1978), but that is not justified. They studied the effect of naloxone on a placebo reduction of experimental ischaemic pain. Each subject was tested on three occasions at one-week intervals. On the first two tests, naloxone had no effect on the placebo response, but by the third week the high dose of naloxone produced a partial decrease of the placebo response. I believe the most generous reading of these four experiments is that the question remains open.

The placebo effect may be dissected away to reveal the pure therapeutic action

For this to be true, the therapeutic effect of an active compound would have to be free of its own additional placebo component. Strong evidence shows that the two responses are not separable in practical tests. In an extensive series of tests on postoperative pain, Lasagna et al (1954) identified placebo reactors and non-reactors. They then gave a fixed dose of morphine to the two groups and found an adequate analgesic response in 95% of the placebo reactors and only 55% of the non-reactors. A much more subtle problem was revealed by Beecher (1968) on examination of the matrix of results from double-blind cross-over studies of morphine versus saline. If the first administration contained morphine, the patient learned that this trial involved powerful medicine and tended to give a strong response to the second administration which was saline. If the first test dose was saline, the response to the second which contained morphine was weak. It is obvious that this problem will also affect the results of trials where the relative effects of two active compounds are being compared. There will be a carry-over effect of the first trial on the results of the second.

It is apparent that the patient or subject is searching for subtle hints of what to expect and that these expectations affect responses. This raises the question of the comparable nature of the active test and the placebo test. It does not take a connoisseur to distinguish intravenous morphine from saline, because the morphine produces such obvious immediate side effects. This problem has led to the use of placebos that produce some obvious effect, such as vasodilatation, which are assumed to have no direct therapeutic effect but give the subject an impression of receiving powerful medicine. The introduction of active placebos produces a series of problems: the placebo and active compound rarely precisely mimic each other; the specific inactivity of the placebo is questionable; the patient may find the placebo's effects distasteful. These problems apply even more to other forms of therapy. What is a comparable manoeuvre against which to test acupuncture? The nature of acupuncture is well known to 90% of the world's population.

Because, as we shall see, it is the expectation of the subject which is crucial, the obverse is the question of secrecy. It is assumed in therapeutic trials that the subject is not aware of the expectation of the proponent. Can that be achieved in practice? Sometimes the secrecy is shattered in obtaining consent: 'We would like you to help us in a trial of a new, safer form of aspirin'. Almost always, the person who administers the therapy, who may not know which pill is blank and which is 'true', will be aware of the general nature of what is being tested. This person's expectations can be covertly infectious. Patients talk to each other and reach a consensus; the strong effects of this covert expectation are shown by Evans (1974). He examined the relation between the relative effect of a range of analgesics versus placebos in 22 published double-blind trials. If the placebo effect was independent of the therapeutic effect, the placebo fraction of responders would have been the same in all trials while the drugs ranged in a series of therapeutic potency. The results all show that the stronger the drug, the stronger the placebo response. Evans divided the pain reduction produced by the placebo by the reduction produced by the drug. The answer is a fixed 55–60% over the entire range from weak to strong analgesics. So much for the blindness of these double-blind trials. So much for the clear separation of placebo and therapeutic effects.

I have described seven reasons why we need to avoid diversions, which are seven reasons why we need to consider the placebo effect with respect as a powerful phenomenon.

Classes of explanation

Affective

Gracely et al (1978) propose that the placebo effect works on the unpleasantness of pain while leaving the intensity dimension unaffected. I gave reasons above to believe that their experiments represent a special case which does not apply universally, especially in clinical cases. Evans (1977) proposes that the placebo operates by decreasing anxiety. However, the results show that there is a weak and variable interaction with various types of anxiety and it is not clear that anxiety reduction is not a component of the placebo effect rather than the cause of it.

Cognitive

By far the commonest proposal is that the placebo effect depends on the expectation of the subject. There is nothing subtle about this. Placebo reactors can be identified before the trial by simply asking the subject what they expect to be the outcome of the therapy. Those who doubt do not respond to the placebo, while those with high expectations do (reviewed by Bootzin 1985). Lasagna et al (1954) investigated many aspects of postoperative patients who responded to placebos and to analgesic drugs and conclude: 'a positive placebo response indicated a psychological set predisposing to anticipation of pain relief'. They add: 'It is important to appreciate that this same anticipation of pain relief also predisposes to morphine and other pharmacologically active drugs'. In a trial of two drugs versus placebos on one hundred patients, Nash & Zimring (1969) tested specifically for the role of expectation. The two drugs had no effect which would differentiate them from the placebo, but there was a strong correlation between the measured expectation and the placebo effect. Expectation is given a number of related names, such as belief, faith, confidence, enthusiasm, response bias, meaning, credibility, transference, anticipation, in 30 of the papers in the bibliography of Turner et al (1980).

Expectation is a learned state and therefore young children do not respond to placebos as adults do, because they have had neither the time nor the experience to learn. Similarly, in adults, the learning of expected effects will depend on culture, background, experience and personality. A desire to believe, please and obey the doctor will increase the effect while hostility decreases it. Obviously, part of the expectation of the patient will depend on the expectation, enthusiasm and charisma of the therapist and there are many reports on this doctor–patient interaction. Expectation in a laboratory experiment may be more limited than in a clinical setting, which may explain why rates and intensities of placebo effects tend to be less in the laboratory than in the clinic (Beecher 1959).

Conditioning

There are many reports of drug anticipatory responses in animals (Herrnstein 1965, Siegel 1985). These come in two forms. In the first, the animal has been given one or more trials on an active drug and is then given a saline injection; it proceeds to mimic the behavioural or physiological response which was observed after the active drug. In the second type, the animal mimics the actions which it mobilizes to neutralize the effect of the active compound. For example, if animals have experienced a series of injections of insulin which lower the blood sugar, a saline injection in the same setting as the insulin injection results in a rise of blood sugar which would be one of the animal's reactions to counteract the insulin-induced decrease (Siegel 1975). In cultures not raised on *Winnie the Pooh*, *The Wind in the Willows* and *Watership Down*, it is customary to deny animals the luxury of cognitive processing and to ascribe such phenomena to classical Pavlovian conditioning.

This led to the proposal that the human placebo response had the characteristics of a conditioned response (Wickramasekera 1980, Reiss 1980). The idea is that active powerful drugs produce a powerful objective physiological response in the same manner that food produces salivation, the unconditioned stimuli and responses. However, giving the drug is inevitably associated with a pattern of other stimuli, such as a hypodermic injection. It is proposed that these are the equivalent of unconditioned stimuli coupled with the conditioned stimulus. It is then proposed that if these incidentally coupled stimuli are given alone, they will provoke the same response as the original drug, just as in the dog, coupling a bell with food eventually leads to the ability of the bell by itself to provoke salivation. The similarity goes beyond the proposed production of a conditioned response. If a placebo is given repeatedly in some, but not all, trials, the effect declines. This is a characteristic of Pavlovian responses, where simple repeated ringing of the bells leads to a steady decline of the salivation unless the conditioning is reinforced by occasional coupling of the bell with food.

All such comparisons between widely differing processes lead to argument about similarities and differences, identities and analogies (Wall & Safran 1986). However, the idea led to a series of clever experiments by Voudouris et al (1989, 1990). The first stage was a repeat of a type of trial which had been reported many times before. Volunteer subjects were given rising electric shocks and the current was established, in full view of the subject, at which the shock became painful and the level at which it become intolerable. Then a bland cream was rubbed on the area, the subjects were assured that it was a powerful anaesthetic, and the shock trial was run a second time. A small fraction of the subjects demonstrated a placebo response by reporting pain and intolerable pain at a higher shock level than they had on the first trial. This established the placebo response rate in these circumstances. They then started again with a new group of subjects and determined their threshold and tolerance shock levels. The cream was applied and, now came the clever and novel part of the experiment, the strength of the electric shocks was secretly reduced, unknown to the subject and observer. When the trial was now run, the subject observed that much higher numbers on the shock machine were achieved before pain was felt and before the pain reached the tolerance limit. These subjects believed that they had tested on themselves the truth of the remarkable anaesthetic properties of the cream. Next, after one such apparent demonstration of the efficacy of the cream, a trial was run in the original conditions, i.e. the strength of current was returned to its original level. The cream was put on and the shock level raised. On this trial, large numbers of the subjects became placebo reactors. The only difference in these newly produced placebo responders was that they had 'experienced' in some fashion the apparent anaesthetic properties of the cream. Clearly, this result can have important practical implications. Whether the change in the subjects was cognitive or conditioned must remain an issue for debate and further experiment. Brewer (1974) concludes that 'there is no convincing evidence for operant or classical conditioning in adult humans' which is free of cognitive awareness of the situation. It may be that the passionately maintained differences between cognitive and conditioned responses will collapse.

Response-appropriate sensation

I wish to introduce a novel proposal, which is that certain classes of sensation are locked to the response that is appropriate to the situation, in contrast to the classical view that sensation is always locked to a stimulus which provokes it. I refer *only* to certain types of body sensation and not to those sensations related to the outer world, such as sight and sound, where psychophysics shows a precise lawful relation between stimulus and sensation. However, the psychophysics of pain differs wildly from that of other senses (Sternbach & Tursky 1964). This special class includes pain, hunger, thirst, vertigo, fatigue, sleepiness, feeling too hot and too cold. In this class of sensations, each member is associated with disease where the sensation is not coupled with the appropriate stimulus. For pain, this is a major clinical problem to be discussed below. This proposal for a separate class of sensations has been approached in a series of steps (Wall 1974, 1979).

In diseases where overt pathology is an integral part of the diagnosis, such as osteoarthritis, the amount of pain is poorly related to the amount of pathology. In other diseases, such as angina pectoris, an appropriate evocative pathology, such as occluded coronary arteries, is obvious in some cases but not all. In other painful conditions, no appropriate peripheral pathology has been identified. These include trigeminal neuralgia, migraine, atypical facial neuralgia, temporo–mandibular joint syndrome, post-encephalitic myalgia syndrome and fibromyalgia. The most extreme example of an uncoupling of pain from injury occurs in emergency analgesia following abrupt injury. Beecher (1959) reported that 70% of soldiers admitted to a forward hospital with severe battle injuries did not complain of pain. In the less dramatic setting of a city hospital, 40% of patients admitted after the common accidents of civilian life reported no pain at the time of the accident (Melzack et al 1982); another 40% reported high levels of pain. There was no obvious relation between the location or severity or nature of the injury and the amount of pain reported at the time of the injury. Three characteristics of this analgesia are crucial to its understanding. (1) The patient is usually fully aware of the injury and its consequences but describes the initial sensation in neutral words, such as 'blows' or 'thumps'. (2) In hospital, the analgesia is precisely located only to the original injury and does not apply to subsequent stimuli such as the introduction of an intravenous line. (3) By next day all are in the expected pain. Similar behaviour is observed in animals after injury (Wall 1979).

While the body sensations under discussion appear poorly related to a provocative stimulus, each is inevitably linked with attention and with a predictable response. For hunger, eating; for thirst, drinking, etc. For pain, three phases of response are observed: to attempt to avoid further injury, to seek aid and safety, and recovery from injury (Wall 1979). The third phase includes immobilization of the painful part, avoidance of contact on the painful area, withdrawal and sleep. All three response patterns are observed in animals as well as in humans.

If, then, pain and the other sensations discussed are variably linked to the provocative stimulus but reliably locked to the response, would it not be reasonable to propose a brain mechanism by which the brain analyses some internal body states in terms of the biologically relevant behaviour and that certain sensations signal the outcome of that analysis rather than the input on which the analysis was based? Just such a brain mechanism has been explored by the ethologists who followed Hess, Tinbergen and Lorenz. In these animal schemata, the brain continuously monitors the flow of information from the internal and external sensory apparatus. Next, a biological priority is assigned to a fraction of the input and the appropriate motor pattern is released. Let us propose that humans, too, incorporate such an apparatus in their brains and that the initial stages do not necessarily intrude on consciousness. Let us propose further that conscious pain appears only after the priority assignment stage and that pain is sensed consciously at the same time as the release of the motor pattern. The ethological motor patterns of vertebrates are *not* fixed action patterns or reflex discharges; they require reference to the sensory system in order to shape the correct response. The combination of an empty stomach and the sight of a nearby bill release the herring gull pecking motor pattern. However, the herring gull chick still needs to use its sensory apparatus to locate the red spot on the mother's bill in order to peck at it. In other words, there are two sequential uses of the sensory input. The first is to assign priority and the second to guide the motor behaviour. It is proposed here that pain appears as a conscious phenomenon only in the second epoch of sensory analysis after the period during which priority was established but consciousness is not alerted.

For pain and the placebo response, I propose that before the placebo, the unconscious priority decision mechanism had assigned priority to the motor pattern and sensation of pain: after the placebo, which is a stimulus with its learned powerful association with pain relief, the unconscious priority decision mechanism reverts to selecting a non-pain state. This new situation assigns a lower priority to pain and allows the release of the next most biologically appropriate pattern. This two-stage analysis process could also provide a rational basis for the other apparently paradoxical absence of pain, emergency analgesia. Pain is the obvious reaction to overt injury but other actions and sensations may take precedence. For the soldier in action, impending death has the well known property of 'concentrating the mind' and much more elaborate life-preserving actions and reactions take precedence over the reaction to localized injury. This begs the obvious question of why one sensation should take precedence over another. Why could they not both be felt simultaneously or at least rapidly alternating? The probable answer reinforces the linking of this type of sensation to motor pattern. It is not biologically permissable to release two motor patterns simultaneously. It would be disastrous to attempt to advance and retreat at the same time. Animals in ambiguous situations exhibit what Tinbergen called displacement activity. A herring gull in a threat posture suddenly switches on a nest building motor pattern and rips up tufts of grass. Obviously, sensation should not be considered to result from an all-or-none switch. Priorities would have a strength and a duration which would be mirrored in the strength and persistence of attention and of sensation.

For an hypothesis to be useful it has to be more than an analogy (Wall & Safran 1986), it has to be both testable and deniable. For the placebo response, this requires probing inside the brain, but that itself requires a definition of what would be the object of the search, which leads me to the final section.

The philosopher's brains

Anyone thinking about thinking inevitably produces a scheme that incorporates cause and effect. Experimentalists also require a plan on which to organize their questions and, usually implicitly without statement, adopt one of the philosophical schemata. With almost vanishing rarity, the experimental findings have affected philosophical thought. There are four classical plans upon which experiments to discover the nature of sensory processing have been based and I wish to propose a fifth for the future. The four plans are complementary and each has generated undoubted facts that have to be incorporated in any plan.

Dualism

This scheme remains the main basis on which most neurophysiology is based. It predicts that identifiable components of the brain will reliably detect, transmit and deliver specific fractions of sensation. My own and many others' inability to detect any such system which could be reasonably labelled a pain system led me to reject the plans as a plausible generator of the sensation of pain (Wall & Jones 1992). Light pressure on the skin usually provokes a sensation of touch but in other circumstances, i.e. tenderness, the same stimulus to the same skin is very painful. The plasticity of the relation of the stimulus to response and the changeable properties of the neurons made it impossible to view this sensory system as line-labelled, modality-dedicated and hard-wired as required by the Cartesian system. From Descartes on to Eccles and Popper, an absolute separation is made between the reliable body machinery which produces sensation and the subsequent mental process of perception (Fig. 1).

<u>DUALISM</u>

Descartes to Eccles and Popper

STIMULUS ⟶ TRANSMISSION ⟶ SENSATION ⟶PERCEPTION

FIG. 1.   Dualism.

Hierarchies

Two hundred and fifty years after Descartes and contemporary with Darwin, a scheme for subdivision of the nervous system into higher and lower levels was introduced (Fig. 2) but it has been interpreted incorrectly in three ways. First, it has been taken to mean that 'higher' is the same as 'more recently evolved'. This, in turn, is taken to justify the dogma that the mind is in the cerebral cortex. What a leap (in the dark)! Second, while evolution is much discussed in Hughlings Jackson's writing and while his guru Spencer originated the phrase 'survival of the fittest', they used evolution to mean something quite different from Darwin. Spencerian evolution relates to thermodynamics and to entropy and is therefore reversible, while Darwinian evolution is not reversible. The third incorrect interpretation was a trivialization that has dominated the use of the scheme in the 20th century. Three crucial discoveries had been made by Jackson's time. There are anatomically separate inputs and outputs to the central nervous system (Bell and Magendie). There are anatomically separate input and output pathways within the central nervous system (Brown–Sequard). There are reflex pathways within the spinal cord which link inputs and outputs (Sechenow). Even the simplest neurologist and the most sophisticated text book writer could cope with these three ideas. Therefore they took Jackson and his subtle followers to mean that there was a short reflex pathway which runs through the spinal cord, a longer one through the brain stem and the longest one which looped through the cortex. In fact, Jackson and Sherrington were very specific that there were internal loops connecting the various levels, which makes a considerable difference from a simple set of reflex loops. Jackson's greatest neurological discoveries came from epileptics. In the commonest form of grand mal epilepsy, the convulsive phase of the attack is preceded by a sensory aura in which the patient has a sensory experience. This can vary among patients from a simple tingling on one finger to an elaborate scene with people, music and a landscape. These are not hallucinations in the sense that the patient believes they are actually happening. On the contrary, the patient is angry and terrified because they know they are about to have a fit. Auras are brilliantly described by Dostoevsky, himself an epileptic, in *The Idiot*. The importance for our present discussion is that the brain is capable of creating virtual reality without reference to or stimulation from the sensory nervous system. This depends on

HIERARCHIES

Hughlings-Jackson and Herbert Spencer to Sherrington

STIMULUS⇆ SPECIFICS⇆ INTEGRATION⇆ HIGHER CENTRES

FIG. 2.   Hierarchies.

long-range feedback mechanisms within the central nervous system, which do not reach out into the periphery.

Cybernetics

Claude Bernard was concerned with the maintenance of a stable internal environment. As he and those who followed studied how stability was achieved, they began to realize that a series of components must exist. This was formalized by Norbert Wiener as cybernetics (Fig. 3). First, there had to be an internal standard which was compared with the actual situation. A comparator measured the mismatch between a sensory input which signalled the actual situation and an internal standard which signalled the ideal situation. This mismatch signal was amplified and triggered a series of graded output patterns which, in turn, fed back onto the actual input to reverse its trend and thereby to reduce the mismatch signal. Physiologists have identified many of the components. In cooling, for example, the dropping temperature is the stimulus which deviates from the standard. The mismatch difference signal triggers an orchestrated series of output patterns as the difference grows—vasoconstriction, piloerection, release of thyroid hormone, insulin and adrenaline to increase metabolism, shivering, rigors.

CYBERNETICS

Claude Bernard and Cannon and Wiener

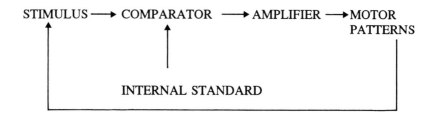

FIG. 3.   Cybernetics.

Ethology

This spectacular development of old-fashioned nature study which I have discussed above defined a series of stages between stimulus and response (Fig. 4). The sensory input is used twice, to decide first what to do and then how to do it. In the initial stage, a combination of sensory signals from outside and from inside assigns a priority to one feature in the behavioural repertoire. This

ETHOLOGY

Hess, Tinbergen and Lorenz

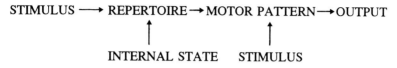

FIG. 4.   Ethology.

releases the motor pattern which is most relevant to the biological situation. The successful achievement of this motor pattern requires a second consultation with the sensory system. Where is the enemy, mate, nest or chick and is it being approached on the optimal course? Experimental studies have been very successful in identifying the sensory patterns and the motor pattern generators but less so the priority-assignment mechanism.

Reality–virtual reality

I wish to propose here that advanced brains contain both the Jackson version of a hierarchical system and the Tinbergen–Lorenz version of an ethological system. The ethological component sequence of repertoire–priority–motor pattern contains an inherent fraction of species-specific components heavily modified by experience and learning. This machinery is entirely responsible for the domestic and skilled actions of everyday life and does not involve consciousness. However, on occasions, a combination of internal and external stimuli occur for which there is no biologically appropriate response available in the repertoire–priority–motor pattern system. When this mismatch occurs, an attentional switch diverts the input into a quite different system. Before going further I wish to give two illustrative examples.

The phantom limb has been a challenging paradox for philosophers and neurologists. Descartes was aware that he had set a trap for himself in the very rigidity of his proposed sensory mechanism. He writes (1641) in *Meditations on First Philosophy*: 'It is manifest that notwithstanding the sovereign goodness of God, the nature of man, in so far as it is a composite of mind and body, must sometimes be at fault and deceptive. For should some cause, not in the foot but in another part of the nerves that extend from the foot to the brain, or even in the brain itself, give rise to the motion ordinarily excited when the foot is injuriously affected, pain will be felt just as though it were in the foot and thus naturally the sense will be deceived: for since the same motion in the brain cannot but give rise in the mind always to the same sensation and since this sensation is much more frequently due to a cause that is injurious to the foot than by one acting in another quarter, it is reasonable that it should convey to the mind pain as in the foot'. The brilliance of Descartes here introduces the idea of the false signal but at the same time has to define the mind as a passive slave of the sensory apparatus. Three centuries later, Bromage & Melzack (1974) considered the results of adding local anaesthetic to nerves supplying a body part. Far from producing signals, these agents block the normal trickle of signals which reaches the brain. A startling phantom phenomenon appears in the area of anaesthesia. This phantom is not an imitation of the real limb, it is more real, swollen and attention grabbing. On the scheme under discussion, the repertoire–priority component of the brain is presented with a sensory input which is simply not in the repertoire. In that situation, the attention switch operates to bring into action the sensation perception mechanism, which, in the absence of a sensory input, creates a virtual limb. Seeking a confirmatory sensory input, the patient visually explores the limb and palpates it and the phantom disappears.

The second example comes from the work of Dubner et al (1981), Bushnell et al (1984) and Duncan et al (1987), which is so startling and novel that it has yet to intrude on theory. They recorded in monkeys from first-order central cells which receive information from nerve fibres from the skin. By all classical criteria, these cells fulfil perfectly the requirements of Cartesian sensory transmission cells—their discharge rigidly and reliably reflects a particular stimulus applied to a unique area of skin. The cells signal in a lawful fashion the location, intensity and nature of the stimulus with such reliability that the signal was the same in awake or anaesthetized monkeys. These workers then trained the animals to use a stimulus in a discrimination task in which the correct response was rewarded. The form of the trial was that the animal was first given a warning signal that the trial was about to begin, then the stimulus was applied and then the animal was rewarded with a drink of orange juice if it reached out and pushed a button if, and only if, the stimulus was of a particular intensity. When the training began, of course, the cell responded only to the skin stimulus and not to the warning signal or any of the other events. However, when the animal had successfully solved the problem and was fully trained, most of the cells produced a brief burst of activity after the warning signal. This novel period of cell discharge mimicked the discharge of the cell which always occurred after the stimulus to be discriminated was presented. This means that the trained brain had created a virtual input which ran over the same pathway as the input provoked by the real stimulus. A precise model of the expected input precedes the input actually provoked by the expected stimulus. The literature contains several examples of this creation of inputs without stimuli in classical and operant conditioning.

Returning to the scheme, it proposes that the brain is capable of generating a virtual reality (Fig. 5). It is further proposed that this experimental theatre is

REALITY - VIRTUAL REALITY

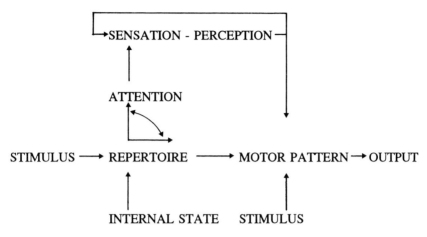

FIG. 5.   Reality–virtual reality.

brought into action only when the repertoire–priority system fails to provide a biologically appropriate motor pattern. The Jacksonian reality–virtual reality experimental theatre is simultaneously author, director, stage, actors and audience. In the situation of a fully mastered discriminant task, the expectations of the stage play precisely mimic reality. That is pantomime. In chronic pain, no amount of rewriting or changing of cast and scenery provides a resolution to match and cancel reality. That is tragedy.

References

Amsterdam EA, Wolfson S, Garlin R 1969 New aspects of the placebo response in angina pectoris. Am J Cardiol 24:305–306

Beecher HK 1955 The powerful placebo. JAMA (J Am Med Assoc) 159:1602–1606

Beecher HK 1959 Measurement of subjective responses. Oxford University Press, New York

Beecher HK 1968 Placebo effects: a quantitative study of suggestibility. In Beecher HK, Lasagna L (eds) Non-specific factors in drug therapy. Thomas Publishers, Springfield, IL, p 27–39

Bootzin RR 1985 The role of expectancy in behaviour change. In: White LP, Tursky B, Schwartz GE (eds) Placebo: theory research and mechanisms. Guilford Press, New York, p 121–134

Brewer WF 1974 There is no convincing evidence for operant or classical conditioning in adult humans. In: Weimer WB, Palermo DS (eds) Cognition and the symbolic process. Wiley, New York, p 1–42

Bromage PR, Melzack R 1974 Phantom limbs and the body schema. Can Anaesth Soc J 21:267–274

Buchaleq LW, Coffield KE 1982 An investigation of drug expectancy as a function of colour, size and preparation. J Clin Pharmacol 2:245–248

Bushnell MC, Duncan GH, Dubner R, He LF 1984 Activity of trigeminothalamic neurons in monkey trained in a thermal discrimination task. J Neurophysiol 52:170–187

Cobb LA, Thomas GI, Dillard DH, Merendino KA, Bruce RA 1959 An evaluation of internal mammary artery ligation by a double blind technique. N Engl J Med 20:1115–1118

Department of National Health and Population Development, Republic of South Africa 1992 Epidemiological Comments, no 193

Descartes R 1641 Meditation on a first philosophy. Paris

Descartes R 1644 L'Homme. Paris

Dimond EG, Kittle CF, Crockett JE 1958 Evaluation of internal mammary ligation and sham procedure in angina pectoris. Circulation 18:712–713

Dubner R, Hoffman DS, Hayes RL 1981 Task related responses and their functional role. J Neurophysiol 46:444–464

Duncan GH, Bushnell MC, Bates R, Dubner R 1987 Task related responses of monkey medullary dorsal horn neurones. J Neurophysiol 57:289–310

El-Sobky A, Dostrovsky JA, Wall PD 1979 Lack of effect of naloxone on pain perception in humans. Nature 263:783–784

Evans FJ 1974 The placebo response in pain reduction. In: Bonica JJ (ed) Pain. Raven Press, New York (Adv Neurol 4) p 289–296

Evans FJ 1977 The placebo control of pain. In: Brady JP, Mendels J, Reiger WR, Orne MT (eds) Psychiatry: areas of promise and advancement. Plenum Publishing Corporation, New York, p 249–271

Farrer GR 1964 Psychoanalytic theory of placebo. Dis Nerv Syst 35:655–662

Finkel MJ 1985 Placebo controls are not always necessary. In: White LP, Tursky B, Schwartz GE (eds) Placebo: theory research and mechanisms. Guilford Press, New York, p 419–422

Finneson BE 1969 Diagnosis and management of pain syndromes. Saunders, Philadelphia, PA

Gracely RH 1989 Psychophysical assessment of human pain. In: Chapman CR, Loeser JD (eds) Issues in pain measurement. Raven Press, New York (Adv Pain Res Ther 12) p 211–229

Gracely RH, McGrath P, Dubner R 1978 Validity and sensitivity of ratio scales. Manipulation of affect by diazepam. Pain 5:19–29

Gracely RH, McGrath P, Dubner R 1979 Fentanyl reduces the intensity but not the unpleasantness of painful tooth sensations. Science (Wash DC) 203:1261–1263

Gracely RH, Woskee PJ, Deeter WR, Dubner R 1982 Naloxone and placebo alter postsurgical pain by independent mechanisms. Soc Neurosci Abstr 8:264

Grevert P, Albert LH, Goldstein A 1983 Partial antagonism of placebo analgesia by naloxone. Pain 16:126–143

Hashish I, Feinman C, Harvey W 1988 Reduction of postoperative pain and swelling by ultrasound: a placebo effect. Pain 83:303–311

Herrnstein RJ 1965 Placebo effect on the rat. Science (Wash DC) 138:677–678

Holroyd KA, Holm JE, Keefe FJ et al 1992 A multi-center evaluation of the McGill pain questionnaire: results from more than 1700 chronic pain patients. Pain 48: 301–312

Koes BW, Bouter LM, Beckerman H, van der Heijden G, Knipschild PG 1991 Exercises and back pain, blinded review. Br Med J 302:1572–1576

Koes BW, Bouter LM, Beckerman H 1992 Randomised clinical trials of manipulative therapy and physiotherapy. Br Med J 304:601–606

Lasagna L, Mosteller F, von Felsinger JM, Beecher HK 1954 A study of the placebo response. Am J Med 16:770–779

Levine JD, Gordon NC, Fields HL 1978 The mechanisms of placebo analgesia. Lancet 2:654–657

Levine JD, Gordon NC, Fields HL 1979 Naloxone dose dependently produces analgesia and hyperalgesia in postoperative pain. Nature 278:740–741

Liberman R 1964 An experimental study of the placebo response under three different situations of pain. J Psychiatr Res 2:233–246

MacArthur C, Lewis M, Knox EG 1992 Investigation of long term problems after obstetric epidural anaesthesia. Br Med J 304:1279–1282

Melzack E, Casey KL 1968 Sensory, motivational and central control determinants of pain. In: Kenshalo D (ed) The skin senses. Thomas Publishers, Springfield, IL, p 423–443

Melzack R, Torgerson WS 1971 On the language of pain. Anesthesiology 34:50–59

Melzack R, Wall PD, Ty TC 1982 Acute pain in an emergency clinic, latency of onset and descriptive patterns. Pain 14:33–43

Merskey J 1989 Pain and psychological medicine. In: Wall PD, Melzack R (eds) Textbook of pain. Churchill Livingstone, Edinburgh, p 656–669

Nash MM, Zimring FM 1969 Prediction of reaction to placebo. J Abnorm Psychol 74:568–573

Rawlinson MC 1985 Philosophical reflections on the use of placebos in medical practice. In: White LP, Tursky B, Schwarz GE (eds) Placebo: theory, research and mechanisms. Guilford Press, New York, p 403–419

Reiss S 1980 Pavlovian conditioning and human fear. An expectancy model. Behav Ther 11:380–396

Sherman RA, Sherman CJ, Gall NG 1980 A survey of current phantom limb pain treatment in the United States. Pain 8:85–99

Siegel S 1975 Conditioning insulin effects. J Comp Physiol Psychol 89:189–199

Siegel S 1985 Drug anticipatory responses in animals. In: White LP, Tursky B, Schwarz GE (eds) Placebo: theory, research and mechanisms. Guilford Press, New York, p 170–194

Sternbach RA, Tursky B 1964 On the psychophysical power functions in electric shock. Psychosomat Sci 1:217–218

Turner JL, Gallimore R, Fox-Henning C 1980 An annotated bibliography of placebo research. J Suppl Abstr Serv Am Psychol Assoc 10:22

Tyler DB 1946 The influence of a placebo and medication on motion sickness. Am J Physiol 146:458–466

Voudouris NJ, Peck CL, Coleman G 1989 Conditioned response models of placebo phenomena. Pain 38:109–116

Voudouris NJ, Peck CL, Coleman G 1990 The role of conditioning and verbal expectancy in the placebo response. Pain 43:121–128

Wall PD 1974 'My foot hurts me', an analysis of a sentence. In: Bellairs R, Gray EG (eds) Essays on the nervous system. Clarendon Press, Oxford, p 391–406

Wall PD 1979 On the relation of injury to pain. Pain 6:253–264

Wall PD, Jones M 1992 Defeating pain. Plenum Publishing Corporation, New York

Wall PD, Safran JW 1986 Artefactual intelligence. In: Rose S, Appignanesi L (eds) Science and beyond. Blackwell Publishers, Oxford, p 115–130

White L, Tursky B, Schwarz GE (eds) 1985 Placebo: theory, research and mechanisms. Guilford Press, New York

Wickramasekera I 1980 A conditioned response model of the placebo effect. Biofeedback Self-Regul 5:5–18

DISCUSSION

Harnad: I would like to generalize what you have described. It is not just placebo that behaves this way. Diabetics will sometimes get into acute hypoglycaemic states: they keep sugar in their pockets, and as soon as they pull the sugar out and lick it, their hypoglycaemia vanishes. This, of course, can't be because of a direct contribution to their systemic glucose levels. In fact, one can achieve the same effects with saccharin. This is also true in ordinary metabolism. The glucostat turns off your hunger well before the requisite homeostasis has been re-established. So it seems that the whole nervous system is geared towards huge anticipatory physiological responses, all based on experience and habit. However, you can very quickly extinguish the remedial effect of licking saccharin by doing it repeatedly without following it with a real increase in blood sugar.

I have two questions. Is there any evidence for chronic placebo effects? Second, is there a possibility that the 33% predictability (if there is some reality to this figure) is anomalous only in the sense that perhaps if a subpopulation is hypnotically susceptible, they don't extinguish placebo effects the way everybody else does?

Kihlstrom: There is no relationship between the placebo response and hypnotic susceptibility.

Harnad: Not the placebo response in general; I am asking about chronic placebo or non-extinction of placebo.

Wall: That was why I gave the example of surgery for angina. The effect of the sham operation remained throughout the six month period of observation. There are many other examples. When an ineffective drug is withdrawn, there is always a large number of patients addicted to the placebo. So there is a chronic placebo effect.

Fenwick: Much depends on our models of explanation. We often have quite the wrong idea of how the system works. The conventional idea of epilepsy is that cell discharges cause seizures, are seizures. What is not asked is: how do these seizures arise? In focal epilepsy, the seizure pacemaker cells are firing all the time, but patients don't have seizures all the time. So what causes the activity of the pacemaker cells to spread into groups of surrounding cells? One important factor is learning—learning to have seizures. There are fascinating accounts in the literature of seizures in cats being conditioned to a flashing light. This is an amazing process: a flash on the retina can apparently produce synchronization of cells around a focus which is not in any way connected to the visual system. Thus, in epilepsy, by a similar mechanism, it is possible to learn both to have, and not to have, seizures. The placebo responses in epilepsy can be explained this way, as alteration of a mental construct. This directly alters the excitability in populations of cells surrounding the epileptic focus, and thus alters the probability of a seizure occurring.

I chose epilepsy on purpose because you frequently get dramatic placebo responses. Some time ago a series of patients at the Maudsley hospital were implanted with cerebellar electrodes. It was hoped that stimulation of these electrodes would stop their seizures. The response from the first patient was excellent, as the stimulation appeared to stop seizure activity. The second patient was equally successful but in a rather different way, and here the placebo response was most important. The electrode array was implanted in the patient's cerebellum and the leads taken down to the chest, but no stimulator was implanted. The patient, without any stimulation, did not have another seizure. This is a maximal placebo response. I think there are very precise mechanisms which underlie this placebo response. Many patients have mechanisms whereby they can stop seizure activity by changing the levels of excitation and inhibition surrounding a focus. In most patients this occurs unconsciously. I suspect it was a similar mechanism that stopped our patient from having fits. There seems to be a close relationship between mind and brain.

Searle: The analogy that you gave with the warning does rather fit the text book story. The suggestion is, habituation affects the physiology in such a way as to create a new circuit. In the case of the warning signal, the warning has the same consequences in the circuitry as the real thing. That would seem to fit the morphine case, where there is a whole set of surrounding stimuli that go with the pharmacology of the morphine. The guy regularly sticks a needle in your arm, and he squirts some stuff in you. According to text book physiology, that's going to create new circuitry. You can activate that circuitry simply by injecting a saline solution. You don't need the pharmacology because the circuit is already there. But, I think you want to say something much more exciting than that. You want to say that the story about the circuitry won't work in any simple way for a first time placebo. Your model of the warning signal won't work for the people who have the placebo operation.

Wall: The placebo stimulus occurs on the background of a long history of the individual's experience of medical treatment. Placebos that work on adults don't work on five year olds. 'Mummy will kiss it better' works on a five year old. That placebo habituates for various reasons (what you think about your mother) and you substitute another set of stimuli as being associated with effective therapy.

In the animal experiment, the animal slowly learned to associate three events: the warning stimulus, the stimulus to be discriminated and the stimulus provided by the reward. After the association is established, the warning signal is followed by nerve impulses in the same cells that respond to the stimulus to be discriminated. The first volley of impulses represent virtual reality created by brain mechanisms followed by a volley representing the reality of an external stimulus.

Gray: But what John Searle has just said remains correct. The animal cases, the morphine injection and the button press can all be understood as classical

conditioning. The only difference depends upon whether the conditioned
response is in the same direction as the drug effect—as in the morphine
case you described—or whether it is an opponent process counteracting the
direct drug effect (Siegel 1983). It is actually very difficult to figure out the
conditions which give rise to one or the other, but they are both familiar
processes.

I think the issue is whether, when you are dealing with the prestige of a doctor
with a white coat who is giving an intravenous injection, that fits the model.
It is not a first time placebo, it clearly depends on a great deal of knowledge
about doctors and intravenous injections and so on. But it might not be classical
conditioning, because those precise circumstances need not necessarily have
occurred before in just the way they are occurring now.

Dennett: You can test the classical conditioning hypothesis directly, and rule
it out, by administering the placebo or the drug under rigidly controlled, nearly
identical stimulus circumstances in which you vary just one parameter. Suppose
each time you do it, there is somebody in the room who says something.
Sometimes he says, 'The Red Sox lost the ball game last night'. Another time
he says, 'I think it's going to rain tomorrow'. The third time he says, 'We have
run out of morphine, give him the saline'. Then you see a marked reduction
of the placebo effect. It clearly depends on the subject recognizing the meaning
of the words.

Gray: That will not work. There were experiments in the 1940s and 1950s
which showed semantic conditioning, that is, generalization of Pavlovian
conditioned reflexes along dimensions of meaning (Razran 1971). This
phenomenon allows one to analyse the effects of a statement such as, 'We have
run out of morphine', while remaining within the framework of classical
conditioning. I'm not saying that is the way such effects are produced, only
that your thought experiment does not rule conditioning out.

Wall: When the placebo effect first became apparent, people said, 'This is
clearly a mental process, it's something to do with the perceptive failures of
the subjects'. Now you say it's conditioning. I don't think either of those
statements is more than labelling an unknown process.

Gray: I'm not saying that. There are some analysed cases that are
conditioning.

Searle: The question then is, how do you think it works?

Wall: In the first place, I would like to admit the possibility of generating
an effective reality.

Nagel: Is part of your message that ordinary cases of feeling or no longer
feeling pain have a much more global explanation than might originally have
been thought? Even in the case in which you stub your toe, the picture of the
impulse creating a sufficient condition for pain in a localized place is inaccurate,
because there too, you are creating a virtual reality.

Wall: I agree.

Humphrey: Why do you think that these phenomena occur more dramatically in the realm of touch than they do in vision? If you sound a warning bell and flash a spot of red repeatedly on the retina, it will never happen that when the bell sounds there is a sensation of red. I like your model of virtual reality, and I would like to be able to generalize it much further than just the pain situation, but it doesn't seem to generalize. What do you think is so special about touch and pain?

Wall: I think you have two types of sensory experiences, one of which implies that you are going to do something, and a second which may be completely neutral. To feel hunger or thirst or pain implies that you are going to try to abolish those sensations. Whereas 'I see a light, I feel touch' can be utterly neutral with no predictive qualities. I propose that the first type is open to manipulation when some other predicted behaviour is more biologically appropriate for the individual.

Kihlstrom: I have always thought the placebo response was especially interesting for the reverse of the conventional way of thinking about the mind–body problem. We usually think about mental states as emerging from physiological processes. In placebo, there is a mental state that seems to alter physiological processes. I don't want to push that too far, but psychosomatic effects of all sorts have that quality.

There is another category of effects that are expectation driven and that are also perceptual in the way that pain is perceptual. We know that expectations have profound effects on things like visual perception. In what sense are these kinds of things different from those sorts of expectation-driven percepts?

Wall: Don't forget, the placebo effect is initiated by an action from the outside. The interesting question is: could one generate a therapy in which the equivalent of a placebo could be generated internally?

Kihlstrom: One most likely could. I was a student of Fred Evans, who showed that the effect of the placebo compared to the active agent was a constant, regardless of the agent to which it was being compared (Evans 1974). Placebo compared to aspirin is 0.54 as effective as aspirin. Placebo compared to morphine is 0.56 as effective as morphine. So if you had a pain that could be effectively treated with aspirin, you could think you were giving morphine and get complete pain relief! Evans suggested a remarkable way of titrating placebo effects to good effect.

Wall: The implications of those results are not precisely what you have suggested. The implications are that it is exceedingly difficult to do a blind experiment in which all clues of expectation are hidden from the patient.

Kihlstrom: I am sure it also disrupts the placebo effect. Because the physician has to believe in what's being given as well as the patient or the treatment will not work.

Marcel: In 1838, Johannes Müller proposed the doctrine of specific nerve energies. That is, the type or modality of your experience would be a function of the nature of nerve involved, which is sensitive only to a particular type of input. Clearly, this is wrong. The consciously felt modality and type of sensation are at least partly the result of attribution. How far are we willing to push the role of tacit beliefs? This is related to the concept of somatization. How many types of somatization are there? There is most trivially the metaphoric type, where 'pain' is just a metaphoric term. There are also two other senses. First, all sensations felt in the body are mental, in so far as they are felt. The second is due to how a culture contructs selfhood. One culture constructs certain types of mental events as bodily, another constructs them as existential. In the former, you will experience a situation as pain, in the latter as mental suffering (Kleinman 1986).

To what extent are qualitative properties (qualia, sensations) actually a function of certain types of beliefs?

Wall: Hysterics create a sensory state within themselves that they cannot distinguish from reality, unlike the epileptic's aura, which the patient rapidly learns does not reflect reality.

Marcel: It really is felt, it really is a pain. What's to distinguish it?

Wall: I agree it's creating a state which is indistinguishable from what would happen had there been an input. I agree with Libet that the hysteric appears to produce false signals half way down the line. It would be useful therapeutically if we could learn how to produce apparently true signals without there being an input to produce them.

References

Evans FJ 1974 The placebo response in pain reduction. In: Bonica JJ (ed) Pain. Raven Press, New York (Adv Neurol 4) p 289–296

Kleinman A 1986 Social origins of distress and disease. Yale University Press, New Haven, CT

Müller J 1838 Handbuch der Physiologie des Menschen, vol 2. Hölscher, Koblenz

Razran G 1971 Mind in evolution. Houghton Mifflin, Boston, MA

Siegel S 1983 Classical conditioning, drug tolerance and drug dependence. In: Smart RG, Glaser FB, Israel Y, Kalant H, Popham RE, Schmidt W (eds) Research advances in alcohol and drug problems. Plenum Publishing Corporation, New York, vol 7:207–246

The neuronal basis of motion perception

William T. Newsome and C. Daniel Salzman

Department of Neurobiology, Stanford University School of Medicine, Sherman Fairchild Science Building, Stanford, CA 94305-5401, USA

Abstract. The central nervous system of humans supports a range of cognitive functions that contribute to conscious mental states. The neural systems underlying several of these cognitive functions, including perception, memory, planning and action, are proving susceptible to experimental analysis in lower primate species such as rhesus monkeys. In particular, recent investigations have generated striking new insights concerning the neural mechanisms that mediate visual perception. We briefly review the functional organization of the primate visual pathways and describe new experiments that demonstrate a causal link between neural activity in one of these pathways and a specific aspect of perceptual performance. The experiments illustrate an incisive method for linking perceptual abilities to their neural substrates. This approach may prove applicable to the analysis of other cognitive functions as well.

1993 Experimental and theoretical studies of consciousness. Wiley, Chichester (Ciba Foundation Symposium 174) p 217–246

All visual information reaches the brain in the form of brief electrical impulses carried by the 1.5 million nerve fibres that originate in the retina of each eye. Thus, our unified percept of the visual scene, including the rich array of objects, colours and motions that we routinely and effortlessly see, must be constructed from the fragmented bits of electrical information transmitted through the fibres of the optic nerves. In humans, this remarkable synthetic feat occurs primarily within several cortical visual areas near the back of the brain. Visual information reaches the primary cortical visual area (V1, or striate cortex) from the optic nerves via a relay connection in the thalamus. A great deal of sophisticated processing occurs in striate cortex and information is then transmitted to adjacent 'extrastriate' visual areas for further analysis. Near the turn of the century, the functional specialization of posterior neocortex for vision became clear to neurologists, who observed that destruction of posterior neocortex creates a state of near-blindness in humans even though the eyes and retina continue to function normally.

Complementing this observation in dramatic fashion, a number of later investigators showed that human subjects can see small patches of light when electrical stimulation is applied directly to the visual cortex. Fig. 1 shows an X-ray

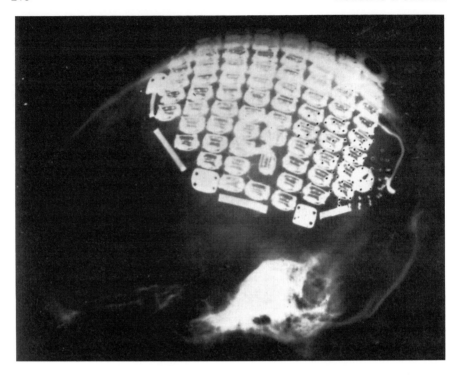

FIG. 1.   A lateral X-ray photograph of the electrical stimulation implant used by Brindley
& Lewin (1968). The large white objects are an array of 80 radio receivers, embedded
in silicone rubber and implanted extracranially. An array of 80 stimulating electrodes
(each 800×800 μm) was positioned intracranially against the surface of the visual cortex
using a cap of silicone rubber moulded to fit the contours of the cortical surface. The
electrodes appear as an array of tiny dots on the right-hand side of the implant. The
shadows of most of the dots were retouched in the original photograph and appear as
black dots. Each radio receiver was connected to an individual stimulating electrode by
a fine, insulated wire. Radio signals could be pulsed to any receiver by means of a
transmitting coil tuned to an appropriate frequency. Pulses were usually 200 μs,
delivered at an overall rate of 100 Hz. Reproduced with permission from Brindley &
Lewin (1968).

photograph of an array of stimulating electrodes and radio receivers surgically
implanted over the visual cortex of a blind human patient. Brindley and his
co-workers in England undertook these experiments to assess the feasibility of
developing a prosthetic device that could permit rudimentary vision in persons
who were made blind by an injury to the eyes or optic nerves (e.g. Brindley
& Lewin 1968); Dobelle and his colleagues have performed similar experiments
in the United States (e.g. Dobelle & Mladejovsky 1974). The array of stimulating
electrodes, each separated by 2.4–3.4 mm, was placed on the surface of visual
cortex on one side of the brain. The stimulating electrodes appear in Fig. 1 as

small black or white dots toward the right-hand side of the implant; the large white objects in the photograph are the radio receivers, each of which communicates with a single electrode via a small insulated wire. By activation of the appropriate receiver with a transmitting coil placed over the scalp, visual cortex could be stimulated through any electrode in the array. When stimulated in this manner, subjects reported seeing bright patches of light that were described variously as resembling stars in the sky, small bright clouds, or elongated blobs of light. These visual sensations, or 'phosphenes', commenced when electrical stimulation began and terminated abruptly when stimulation ended.

These experiments showed that visual cortex is not only *necessary* for normal visual experience, but that activation of visual cortex is *sufficient* to generate subjective visual sensations even though no corresponding activity exists in the retina or optic nerve. Besides the potential importance of these experiments for the development of visual prosthetics, the results are of substantial theoretical importance because they demonstrate a causal relationship between neural activity in the cortex and visual sensations that can be consciously perceived and described by human subjects. While the patterns of light perceived in the experiments of Brindley and Dobelle were relatively simple, the data nevertheless raise the enticing prospect of linking more complex percepts to specific patterns of cortical activity. (Penfield and his associates have shown that electrical stimulation with a single electrode can lead to subjective impressions of remarkable specificity (e.g. Penfield & Perot 1963), but the locations of his electrodes suggest that the neural circuits activated in those experiments are related more to memory of past events than to the synthesis of novel percepts).

How might this prospect be realized? One key step is to design experiments that take advantage of contemporary knowledge concerning functionally specialized circuits within the visual cortex. V1 is composed of a large number of processing modules called hypercolumns. Each hypercolumn occupies about 2–4 mm² of the cortical surface. A single hypercolumn contains specialized circuits for analysing contour, colour and motion within a small patch of the visual image. Because adjacent hypercolumns analyse adjacent patches of space, V1 contains an orderly map of the visual field.

Fig. 2, taken from the work of Livingstone & Hubel (1984), illustrates the current conception of the internal organization of a hypercolumn. A slab of visual cortex, like all neocortex, is composed of several layers of cells occupying a total thickness of 1–2 mm. A conventional numbering scheme for the layers is provided along the right-hand edge of the figure. The functional organization of a hypercolumn can be explored by lowering a microelectrode into the cortex and recording the electrical impulses (or action potentials) generated by single neurons in response to visual stimuli projected onto the retina. Experiments of this nature have shown that each hypercolumn is composed of a set of smaller columns with distinct physiological characteristics. For example, each hypercolumn contains two large slabs (or 'columns') of neurons, each dominated by inputs from one eye ('L' and 'R' in Fig. 2). Running orthogonally to these 'ocular dominance' columns is a set of smaller 'orientation' columns containing neurons that encode information about the orientation of local contours within the visual scene. These neurons are called 'orientation selective' because they respond optimally to an edge or slit of light of a particular orientation; neurons within a single column share a common 'preferred' orientation. As indicated by the small icon at the top of each orientation column in Fig. 2, the preferred orientation shifts systematically from column to column so that all possible orientations are represented within a set of columns occupying 1–2 mm of cortical surface area (for a general review see Hubel 1988).

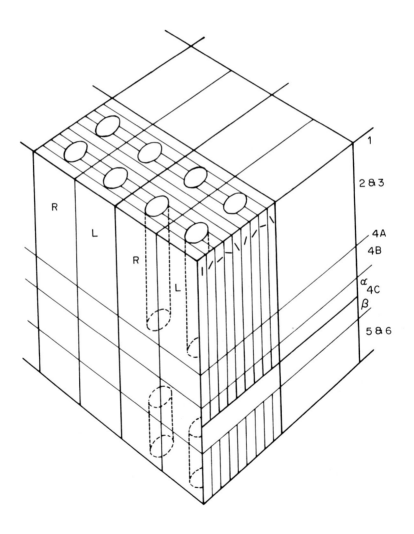

Specialized circuits for the analysis of motion and colour also exist within the hypercolumn. Layer 4B, for example, is dominated by direction selective cells which respond only when a visual stimulus moves in a particular direction through the region of space analysed by the neurons. Similarly, neurons within the cylindrically shaped columns in Fig. 2 appear to be specialized for analysing the wavelength composition of visual stimuli. Thus, each hypercolumn contains the neural machinery required to process inputs from both eyes and to analyse a particular patch of the visual scene for oriented contours, motion and wavelength.

Given the intricacies of local circuit structure at the level of the hypercolumn, it is not surprising that electrical stimulation yielded relatively crude visual sensations in the human subjects tested by Brindley and Dobelle. Both the electrodes and stimulating currents used in the early experiments were sufficiently large that neurons were probably activated over 1–3 mm^2 of the cortical surface, an area that would include all of the elegantly complex local circuits of one or more hypercolumns. On the basis of current knowledge, then, it is tempting to speculate that more refined percepts of orientation, motion and colour could be generated were the local circuits stimulated in a more selective fashion.

Current techniques enhance the prospects of success in such experiments, since very small intracortical electrodes (20 μm in length as opposed to the 800 × 800 μm surface electrodes used by Brindley) can be used to characterize neurons physiologically and to stimulate the same region of cortex by passing pulses of

---

FIG. 2. The current conception of a V1 hypercolumn, taken from the work of Livingstone & Hubel (1984). The diagram illustrates an idealized slab of cortex from V1, showing the orthogonally intersecting systems of ocular dominance columns and orientation columns that constitute a hypercolumn. Neurons within the ocular dominance columns are dominated by inputs from the left eye (L) or right eye (R). Neurons within an orientation column respond optimally to local contours of a particular orientation, and the preferred orientation shifts systematically from column to column as indicated by the small icons at the top of each orientation column. A hypercolumn comprises one set of right and left ocular dominance columns and a complementary set of orientation columns; thus the diagram illustrates two hypercolumns in detail. Each hypercolumn is approximately 1–2 mm wide. The cylindrical structures signify regions of the cortex that stain heavily for the enzyme cytochrome oxidase. In the macaque monkey, these structures are thought to be specialized for analysing wavelength information. All neocortex consists of recognizable layers of neurons, and a conventional numbering scheme for the cortical layers of V1 is illustrated to the right of the diagram. The direct pathway from the retina via the thalamic relay nucleus terminates predominantly in layer 4C of V1, though a few fibres terminate in layer 6 and the lowest portion of layer 3. Neurons in the upper layers send information primarily to other cortical areas. A very high proportion of neurons in layer 4B are direction selective neurons, suggesting that this layer is concerned primarily with motion analysis. Reprinted with permission from Livingstone & Hubel (1984).

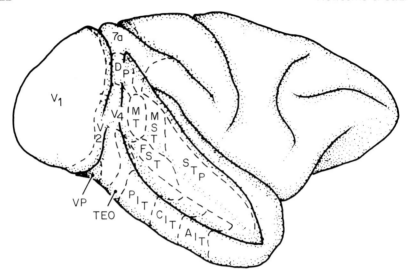

FIG. 3.   A lateral view of the cerebral hemisphere of a macaque monkey illustrating the boundaries of currently identified cortical visual areas. Visual cortex in the macaque occupies a large portion of the occipital, parietal and temporal lobes, covering approximately 50% of the cortical surface in all. The primary visual area, V1, is located at the posterior pole of the hemisphere (far left in the diagram) and the middle temporal visual area (MT) resides in the depths of the superior temporal sulcus. This sulcus was artificially 'opened' in the diagram so that the location of MT and neighbouring visual areas could be seen. MT and an adjacent area, MST (medial superior temporal area), are specialized for analysing visual motion information. Other areas buried within adjacent sulci also contribute to the motion pathway. AIT, anterior inferotemporal area; CIT, central inferotemporal area; DP, dorsal prelunate area; FST, floor of the superior temporal sulcus; PIT, posterior inferotemporal area; STP, superior temporal polysensory area; TEO, TE occipital area; VP, ventral posterior area.

electrical current. Furthermore, the experiments can be performed in extrastriate cortical areas where functionally specialized circuits are more accessible than in the intricately organized hypercolumns of striate cortex. We have begun to examine the perceptual effects of applying microstimulation to extrastriate cortex by training rhesus monkeys on visual discrimination tasks so that they can report what they see. The rhesus monkey (*Macaca mulatta*) is an appropriate subject for our experiments because: (1) this species can be easily trained to perform visual discrimination tasks, (2) there exists an extensive base of knowledge concerning the structure and function of its central visual pathways, and (3) the basic perceptual capacities and the structure of its visual system are similar to those of humans.

The middle temporal area and the motion pathway

Fig. 3 depicts a lateral view of the cerebral hemisphere of a rhesus monkey; the figure indicates the boundaries of several cortical visual areas as we now conceive them. Striate cortex is situated at the posterior pole (far left) of the hemisphere, and visual information from this area is distributed (directly and/or indirectly) to more than 20 extrastriate visual areas in nearby cortex of the occipital, temporal and parietal lobes (reviewed by Van Essen 1985, Felleman & Van Essen 1991).

Several of the extrastriate areas appear to be specialized for processing specific sorts of visual information, but the best example of functional specialization is an extrastriate pathway comprising several visual areas that preferentially analyses visual motion information (Maunsell & Newsome 1987). This pathway was originally linked to motion processing because a large majority of its neurons were found to be directionally selective in the same manner described above for cells in layer 4B of striate cortex (Zeki 1974, Van Essen et al 1981). The best studied area of the motion pathway is the middle temporal area (MT, or V5), which is situated on the posterior bank of the superior temporal sulcus (this sulcus has been 'opened' in Fig. 3 so that MT can be visualized). Fig. 4 shows that MT has a columnar structure for direction of motion similar to that in striate cortex for contour orientation (Albright et al 1984). Thus, a microelectrode that passes vertically through MT typically encounters a sequence of direction selective neurons responding optimally to the same direction of motion. If the electrode passes tangentially through MT, the direction of motion preferred by single neurons changes systematically as the electrode moves from column to column.

The columnar organization in MT allows one to position a microelectrode within a directionally specific column of neurons by advancing the electrode in small steps, recording the responses of clusters of neurons at each step and noting the points of transition from one preferred direction of motion to another. When the electrode is positioned properly within a column, surrounding neurons can be stimulated selectively using weak current pulses (10 μA) whose spread within the cortex is limited to dimensions approximating those of a cortical column (Stoney et al 1968). If a monkey's perception of motion direction is based on the outputs of such neurons, one would expect microstimulation to cause the monkey to perceive motion in the direction encoded by the stimulated neurons.

Microstimulation of the middle temporal area

To examine the effects on perceptual performance of applying microstimulation in MT, we trained several monkeys on a direction discrimination task using operant conditioning techniques. During experimental sessions, a monkey sat in a primate chair and viewed computer-generated visual stimuli presented on a TV screen directly in front of it. The visual stimuli were flickering random dot patterns designed to activate direction selective neurons in the brain. The random dot display could take several forms in which the strength of the motion

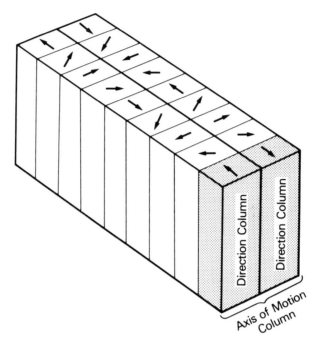

FIG. 4. An idealized diagram of the columnar structure of the middle temporal area (MT) taken from the work of Albright et al (1984). The diagram illustrates the pattern of direction columns within a slab of cortex in MT. Neurons in each column respond optimally to motion in a particular direction, and the preferred direction of motion shifts systematically from column to column as shown by the small arrows at the top of each column. A complete set of direction columns, encompassing all possible directions of motion, occupies 1–2 mm of cortex. Adjacent columns in MT may sometimes have *opposite* preferred directions of motion. In order to introduce a directionally specific signal into the cortical circuitry, therefore, one must restrict electrical stimulating current as closely as possible to a single column. Reprinted with permission from Albright et al (1984).

signal in the display was varied. At one extreme, the direction of motion of individual dots was entirely random and there was no coherent motion signal in the display; this form of the display looks like the visual noise on a domestic television tuned between stations. Coherent motion can be introduced to the display by specifying a small proportion of the dots to move in a particular direction while the remaining dots continue to move randomly. In this form, the entire display appears to drift in the direction of the coherent motion signal. If the percentage of dots in coherent motion is low, the global motion percept is weak and its direction of motion is frequently identified incorrectly. As the percentage of dots in coherent motion increases, the percept becomes stronger and its direction of motion is easily identified. Monkeys typically perform as well as humans at discriminating the direction of motion in the display. This stimulus is ideal for our purposes, because the effects of microstimulation on directional judgements are most obvious when the monkey attempts to discriminate a weak motion signal whose direction is uncertain.

Our experimental paradigm is illustrated in Fig. 5A. On an individual trial, the monkey was required to fix its gaze on a small point of light (FP) while it viewed the random dot display for one second. In the present experiments, the coherent motion signal could occur in any of eight directions equally spaced around the clock at 45° intervals. The dot display was presented within a circular aperture (solid circle in Fig. 5A) that was superimposed on the region of the visual field analysed by neurons at the stimulation site. Thus, the monkey attended eccentrically to the display while maintaining his gaze on the fixation point. At the end of the one second viewing interval, the monkey reported the direction of the coherent motion signal by moving his eyes from the fixation point to one of eight light-emitting diodes (target LEDs) that corresponded to the eight possible directions of motion. The monkey sat within a magnetic search coil apparatus that provided a precise measure of eye position throughout the experiment. Correct answers were detected by the computer and reinforced with a liquid reward; incorrect answers were punished by a brief time-out period between trials. The reward contingencies were the same whether or not microstimulation was applied on a given trial.

We obtained data in blocks of trials in which motion occurred with equal probability in any of the eight directions and over a range of signal strengths (percentage of dots in coherent motion). All trial conditions were presented in random order; the monkey had no basis for predicting the direction or strength of the motion signal on a given trial. Microstimulation was applied on half the trials for each condition (chosen randomly), and the stimulating pulses (10 μA, 200 Hz, biphasic pulses) began and ended simultaneously with the onset and offset, respectively, of the random dot display. In this manner, we attempted to introduce a directionally specific signal into the cortical circuitry that would influence the monkey's perceptual judgements in a predictable way. We assessed the influence of microstimulation by comparing the monkey's choices on 'stimulated' versus 'non-stimulated' trials. (Detailed descriptions of the visual stimuli and our physiological and behavioural methods can be found in prior publications from this laboratory: Newsome & Pare 1988, Salzman et al 1992.)

Figs 5B and 5C illustrate data from one experiment. The polar plot in Fig. 5B shows the visual responses recorded from neurons near the electrode tip before the stimulation experiment began. The visual stimuli in this phase of the experiment were random dot patterns with a maximum strength motion signal (all dots moving coherently) that moved across the receptive field in each of eight possible directions. The angle of each data point with respect to the centre of the polar plot indicates the direction of motion of the visual stimulus. The distance of each data point from the centre of the polar plot shows the intensity

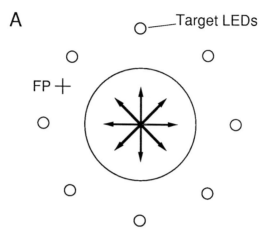

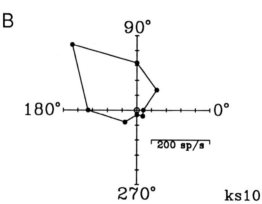

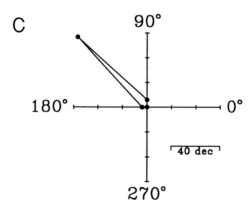

of the neural response recorded for that direction of motion. Thus the 'tuning curve' illustrated in Fig. 5B shows that the electrode was positioned within a group of directionally selective neurons whose preferred direction was up and to the left (135° by laboratory convention). This tuning curve, like those of most MT neurons, was somewhat broad since the neurons also responded well to adjacent directions of motion on either side of the preferred direction.

Fig. 5C illustrates the behavioural data obtained during the microstimulation phase of the experiment. Because we were primarily interested in learning how microstimulation *changes* the pattern of choices made on the direction discrimination task, we subtracted the number of choices made in favour of each direction of motion during non-stimulated trials from the number of choices made for the corresponding direction of motion during stimulated trials. Positive differences from this subtraction reveal the directions that the monkey chose more frequently as a result of microstimulation, and these positive differences are illustrated as a function of direction in the polar plot of Fig. 5C. In this experiment, microstimulation elicited a massive increase in decisions favouring motion at 135°, but little or no increase in favour of any other direction. Two aspects of the data in Fig. 5C are particularly noteworthy: (1) the preferred direction of the 'behavioural tuning curve' corresponds closely to the preferred direction of the visual tuning curve in Fig. 5B, and (2) the width of the behavioural tuning curve is much narrower than the width of the visual tuning curve. Both of these results are typical of the data obtained in 25 other experiments in which microstimulation yielded substantial effects on the monkey's behaviour in the eight-choice task (Salzman & Newsome 1991).

FIG. 5.   The results of a recording and microstimulation experiment in the middle temporal area (MT). (A) Methods employed in the microstimulation experiment. The monkey fixated a point of light (FP) and motion was presented in one of eight possible directions (arrows) within an eccentric aperture (large circle). The aperture was positioned so as to cover the portion of visual space analysed by neurons in the stimulated column in MT. The monkey viewed the dot pattern for one second, then revealed its judgement of the direction of coherent motion by making a quick eye movement to one of eight light-emitting diodes (Target LEDs) corresponding to the eight possible directions of motion. (B) Multi-unit recording of visual responses from a directional column in MT. The diagram is a polar plot showing the intensity of response (in total spikes) as a function of the direction of motion of the visual stimulus. This cluster of neurons responded optimally to motion up and to the left (135°), but robust responses occurred for motion at 90° and 180° as well. (C) The results of electrically stimulating the column for which the visual responses are illustrated in panel B. The polar plot indicates the number of choices made by the monkey as a function of direction. The number of choices plotted for each direction is the *positive difference* between the number of choices made on stimulated trials and the number of choices made on non-stimulated trials. Negative differences are not shown. Twenty trials were presented in each of eight directions for both the stimulated and non-stimulated conditions (320 trials total). Microstimulation resulted in an increase of 80 choices toward the LED at 135°, corresponding nicely to the preferred direction of neurons at the stimulation site (panel B).

The consistent correspondence in preferred direction between the two tuning curves shows that the microstimulation-induced changes in the choices made by the monkey can be *predicted* from the visual tuning properties of the stimulated neurons. Thus, microstimulation introduces a directional signal into the cortical circuitry that is interpreted in a meaningful fashion by the monkey as it performs the discrimination task. The disparity in the bandwidths of the two tuning curves is also interesting. The monkey's behaviour suggests that it has access to a very precise directional signal that is computed from the activity of broadly tuned MT neurons. Neurophysiologists investigating motor systems have proposed population models in which precise movements of the eyes and limbs can emerge from the collective activity of broadly tuned neurons in motor regions of the brain (Georgopoulos 1990, McIlwain 1991). A similar population coding strategy for visual motion may occur in MT.

Concluding remarks

The primary significance of these results is that they establish a causal relationship between the activity of direction selective neurons in the cortex and a monkey's perceptual decisions on a direction discrimination task. Clearly, our success in this particular experiment raises the hope that similar links between physiology and performance can be established for other classes of cortical neurons such as those selective for orientation and colour. Our experimental approach, which combines multi-unit physiological recording, electrical microstimulation and an appropriate psychophysical task, may be applicable wherever neurons with similar physiological properties are clustered together in columns or patches within the cortex. This arrangement permits one to stimulate simultaneously enough neurons to elicit behavioural effects without sacrificing functional specificity. Ultimately, however, more sophisticated approaches will be required to identify the neural substrates for complex perceptual capacities that require simultaneous modulation of activity in large numbers of circuits.

Our experiments are similar in spirit to the brain stimulation studies of pioneering investigators like Penfield, Brindley and Dobelle, who established the principle that subjective visual sensations can be elicited by electrical activation of neural tissue within the visual cortex. The present study extends this principle significantly by showing that a specific aspect of perceptual performance can be linked empirically to activity within physiologically specialized circuits. These circuits, though small and intricately organized, can be accessed and manipulated with modern neurophysiological techniques, and the perceptual consequences of this manipulation can be measured quantitatively.

A major distinction between the earlier studies and our own is the difference in experimental subjects. Whereas human subjects can report what they see in a reasonably direct manner (through language), our inferences concerning the monkey's visual experience are less certain. It remains possible, for example, that electrical microstimulation of MT influences what the monkey *decides* on a given trial without influencing what it *sees*. Several aspects of our results, which are beyond the scope of the present publication, suggest that the primary effect of microstimulation in MT is to affect the sensory representation of the stimulus rather than the 'decision process' which presumably operates at a higher level of cortical processing (Salzman et al 1992). Thus, our results are highly suggestive of a causal link between neural activity in a physiologically classified set of neurons and a particular mental process (the perception of motion), but data confirming this link cannot be obtained until equivalent experiments can be carried out in human subjects.

While our efforts are directed towards understanding the neural mechanisms underlying visual perception, other neurophysiologists are producing exciting insights into the neural substrates of cognitive functions such as memory, attention and motor planning (e.g. Moran & Desimone 1985, Miyashita & Chang 1988, Georgopoulos et al 1989, Barash et al 1991, Corbetta et al 1991, Maunsell et al 1991, Miller et al 1991). Such 'bottom-up' approaches to cognitive function will complement and extend the 'top-down' approaches of cognitive psychologists and philosophers. Ultimately, this combination of efforts may provide a clearer understanding of the self-aware and reflective mental state that we refer to as consciousness. As will be clear from other papers in this volume, it is arguable whether our most incisive approaches and our best efforts will ever yield a completely satisfactory account of our own conscious states. Nevertheless, it seems both a prudent and enjoyable goal to push these approaches as far as they will take us.

Acknowledgements

We are grateful to Judy Stein for excellent technical assistance and to Drs K. H. Britten and M. N. Shadlen for helpful discussion during the course of the experiments. We also thank Dr J. H. R. Maunsell for providing the updated diagram of cortical visual areas used in Fig. 3. The work was supported by the National Eye Institute (EY 5603) and by a Medical Student Training Fellowship from the Howard Hughes Medical Institute.

References

Albright TD, Desimone R, Gross CG 1984 Columnar organization of directionally selective cells in visual area MT of macaques. J Neurophysiol 51:16–31

Barash S, Bracewell RM, Fogassi L, Gnadt JW, Andersen RA 1991 Saccade-related activity in the lateral intraparietal area: I. Temporal properties; comparison with area 7a. J Neurophysiol 66:1095–1108

Brindley GS, Lewin WS 1968 The sensations produced by electrical stimulation of the visual cortex. J Physiol 196:479–493

Corbetta M, Miezin F, Dobmeyer S, Schulman G, Petersen S 1991 Selective and divided attention during visual discriminations of shape, color, and speed: functional anatomy by positron emission tomography. J Neurosci 11:2383–2402

Dobelle WH, Mladejovsky MG 1974 Phosphenes produced by electrical stimulation of human occipital cortex, and their application to the development of a prosthesis for the blind. J Physiol 243:553–576

Felleman D, Van Essen D 1991 Distributed hierarchical processing in the primate cerebral cortex. Cortex 1:1–47

Georgopoulos A 1990 Neural coding of the direction of reaching and a comparison with saccadic eye movements. Cold Spring Harbor Symp Quant Biol 55:849–859

Georgopoulos A, Lurito J, Petrides M, Schwartz A, Massey J 1989 Mental rotation of the neuronal population vector. Science (Wash DC) 243:234–243

Hubel D 1988 Eye, brain and vision. WH Freeman, Oxford (Sci Am Lib, NY)

Livingstone MS, Hubel DH 1984 Anatomy and physiology of a color system in the primate visual cortex. J Neurosci 4:309–356

Maunsell JHR, Sclar G, Nealey TA, DePriest DD 1991 Extraretinal representations in area V4 in the macaque monkey. Visual Neurosci 7:561–573

Maunsell JHR, Newsome WT 1987 Visual processing in monkey extrastriate cortex. Annu Rev Neurosci 10:363–401

McIlwain J 1991 Distributed spatial coding in the superior colliculus: a review. Visual Neurosci 6:3–14

Miller E, Li L, Desimone R 1991 A neural mechanism for working and recognition memory in inferior temporal cortex. Science (Wash DC) 254:1377–1379

Miyashita Y, Chang H 1988 Neuronal correlate of pictorial short-term memory in the primate temporal cortex. Nature 331:68–70

Moran J, Desimone R 1985 Selective attention gates visual processing in the extrastriate cortex. Science (Wash DC) 229:782–784

Newsome WT, Pare EB 1988 A selective impairment of motion perception following lesions of the middle temporal visual area (MT). J Neurosci 8:2201–2211

Penfield W, Perot P 1963 The brain's record of auditory and visual experience. Brain 86:596–696

Salzman C, Newsome W 1991 Microstimulation of MT during an eight-alternative motion discrimination: directional tuning of the behavioral effect. Soc Neurosci Abstr 17:525

Salzman CD, Murasugi CM, Britten KH, Newsome WT 1992 Microstimulation in visual area MT: effects on direction discrimination performance. J Neurosci 12:2331–2355

Stoney SD Jr, Thompson WD, Asanuma H 1968 Excitation of pyramidal tract cells by intracortical microstimulation: effective extent of stimulating current. J Neurophysiol 31:659–669

Van Essen DC 1985 Functional organization of primate visual cortex. In: Peters A, Jones EG (ed) Cerebral cortex. Plenum Publishing Corporation, New York, p 259–329

Van Essen DC, Maunsell JHR, Bixby JL 1981 The middle temporal visual area in the macaque: myeloarchitecture, connections, functional properties and topographic representation. J Comp Neurol 199:293–326

Zeki SM 1974 Functional organization of a visual area in the posterior bank of the superior temporal sulcus of the rhesus monkey. J Physiol 236:549–573

DISCUSSION

Marcel: I would like to describe one patient, the Munich patient, in whom we know the only damage is in MT and V5. That patient does not see movement; she sees 'a series of stills'. Secondly, if you do selective attention experiments, where normal people benefit from segmentation by perceived movement, this patient does not benefit from that (McLeod et al 1989). But, if you throw a ball, she will catch it. So it does look as though, for the human, MT is giving phenomenal movement and that on which judgements are based, but actions which are direction sensitive, in the sense of intercepting a ball, can be performed in the absence of a functional MT.

Newsome: Ultimately, it would be highly desirable to analyse the functional roles of MT and other visual areas by studying human patients, and I certainly pay close attention to clinical studies such as the one you mention. It is probably premature, however, to conclude that this patient has a selective ablation of MT. As I understand it, she has damage to cortical and subcortical grey matter in both hemispheres and to white matter tracts as well. The fact that her deficits appear reasonably selective for motion vision certainly suggests that her lesions involve a pathway that is analogous to the motion pathway identified in monkeys. Even in monkeys, however, this pathway is composed of several visual areas, and it is not yet clear whether the patient's lesions actually involve a homologue of macaque MT. For the present, then, I would avoid the strong conclusion that her perceptual phenomenology gives us unambiguous information about the role of MT in motion perception in humans.

Humphrey: A monkey without the striate cortex, and therefore lacking any of these motion-detecting cells in MT, can catch a moving fly. So although I would want to describe that monkey as having blindsight and not having phenomenal experience of seeing movement, it can use movement information.

Newsome: Let me add a cautionary comment concerning the interpretation of lesion experiments. While I believe that lesion experiments are very useful, we must remember that a damaged cortex may invent new ways to solve problems that are not characteristic of a normal cortex. For example, we have shown that a monkey's thresholds on our direction discrimination task were dramatically (and selectively) elevated during the first few days following a complete unilateral lesion of MT. After three weeks of practice, however, the monkey recovered nearly to pre-lesion standards, although some permanent deficit remained. To interpret this result properly, one must remember that MT is only one visual area in an extended cortical pathway that processes motion information. For example, MT sends motion-related outputs to two higher-level visual areas, the medial superior temporal area (MST) and the ventral posterior area (VP), near the juncture of the parietal and occipital lobes. Both MST and VP, however, receive additional inputs from antecedent areas on the motion pathway other than MT, mostly notably V3 and V2. Thus MT may be a critical centre for processing motion signals in the normal cortex, but in a damaged cortex MST and VP may be able to employ inputs from V2 and V3 to accomplish many tasks in a reasonably normal way. This does not mean that MT plays only a minor role in normal motion vision; rather, it indicates that damaged cortices may be very resourceful in developing new ways to solve sensory problems.

Nick Humphrey has described a most interesting case (p 160), that of the monkey, Helen, who has a complete lesion of striate cortex yet can perform many visually guided tasks in a surprisingly normal way. I understand, however, that it took this monkey many weeks, if not months, to develop these behaviours after the lesion, a period in which a great deal of reorganization could take place. In some ways, then, a visual system that has had a great deal of time to recover from a lesion may represent a novel system that informs us more about neural plasticity than about normal visual function.

Gray: In the microstimulation experiment, the stimulation was applied on half the trials and you said that the animal was not rewarded on the stimulated trials. This puzzles me, because it means that the monkey was on a 50% reinforcement schedule. Did you see any behavioural reactions on the part of the animal that would distinguish his response on trials when he was rewarded or not rewarded?

Newsome: The animal is always rewarded for a correct choice, regardless of whether it's a stimulated trial or non-stimulated trial.

Gray: When you say correct response on the stimulated trial, the stimulation on those trials is different from the display?

Newsome: That's right. We rewarded him for detecting what was on the display.

Gray: From his point of view, that could be non-reward for a correct response.

Newsome: You raise an important point, and I want to address it in two parts. I agree that on stimulated trials the monkey is sometimes not rewarded for what is a correct response from his point of view. We were concerned at first that such trials might essentially 'de-train' the animal and cause him to answer in unpredictable ways. This seems not to be the case, however, for a couple of reasons. First, stimulated trials are randomly interleaved with non-stimulated trials, and the monkey is therefore rewarded correctly for veridical reports on half of the trials in a block. Second, the absence of a reward for an answer that was 'correct' from the monkey's point of view is precisely what happens to animals who work on a variable reinforcement schedule, and such reinforcement schedules do not appear to exert untoward influence on an animal's choice strategy.

The second thing I want to point out is that microstimulation occasionally gives the monkey extra rewards because it causes him to answer correctly on a trial on which he might otherwise choose incorrectly (if, for example, the display contains a weak motion signal in the preferred direction of the stimulated column of cells). The frequency of these two events—stimulation causing a 'mistake' and stimulation causing a 'correct' answer—is about equal in our two-alternative, forced-choice task, and the overall reward rate remains fairly stable throughout a block of trials.

In the eight-alternative task, however, the frequency of induced mistakes is greater than the frequency of induced correct responses, and the overall reward rate on the stimulated trials decreases. We were concerned for a while that the monkey's motivation might deteriorate because of the drop in reward rate, with the unpleasant prospect that our data might be compromised. This seems not to be the case. The monkey continues to perform in a motivated fashion throughout the microstimulation experiments, and his accuracy on non-stimulated trials remains quite good. It helps in this context to realize that random performance in the eight-choice task would be 12% correct (an abysmal percentage), so the monkey has a lot to gain by performing in a motivated fashion, even if microstimulation causes a modest decrease from his usual reward rate.

Gray: Have you looked at the following two aspects of your data from this point of view? If the stimulus that you are providing is exactly like the real stimulus out there in the world, you might expect the monkey, on those trials where he's responding, from his own point of view, correctly but not getting rewarded, to show some signs of surprise. I would think in a monkey this would be easily detectable. Conversely, if the stimulation you are providing is very similar to what's coming in from the real world, but discriminably different (I suppose a more plausible hypothesis), you might expect him, over a course of trials, to begin to learn the difference. In other words, you might get a trend over trials for the monkey to perform better at the beginning than at the end. Did you see either of these two phenomena in your data?

Newsome: To answer your first question, I have not noticed subjective responses related specifically to stimulation trials. Monkeys sometimes become frustrated when they fail to get rewarded on a trial, as evidenced by a vocalization or by a sudden movement in the primate chair. (There are New York monkeys and California monkeys—New York monkeys hate to miss a single trial whereas California monkeys take a much more relaxed approach!) But I have not noticed an increase in such behaviour on stimulated trials relative to non-stimulated trials.

Your second point is an excellent one, and we were very concerned about this possibility at the beginning of the experiments. Because the monkey experiences a decrease in reward rate on stimulated trials, he might be motivated to develop a different discrimination strategy on the stimulated trials in order to return the reward rate to normal. If, as you suggest, the monkey can subjectively distinguish stimulated from non-stimulated trials, he might compensate for the effect of the stimulating current by adjusting his criterion for reporting preferred direction motion. In other words, the monkey might insist on an unusually strong sensation of motion before he is willing to report the preferred direction. If the monkey adopted such a strategy, however, we would expect our microstimulation effects to disappear with time as the monkeys became more adept at recognizing stimulated trials and applying the new strategy. We have now run three animals for 6–18 months on this experiment, and we have observed no such decrease in the frequency or quality of the stimulation effects in any of the three animals. We believe, therefore, that the monkey cannot subjectively distinguish stimulated from non-stimulated trials, and that the existence of occasional trials with incorrect reward contingencies (from the monkey's point of view) has no significant effect on our results. More generally, it is comforting to realize that large microstimulation effects are obtained despite an overall decrease in the monkey' reward rate. If the monkeys received an increased reward rate for generating the result we wanted to see, I would suspect an artifact and probably lose considerable sleep over it.

Gray: Why did you choose the stimulus parameters that you did? *A priori*, you could have equally well made the exact opposite hypothesis. You could have said: 'If I stick an electrode in the middle of the right column and I put on a burst of high frequency stimulation, I'm going to disrupt whatever firing of those neurons would count as normal, and the system rather than use information from this column would actually stop using it.' Did you choose your stimulus parameters in the light of some knowledge of the normal firing patterns of those neurons?

Newsome: The stimulation parameters were chosen carefully. We decided on 10 µA current pulses because a prior study in the motor cortex of monkeys by Asanuma and colleagues had demonstrated that pulses of this size would directly activate neurons within about 85 µm of the electrode tip (Stoney et al 1968). This distance is roughly similar to the width of a cortical column, and we therefore hoped that the 10 µA pulses would activate a small number of columns in a fairly selective manner. We selected 200 Hz as our default stimulation frequency because 200 Hz approximates the largest firing rate we have seen from MT neurons in response to our random dot patterns; we wanted a frequency that would be physiologically plausible yet give us the best chance of seeing an effect.

We have recently explored the effects of changing current amplitude and frequency. We can obtain significant microstimulation effects for current amplitudes as low as 5 µA or with stimulating frequencies as low as 25 Hz. Interestingly, the 5 µA figure compares favourably with current thresholds for eliciting muscular contraction from stimulation in motor cortex, superior colliculus or frontal eye fields; it is a very small amount of current. The fact that 25 Hz pulses can influence the monkey's choices shows that effects can be obtained with frequencies that are well within the normal range of firing rates for most MT neurons. If we stimulate with large current pulses—80 µA, for example—the directional bias in the monkey's choices disappears and a simple reduction in psychophysical sensitivity (increased thresholds) occurs. The most likely explanation for this is that large current pulses activate a large array of columns encoding divergent directions of motion. Thus, the large current pulses degrade the specificity of the directional signal within the cortex and simply impair the monkey's performance on the direction discrimination task.

Your final point is quite interesting. There seemed little reason *a priori* to believe that stimulation with an extracellular microelectrode would do much more than disrupt the normal pattern of activity within a column and thus impair the monkey's performance. Cortical columns are complex processing units whose normal workings seem to involve a delicate interplay between excitatory and inhibitory inputs of multiple origins. It is remarkable to me that our relatively crude intervention with a single stimulating electrode can have large and coherent effects on the animal's behaviour. Perhaps a motor physiologist would tell us that all of this is old hat—that there is no more reason to be surprised at this result than there is to be surprised that single muscles twitch in response to microstimulation of motor cortex. But I am surprised anyway. In this context, it is probably important to remember that not all of our experiments yield positive results; we probably have about a 60% success rate overall. It may be that some of the failures result from the fact that the microstimulation sometimes shuts down the outputs from a column, perhaps by activating inhibitory circuits, rather than exciting it.

Harnad: What about selective inhibition by stimulating the MT column in one direction while the sensory stimulus is in the opposite direction?

Newsome: That situation is built into the task I described. Motion can appear in any of eight different directions and we apply stimulation to a single column during each condition. At some time during the experiment, therefore, visual stimulus motion is going downward while we are stimulating a column that signals upward motion. This creates the condition for a very interesting experiment in which we attempt to 'null' the directional signal created by stimulation of the 'up' column by gradually adding a stronger downwards signal (i.e. more correlated dots) to the visual stimulus until the monkey acts as if no motion at all is present in the stimulus (chooses either direction with equal probability). This allows us to quantify the strength of the microstimulation-induced signal by expressing its worth in units of the visual stimulus—percent correlated dots. In our largest effects, microstimulation can be 'worth' 50–100% correlated dots, an intensity that is well above the psychophysical threshold for discriminating motion direction. For many experiments, however, microstimulation is 'worth' only 3–7% correlated dots, a value that is near or sometimes below the psychophysical threshold.

Marcel: Do you observe streaming effects? You are saying that a receptive field detects dots going in non-coherent directions and in some way sums the effect to determine which way it responds. But when we consciously see the moving dots, we are aware of streams. I see a stream of dots going one way and a stream of dots going another way. It's not that I see the sum of the different streams as being movement in a particular direction, I see movement in different directions. The interesting point is: do I see movements in two different directions or do I see movement in one direction on a background, i.e. is there a figure–ground effect?

Newsome: That is an important question, but I don't know the answer to it. The monkey cannot describe to me what he sees, and I therefore don't know what it is 'like' to be the animal and be stimulated.

Marcel: Alan Cowey has proposed ways of asking monkeys, for some things, a 'what it's like' question. One example is to use the animal's choice of a reinforcement schedule; for example, to ask whether a monkey has blindsight or not you allow the monkey a choice. You train the monkey such that, if it makes no choice whatsoever it will get 75% reward. If the monkey chooses correctly, it will get 100%; if it chooses incorrectly it gets 50%.

The question is whether the monkey is experiencing something or not. The monkey can choose on the basis of how confident it is that it is seeing something, or it can choose just to receive a reward where it doesn't have to base a choice on a visual discrimination.

Newsome: There may be some approaches along those lines that we should think about. Ultimately, though, I am very sceptical about our ability to know what a monkey's internal sensory experiences are like, especially ones that are caused by 'unnatural' intervention such as an experimenter's electrode. The most satisfactory approach would be to side-step this problem by doing similar experiments in humans. If one could reproduce the behavioural result in a human, and the human in addition responded, 'By golly, I see motion upward when you stimulate', the thorniest difficulties of subjectivity would be circumvented to my satisfaction. This is not altogether a pipe dream, because electrical stimulation experiments are sometimes done with the cooperation of conscious humans who are undergoing surgery for treatment of epilepsy or other neurological conditions. I would want to have a very good idea where MT is in a human before trying such an experiment, however.

Having expressed my reservations, I will say that I believe the monkey probably experiences a sensation of motion during large stimulation effects. Perhaps the best way to think about this is to consider a perceptual illusion called the motion after-effect or waterfall illusion. If you stare at a waterfall for 30 seconds or so and then look at the cliff face to the side of the water, you get a compelling sensation that the cliff face is moving upward at a slow rate. This occurs even though you know cognitively that the cliff cannot possibly be moving. This is a very revealing observation because it shows that motion can be computed independently in the brain and, in essence, 'assigned' to objects in the environment that may not be moving at all. I suspect that something akin to this may be going on when we stimulate MT. The monkey may 'see' motion by attributing this internal sensation to the dots on the screen. If this is the case, that subjects undergoing microstimulation actually see coherent motion, I would feel justified in saying the brain pathway being stimulated plays an important role in conscious awareness.

Kinsbourne: When you stimulate the columns, do you get eye movement?

Newsome: No, microstimulation in MT seems to have no direct effect on motor circuits that control eye movements. If we apply microstimulation during the intertrial interval (for one second at 200 Hz, just as we do during the actual experiments), we do not elicit eye movements of any kind—saccadic, pursuit or other. In the context of our experimental paradigm, of course, microstimulation in MT ultimately affects oculomotor neurons, because the monkey must report the outcome of his decision with an eye movement, but that influence is indirect. In order for microstimulation in MT to affect the oculomotor system, the monkey must be performing the experimental task.

Kinsbourne: If you are getting phenomenal movement in one direction and maintain it, why would you not get optic nystagmus?

Newsome: We don't see optokinetic nystagmus in the normal experimental situation or during microstimulation. Remember that the monkey is required to fixate a stationary point and attend to the motion stimulus at a restricted peripheral location. If the motion stimulus is presented over the fovea, we do see optikinetic nystagmus, but when it is presented peripherally we generally do not.

Kinsbourne: You could set the experiment up so that the monkey should 'see' streaming in one direction; then you should get optokinetic nystagmus.

Harnad: This point is again related to hermeneutics. The reason I left the field of laterality (Harnad et al 1977) was the disproportionate importance assigned in that field to what look like trivial data. Consider, for example, a 50 ms speed advantage that may occur when a stimulus is presented in the left rather than the right visual field in some perceptual task. If the same 50 ms advantage had instead been exhibited in the running speed of one group of kids compared to another, the effect would rightly be dismissed as trivial. But when such differences can be annointed with the mystique of being related to 'the brain' in some way (even something as vague as being on the left or the right), their significance and explanatory power are immediately elevated by interpretations (in terms of grand left-brain/right-brain theories) vastly out of proportion to their actual empirical content.

By way of analogy, suppose that instead of being recorded from the brain, Bill Newsome's findings had been read off an oscilloscope stuck into a simple artificial optical recognition system that was capable only of detecting orientation; and suppose one found in this system a unit that was selectively responsive in just the way Bill has described. One would not feel one had made an inroad on the mind–body problem. So why should one feel that one has done so when one happens to find this in the brain?

I am not suggesting that Bill's finding is trivial *as neurophysiology* (as some of the laterality findings are). But it certainly does not seem to cast any new conceptual light on the mind–body problem along the lines Tom Nagel has here expressed optimism about eventually achieving, as we get closer to scientific Utopia.

Newsome: I don't know, I'm asking you! This is one reason I would like to do these experiments in humans. If the human reported, 'I see motion' and it impinged upon their conscious awareness and their subjective experience of who they are, then I would feel I had done something to affect the stream of awareness that we call 'mind'.

Nagel: But it must have some effect on the experience. Wouldn't the question be: what are the options? I suppose the stimulation could affect the monkey's choices, not by affecting its visual experience but by somehow affecting, as it were, the inference it makes about what is actually going on from its visual experience. Are you sceptical that these results show that the stimulation affects the monkey's experience at all?

Newsome: The stimulation certainly affects the monkey's behaviour; it affects the choices he makes very dramatically. I don't know whether the monkey feels that it saw up and reported up but we didn't reward him.

Searle: It seems to me, Bill, that you have some legitimate hesitations and I think that's commendable. But you are perhaps over-cautious with some forms of scepticism. Let me give a blunt commonsense, philosophical answer to your question. We have pretty good evidence that it's because of the impact of the stuff that comes in through the eyeball on the rest of the brain that we have visual experiences at all. We also have pretty good evidence that the visual cortex plays a special role in the production of visual experience. So I think you are too cautious, if you suppose that you really don't know anything about the vision of the monkey on the basis of this research. I think the research is terrific and I think it is exactly the kind of thing we need to know in order to understand vision.

But there are some dangers. The greatest danger is, roughly speaking, that we may be committing a combination of the homunculus fallacy and the atomistic fallacy. It's ironic that something very like this discussion took place in this very room when we had a Ciba Foundation symposium on Brain and Mind in 1978. Creutzfeldt gave a display of the pattern of firings exhibited by the Hubel–Wiesel cells in the visual cortex of a bird. When he projected a picture on the screen of the pattern of individual neurons that were firing, the atomistic points on the screen made a pattern that he thought was a representation of the bird's visual experience. It seems to me that he was making two fallacies. One was the fallacy of supposing that the pattern of individual nerve firings adds up to a picture that is seen. The second was the tacit assumption that there must be some little homunculus inside the brain that looks at this pattern of neural firings. Those are very tempting fallacies, but I don't think you are making either of them. So, if we can avoid these fallacies, what is the next step? Obviously, we want more research of the type that you are doing, but the next hard question is: how does the brain integrate all of this into a conscious visual experience?

Newsome: 'All of this' meaning . . .?

Searle: All the stuff that comes in through the lateral geniculate nucleus to the cortex. Furthermore, how does the rest of the information in the cortex get into visual experience? The fascinating thing about vision is that you don't just see a body moving but, for example, you might see a Mercedes 300 driving down Portland Place. That is, in fact, how I would characteristically see something. But I don't have a special Mercedes detector in my brain. If I don't have a Mercedes detector and yet I can see a Mercedes, there must be a whole lot of information elsewhere in my brain that is being used directly in the formation of visual experiences.

Newsome: I agree that the problem of integration is one of the most important and difficult ones facing visual neuroscience. This, however, is not the problem being addressed in our experiments, and we have done everything possible to avoid that problem. We have designed the task so that the monkey can perform it simply by using information that is encoded in those columns in MT. By using a stochastic stimulus, we tried to eliminate any extraneous features or position cues that might provide the monkey with an alternate strategy for solving the problem. Thus, we are really trying to tap directly into the brain mechanisms that 'do' motion. Now, if we changed the task so that the monkey was required to discriminate a red square moving upward from a green triangle moving leftward, all hell would break loose. Then we would have an integration problem. While we are making no attempt to address this problem in our current experiments, I certainly agree that a satisfactory visual science will ultimately require a solution to the problem.

Gazzaniga: If you make a microlesion in the cell that you are affecting, my guess is that you would not see a raised threshold in that part of the visual field. This would suggest that your stimulation is sending output to some other critical structure that's actually doing the computation that's assisting discrimination.

Newsome: I suspect that a microlesion of the column we are stimulating might raise thresholds very transiently, but I don't even know whether the impairment would last long enough for us to measure it well. I believe there exist other columns in MT and other visual areas as well that can pick up the load if any single column or group of columns is damaged (we actually have evidence to this effect from MT lesion experiments).

Certainly, information must emerge from MT and affect other structures in order for stimulation in MT to influence behaviour, and we have little idea at present how large that network of affected structures might be. The question is important because its answer would ultimately include a description of the processes by which sensory signals emerge from MT, decisions are made regarding the direction of motion, and operant responses (eye movements in our case) are programmed and executed. We think loosely about decision processes in the following fashion. If a monkey is performing an up versus down discrimination, a measurement of neuronal activity is made from a group of 'up' columns and a group of 'down' columns. These two measurements are compared and the decision is made in favour of the direction yielding the largest signal. An appropriate operant response is then planned and executed.

Interestingly, we know a lot now about the brain centres that encode direction of motion and about the brain centres that plan and programme saccadic eye movements. The real mystery is the decision process between the two that links sensation to action. In some sense then, that may be the most important part of the network you are asking about—this downstream comparator that selects one of the directional signals and links it in an appropriate manner to a motor response. This machinery must lie somewhere between MT and the oculomotor system, and we know roughly the anatomy linking the two. By recording in these linking structures while the monkey performs the discrimination task, we may be able to get some hints about the physiological structure of the decision process. This is perhaps the most important sequel to the present experiments.

Kihlstrom: How do you think that your results contribute more than the inferences that can be drawn from the earlier Hubel & Wiesel type of experiments?

Newsome: I would say that the key contribution of our experiments is to establish causality. We not only show that a certain type of neuron is impressively correlated with a particular aspect of perceptual performance, but that manipulation of that type of neuron *causes* predictable changes in performance.

Kihlstrom: Do you have any qualms about the Hubel & Wiesel experiments that you are still not satisifed about on the basis of your present experiment?

Newsome: Sure. Establishing an empirical link between direction selectivity and motion vision does not accomplish the same for orientation selectivity and form vision. For years, physiological (and, increasingly, computational) studies have been based on presumed connections between cortical cell types and perceptual experience. In principle, our experimental approach can be extended to these other cell types as well.

Humphrey: I would like to describe a similar situation that arose in ethology in relation to the dance of bees. Von Frisch originally noticed the correlation between the speed of waggling and the distance of the food source from the hive. It was assumed that this information was being used in a communicative way. Then some critics said that although there is a correlation, the bees don't use this information, they actually use other cues. It wasn't until people made a little mechanical bee that could waggle, and showed that they could manipulate the foraging behaviour of other bees which had observed it, that people finally became convinced that Von Frisch's conjecture is correct.

I think exactly the same thing arises with the results of Hubel & Wiesel. It looked as though all the information was there in the selective responses of individual cells, then people like Fergus Campbell said: 'The information is there, but it's not being used'. Experiments like Bill Newsome's really do suggest that the information is being used. This is very important.

Newsome: The information is indeed being used and in a manner that fits our intuition. After seeing these data for the first time, Torsten Wiesel commented to me, 'It is a lovely experiment, but I could have told you the answer before you did it'!

Searle: This is the answer to Stevan Harnad's scepticism. Of course, you can build an artificial system that will detect movement. You can, for example, put a unit into the system that is sensitive to lateral motion. That shows that it is *possible* that the brain works this way. Bill Newsome has given us good evidence that there is a part of the system that actually *is* responsive in the way he describes.

Marcel: If you don't have visual cortex on one side, it does not prevent you from having visual experience in the corresponding area of experienced visual field. That doesn't mean that area doesn't play a part in visual experience, it just means it's not necessary. There are visual hallucinations in cortically blind subjects where you know from the evoked potential of the cortex and from scanning that that area of cortex is dead. This is very important for interpretations of the sort that you are interested in—of what the functional role is, at least in experience, for certain areas of cortex.

Boden: John Searle asked earlier, what would it be like to understand the mind–body relation? He said it would be to have a neurophysiological theory which told us that when such and such happened in the brain, something must go on in the mind. What is the nature of this 'must'? And what sorts of things could offer it to us? Clearly, a mere correlation isn't enough. Descartes himself would have said that when you have the experience of something occurring in a certain way, there's something happening in your brain different from when you experience something occurring in a different way. If by 'must', you mean 100% reliable regularity, Descartes would have been perfectly willing to say 'must', but he wouldn't have said it was in any sense intelligible.

There needs to be some sort of mapping, not just temporal correlations of events in the two spheres, but some sort of shared abstract logical structure, like in Bill Newsome's columns in the visual cortex. Not only are the physical motion directions apparently stored in particular groups of cells in the brain, but the relationships between the different orientations and the cells in this part of the brain are themselves mapped in a very systematic way. If you have that sort of abstract relationship, as well as a mere correlation—these cells fire when we see that—then perhaps you are nearer to something which one might call an intelligible 'must', rather than what you might call a brute fact 'must', with which Descartes would have been perfectly happy.

As another example, Crick & Koch (1990) in their paper about consciousness talked about the binding problem with respect to vision. Their theory was that what makes us bind different visually discriminable properties to one and the same thing, and what makes us have a conscious percept in which these things are in some sense unified, is that the different cell assemblies in the parts of the brain which independently respond to these particular properties come to oscillate together. Are they just saying something that would in no way have impressed or surprised Descartes? Or are they trying to say something more than that? Something with the same sort of logic Descartes himself used when he said that unity of consciousness and the senses and so forth must be in the pineal gland because it is in the centre of the body, it isn't doubled, etc. If we are ever to get this intelligible 'must' in our theory, it will have to be via some shared abstract structural properties of that sort, rather than mere correlation.

Gray: You are absolutely right. Can I set the standard one notch higher? In a sense, as Max Velmans has emphasized, we have the problem of putting together two sides of the dual aspect problem. We could call this putting together the third- and first-person perspectives. I much prefer the way John Searle approaches the problem—that is, putting together the neurophysiology on the one hand and the conscious experience on the other.

The big example we have of a dual-aspect theory that works is the duality of particle and wave in quantum mechanics. That is an abstract theory which not only works and produces an 'intelligible must', but comes up with a whole lot of predictions that could not have been made without the theory. The problem we face at the moment, in not having such a theory of consciousness, is that we can work only at the level of refining these kinds of correlations. Experimentally, we have gone beyond correlations—the beauty of Bill Newsome's experiment, which impresses me enormously, is precisely that it does go beyond correlation and into causation. But even given causation in experimental terms, there is still only the brute fact of being able to say: action here produces conscious experience of apparent motion, and action somewhere else produces apparent colour experience or whatever, and action in yet a third place, in the superior colliculus or in the optic tectum, has nothing that looks like a conscious correlate. The gathering of these kinds of data must be a major empirical issue for a long time to come. From them, one supposes that the conditions will gradually emerge which will facilitate the creation of the kind of theory that Margaret Boden has just been talking about.

Humphrey: I think the example you have just given is a very unfortunate one. The wave and particle aspects of matter are not logically isomorphic in the way that Margaret Boden seems to be asking for. As I understand, she wants a theory which says that the physiology has certain logical abstract properties and the phenomenology has the same properties, therefore they go together. That would be wonderful and would get towards what Tom Nagel describes as an objective phenomenology. But the example you gave, Jeffrey, of dual aspects where matter can be both wave and particle at the same time, doesn't seem to involve any such isomorphism. It just happens to be a brute fact of nature.

Harnad: In any case, puzzles are not resolved by further puzzles. The strength of quantum mechanics is the broad range of empirical data it successfully predicts and explains. The quantum puzzles, on the other hand, are still a source of frustration and perplexity to most physicists (and philosophers) who give them any thought. The puzzles are certainly not the triumphant aspect of quantum mechanics. Rather, one reluctantly reconciles oneself with them in exchange for quantum mechanics' enormous empirical power. Physicists would no doubt be delighted to jettison all the quantum puzzles (duality, complementarity, uncertainty) for a Grand Unified Theory with all the power of quantum mechanics but none of its paradoxes. Those who would like to import those paradoxes alone to another field are trading in the weaknesses of quantum mechanics rather than its strengths.

Nagel: Margaret Boden's suggestion that the discovery of isomorphisms is an essential step on the route to intelligibility must be right. But, it raises the following question. Bill Newsome's results are very specific; of course, anything one is likely to get at this stage is going to be very specific. But even something as specific as motion perception, I would think, can exist only as part of a more global visual experience. So there is always going to be a problem with the interpretation of highly specific results like this. Bill, do you feel that a large background must be assumed to make sense of the connection that you have found? Or do you think we could do it point by point and get the large, more global picture by construction out of the points? I'm prompted here by Pat Wall's more global orientation.

Newsome: This specific experiment emerged from a substantial background of work and thought about the way the visual system is organized and might function. That background, however, is not particularly arcane. With the assistance of a few diagrams on a napkin, I can explain the key concepts to an intelligent layperson in about half an hour. One must accept (at least as a working hypothesis) that the primary function of a brain is to mediate behaviour and that this task is accomplished by normal rules of cause and effect. Given this intellectual (philosophical?) commitment, everything else that led to our experiments is empirical. We have formulated no fundamentally new concepts here. We have put together several traditional physiological ideas—receptive fields, topographic maps, cortical columns, direction selectivity—in an experiment that brings them to life and validates them in a compelling fashion. The power of the experiment comes from the repeatable changes in behaviour that follow a fairly precise manipulation of a neuronal system. This is not dissimilar to the situation in molecular biology where the power of an experiment lies in the changes in the amino acid composition of a protein following manipulation of the genome. In systems neurobiology, however, the ultimate test of a linking hypothesis lies in the realm of measurable behaviour rather than in protein sequences!

Searle: Remember the bunch of lines that we see as human face (Searle, this volume, Fig. 1). The stimulus doesn't literally look like a human face. The implication is that the contribution of the brain to the visual perception is enormous. I think that is part of what Tom was getting at.

Newsome: I am fully committed to the idea that perception is a constructive process. I think the Gestalt psychologists demonstrated this well. Most of the time the brain's construction is fairly accurate and we operate well within our visual world. At other times the brain makes mistakes, as we know from various perceptual illusions. We would very much like to know how this constructive process works in physiological terms, and there are a few laboratories around the world that are actually addressing this problem. The work of Rudiger von der Heydt and Esther Peterhans on the responses of visual cortical neurons to illusory contours is one example. A satisfactory visual neuroscience must certainly account for these phenomena in the long run.

Lockwood: Could I say something about isomorphism before we lose this point? I was studying psychology at the time the early Hubel & Wiesel work was published. This established the existence of cells in the primary visual cortex that fire preferentially in response to bars and edges with a particular orientation, and certain specific directions of motion. A friend of mine, who was a philosopher, told me how marvellous he thought this work was. He said: 'That's exactly what vision feels like'. This remark struck me as a perfect statement of what I did not feel about Hubel & Wiesel's work!

The trouble with this notion of isomorphism is that it's very difficult to get a firm grasp on what kind of isomorphism is required here. There's a sense in which anything that could be regarded as holding all the information that is present in one's phenomenology could be said to be isomorphic with the phenomenology itself—there would be, after all, a systematic mapping from one to the other. But it seems to me implausible to suppose that just any such isomorphism would be good enough. Suppose that when we looked at the brain, it turned out to be a digital computer, and what corresponded to any particular phenomenological state was just a bit string. There would be one sort of bit string that tends to come up, perhaps, in the auditory cortex, another type in the visual cortex. All the information would be there. Yet this does not seem to work as an explanation of the phenomenology and the differences that are to be found within it. Appealing to different arrangements of ones and zeros does nothing whatever to render the phenomenology, and the differences within it, rationally intelligible. So not just any isomorphism will do. On the other hand, the idea of an 'intelligible' isomorphism is itself not, in our present state of understanding, a particularly intelligible concept.

Dennett: Margaret talked about the Crick & Koch paper. The reason their claim about binding leaves us unsatisfied is that in their paper they do not address the question: And then what happens? The same is true when you say, 'Suppose we discover that all this information is encoded in a bit string'. What we want to know is: And then what happens? I submit that if there is an intelligible answer to this question that shows how the information in that bit string manages to accomplish the work that has to be done as revealed in the reports and behaviour of the subject, then it becomes intelligible. The fact that it's a bit string does not disqualify it: what disqualifies it for the moment is that you don't have any answer to the question: And then what happens?

Harnad: Becomes intelligible *as what*? One of the effects of this very interesting talk is that some of the fragile alliances that had formed at this symposium have been shattered; people who thought they could make common cause are now clearly going their own ways!

When I wear my cognitive psychologist's or neuroscientist's hat, I find Bill Newsome's results very interesting, because I see them as telling me how the brain works and perhaps how to make a visual system in principle work. But if I put on a philosopher's hat, it's another story. Bill Newsome has gone 75% of the way; let's pretend he has also done the ablation study and the human study so that he has really established that this unit is necessary and sufficient in this particular mechanism for motion detection. That would be an empirical step, but it would be just a piece in a much larger puzzle, and you all agree that there are many other relevant things we need to know. One of the things Maggie Boden suggested was that it is not even enough that there should be a completed big puzzle: there even has to be isomorphism—the whole structure we eventually discover that is necessary and sufficient to do all the vision must, in addition, square with the subjective phenomenology of vision, and all the rest.

I want to question the slight epiphany that we get when we manage to capture a necessary and sufficient unit such as Bill Newsome's. I'm suggesting that our epiphany is spurious. Why should our reaction to this unit be different to our reaction to a clear non-starter, such as the computer vision system I mentioned earlier? Why do we go 'Aha' with this unit and not with a functional equivalent that has essentially the same properties, but neither aspires to be human nor resides in one? Not only do I not see any justification for an 'Aha' in the one case when it is so clearly unjustified in the other, but I don't even see anything suggesting the road leading to an 'Aha' in anything along those lines (including Maggie's isomorphisms and Dan's heterophenomenology).

Newsome: I agree. I believe our data are important from the point of view of neuroscience or cognitive psychology, but I doubt that they raise any fundamentally new questions, or answer any fundamental problems, from a philosophical point of view. When I was invited to this conference, I wanted to come because I wanted to hear what philosophers talk about at meetings of this nature. I doubted, however, whether I had anything to say that was particularly important for a philosopher to hear. I personally believe that the philosophical issues raised and addressed by our experiments are essentially the same as those raised and addressed by the work of Giles Brindley, who elicited subjective sensations of light in blind patients by stimulating visual cortex, or by the work of Wilder Penfield, who elicited organized, complex sensations by stimulating temporal cortex. The important point of those experiments was that focal activation of brain tissue can cause meaningful conscious phenomena even if the activation is achieved by artificial means. At least some conscious phenomena, then, seem to arise in a fairly direct manner from the activity of systems of neurons in the brain. If we assume for the moment that our monkeys actually 'see' motion when we stimulate MT, our experiments simply extend this principle by linking a more specific type of sensation to more precisely defined circuits within the brain.

Hopefully, this incremental approach will bring more and more of our subjective experience within the domain of empirical investigation as research continues. I must admit that I am less optimistic about obtaining really satisfying answers to other questions about sensory experience. For example, why are the subjective sensations that accompany stimulation of visual and auditory cortex so radically different? Why is it that the first cause in me the subjective quality associated with 'seeing' whereas the second cause the quality of 'hearing'? I think this is a very difficult issue and I am always embarrassed when an undergraduate or first-year medical student asks this question, because I have no good answer. Neurophysiologists tend to mumble things about labelled lines in reply to such questions because that is the best we can do, but I've never been convinced that that emperor is well clothed.

Gray: There is one further point—you are doing these experiments in a monkey. If you end up getting, as you will, evidence that is compatible with the hypothesis that the monkey perceives motion in the sense that we see motion—maybe you could show the waterfall illusion being affected by your stimulation—then we would have strong grounds to say monkeys have conscious experience. I'm not sure that you can at present demonstrate that.

Searle: The point is, Bill, philosophically, one is never satisfied until one knows exactly how it works. That's why your work is philosophically important.

References

Crick FHC, Koch C 1990 Towards a neurobiological theory of consciousness. Semin Neurosci 2:263–275

Harnad S, Doty RW, Goldstein L, Jaynes J, Krauthamer G (eds) 1977 Lateralization in the nervous system. Academic Press, New York

McLeod P, Heywood C, Driver J, Zihl J 1989 Selective deficit of visual search in moving displays after extrastriate damage. Nature 339:466–467

Searle JR 1993 The problem of consciousness. In: Experimental and theoretical studies of consciousness. Wiley, Chichester (Ciba Found Symp 174) p 61–80

Stoney SD Jr, Thompson WD, Asanuma H 1968 Excitation of pyramidal cells by intracortical microstimulation: effective extent of stimulating current. J Neurophysiol 31:659–669

Brain mechanisms and conscious experience

Michael S. Gazzaniga

Center for Neuroscience, University of California, Davis, CA 95616, USA

Abstract. The human brain enables a variety of unique mental capacities. Our special capacities for inference, personal insight into the reasons for our actions, deception, high level problem solving, for literally dozens of activities represent specialized systems that most likely reflect specialized neuronal circuits that have accumulated in our brain by selection processes over thousands of years of evolution. I believe many of these enriching capacities are not so much the advantageous computational products of a large neuropil as they are the product of a brain that has accumulated specific algorithms for adaptation. Our awareness, our consciousness of these capacities, is nothing more or less than a feeling about them. A correlate of this view is that there are many processes supporting human cognition of which we are neither aware nor conscious. When conscious appreciation or feeling is involved for a modality of sensation or action, neural pathways communicating this information must be intact, normally to the left hemisphere. This paper reviews evidence that supports this view of consciousness that distinguishes special human capacities and feelings about those capacities from the neural substrates that underlie these distinctions.

1993 Experimental and theoretical studies of consciousness. Wiley, Chichester (Ciba Foundation Symposium 174) p 247–262

The British neuroscientist, philosopher, physicist, theologian and friend, Donald M. MacKay, once commented that it is easier to understand how something works when it is not working properly. He was drawing upon his experience in the physical sciences and simply wanted to note that an engineer could decipher more quickly how something like a television worked if the picture was fluttering than if it was working normally. It is a helpful insight and one that I subscribe to. I study broken human brains. I think they can teach us a lot about that thorny topic, human consciousness.

For me, the topic of consciousness is productively approached from the neurological side. Clearing the throat, setting up formal arguments, making seemingly important distinctions between this and that, reviewing and trying to remember who said what about what before you, are all exercises that do not prepare you for seeing human patients with broken brains. The phenomenon of human consciousness as seen in patients with alterations in normal neural organization is as riveting as understanding the message is challenging. Brain scientists hope to interest philosophers in our primary observations. We also hope to avoid getting them excited about our observations for the wrong reasons—namely errors in our logic!

General background

More and more, it is time for neuroscientists to consider their field and their observations in an evolutionary context (Gazzaniga 1992). They are massively guilty of ignoring context—of ignoring the history of our species. That history, I believe, provides major clues to how our brains go about their business.

I will argue that forces of Darwinian selection established specialized circuits in our brains that are dedicated to carrying out the variety of mental functions we enjoy. These circuits reflect adaptations that were established thousands of years ago, most likely during the Stone Age. These adaptations were of cognitive mechanisms—mechanisms that allow the formation of more general hypotheses in response to environmental challenges. There is an important distinction between behavioural adaptations and cognitive adaptations (Tooby & Cosmides 1987, 1990). If our brains had merely accumulated the capacity for certain behavioural adaptations, our species would possess a dizzying array of specific capacities that could show little latitude in responding to challenges. The *sine qua non* of the human is the variation we show in response to common challenges.

The argument for specialized structures would suggest focal brain lesions or surgical interventions that disconnect one region of the brain from another might disrupt specific processing mechanisms critical to human cognition. I will illustrate this point with several examples. However, discovering that the human brain is full of specialized processors does not seem to illuminate an answer to the problem: What is consciousness?

My own view of the matter reduces to a simple truth. When all is said and done, what we mean about being conscious is that we feel about things—about capacities. Consciousness is not the capacity to see colour or shapes, or to feel pain or make inferences, interpret our actions, appreciate art and music. Those capacities reflect specialized systems in the brain that have evolved and are present as individual systems. When thinking about the phenomenon of consciousness, it is important to distinguish mental capacities which are truly wondrous and our sense of those capacities. The distinction becomes blurred and, in part, it is due to one of the specialized systems in the human brain, the interpreter module. This special left hemisphere system that provides a running account of our actions, thoughts and feelings about our specialized capacities tends to blend our actual modularity into a sensation of unity.

This view is not that different from what I take to be the view of William James. He made five points about the problem of consciousness. He felt it was subjective; it changed; it was continuous; it had 'aboutness'; and it was selective. I accept all those characteristics and propose the brain mechanisms outlined below are consistent with his view. If the human brain comprises a constellation of specialized circuits more or less dedicated to carrying out specific mental functions and if one of those systems is dedicated to interpreting the actions of the other specialized systems, then one can nearly predict the characteristics that James outlines for the nature of human consciousness as a direct consequence.

Evidence for specialized circuits

Consider the human brain. It has two halves, the left and the right. We know the left cortex is specialized for language and speech and the right has some specializations as well. Yet, each half cortex is the same size and has roughly the same number of nerve cells. The cortices are connected by a large structure called the corpus callosum. The total, linked cortical mass is assumed somehow to contribute to our unique human intelligence. What do you think would happen to your intelligence if the two half brains were divided? Would you lose half of your intelligence because the part of the brain talking to the outside world would lose half of its support staff? To answer this, consider the evidence from surgical interventions where the left brain is disconnected from the right. This procedure is called split-brain surgery and is performed in patients who suffer from epilepsy. I have been studying patients with hemispheric disconnection for years.

A cardinal feature of split-brain research is that following disconnection of the human cerebral hemispheres, the verbal IQ of the patient remains intact (Gazzaniga et al 1962, Nass & Gazzaniga 1987, Zaidel 1990) and the problem-solving capacity remains unchanged. While there can be deficits in recall capacity and on some performance measures, the overall capacity for problem solving seems unaffected. In other words, isolating essentially half of the cortex from the dominant left hemisphere causes no major change in intellectual function. This represents strong evidence that simple cortical cell number cannot be related to human intelligence.

The notion of special circuitry is supported by a vast number of observations on patients with focal brain disease as well as a host of studies from split-brain patients. For example, most patients with a disconnected right hemisphere are seriously impoverished on a variety of tasks (Gazzaniga & Smylie 1984). While the isolated right hemisphere remains superior to the isolated left hemisphere for some activities such as the recognition of upright faces, some attentional skills and perhaps also emotional processes, it is poor at problem solving and many other mental activities.

Specialized circuits for human capacities

If one accepts that the human brain has special circuits for its various mental functions, one can consider the different levels of organization within the nervous system where these circuits might appear. I shall argue that the cerebral cortex is the custodian of new circuits critical for human cognitive processes. In this light, it is commonly observed that the overall plan of the mammalian brain seems quite similar across a variety of species, particularly when one compares the primate and human brain. One of the reasons comparative studies are carried out is the belief that homologous brain structures may serve common functions in the primate and human. Yet, the human brain, quite simply, is different from the monkey brain. There are many structures that carry out different functions in the two species. Let me review work on two structures that we have studied directly and indirectly in our laboratory—the anterior commissure and the superior colliculus.

The literature on animal studies clearly shows that the anterior commissure transfers visual information between hemispheres. In cats, interocular transfer occurs via the callosum alone, whereas the anterior commissure was found to be involved in visual transfer in chimpanzees and rhesus monkeys (Gazzaniga 1966). This would suggest that the same might be true for humans. However, in humans, when the callosum is cut but the anterior commissure is spared, there is no transfer of visual information of the kind seen in the monkey and chimp (Gazzaniga 1988, Gazzaniga et al 1985). Thus, the anterior commissure, although clearly able to transfer visual information in the monkey and chimp, does not do so in the human.

The difference seen with fibre tract systems is also apparent in more nuclear structures, such as the superior colliculus. There is clear evidence from the monkey that this structure is crucially involved in the control of eye movements. Mohler & Wurtz (1977), for example, demonstrated that primates with lesions of the primary visual cortex were able to detect and direct their eyes in response to visual stimuli presented in the scotoma, the blind spot in the visual field caused by the lesion. They suggested that the superior colliculus, working alone or in complementary fashion with the visual cortex, could carry out these functions for stimuli that fell within the scotoma. Others have claimed even higher order functions are possible after such occipital lesions (Weiskrantz et al 1977, Pasik & Pasik 1971). While similar claims have been made for the human (Weiskrantz 1990), we have not succeeded in demonstrating residual function following lesions to primary visual cortex. More recently, we have carried out microperimetry of patients with occipital lesions using an image stabilizer (Wessinger et al 1991, Fendrich et al 1992). These studies have clearly shown that patients with homonymous hemianopia can have small islands of spared vision, in which there is visual function. In most of the scotoma, however, there is no visual function, as reported by Holtzman (1984). In short, when visual function is possible, there seems to be spared visual cortex. This observation was confirmed with magnetic resonance imaging. Overall, these results suggest that the spared superior colliculus in the human is not able to carry out the kinds of oculomotor functions that are possible in the monkey.

Special human circuits

If the human brain has unique organizational features and appears to have many of its major cortical surface areas specified genetically, then humans may have capacities that other primates do not. The multitudinous extra circuits in the much larger human cerebrum perform activities that other species simply cannot. One such specialization is the capacity to make voluntary facial expressions. This is a unique trait of humans that is easily accessible for study. No other animal, including the chimpanzee, can make such voluntary facial expressions.

There are a variety of beliefs about how the brain is organized to perceive and produce facial expressions. In the perceptual domain, it seems that the right hemisphere has special processes devoted to the efficient detection of upright faces (see Gazzaniga 1989). Although the left hemisphere can also perceive and recognize faces and can show superior capacities when the faces are familiar, the right hemisphere appears specialized for unfamiliar facial stimuli (Gazzaniga & Smylie 1984).

We have recently examined these and related issues in split-brain human patients. Disconnection of the two cerebral hemispheres allows the role that the corpus callosum plays in controlling voluntary and involuntary expression to be assessed. It also allows examination of the ability of each hemisphere to initiate facial expressions.

The pattern of innervation for the upper half of the face is different from that for the lower half of the face; the differences involve both central and peripheral systems. The neural mechanisms involved in voluntary facial postures are controlled by the cortical pyramidal system, while the control of spontaneous postures is managed by the extrapyramidal system (for review see Rinn 1984). This diversity of innervation is reported to be responsible for the preservation of symmetrical spontaneous facial postures in the presence of unilateral damage to motor cortex. Patients with such a lesion will show a contralateral facial droop that will resolve when smiling spontaneously. In this instance, while the pyramidal input to the facial nucleus is destroyed, the extrapyramidal input is not. It is also commonly reported that patients with extrapyramidal disease, such as Parkinson's disease, will display a masked face when at rest and look more normal when smiling to command.

We examined the capacity of each cerebral hemisphere to initiate voluntary facial postures. The results reveal marked differences in the capacities of each hemisphere, indicating that the corpus callosum plays a critical role in the normal production of voluntary symmetrical facial expressions. Examination of asymmetries in smiling to command revealed that when the command to smile was visually presented unilaterally to the left hemisphere, the right side of the mouth dramatically commenced retraction as much as 180 ms before the left side responded. When the command to smile was presented to the right hemisphere, none of the patients was able to respond. In another series of tests on patients J.W. and D.R., a drawing of a 'happy face' or a 'sad face', presented exclusively to either hemisphere, found the right hemisphere giving the correct response at a frequency no better than that obtainable by chance. On trials in which an incorrect response had been made, as in frowning to a happy face, J.W. was nonetheless able to draw a picture of the given stimulus with his left hand.

These kinds of observations emphasize the superiority of the left hemisphere in interpreting events and its dominant role in organizing responses to those events. In the present context, high level evaluative processes must be invoked to override a potentially spontaneous facial expression such as smiling. Such processes would appear to occur only in the left hemisphere, i.e. the hemisphere that appears to control voluntary expression. This sort of 'voluntary' control would appear different and involve more complex processes than those associated with adopting 'voluntary' hand or foot postures in response to a cue. Therefore, where evaluations involve more psychological aspects of a person's expressions, the left hemisphere appears dominant.

Cognitive similarity/neural similarity?

For the past few years we have been examining the brains of monozygotic twins to investigate whether monozygotic twins are more similar in cortical organization than are unrelated individuals. We first examined the corpus callosum, where we showed that this enormous fibre tract system was more similar in area and shape in monozygotic twins than in unrelated pairs (Oppenheim et al 1989). Using a new method of assessing the cortical surface areas of the human brain (Jouandet et al 1989, Loftus 1991), we have now studied the cortical surface of both male and female monozygotic twins (Thomas et al 1990, Green et al 1992, Tramo MJ et al, unpublished 1992). Such twins look alike, talk alike, behave similarly, think similarly and so on. Are their brains alike? Normally, there is great variation in the gross morphology of the brain: while all brains have a similar overall plan, they vary tremendously in the details. Some brains have bigger frontal lobes than others. The patterns of how the cortex appears, called the gyral/sulcal pattern, varies and that variation presumably reflects differences in the underlying brain organization. Is the great similarity in the overall cognitive skills of monozygotic twins due to physically more similar brains?

Until recently, no one has had information on this crucial point. Our laboratory has been working on ways of quantifying magnetic resonance images in a way that would allow one to examine various regions in each half brain and to assess their similarity in surface area. Fifty slices are made of the brain and these slices are reconstructed to make maps of the human cerebrum. With the maps, it becomes easy to measure the cortical areas of the various major lobes of the brain. We now estimate the surface area from the three-dimensional reconstruction of the cortical surface itself. We discovered that there is a significant effect of monozygosity for frontal, parietal and occipital cortical surface area. Additionally, monozygosity significantly affects regional cortical surface area and involves twice as many areas in the left hemisphere as in the right. Overall, we can conclude that the brains of monozygotic twins are more alike than those of unrelated individuals.

The final, very important factor is that if our brain represents an assembly of specialized circuits, we have to explain William James' primary observations. We do feel unified and whole and we do have integrated feelings (usually) about all of our actions, thoughts and behaviours. There must be a specialized process in the brain that contributes to this undeniable aspect of our conscious experience.

Left brain interpreter

Several years ago we began to make observations on how the left, dominant speaking hemisphere dealt with the behaviours we knew we had elicited from the specialized circuits in the disconnected right hemisphere. We first revealed the phenomenon using a simultaneous concept test. The patient is shown two pictures, one exclusively to the left hemisphere and one exclusively to the right, and is asked to choose from an array of pictures placed in full view in front of him/her the ones associated with the pictures presented laterally to the left and right brain. In one example, a picture of a chicken claw was flashed to the left hemisphere and a picture of a snow scene to the right hemisphere. Of the array of pictures placed in front of the subject, the obviously correct association is a chicken for the chicken claw and a shovel for the snow scene. Patient P.S. responded by choosing the shovel with the left hand and the chicken with the right. When asked why he chose these items, his left hemisphere replied 'Oh, that's simple. The chicken claw goes with the chicken, and you need a shovel to clean out the chicken shed.' Here, the left brain, observing the left hand's response, interprets that response into a context consistent with its sphere of knowledge—one that does not include information about the left hemifield snow scene.

This same general idea has been observed when the 'left brain interpreter' struggles to deal with mood shifts, produced experimentally by manipulating the disconnected right hemisphere. A positive mood shift triggered by the right hemisphere finds the left interpreting its current experience in a positive way. Similarly, when the right triggers a negative mood state, the left interprets a previously neutral situation in negative terms.

Connecting to the interpreter: all roads do not lead to Rome

Specialized circuits are distributed throughout the cerebral cortex. The neural mechanisms involved with the local processing of particular modalities appear proximal and closely associated with the primary inputs for that modality. Awareness of these modality activities would appear to arise by information being communicated to the left hemisphere via cortical circuits. If the information requires communication from the right to the left hemisphere, the information courses over specific callosal pathways. Our understanding of cortical circuitry comes from considering the effects of lesions to primary cortical structures and pathways. Consider patient A. W. (Baynes et al 1992, 1993).

Patient A.W. suffered a stroke which involved the mid-region of the corpus callosum and other cortical structures in her right hemisphere. She is a very intelligent woman with training in biomedical research. Inspection of her magnetic resonance scans revealed that most of the splenium and rostrum of her callosum had been spared, as well as a ribbon of fibres both dorsal and ventral to her primary lesion in the mid-two thirds of her callosum. What is of particular interest is how she processed information with her left hand.

When processing with her right hand, she behaved completely normally. In this situation, objects would be placed in hand out of view. She quickly named them, as stereognostic information from the right hand was projected directly to the left dominant speaking hemisphere. There, tactile information is in close proximity to language and speech mechanisms and the results of tactile information processing can be communicated to the examiner. Needless to say, the right hand can match objects as well. Thus, an object placed in the right hand can subsequently be retrieved by the right hand when placed in a grab bag of items.

The dramatic effects of callosal disconnection surgery can be seen when the patient attempts to retrieve with the left hand an object originally placed in the right hand. A.W.'s performance falls to near chance. At the same time, an object placed in the left hand can also be easily retrieved by the left hand when placed in a grab bag of other objects. This indicates the right cerebral hemisphere has intact those neural circuits associated with the processing of stereognostic information projected to the right hemisphere from the left hand. This information, however, cannot be communicated to the left hemisphere. Callosal disconnection produces intriguing and fascinating behaviours.

An eraser can be placed in the left hand. The left hemisphere, when queried by the examiner, says it doesn't feel anything or doesn't know what the object is. Nonetheless, the left hand can easily find the matching stimulus from the grab bag. Thus, the correct object has been retrieved by the right hemisphere. The left hand is holding the correct object, but all of this activity remains known only to the right hemisphere. Further, it remains known only to the right hemisphere even though the right hemisphere is connected to the left through millions of remaining callosal fibres: this complex experience cannot be communicated to the left through these remaining fibres. Tactile experiences must be communicated through callosal fibres dedicated to communicating tactile information and those have been damaged. In short, our awareness of experiences is tied to specific fibre systems.

Summary

There is, it seems to me, the belief that understanding something like human consciousness will be achieved as we learn more and more about the vast computational capacities of the human brain. Somehow, the argument goes, the complex neural activities of the huge cerebral mantle hold the answer to this perennial issue. Biologists, psychologists and evolutionists are forever talking about big brains and the secret big brains must hold for understanding the special feeling we hold dear as being conscious humans.

The argument put forth here would see our big brains housing specialized circuits that are involved with specific functions. The functions relating to human cognition are mostly housed in the left hemisphere and can proceed essentially normally after being disconnected from half of the cortical mantle. Further, it is argued that consciousness reflects feelings about these capacities. The feelings about these capacities are largely managed by cortical circuitry that must have connections to the left hemisphere's interpreter system, if they are to enter into our awareness and be incorporated into our beliefs about the nature of our personal reality.

Acknowledgements

Aided by NIH grants NINDS 5 RO1, NS22626-06 and NINDS 5 PO1 NS 17778-09 and the James S. McDonnell Foundation. Parts of this chapter appeared in Conceptions of the human mind, papers from a conference held at Princeton University in honour of George A. Miller edited by Gilbert Harman; Lawrence Erlbaum, Hillsdale, New Jersey.

References

Baynes K, Tramo MJ, Fendrich R, Reeves AG, Gazzaniga MS 1992 Specificity of interhemispheric transfer following a partial lesion of the corpus callosum. Soc Neurosci Abstr 18:1207
Baynes K, Tramo MJ, Reeves AG, Gazzaniga MS 1993 Isolation of a right hemisphere cognitive system following watershed infarcts: implications for the anarchic hand phenomenon. Manuscript in preparation
Fendrich R, Wessinger CM, Gazzaniga MS 1992 Residual vision in a scotoma: implications for blindsight. Science (Wash DC) 258:1489–1491
Gazzaniga MS 1966 Interhemispheric communication of visual learning. Neuropsychologia 4:183–189
Gazzaniga MS 1988 Interhemispheric integration. In: Rakic P, Singer W (ed) Neurobiology of neocortex. Wiley, New York (Dahlem Workshop, Berlin, May 1987)

Gazzaniga MS 1989 Organization of the human brain. Science (Wash DC) 245:947–952

Gazzaniga MS 1992 Nature's mind. Basic Books, New York

Gazzaniga MS, Smylie CS 1984 Dissociation of language and cognition: a psychological profile of two disconnected right hemispheres. Brain 107:145–153

Gazzaniga MS, Smylie CS 1990 Hemispheric mechanisms controlling voluntary and spontaneous facial expressions. J Cognit Neurosci 2:239–245

Gazzaniga MS, Bogen JE, Sperry RW 1962 Some functional effects of sectioning the cerebral commissures in man. Proc Natl Acad Sci USA 48:1765–1769

Gazzaniga MS, Holtzman JD, Deck MDF, Lee BCP 1985 MRI assessment of human callosal surgery with neuropsychological correlates. Neurology 35:1763–1766

Green RL, Tramo MJ, Loftus WC et al 1991 Regional cortical surface area measurements in monozygotic twins discordant for schizophrenia suggest a left hemisphere basis for the disease. Soc Neurosci Abstr 17:1455

Holtzman JD 1984 Interactions between cortical and subcortical visual areas: evidence from human commissurotomy patients. Vision Res 24:801–813

Jouandet ML, Tramo MJ, Herron DM et al 1989 Brainprints: computer-generated two-dimensional maps of the human cerebral cortex in vivo. J Cognit Neurosci 1:88–117

Loftus WC 1991 Three dimensional minimal surface area reconstructions from planar contours using dynamic programming. Technical Report 100.2, Program in Cognitive Neuroscience, Dartmouth Medical School, Hanover, NH

Mohler CW, Wurtz RH 1977 Role of striate cortex and superior colliculus in visual guidance of saccadic eye movements in monkeys. J Neurophysiol 40:74–94

Nass R, Gazzaniga MS 1987 Lateralization and specialization of the human central nervous system. In: Plum F (ed) Handbook of physiology, Section 1. The nervous system, vol 5: Higher functions of the brain. Williams & Wilkins, Baltimore (Am Physiol Soc, Bethesda) p 701–761

Oppenheim JS, Skerry JE, Tramo MJ, Gazzaniga MS 1989 Magnetic resonance imaging morphology of the corpus callosum in monozygotic twins. Ann Neurol 26:100–104

Pasik T, Pasik P 1971 The visual world of monkeys deprived of striate cortex: effective stimulus parameters and the importance of the accessory optic system. Vision Res (suppl 3) 7:419–435

Rinn WE 1984 The neuropsychology of facial expression: a review of the neurological and psychological mechanisms for producing facial expressions. Psychol Bull 95: 52–77

Thomas CE, Tramo MJ, Loftus WC, Newton CH, Gazzaniga MS 1990 Gross morphometry of frontal, parietal and temporal cortex in monozygotic twins. Soc Neurosci Abstr 16:1151

Tooby J, Cosmides L 1987 From evolution to behavior: evolutionary psychology as the missing link. Dupre J (ed) The latest on the best: essays on evolution and optimality. MIT Press, Cambridge, MA, p 277–306

Tooby J, Cosmides L 1990 On the universality of human nature and the uniqueness of the individual: the role of genetics and adaptation. J Pers 58:17–67

Weiskrantz L 1990 The Ferrier Lecture 1989. Outlooks for blindsight: explicit methodologies for implicit processes. Proc R Soc Lond B Biol Sci 239:247–278

Weiskrantz L, Cowey A, Passingham C 1977 Spatial responses to brief stimuli by monkeys with striate cortex ablations. Brain 100:655–670

Wessinger CM, Fendrich R, Gazzaniga MS 1991 Stabilized retinal perimetry with a hemianopic patient: implications for blindsight. Soc Neurosci Abstr 17:846

Zaidel E 1990 Language functions in the two hemispheres following complete cerebral commissurotomy and hemispherectomy. In: Boller F, Grafman J (eds) Handbook of neuropsychology, vol 4. Elsevier Science Publishers, Amsterdam

DISCUSSION

Gray: I would like to probe the analogy with language. You could be saying consciousness is like the innate language system that only the human possesses, as far as we know, even though you can teach other animals a bit of linguistic skill. Therefore, only human beings are conscious.

Gazzaniga: No, I wasn't saying that.

Marcel: Jeffrey, in this case, clearly Mike Gazzaniga is talking about reflexivity when he talks about consciousness. He is not talking about phenomenal experience. Consciousness for him is 'the feelings we have about our capacities'. Not everybody here has the same referent when they talk about consciousness; we are not all talking about the same thing.

Secondly, Mike, you suggest that consciousness is not learned. How do you know? What about different forms across cultures? You are talking about an interpreter of conscious experience. There is a long tradition— Helmholtz, Dan Dennett, Max Velmans, me—of viewing consciousness as the result of an account. But the accounts that you are talking about are communicative verbal accounts. For example, if you are going to say that our visual experience is an account, do you want to say that the interpreter is in the left hemisphere?

Gazzaniga: This starts the puzzle category. Puzzle one: why is it when you split someone's brain, after they wake up and look at you, and say 'Hi', they don't say, 'I don't see half your face', which they don't from the left hemisphere? It's as if the sense that they should see half of your face is located elsewhere. That is, of course, preposterous. Yet, why isn't there a protest from prior experience that something is radically different?

Marcel: That is like patients with anosognosia.

Gazzaniga: No, the information is there; the information is working happily in that hemisphere, it's not damaged.

Marcel: You are discussing a reaction to what one is experiencing. I am talking about experience itself. The reaction 'My experience is funny', is a second-order event.

Gazzaniga: I am suggesting there may be another quality to that, more than just a second-order event.

Marcel: If that were the case in the left hemisphere, why do patients with anosognosia fall into this category? Such patients more often have *right* brain damage. Therefore, that second-order capacity cannot reside *only* in the left hemisphere. Maybe the linguistic accounts, communicative ones, do.

Nagel: Do patients with scotomas that are caused by retinal damage also not notice them?

Gazzaniga: Those are noticed immediately.

Gray: Do the split-brain patients not adopt any changed visual habits that would allow them to see your whole face? Do they adopt habits of keeping their eyes or head turned in some direction or other?

Kinsbourne: A patient with neglect does not adopt such habits. You can only know something is missing if there's a mismatch between your representation of what should be contained within the domain in question and incoming information. If the representation itself isn't accessible, there is no mismatch signal which says something is missing.

Gazzaniga: Except the memory.

Kinsbourne: There is the completion phenomenon, which has been shown for a few split-brain patients (Trevarthen 1974). If you give them half a figure in the right half field, they will report seeing a whole figure, as if they were inferring unconsciously its extension into the left half field. So there is no experiential shock.

Gazzaniga: If you give these patients a left half figure to the left visual field, and ask them to draw what they see, the right hemisphere again draws a half figure, it doesn't complete—as if the interpreter again is not doing anything beyond . . . .

Kinsbourne: But once it has drawn a half, it sees a whole, because it completes.

Gazzaniga: No, the left hemisphere does that but not the right.

Harnad: Is there any evidence that patients with a right hemispherectomy are more literally minded about input than are patients with a left hemispherectomy, along the lines of the effects in the left and right hemispheres of split-brain patients?

Gazzaniga: If you are going to get any kind of function from the right hemisphere, the damage to the left would have to occur very early. This is also an issue with patients with hemispherectomies and residual vision. If the tests have been done correctly, these patients with hemispherectomies seem to have residual vision. But we know that early lesions of the brain lead to such reorganization of the brain that you are no longer testing the normal visual system. This occurs dramatically in cases of agenesis of the corpus callosum: there is transfer of information within the brain.

Harnad: I was thinking of late hemispherectomy.

Gazzaniga: If you take off the left hemisphere late, there is not much going on afterwards.

Newsome: One of the cardinal features of blindsight is that the classic blindsight patient denies seeing what they manifestly can see, as shown behaviourally. Do your patients with the tiny islands of spared vision deny seeing things in those islands? Or if you asked them to make a visual discrimination, would they say, 'Ah, I have a little patch out there where I can see a signal'?

Gazzaniga: That's a real hornet's nest. We can get confidence ratings of 1–5 after running patients on each trial. First, there is no question that the patient is responding to each trial and discriminating the shapes. When we set these tests up, the stimulus is presented into what is clearly a residual vision area, and we also put the same stimulus on other trials into the good visual field, as well as some marginal zones. With a 1–5 scale, the patient obviously assigns 5 to what's clearly seen, they assign 2 and 3 to what may be vaguely seen, and they assign 1 to what is really difficult. When you then ask them, 'What do you really mean by 1?', they may reply either 'I saw something' or 'I didn't see anything at all'.

If you test normal people and show them a display where you vary the signal:noise ratio on a display, and you ask for confidence ratings, you also get this range. From those data, you wouldn't argue for parallel pathways and the like. A range of confidence ratings is a property of the task—that could be all that is happening here.

Searle: Mike, the way I heard your description of the island cases is they have a blank spot in the visual field with points of light in it. Is there any reason to suppose that's not right? The data that you just gave may mean that if the stimulus is degenerate enough, the patient would say, as a person with normal vision would, either 'I didn't see it at all' or 'I just saw something vaguely'. It seems to me we have good reasons to suppose there was a conscious visual experience of those points; whereas in a standard blindsight case, there's good reason to suppose there isn't any conscious visual experience.

Gazzaniga: If you are studying blindsight in the human, you have to do microperimetry of the visual field to find out what it is like. We are studying a second patient now. When we put her in the eye-tracker, her field is like spaghetti! There's vision here, vision there. Generally, the vision is hugely impaired, no question about that. But when we place stimuli in the spaghetti lines, we get perfectly fine performance.

Dennett: What do you mean by performance in this regard? Does this patient react to stimuli without a prompt? Are you sure it's not just a forced-choice test?

Gazzaniga: We are doing our work from the ground up. We are establishing a two-alternative forced-choice, detection task.

Marcel: Forced-choice? So they don't spontaneously see consciously what is in their scotoma?

Gazzaniga: I'm not saying that. They do make a conscious choice in response to the stimulus. It's in the nature of the experiment. However, they may have low confidence about their judgement.

Dennett: So if you said, 'Press a button if you ever see a spot of light in this field', we don't know whether they would ever press the button.

Gazzaniga: Consider the visual field of the patient and consider the approximately 60 points we test where the patient is completely blind. They have the anatomy intact that should support blindsight. In tests using the most sensitive method known to detect any residual vision, we find that they see nothing.

Velmans: Doesn't that just show that those particular sensitive spots are sufficient to support a form of visual discrimination? It doesn't in itself show those spots are sufficient to support a phenomenal experience.

Gazzaniga: Related phenomena occur all the time in normal college sophomores. I have tested them on spatial tasks where they have to point to a sequence of events occurring within a grid of nine squares. When we increase the speed of presentation of stimuli, subjects swear that they are not performing above chance, yet their performance is above chance. What do you make of that?

Kihlstrom: It's the kind of thing that you can understand in terms of a distinction between explicit and implicit cognition. These effects are emerging on a two–alternative forced-choice test, where you make the person make a decision, even in the absence of phenomenal experience that would support some kind of spontaneous speech act or something. Those are the kinds of conditions under which implicit perception and implicit memory appear. So maybe there isn't phenomenal experience, maybe something is being processed nonetheless. That leads me to the question about the role of the anterior commissure here. Is there any evidence for implicit perception or implicit memory in the other hemisphere?

Gazzaniga: No.

Kihlstrom: Has it been looked at with an implicit memory test?

Gazzaniga: It's worse than that. Using the image stabilizer, you can leave the stimulus in the left visual field for five seconds. In our test, all the right hemisphere has to do is decide whether or not the left hemisphere stimulus is horizontal or vertical lines, or an apple or orange. Performance is still at chance.

Libet: With the differences you have been describing between the right and left hemisphere, and the role of the 'interpreter' in the left hemisphere, are you suggesting that the person or the self is really in the left hemisphere?

Gazzaniga: I'm saying that the special module that we have that interprets our actions is in the left hemisphere.

Humphrey: You said that consciousness was innate. We know that people with left hemispherectomy apparently can function quite normally and I think we would want to say that they are conscious. In the ordinary sense of innate, one would say that if consciousness is innately in the left hemisphere, then the brain won't re-adapt and compensate for changed circumstances. I would like Dan Dennett to come in on this issue, because Dan's view of consciousness as a virtual machine imposed on the hardware of the brain makes consciousness a learned phenomenon. I think all of us would agree that the hardware has very important innate characteristics; but I think few people would want to say that consciousness is innate.

Gazzaniga: I would love to.

Nagel: The idea that consciousness is learned is bizarre.

Searle: My interpretation of what Mike Gazzaniga said is: both hemispheres are conscious, it's just that the right one is pretty dumb. Mike makes it sound like a computer: it just gives you back what you put in. Whereas there are many other kinds of activities going on in the left hemisphere. As far as consciousness is concerned, both hemispheres are conscious. It is innate to the mechanisms of those hemispheres that they produce consciousness. Is that the position?

Gazzaniga: Yes.

Fenwick: After split-brain surgery, one of the most disabling problems is the fact that the two hemispheres fight with each other.

Gazzaniga: No they don't. That was an early mistake. In the first case, W.J., there was a lot of frontal lobe damage in addition to the callosal surgery, so there was very poor ipsilateral control of the limbs in that patient. Thus, when the left hemisphere wanted to do something, it could control the right hand; when the right hemisphere wanted to do something, it could control the left hand. But the left hemisphere had very poor control of the left hand and the right hemisphere had very poor control of the right hand. So there could be antagonism. In subsequent patients, who haven't suffered extracallosal damage, one doesn't see that situation at all. You can demonstrate the ipsilateral deficit by subtle testing of distal musculature, but the fighting between hemispheres that you are referring to was really an aspect of the first case.

Fenwick: I have recently reviewed the epilepsy literature and the split-brain studies. It is not just in one case, this antagonism is widely reported.

Gazzaniga: You have to trust me a little. I have seen these cases, all of them. Every once in a while you get some visiting medic who listens to a random story of a patient. One such medic gave a lecture at my school about one of our patients. She said: 'You don't need a tachistoscope to do visual testing, just show V.P. her closet, and you will see she has the hardest time picking out her dress. There is a deep conflict between the hemispheres.' She hadn't seen V.P. preoperatively trying to pick out her dress!

Dennett: Mike, you mentioned that there is no change in IQ after surgery. But are the IQs of patients with split-brains well below the normal range?

Gazzaniga: No, we have smart split-brain patients and their IQs don't change.

Shevrin: You mentioned the amazing conformity between monozygotic twins in their brain structure. There is also considerable evidence that their evoked potentials are very similar (Shevrin et al 1970).

What is the current status of Galin's (1974) hypothesis that the right hemisphere is more closely related to dreaming and unconscious processes in general?

Gazzaniga: I think that was fun back in the early days of thinking about left brain/right brain. Traditional dreaming studies have been done with patients after split-brain surgery. When they are woken during REM sleep and asked if they were dreaming, they reply that they were dreaming.

Shevrin: So earlier reports that the dreams of split-brain patients have a poverty of imagery and so on don't stand up?

Gazzaniga: No.

Searle: There was a period when we got a lot of pop science literature to the effect that the right brain did poetry, music, falling in love and deconstruction; and the left brain did logic, mathematics, analytic philosophy and truth-seeking. What I hear from you is that that's a load of nonsense.

Gazzaniga: The new dichotomy is Bush/Quayle.

References

Galin D 1974 Implications for psychiatry of left and right cerebral specialization: a neurophysiological content for unconscious processes. Arch Gen Psychiatr 31:572–583

Shevrin H, Smith WH, Fritzler D 1970 Subliminally stimulated brain and verbal responses of twins differing in repressiveness. J Abnorm Psychol 76:39–46

Trevarthen C 1974 Functional relations of disconnected hemispheres with the mainstream, and with each other: monkey and man. In: Kinsbourne M, Smith WL (eds) Hemispheric disconnection and cerebral function. Thomas, Springfield, IL, p 187–207

Consciousness, schizophrenia and scientific theory

Jeffrey A. Gray

Department of Psychology, Institute of Psychiatry, De Crespigny Park, Denmark Hill, London SE5 8AF, UK

Abstract. The positive symptoms of acute schizophrenia are, of their very nature, aberrations of conscious experience. A recent theory of the mechanisms underlying their occurrence spans four levels: neuroanatomical, neurochemical, cognitive and the symptoms themselves. The theory is capable of being tested in animals and human subjects, and it has passed a number of experimental tests at both levels with success. Implications of the theory for the scientific treatment of consciousness are considered. Although the theory permits useful questions relating to consciousness to be put and even to some extent to be answered, it leaves the most basic issue—the theoretical link between the occurrence of conscious experience and the neural substrate of the brain—unresolved, as do all similar theories so far.

1993 Experimental and theoretical studies of consciousness. Wiley, Chichester (Ciba Foundation Symposium 174) p 263–281

In this paper I shall use the aberrations of conscious experience that are symptomatic of schizophrenia to illustrate the problems that face contemporary science in the attempt to bring such phenomena into its network of causal explanation. In doing so, I shall assume that there *is* a problem of consciousness (i.e. that no-one has yet succeeded in either arguing it away or solving it); that it is a problem of *consciousness*, not a mind–body problem (since there is no difficulty in principle in understanding how physical systems can carry out mental operations that remain unconscious); and that it is a *scientific*, not a purely philosophical problem (though one which still awaits a general conceptual solution to which philosophy can contribute, not one that can be solved simply by the accumulation of data or improved technology) (for justification of these assumptions, see Gray 1987). The detail of the argument rests heavily upon a recent theory of the neural and psychological bases of the symptoms of schizophrenia (Gray et al 1991a,b), which I shall first summarize. My chief concern, however, is not to set out this theory as such, but rather to draw from it certain inferences as to the limits that attach at present to any attempt to provide a scientific account of conscious phenomena of any kind. Even if, as is plausible, our particular theory of the neuropsychology of schizophrenia is partly or wholly wrong, the inferences I wish to draw concerning these limits will, I believe, remain substantially correct.

Abnormalities of consciousness and cognition in schizophrenia

The theory of the neuropsychology of schizophrenia that my colleagues and I have developed (Gray et al 1991a,b) is intended to span the complete range of explanation from a malfunction in the brain to the psychological symptoms of the condition. It can be regarded as integrating four levels of description (Fig. 1). (1) A structural abnormality in the brain (specifically, in the limbic forebrain, affecting the hippocampal formation, amygdala, and temporal and frontal neocortex) gives rise to (2) a functional neurochemical abnormality in the brain (specifically, hyperactivity of transmission in the ascending mesolimbic dopaminergic pathway). (3) This, in turn, disrupts a cognitive process (specifically, the integration of past regularities of experience with current stimulus recognition, learning and action) and so produces (4) the positive symptoms characteristic of acute schizophrenic psychosis.

Notice that, if the explicandum (step 4) in this chain were definable in ordinary biological terms (e.g. a failure in thermoregulation), this type of integrative neuroscientific explanation would be familiar and pose no theoretical or philosophical problems. Step 3 poses no problem, because this need not involve consciousness in any way. To see that this is so, consider the thermoregulation example more closely.

If an animal is regularly placed in a distinctive environment in which it is exposed to a cold temperature, it will learn to adapt to that environment, changing thermoregulatory processes appropriately and immediately upon entering the environment. This type of adaptive change (familiar to us as Pavlovian conditioning) is an example of the control of current stimulus recognition (the environment associated with cold) and action (altered thermoregulation) in the light of past experience, so that it instantiates step 3 in Fig. 1. Yet a failure in such learned anticipatory thermoregulation which was due, for example, to a structural abnormality in the hypothalamus, leading to altered neurotransmission and so to an impairment in the capacity to sustain the relevant learning processes, could clearly be explained by standard paradigms in behavioural neuroscience. This simple state of affairs does not imply, however, that consciousness is ruled out by such explanatory paradigms. For all we know, an animal in such an experiment is fully conscious of the relationship between the distinctive environment and a cold temperature (as we might be, say, in an Alpine hut). It is rather that the paradigm is entirely silent on the issue of consciousness: it can be subjected to a comprehensive theoretical and experimental scrutiny that will fully determine its credentials as a valid scientific explanation without reference to the issue of conscious experience.

Unlike thermoregulation, however, the 'positive' (Crow 1980) symptoms of schizophrenia (to which Gray et al's 1991a theory is addressed) are necessarily linked to conscious experience. It is true that one knows about many of these symptoms only by having the patient describe them; it also true that schizophrenia involves oddities of language. But I doubt that, even in the heyday of radical behaviourism, anyone has ever proposed that the strange subjective experiences so characteristic of schizophrenia can be dismissed as mere oddities of 'verbal behaviour'. Freedman (1974) has distilled a summary of some of these experiences from about 60 autobiographical accounts written by schizophrenics during or after their psychotic episodes. They include feelings of enhanced sensory awareness, reports of visual illusions, changes in depth perception, reports of racing thoughts each with an increased range of associations, descriptions of loss of meaning of words or objects, reports of difficulty in focusing attention and concentrating—not to mention the classic symptoms of auditory hallucinations and delusional beliefs. It is clear from this catalogue that any account of schizophrenia that makes no reference to conscious experience is, to say the least, limited in its ambition. But, if we are to overstep this limit, we need some way of linking conscious experience to the rest of the explanatory chain illustrated in Fig. 1. Does any such way exist?

The answer to this question can be 'yes' or 'no', depending upon how it is put. Let me first pose it in a way that permits the optimistic, positive answer.

Tying in consciousness to the theory of the neuropsychology of schizophrenia: the optimistic answer

Can an account of the neuropsychology of the positive symptoms of schizophrenia which encompasses the whole explanatory chain of Fig. 1 be tested experimentally? Can we go even further and, given the obvious ethical and practical problems of testing theories about brain function in human beings, investigate this account in animals? We believe these objectives can be achieved with the theory we have proposed (Gray et al 1991a,b).

The key move (one to which we shall need to return) in this achievement is to reduce the specific subjective experiences that constitute the positive symptoms of schizophrenia to a malfunction in one general cognitive process. This move was made by my colleague, David Hemsley (1987), drawing upon previous formulations by others (Table 1). His proposal is that the positive symptoms of schizophrenia can all be seen as arising from 'a weakening of the influence of stored memories of regularities of previous input on current perception'. Hemsley (1987, 1990) has justified this proposal in detail and I shall not repeat his arguments. It is in any case the general form of this type of explanation that is relevant here, rather than the specific details. Indeed, similar accounts have been proposed which could serve our purposes equally well, e.g. Frith's (1987) hypothesis that 'willed intentions are not monitored correctly in

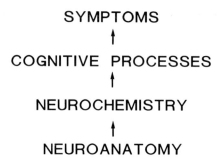

FIG. 1.   An integrative theory (Gray et al 1991a) of positive schizophrenic symptoms (top), seen as arising from a structural abnormality in the brain (bottom), which gives rise to a functional neurochemical abnormality, and hence an abnormality in cognitive processing.

schizophrenia'. What such accounts do is substitute for references to essentially conscious phenomena (schizophrenic symptoms) reference to a cognitive process which *may or may not be conscious* without affecting either the explanation or the means for testing it. For, in spite of the mentalistic language (Hemsley's 'stored memories' or Frith's 'willed intentions'), these are cognitive processes that can in principle be turned into computer programs or built into machines (whereas we have no idea how to approach such computing or engineering feats when it comes, say, to hallucinations). From here on, it is relatively straight forward. So much so, in fact, that some of the most important evidence on which the theory is based is drawn from experiments with animals; indeed, once Hemsley's key move has been made, it is almost as easy to conduct relevant experiments with animals as with human subjects. This is an important point: as we shall see, it permits an approach to the very difficult issue of the presence (or absence) of conscious experience in animals. It is worth considering, therefore, the specifics of the theory in order to illustrate the relationship between animal and human experiments.

Outline of a theory of the neuropsychology of schizophrenia

At the neuroanatomical level the theory draws upon evidence from the post-mortem schizophrenic brain that shows pathology in the limbic forebrain. Neuro-chemically, the theory draws upon evidence from drugs with psychotomimetic or anti-psychotic properties, which shows a relationship between dopaminergic transmission and the positive symptoms of schizophrenia. These two lines of evidence are used to propose a correspondence (Fig. 2) between (1) the stored regularities and current perception/action of Hemsley's cognitive processing (Fig. 2A) and (2) the links between the subiculum (part of the limbic forebrain) and the nucleus accumbens (Fig. 2C) (to which the mesolimbic dopaminergic

TABLE 1   Current views on the nature of schizophrenics' cognitive impairment

'The basic cognitive defect . . . is an awareness of automatic processes which are normally carried out below the level of consciousness' (Frith 1979, p 233).

'There is some suggestion that there is a failure of automatic processing in schizophrenia so that activity must proceed at the level of consciously controlled sequential processing' (Venables 1984, p 75).

Schizophrenics 'concentrate on detail, at the expense of theme' (Cutting 1985, p 300).

Schizophrenics show 'some deficiency in perceptual schema formation, in automaticity, or in the holistic stage of processing' (Knight 1984, p 120).

Schizophrenics show a 'failure of attentional focusing to respond to stimulus redundancy' (Maher 1983, p 19).

'Schizophrenics are less able to make use of the redundancy and patterning of sensory input to reduce information processing demands' (Hemsley 1987).

Schizophrenics 'do not maintain a strong conceptual organization or a serial processing strategy . . . nor do they organize stimuli extensively relative to others' (Magaro 1984, p 202).

system projects). The correspondence relies on several assumptions. (1) That the limbic forebrain uses stored regularities of previous input to compute a prediction as to the 'next' (time being divided into quanta of approximately 0.1 seconds) state of the world, given the subject's current motor programme. (2) That the limbic forebrain compares this prediction to the actual state of the world in the following time quantum. (3) That the outcome of this matching operation is transmitted via the projection from the subiculum to the nucleus accumbens. (4) That this nucleus forms part of a motor programming system in the basal ganglia; that the motor programming system uses a 'match' message from the subiculum to continue the current motor programme and a 'mismatch' message ('something novel/unexpected has occurred') to interrupt it. (5) That schizophrenia entails a disruption of the normal input from the subiculum to the nucleus accumbens leading, neurochemically, to a functional imbalance equivalent to hyperactivity in the dopaminergic projection to the nucleus accumbens and, psychologically, to an 'over-occurrence' of apparently novel events. (6) That finally (by Hemsley's move), this gives rise to positive schizophrenic symptoms.

Evidence in support of the theory comes from several directions. Much of it derives from two key behavioural paradigms, latent inhibition and the Kamin blocking effect, both first studied in experimental animals and also demonstrable with human subjects. Here, I shall consider only latent inhibition (Lubow 1989). This is an extremely simple phenomenon: if a potential conditioned stimulus (CS) (e.g. a light or tone) is given to a rat a number of times (typically, 20–40) without consequence, this pre-exposure retards subsequent learning when the stimulus does have consequences (when it predicts a second stimulus, for example, food or foot-shock). In Hemsley's terms a past regularity (CS with

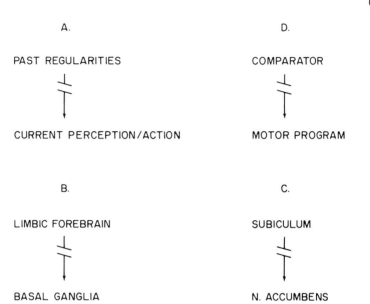

FIG. 2. A further illustration of the theory of schizophrenia proposed by Gray et al (1991a). (A) The abnormality of cognitive processing consists of a failure to integrate past regularities of experience with the current control of perception and action. (B) This reflects a dysfunctional connection between the limbic forebrain and the basal ganglia. (C) The specific pathway carrying the dysfunctional connection is from the subiculum (in the limbic forebrain) to the nucleus accumbens (in the basal ganglia). (D) The computing functions thus disrupted are the passage of information from a comparator system utilizing stored traces of past regularities (limbic forebrain) to a motor programming system (located in the basal ganglia) controlling perception and action.

no consequence) adversely affects the current learning of a new association (CS with unconditioned stimulus, UCS). The potential significance of this phenomenon for the study of schizophrenia was first pointed out by Solomon et al (1981) and Weiner et al (1981). Both these groups demonstrated that the indirect dopamine agonist and psychotomimetic, amphetamine, blocked latent inhibition in the rat. It did this by increasing learning in animals that had been pre-exposed to a CS with no consequence to the level shown by undrugged controls that had not been pre-exposed. In other words, drugged animals behaved as though the past regularity, CS with no consequence, failed to influence their current learning. Both Solomon et al (1981) and Weiner et al (1981) suggested, therefore, that the blockade of latent inhibition by amphetamine might constitute an animal model of the psychotic symptoms of schizophrenia (which, for reasons which will be apparent from the nature of these symptoms, may justly be regarded as the Mount Everest of animal models).

    Subsequent work (references in the reviews by Gray et al 1991a,b, unless others given) has provided considerable support for this hypothesis, including the following observations. The blockade of latent inhibition by amphetamine in the rat is due to dopamine release specifically in the nucleus accumbens. A CS to which the rat has not been pre-exposed causes release of dopamine in the nucleus accumbens, and this conditioned release is strongly reduced by pre-exposure (Young et al 1992). Latent inhibition can also be blocked in the rat by damage to the hippocampal formation or by disconnection of this structure from the nucleus accumbens (Tarrasch et al 1992). Latent inhibition can be blocked in normal human subjects by amphetamine (Gray et al 1992a). Finally, and critically, as initially reported by Baruch et al (1988) and replicated by Gray et al (1992b), latent inhibition is absent in the early stages of an acute schizophrenic episode, before medication with neuroleptics (anti-psychotic drugs which act by blocking dopamine receptors) has succeeded in controlling psychotic symptoms.

There are two important features to note in the experiments with human subjects. The first is that acute schizophrenics in the pre-exposed condition learn the CS–UCS association *faster* than do pre-exposed normal control subjects. This eliminates the possibility that the aberrant cognitive performance of acute schizophrenics is an artifact due to interference from some aspect of their illness (hearing voices in the head, lack of cooperation or motivation, etc). The second is that the human latent inhibition paradigm shares with the animal paradigm only a conceptual similarity, but virtually no concrete features (stimuli, responses, etc): in the animal paradigm (Weiner et al 1981), conditioning is measured as the degree to which a tone (pre-exposed or not) that has been associated with foot-shock is able to suppress licking for water; in the human paradigm (Baruch et al 1988), for both normal and schizophrenic subjects, conditioning is measured as the speed of identifying the predictive relationship between a burst of white noise (pre-exposed or not) and an increment on a counter display.

Implications of the theory for consciousness

These findings offer strong support for the theory. But our concern here is rather with the *form* of the theory and with the *nature* of the evidence by which it is supported. Consider in particular the comings and goings between observations made with human beings and animals.

The work I have described starts with observations on human beings: the symptoms of schizophrenia and the finding that these symptoms can be induced or exacerbated by the drug, amphetamine. As already noted, these symptoms necessarily involve reference to conscious events. Next, there is a theoretical step, invoking cognitive processes that are neutral with respect to consciousness (what I have called 'Hemsley's move'). The focus then moves to animal work, with the demonstration that amphetamine has behavioural effects (blockade of latent inhibition) in rats that are consistent with this cognitive view of schizophrenia. (In the background there was, of course, already much neurochemical evidence, largely gained with animals, concerning the effects on dopaminergic transmission of both amphetamine and neuroleptics.) Studies on animals are then used to explore in depth the neural basis of latent inhibition and the effects of amphetamine on latent inhibition. Finally, the story comes back to humans, with the construction of a human model (latent inhibition with an increment on a counter as the UCS) of the animal model (latent inhibition with foot-shock as the UCS) of schizophrenia, and the demonstrations that amphetamine blocks latent inhibition in human subjects and, critically, that acute schizophrenics do not show latent inhibition.

This procedure is in many respects typical of the construction and testing of scientific theory. As each prediction is verified experimentally, our confidence in the theory is strengthened, as is our willingness to answer questions by reference to it. In particular, verification of the predictions about latent inhibition at the human level validates the use of blockade of latent inhibition in animals as a model of acute schizophrenia. It follows therefore that what is known about the neural basis of the blockade of latent inhibition in animals becomes potentially relevant to understanding the neural basis of acute schizophrenia. Further, since the original assumption that blockade of latent inhibition might constitute a model of schizophrenia derives from a particular view of the cognitive disruption underlying the schizophrenic process, that view too is strengthened. Finally, since the cognitive account of schizophrenia was itself constructed in order to make sense of the subjective experiences described by schizophrenics, it would seem that we are on the way to having a scientifically valid theory of the way in which these experiences come about.

These conclusions also take us well on the way to being able to give a reasoned answer to a question which has often been seen as entirely refractory to such answers: are animals conscious? To the extent that the theory of acute schizophrenia briefly outlined above is correct, the answer to this question (at least for the rat, on which the critical experiments have been performed) must be 'yes'. The form of the theory, combined with the nature of the schizophrenic symptoms that it attempts to explain, strongly implies that the effect of amphetamine in blocking latent inhibition in human subjects should be understood as reflecting a change in conscious experience (taking the form, roughly speaking, that the drug enhances the salience in consciousness of the pre-exposed CS; cf the descriptions, summarized by Freedman 1974, of feelings of 'enhanced sensory awareness' in schizophrenics' autobiographical accounts of their illness). But similar effects require similar explanations, especially if they are encompassed by the same theory based upon the same evidence. It must therefore follow that, if the blockade of latent inhibition by amphetamine in human subjects reflects a change in conscious experience, so it does in the rat. Therefore, rats have at least some conscious experiences. (This is not, of course, a radically new point. It has been possible to make it at least since drugs that are analgesic in humans were shown to raise the threshold for reactions to putative painful stimuli in animals. Indeed, one could argue that the similarity of such reactions, drug or no drug, in animals and humans is itself enough to make the point. The argument here, however, is applied to a range of conscious experiences that are presumably more complex than the perception of pain.)

This theory of the neuropsychology of schizophrenia also gives us a way to frame a general view of the cognitive functions in which consciousness plays an important role (an issue I raise with trepidation, given Velmans' 1991 systematic destruction of every hypothesis so far proposed for what these functions might be). The theory treats heightened schizophrenic awareness (indexed experimentally by blockade of latent inhibition) as being due to disruption of neural messages that ought normally to be transmitted from the subiculum to the nucleus accumbens (Fig. 2C). The role played by these messages is seen as the transmission to a motor programming system of a confirmation (or otherwise) that the last step in the current programme was successfully completed (Fig. 2D), so that it is alright (or not) to proceed to the next (Gray et al 1991a). Disruption of this transmission in the schizophrenic is thought to be the equivalent of a failure to confirm that the motor programme is going according to plan, even when it is: events that ought to be experienced as fully predicted are in fact experienced as being novel. Thus, if the theory is on the right lines, conscious experience is related (though not necessarily exclusively) to dealing with unexpected events. This is hardly a new conclusion; but it may be useful to tie it down to specific neural machinery, to the computing relations between a motor programming system and a comparator system (Gray 1982), and to behavioural paradigms that can be studied in animals as well as in humans.

Tying in consciousness: the pessimistic answer

It would seem, then, that we are making progress. But a closer look casts doubt upon this optimistic conclusion.

The difficulty lies here: nothing in the account of the neuropsychology of schizophrenia that I have sketched above gives the slightest clue why *any* of the events in the brain contained in this account, whether they are described in terms of neuronal functioning (e.g. dopamine release in the nucleus accumbens) or information processing (e.g. transmission of the message, 'something novel'), should achieve or cause *any* form of conscious experience. The phenomena we are trying to explain are, of their essence, conscious; but the processes in the explanation are not. This in itself need not pose any problem. As Searle (1985) points out in an instructive analogy, individual molecules of H_2O do not possess the property of liquidity, but interactions between these molecules confer this property upon water in bulk. So perhaps something about the interactions between the various neural and/or cognitive processes delineated above confers consciousness upon the whole organism, even though these processes individually lack consciousness. Certainly, this is a possibility. But, as I have noted in a critique elsewhere (Gray 1987) of Searle's analogy, we are able to account for liquidity in terms of interactions between molecules of H_2O precisely because theorists have ascribed to the molecules just those theoretical properties needed to provide such an account. But neither the neural nor the informational processes upon which our theory of schizophrenia rests have been endowed with properties that would permit them to account for the occurrence of conscious experiences. The time to make the endowment would have been at the step (Fig. 1) that I have called Hemsley's move. But, at this step, what we did was to finesse the problem of consciousness, by changing terminology from conscious processes to processes that might be conscious or not, preparatory to moving still further down the explanatory chain to processes that are quite definitely not conscious. Nor is this an unfortunate lapse in this particular theory: it can be found in every comparable effort to construct such a theory. For no one has yet proposed any convincing theoretical properties, whether attached to neurons (as Searle 1985, for example, would wish) or to information processes (as wished, for example, by Dennett 1991), from which consciousness can be deduced. (For this reason, too, the choice among neurons, information processes, both or something else as the necessary conditions for consciousness remains arbitrary; see Gray 1987.)

Acknowledgements

I am grateful to my colleague at the Institute of Psychiatry, Dr David Hemsley, for many stimulating discussions of the bizarre phenomena of schizophrenia. The theory of schizophrenia on which this paper is based owes much to him, and to Dr Joram Feldon of Tel Aviv University and Dr Nicholas Rawlins and Professor David Smith of Oxford University.

References

Baruch I, Hemsley DR, Gray JA 1988 Differential performance of acute and chronic schizophrenics in a latent inhibition task. J Nerv Ment Dis 176:598–606
Crow TJ 1980 Positive and negative schizophrenic symptoms and the role of dopamine. Br J Psychol 137:383–386
Cutting J 1985 The psychology of schizophrenia. Churchill Livingstone, Edinburgh
Dennett DC 1991 Consciousness explained. Allen Lane, London
Freedman BJ 1974 The subjective experience of perceptual and cognitive disturbances in schizophrenia. Arch Gen Psychiatry 30:333–340
Frith CD 1979 Consciousness, information processing and schizophrenia. Br J Psychol 134:225–235
Frith CD 1987 The positive and negative symptoms of schizophrenia reflect impairments in the perception and initiation of action. Psychol Med 17:631–648
Gray JA 1982 The neuropsychology of anxiety: an enquiry into the function of the septo-hippocampal system. Oxford University Press, Oxford

Gray JA 1987 The mind-brain identity theory as a scientific hypothesis: a second look. In: Blakemore C, Greenfield S (eds) Mindwaves. Blackwell Publishers, Oxford, p 461–483

Gray JA, Feldon J, Rawlins JNP, Hemsley DR, Smith AD 1991a The neuropsychology of schizophrenia. Behav Brain Sci 14:1–20

Gray JA, Hemsley DR, Feldon J, Gray NS, Rawlins JNP 1991b Schiz bits: misses, mysteries and hits. Behav Brain Sci 14:56–84

Gray NS, Pickering AD, Hemsley DR, Dawling S, Gray JA 1992a Abolition of latent inhibition by a single 5 mg dose of d-amphetamine in man. Psychopharmacology 107:425–430

Gray NS, Hemsley, DR, Gray JA 1992b Abolition of latent inhibition in acute, but not chronic schizophrenics. Neurol Psychiatry Brain Res 1:83–89

Hemsley DR 1987 An experimental psychological model for schizophrenia. In: Hafner H, Gattaz WF, Janzavik W (eds) Search for the causes of schizophrenia. Springer-Verlag, Berlin, p 179–188

Hemsley DR 1990 What have cognitive deficits to do with schizophrenia? In: Huber G (ed) Idiopathische Psychosen. Schattauer, Stuttgart, p 111–127

Lubow RE 1989 Latent inhibition and conditioned attention theory. Cambridge University Press, Cambridge

Knight RA 1984 Converging models of cognitive deficit in schizophrenia. In: Spaulding WD, Cole JK (eds) Theories of schizophrenia and psychosis. University of Nebraska Press, Nebraska, p 93–156

Magaro PA 1984 Psychosis and schizophrenia. In: Spaulding WD, Cole JK (eds) Theories of schizophrenia and psychosis. University of Nebraska Press, Nebraska, p 157–230

Maher BA 1983 A tentative theory of schizophrenic utterance. In: Maher BA, Maher WB (eds) Progress in experimental personality research. Academic Press, New York, vol 12:1–52

Searle JR 1985 Minds, brains and science. BBC Publications, London

Solomon PR, Crider A, Winkelman JW, Turi A, Kamer RM, Kaplan LJ 1981 Disrupted latent inhibition in the rat with chronic amphetamine or haloperidol-induced supersensitivity: relationship to schizophrenic attention disorder. Biol Psychiatry 16:519–537

Tarrasch R, Weiner I, Rawlins JNP, Feldon J 1992 Disruption of latent inhibition by interrupting the subicular input to nucleus accumbens and its antagonism by haloperidol. J Psychopharmacol 6:111

Velmans M 1991 Is human information processing conscious? Behav Brain Sci 14:651–726

Venables PH 1984 Cerebral mechanisms, autonomic responsiveness and attention to schizophrenia. In: Spaulding WD, Cole JK (eds) Theories of schizophrenia and psychosis. University of Nebraska Press, Nebraska, p 47–91

Weiner I, Lubow RE, Feldon J 1981 Chronic amphetamine and latent inhibition. Behav Brain Res 2:285–286

Young AMJ, Gray JA, Joseph MH 1992 Dopamine function in selective attention and conditioning: a microdialysis study using latent inhibition. J Psychopharmacol 6:112

DISCUSSION

Marcel: Jeffrey, may I raise a logical problem about the status of the theory? From your account at the functional level of what gives rise to the positive symptoms, it's not clear to me whether it's a post-conscious rational process or a pre-conscious causal process. If you are saying that delusional beliefs are a 'rational' reaction to phenomenal experience, then you cannot be accounting for phenomenal experience itself with that hypothetical process.

Gray: My main point was that Hemsley's move is a defence against having to answer that question. I'm not saying that what I call Hemsley's move is special to us—it is characteristic of the moves that are always made when psychologists attempt to produce this kind of theory. When you start using the language of cognitive processing, you no longer have to answer the question that you just put to me.

I can also answer your question more specifically with regard to experiments. Shanks (1985) used the Kamin (1968) blocking effect, which provides a good example of the way our theory maps on to the symptoms of schizophrenia. The Kamin blocking effect is as follows. You first teach a subject (an animal or a human being) that one conditioned stimulus predicts an unconditioned stimulus. Then you give the subject a compound stimulus. For example, the first conditioned stimulus might be a tone predicting shock, and the compound stimulus could be a tone plus light still predicting the same shock. Then you ask, has the subject learnt that the light predicts shock? If the subject already expected the shock because the tone predicted it, he does not learn about the light: this is the Kamin blocking effect.

We have done that experiment in humans (Jones et al 1992) and shown that schizophrenics learn just as rapidly whether they have been pre-exposed to the final conditioned stimulus or not. This is an excellent model of the formation of delusional beliefs. We actually think this is the way delusional beliefs are formed, because the schizophrenic will see something that ought to be fully predicted in his life, but to him it is not fully predicted, and he will form a causal delusion (Hemsley 1990).

Humphrey: Hemsley's move moves just a bit too fast for me. I think it is actually a three-part move: (1) schizophrenic symptoms are conscious mental processes; (2) these conscious mental processes can be turned into mental processes which may or may not be conscious; (3) these mental processes can be turned into brain processes that may or may not be mental. It's the second move from conscious mental processes to mental processes which is the tricky one, and which I don't think your kind of theory can address. I think it's a beautiful explanation of how mental states can become disordered; I don't think it says much about the aetiology of consciousness.

Gray: I think whether you wish to say it that way or my shorter way depends upon whether you conceive unconscious mental processes to be something additional to the neurophysiological processes that we choose to describe in information processing terms. I personally accept the conclusion which I felt we were reaching yesterday. This is that there are brain processes and it is scientifically not only valuable, but I think necessary, to describe those neurophysiological processes also in terms of information processing of some kind, such as the syntax that it is necessary to build into language processes. Then some of those become conscious as well. So I think there are two things, not three.

Shevrin: I don't quite follow one further step in the theory. I can see there's a correlation between the difference in the conditioning processes of schizophrenics and normal individuals. But how do you get from that to the experience of an auditory hallucination? Why don't they simply experience the world as novel?

Gray: You didn't understand that because I deliberately didn't try to explain it. David Hemsley (e.g. 1987) has written about this issue. Let's avoid auditory hallucinations, which are the feature Hemsley himself deals less well with; Chris Frith (1987) deals with them excellently in another theory, that has the same logical structure as ours, and indeed almost the same anatomy.

Let's take the case in which a schizophrenic appears to see significance in some perfectly ordinary event. The theory would say that to normal people the event would be very familiar and therefore would not capture attention; to the schizophrenic, however, it would be apparently unpredicted, novel, attention-capturing, and because of that the schizophrenic will need to see a significance in it, and he will begin to think he's getting a message from the gods or something like that.

Shevrin: Would you say that your theory would also generalize beyond schizophrenia to other forms of hallucinatory processes, for example as in paranoid non-schizophrenics? Or to the hallucinatory experience of dreaming?

Gray: I certainly wouldn't want to apply it to dreaming. The boundary conditions of the theory at the moment are awaiting further data. We seem to get a very good fit of the theory to positively symptomatic psychotic schizophrenia. We are currently investigating patient groups, such as manics, who are also positively symptomatic psychotics but belong to a different diagnostic pathway. The theory is applicable in principle to any such positive psychotics' symptoms, but we haven't yet investigated fully patient groups other than schizophrenics.

Harnad: Jeffrey, this was a beautiful piece of integrative cognitive neuroscience, the best kind of work we can hope for. You mentioned previous attitudes towards consciousness in research and suggested that it's time for us to acknowledge the relevance of consciousness to research. Consider the testable, Utopian theory that fits all the kinds of data we can have at so many different levels—neurobiological, behavioural, animal, human, pathological, non-pathological. If the structures and processes in that grand cognitive neurobehavioural theory can be treated as conscious or not, *ad libitum*, how does the issue of consciousness become critical (or even relevant) to the theory building?

Gray: Because I want to know what it is that makes a process conscious or not. My theory very carefully doesn't address that problem, just as every other similar theory doesn't. It leaves it totally opaque, and therefore you can't use it even to ask the question: what makes a process conscious?

Dennett: May I suggest a one-word revision which I think will focus the issue. You should add the word 'apparently', so that it reads 'processes that may *apparently* be treated as conscious or not'. This changes the burden of proof in one way. One doesn't assume that one knows what one means by saying, 'I'm not treating this as a conscious process'. As one develops the theory, the conviction that you are not, in fact, capturing consciousness with your model (which isn't saying it's about consciousness) might lapse.

Let me compare this with a similar move that you might find in biology. Biologists used to say, 'We want to talk about life and about whether something is living or not. We are going to put forward models of processes which can be treated as living or not.' Eventually, when the accounts got good enough, instead of saying, 'This doesn't have to be a living process', they said, 'This is what living processes are'.

Gray: Dan, if you are saying that when we have a fully developed understanding, there will still be processes about which, even given that developed understanding, one won't be able clearly to say this is or isn't conscious, that's fine. I accept that's a reasonable possibility. But it isn't the case that we don't have any idea of what distinguishes life from non-life, just because there are instances which are fuzzy. We know, for example, that life has to have properties like irritability, replication systems and so on.

Dennett: I wasn't talking about the fuzzy cases, I was talking about things like a model of some process in mammals, let's say, at the level of molecular biology. One can treat that without making any assumptions about it being living. You don't have to make assumptions about it being living, because that is implicit in all of the assumptions you have made about the conditions under which these things are happening. If somebody asks, 'Does it have to be alive in addition to all these other things going on?' they are missing the point—this is what it is to be alive.

Gray: But we do have an understanding of what it is to be alive, in a way that we don't have an understanding of what it is to generate consciousness.

Harnad: The revision that Dan Dennett suggested is already there when Jeffrey Gray refers to 'a process that may be treated as conscious or not'. The simplest way of putting it is that a neural process will always be *interpretable* either way— as conscious or not. It's up to you. There's no objective way to settle the matter, and, more important, it really makes no difference to the empirical success of the cognitive neurobehavioural theory of which the process in question is a component. By contrast, this is decidedly not the case with, say, a biological theory of life. To be sure, whether something is alive or not is not just a matter of interpretation (just as it is not a matter of interpretation whether something is conscious—has a mind—or not). But in the case of life, once all the objective empirical questions have been answered, the further question of whether the thing in question is merely interpretable as alive or 'really' alive (whether it's a 'true biome' or an empirically indistinguishable 'abiotic zombie biome') no longer has any content. Its content has been exhausted by the answers to all the empirical questions. In the case of the mind, the counterpart of that last question still has content. You could have Jeffrey's integrative neuroscience empirically completed and still say on the last day that's interpretable this way or that, mindfully or mindlessly; yet we know that *everything*—the very existence of our mental lives—rides on the validity of one of those interpretations and not the other, even though all the empirical theory and data are equally compatible with either one. To put it more succinctly: the Utopian theory of life can answer all the substantive questions about life versus lifeless zombie lookalikes with nothing left over or out, whereas the Utopian theory of mind can answer none of the substantive questions about mind versus mindless zombie lookalikes, and hence leaves everything out.

Dennett: Let me describe a thought experiment that goes back to Descartes. In the preface to his book, *Le Monde*, Descartes said: I'm going to describe a world, not our world. Then he proceeded to describe 'a' world in a science fictional vein. At the end he said, 'Guess what, that's *our* world I have just described to you'. Now imagine a slight variation on this: a biologist says, 'I'm going to describe some very interesting structures to you'. He proceeds to describe—without saying a word about life—DNA replication, locomotion, repair, etc. At the end he says, 'That's what life is'. I'm proposing the same move with regard to consciousness. You describe these robots and all of their capabilities; at the end you say, 'That's what consciousness is'.

Harnad: There is a fundamental disanalogy between (mindless) 'zombie mind' and (lifeless) 'zombie life'. Your thought experiment applies to the latter, but not the former. There is an extra fact of the matter about mind but not about life, except in so far as there is an element of animism implicit in vitalism, which simply reduces it all to the mind–body problem again (Harnad 1992).

Nagel: The disagreement is going to remain with regard to what you understand by treating it as conscious. I agree that one might be able to treat such an entity as conscious, but I think that would be to treat it *as if* something were true of it—something of which the truth is not yet entailed by the things that you have said about it.

Dennett: Nothing entails that there isn't élan vital.

Nagel: I think modern biology does entail that there is no élan vital, because modern biology has produced, at least in outline, a successful reduction of precisely those phenomena which constitute life. Generation, nutrition, growth, reproduction are phenomena of which we have a complete schematic understanding in a way that allows them to be reduced to chemistry. There's no room for the further question—what about élan vital?

Dennett: I think you are wrong, Tom; there is room for that question. Suppose it turned out that on another planet, there were phenomena—organisms?—

that were modelled on an interpretation of modern terrestrial biology *with slight changes*. The question would then arise: Are they alive?

Gray: Dan, there is a crucial difference between élan vital and conscious experience. Élan vital was purely a theoretical term devised by the biologists of the time to account for phenomena. Conscious experience is data.

Velmans: Everything that biologists want to say about the difference between what is life and what is non-life can be described in terms of third-person perspective facts. But in the case of conscious experience and mental life many of us believe that we also have first-person perspective facts, which cannot be reduced to third-person perspective facts.

Dennett: Consider what would be the case if we had the complete third-person theory in place. You may say this leaves out first-person point-of-view facts, but it doesn't leave out what we might call apparent or pseudo first-person facts, because the details of your theory will include positing an apparent first-person perspective to this zombie. There will be a complete duality of facts: for every fact that you attribute to the first-person point-of-view of your conscious schizophrenic, there will be a pseudo first-person point-of-view fact about this zombie schizophrenic. At that stage, bearing in mind that your theory is going to articulate all of this apparent first-person point-of-view material, you have a complete apparent phenomenology, a heterophenomenology, and one can say this is the answer to the question—there really isn't any further issue.

Gray: That approach is very valuable and will take us a long way. But let me illustrate the kind of question which that approach will never answer. People frequently sit around and ask: is a monkey conscious, is a rat conscious, is a goldfish conscious, is an amoeba conscious? At the moment we have no way of answering those questions. I believe the data that I showed already allow me, so long as I think that consciousness is attached to some processes rather than others, to say the rat must be conscious in much the same way as the human being. Our paradigms were deliberately set up to account for conscious symptoms that occur in the schizophrenic. The evidence on which they rest includes, among other things, demonstrations of equivalent drug effects on behaviour in these paradigms in rats (Weiner et al 1988) and human beings (Gray et al 1992). So it is parsimonious to assume that processes that are related to this behaviour and are conscious in humans are also conscious in rats. Your approach, in contrast, makes the question, 'is the rat capable of conscious experience?', an absurd question; you don't want to know the answer.

Marcel: Jeffrey, your claim seems to be at odds with what you identify as the major problem. You say the major problem is phenomenal experience. You fail to give any account of what's responsible for the phenomenality. John Searle says, that's just like liquidity and molecules. But it's not. There is a bridging theory that tells you why, for liquidity, the difference is one of level of description. There's nothing I can see for consciousness that's like a bridging theory which tells me it's a level of description. I really don't see any principled account, outside of science or in science, of what gives you that bridge.

Gray: I agree that a principled theory is missing; it needs to be at the top arrow in Fig. 1. I am further saying that, when we have that principled theory, as I firmly anticipate one day we will, then it will be possible, using the kind of theoretical structure that I've described, to answer questions about whether, for example, the rat has conscious experiences. I don't think Dan Dennett's approach will ever get us to that point.

Harnad: Dan Dennett made a point about what he described as 'heterophenomenology' (the complete functional explanation of not only everything we do, but also how the world looks to us, in every one of its qualitative details). Another way of putting Dan's point is that once you have that complete heterophenomenology, which we would all like to have (but which Jeffrey Gray and I would be inclined to say is not enough), there would be an awful lot of apparently superfluous stuff in there, if it indeed failed to capture *real* phenomenology. Dan could rightly ask: 'If it's not the real thing, but merely 'interpretable-as-if', then what is all that superfluous stuff that's so systematically *interpretable* as our complete phenomenology doing there at all?' It would seem to be multiplying entities vastly beyond necessity to have all that interpretable superfluous structure in a zombie that had no real mental life at all!

Nagel: Nobody is denying that this would provide very strong grounds for ascribing consciousness. The question is: is it an inference or not?

Harnad: No, the issue is not just an *epistemic* one, concerning sufficiency of grounds. There is an *ontic* question about both the real phenomenology and the (ostensibly superfluous) *interpretable-as-if* 'phenomenology' in Dan's complete heterophenomenology. It's already a mystery why we are conscious at all, rather than just zombie lookalikes (because for the Blind Watchmaker—a functionalist if ever there was one, and surely no more a mind-reader than we are—functionally indistinguishable zombies would have survived and reproduced just as well). But Dan's heterophenomenology seems to force a second ontic problem on us, namely, all of the inner stuff a system would have to have in order to reflect systematically all the qualitative minutiae of our subjective lives. We know why a zombie wouldn't bother to have *real* qualia; why would it bother to have all those pseudoqualia? Could it be that every qualitative difference in our repertoire subtends a potentially adaptive functional difference?

Searle: There are two things. The analogy I made with liquidity, like all analogies, is very limited. It had only one purpose, which was to get you to see that you can accept the reality of inner subjective states of consciousness without buying any version of dualism. There's nothing mysterious about higher-level features of physical systems, and there's no reason consciousness can't be a higher-level feature of brain systems. The next point is: how the hell does it work? That is the question I was asking the brain stabbers. But that is an empirical question, including its theoretical aspects, in the broader sense of a factual scientific question. I want to keep that question out of philosophy where it doesn't belong and in the hard sciences where it does belong.

Move number two: there is a clear distinction between the case of élan vital and the case of subjective states of awareness. As far as we know anything about how the world works, once you have told the whole story about the third-person phenomena of DNA and RNA and all the rest, there is nothing else to the story of life, nothing else to the distinction between living and non-living matter. But in the case of, for example, my sensations of pain, once you have told the whole story about my behaviour and my neuron firings, there is something else, namely, the felt sensation of pain. And that felt sensation is a datum, not a theoretical construct.

Dennett: That just begs the question, because there was a time when exactly what you just said could have been said by the believers in élan vital. They could have said that once you have all the biochemical story, there still remains this fact that some things are alive and some are not.

Nagel: What was the corresponding datum, which they could have claimed we were ignoring?

Dennett: Brute fact, heartfelt conviction.

Searle: Why are we having this debate? Historically, from the 17th century on, subjective states of conscious feelings or awareness were not supposed to be part of real science. I am arguing that we should get them into real science, so they are as much a part of our investigation as quarks or muons are. As well as being data, I think it will also turn out that they play a theoretical role. If you incorporate subjective states of consciousness into neuroscience, then a complete theory of the brain won't just be a theory about third-person phenomena, it will be a theory that explains subjective states of awareness—they will now become part of the subject matter of the biological sciences.

This is the real crux of the matter: that science can't include subjective states of awareness, I want to say is pure superstition. If we have a definition of science that excludes subjective states of awareness, then let's change the definition of science.

Nagel: There is an equivocation here on the term 'subjective'. Of course, science has to be about objective facts, but there are objective facts about subjective states of awareness, and they aren't just facts about behaviour and functional role, they are objective facts about how it feels for the subject of an experience to undergo it.

Dennett: There are thousands of objective facts about subjective states that we get from science now: about the differences in our colour preferences, and about such trivia as the fact that when Tony Marcel stands up and I stand up, my eyes are higher off the ground than his are and that affects how the world is to me compared to how the world is to him. One can catalogue these objective facts about subjective states and study them from the third-person point of view. There is no apparent limit to how far you can get. Can we know what it's like to be Tony? Sure we can, in great detail. Your claim, Tom, is that that process does not asymptote at all of it; there is always a residual set of facts about the subjective world, which this process doesn't even close in on. I'm saying it does close in on it, it closes in on it to the point where nothing but mounting boredom would be the proper response to asking for any more of it.

References

Frith CD 1987 The positive and negative symptoms of schizophrenia reflect impairments in the perception and initiation of action. Psychol Med 17:631–648

Gray NS, Pickering AD, Hemsley DR, Dawling S, Gray JA 1992 Abolition of latent inhibition by a single 5 mg dose of d-amphetamine in man. Psychopharmacology 107:425–430

Harnad S 1992 Artificial life: synthetic versus virtual. Artif Life III, Santa Fe Institute, New Mexico, 15–19 June 1992

Hemsley DR 1987 An experimental psychological model for schizophrenia. In: Hafner H, Gattaz WF, Janzavik W (eds) Search for the causes of schizophrenia. Springer-Verlag, Berlin, p 179–188

Hemsley DR 1990 What have cognitive deficits to do with schizophrenia? In: Huber G (ed) Idiopathische Psychosen. Schattauer, Stuttgart, p 111–127

Jones SH, Gray JA, Hemsley DR 1992 Loss of the Kamin blocking effect in acute but not chronic schizophrenics. Biol Psychiatry 32:739–755

Kamin LJ 1968 'Attention like' processes in classical conditioning. In: Jones MR (ed) Miami symposium on the prediction of behavior: aversive stimulation. University of Miami Press, Miami, p 9–33

Shanks DR 1985 Forward and backward blocking of human contingency judgement. Q J Exp Psychol B Comp Physiol Psychol 37:1–21

Weiner I, Lubow RE, Feldon J 1988 Disruption of latent inhibition by acute administration of low doses of amphetamine. Pharmacol Biochem Behav 30:871–878

How does a serial, integrated and very limited stream of consciousness emerge from a nervous system that is mostly unconscious, distributed, parallel and of enormous capacity?

Bernard J. Baars

The Wright Institute, 2728 Durant Avenue, Berkeley, CA 94704, USA

Abstract. Much of the nervous system can be viewed as a massively parallel, distributed system of highly specialized but unconscious processors. Conscious experience on the other hand is traditionally viewed as a serial *stream* that integrates different sources of information but is limited to only one internally consistent content at any given moment. Global Workspace theory suggests that conscious experience emerges from a nervous system in which multiple input processors compete for access to a broadcasting capability; the winning processor can disseminate its information *globally* throughout the brain. Global workspace architectures have been widely employed in computer systems to integrate separate modules when they must work together to solve a novel problem or to control a coherent new response. The theory articulates a series of increasingly complex models, able to account for more and more evidence about conscious functioning, from perceptual consciousness to conscious problem-solving, voluntary control of action, and directed attention. Global Workspace theory is consistent with, but not reducible to, other theories of limited-capacity mechanisms. Global workspace architectures must show competition for input to a neural global workspace and global distribution of its output. Brain structures that are demonstrably required for normal conscious experience can carry out these two functions. The theory makes testable predictions, especially for newly emerging, high-speed brain imaging technology.

1993 Experimental and theoretical studies of consciousness. Wiley, Chichester (Ciba Foundation Symposium 174) p 282–303

Asking the right question can often help organize and simplify an otherwise overwhelming amount of evidence. This paper asks how a narrowly limited conscious stream emerges from a massively parallel, largely unconscious nervous system. Limited capacity mechanisms associated with consciousness appear to be biologically very costly, and one may reasonably ask what biological benefits could possibly accrue from such basic 'architectural' features. 'Global Workspace' theory, described below, suggests one reasonable answer, which when compared to others shows a striking amount of agreement as well as some significant differences (Baars 1983, 1988, Baddeley 1992a,b, Crick 1984, Crick & Koch 1990, Dennett 1991, Dennett & Kinsbourne 1992, John 1976, Kinsbourne 1988, Marcel 1983, Norman & Shallice 1986, Posner 1992, Shallice 1978, Damasio 1989, Edelman 1989).

Limited capacity versus massive capacity

There is increasing agreement that large parts of the human nervous system, such as the neocortex, can be viewed as 'societies' of separable, very specialized unconscious systems (Dennett & Kinsbourne 1992, Kinsbourne 1988, Marcel 1993). The neurobiological evidence for this view comes from anatomical studies (e.g. Mountcastle 1978), as well as physiological experiments and careful studies of patients with brain damage (e.g. Geschwind 1979, Luria 1980, Gazzaniga 1988). Convergent psychological evidence comes from studies of automaticity due to practice (Shiffrin et al 1981), from psycholinguistics and memory theory, and from the study of errors and slips (e.g. Baars 1992). The connectionist movement in cognitive science also suggests that small networks which change connection strength as a function of node activity provide elegant and often powerful models of many local phenomena. Purely functional models combining many independent expert systems have been studied for at least two decades. Indeed, computational models of complex human functions like language comprehension, motor control or visual analysis always contain multiple specialized modules. All these sources suggest that the nervous system has a great number of specialized cell populations which can operate in parallel, unconsciously, and with some autonomy.

Paradoxically, an equally impressive body of evidence points to quite a different nervous system. There is strong and reliable support for a mechanism that is serial rather than parallel, internally consistent at any single moment rather than distributed, very limited in capacity, and strongly associated with consciousness.

Evidence for a limited capacity mechanism comes from three major sources. First, selective attention tasks, in which humans can follow only a single dense and coherent flow of information, such as a spoken message or a basketball game, at one time; any other streams of information are unconscious. Second, dual-task phenomena, where the mutual interference and degradation of simultaneous tasks requires consciousness or mental effort (Shallice 1978, Norman & Shallice 1986). Third, immediate memory, consisting of sensory memories and rehearsable short-term memory, with its known capacity limit of seven plus or minus two separate and unrelated items (Baddeley 1992a,b).

These three sets of phenomena point to a nervous system that is rather slow, prone to error, unable to perform simultaneous tasks, and quite limited—just the opposite of the parallel distributed system described above.

Limited capacity phenomena are strongly associated with consciousness. Selective attention tasks separate two coherent streams of information into a conscious and an unconscious one. In dual-task paradigms, interference between the two tasks depends upon the extent to which both are conscious: the more the tasks become predictable and automatic, the less they interfere with each other (Shiffrin et al 1981). Thus, the more skilled we become in driving along a predictable road, the more easily we can carry on a conversation at the same time. Sensory memory always involves conscious information; short-term memory involves inner rehearsal of numbers or words, in which the items are 'refreshed' by being made conscious every several seconds. The relationship between consciousness and the limited capacity system is therefore very close.

I have suggested that consciousness *underlies* the limited capacity system (Baars 1988). One of the most explicit models of limited capacity is Baddeley's well-developed notion of Working Memory. It has two major content components, the 'phonological loop' (for rehearsing verbal items) and the 'visuospatial sketchpad' (for using visual imagery in planning, for example) (Baddeley 1992a). There is a great deal of solid empirical evidence for both components. However, contrary to expectation, the phonological loop and the visuospatial sketchpad have recently been found to interfere with each other (Baddeley 1992b). This suggests to Baddeley and others that both of these components are aspects of normal conscious experience. (See Baars 1988, chapter 8, for one model relating working memory to consciousness.)

Consciousness 'as such'

The evidence that bears most directly on the issue of consciousness *as such* compares similar conscious and unconscious phenomena. For example, Libet's (1981) work suggests that somatosensory stimuli are represented in the cortex for a considerable time before they become conscious. The bodily location, and perhaps other parameters, of the stimuli, may exist before the onset of conscious experience. Dennett (1991) and Dennett & Kinsbourne (1992) have criticized the notion of 'onset of conscious experience', but this idea does not have to emerge from a naïve Cartesian theatre. Within rather broad time limits, we can probably specify the onset of perceptual consciousness, as indicated by Libet's work (see Libet, this volume).

Another example concerns event-related potentials created by repetitive stimuli which habituate over time, although the habituated representation can be shown to continue after conscious access fades. E. R. John (1976) reports that activity before habituation is widespread throughout a cat's brain, but, after habituation, event-related potentials can be found only in the sensory tract that continues to be stimulated. Recent work with positron emission tomography suggests the same result: that a novel task, of which subjects are conscious in its details, increases metabolic activity all over the brain, whereas the same task performed automatically after practice causes high metabolic activity only locally (Haier 1992).

The remarkable phenomenon of blindsight likewise suggests a natural contrast between visual representations that are conscious and similar representations that are unconscious (Weiskrantz 1988). It is important to distinguish research that compares similar conscious and unconscious events, and therefore tells us about consciousness *as such*, from work that compares different *contents* of consciousness, such as different perceptual experiences, images and inner speech. In comparisons of similar conscious and unconscious phenomena, consciousness is the independent variable (Libet 1981, Baars 1983). On the other hand, if we study the ability of subjects to switch from foveal to non-foveal visual experience, we are not studying consciousness as such, but something that is more accurately called 'attention', i.e. the *control of access to different conscious contents* (Baars 1988, chapter 8). From this point of view, Posner's important work on 'attentional networks' in the brain involves selective or directed attention rather than consciousness (e.g. Posner 1992). Obviously, attention and consciousness are intimately related, but the distinction is vital.

Resolving the limited capacity paradox

The flow of conscious experience is traditionally viewed as a serial *stream*—one that integrates different sources of information, but is limited to a single internally consistent content at any given moment (Baars 1988). But what is this very limited, serial, integrated stream of consciousness doing in an enormous society of parallel and distributed unconscious bioprocessors? Why do people have trouble keeping more than nine items in short-term memory, when an inexpensive calculator can store dozens of long numbers? Over one thousand million years of evolution of nervous systems, why did truly independent conscious streams not develop?

Such questions focus on the functional paradox of limited capacity mechanisms. By any reasonable measure, the conscious stream is biologically very expensive. The human brain consumes about 25% of body glucose and is dependent on an uninterrupted supply of oxygen; because its major input and output functions involve consciousness, a substantial part of this energy investment must go toward supporting limited capacity mechanisms (Lassen et al 1978). There must also be an evolutionary cost in being limited to a single coherent stream of events at one time. Surely if animals could not be *distracted*, i.e. if they could be conscious of multiple streams of events simultaneously, such as guarding against predators, searching for food and interacting with their social group, they would increase their chances for survival and reproduction.

But vertebrates can orient to only a single informative flow of events at any given time. What evolutionary benefits could justify such costs?

There is a class of information-processing architectures that have exactly the form described above—that is, they combine a serial stream with a large, parallel, distributed society of processors—which suggests an answer to the question of cost and benefits. These global workspace architectures have been developed by a number of cognitive scientists for purely pragmatic reasons: not primarily as a model of human functioning, but to solve very difficult problems, such as speech analysis, which involve multiple knowledge sources. They are expensive in terms of processing resources, but they justify their cost because they can combine the activities of many different quasi-autonomous 'specialists' to solve problems that cannot be solved by any single one (Hayes-Roth 1985). Global workspace architectures consist of collections of specialized processors, integrated by a single memory, whose contents can be broadcast to all the specialists. They are publicity systems in the society of specialists. Input specialists (such as perceptual systems) compete for access to the global workspace; once they gain access, they are able to disseminate a message to the system as a whole. When a problem has a predictable solution, it is handled by a specialized processor. But when novel problems arise, or when new, coherent actions must be planned and carried out, the global workspace becomes necessary (Baars 1983, 1988, 1992).

The Global Workspace theory of conscious experience employs this remarkably simple and useful architecture to explain many pairs of matched conscious and unconscious processes, all bearing on consciousness *as such* (see above). The theory currently consists of a series of seven increasingly adequate models which together are able to account for a vast amount of evidence about perceptual consciousness, unconscious problem-solving, habituation and automaticity, voluntary control of action, the role of intentions and expectations, selective and directed attention, contextual influences on conscious experience, and the adaptive roles of consciousness in the nervous system (Baars 1988). Global Workspace theory is consistent with, but not reducible to, other theories of limited capacity.

A global workspace does not perform executive functions, though it can be used by executive systems (Baars 1988, chapter 9). If the global workspace is a publicity organ in a society of specialists, then executive systems resemble a government, or, more flexibly, a variety of processor coalitions that aim at various times to control access to the global workspace in order to control the society as a whole.

Global workspace architectures are somewhat counterintuitive, because the intelligence of the system does *not* reside in the global workspace, but rather in the experts that provide input to and receive output from it. Take the example of spotting errors in a consciously perceived sentence. We can detect errors at many different levels: in acoustics, phonology, lexical choice, syntax, morphology, semantics and the pragmatic goals of the speaker. We rapidly detect such errors in any conscious sentence, *even though we are not conscious of the many complex rule systems that detect the error*. Thus, the detailed intelligence of the system does not become conscious in error-detection.

Global Workspace theory provides a *functional account* of the limited capacity stream of consciousness, because global messages need to reach the whole 'society' of processors, so that any arbitrary knowledge source can be related to any other. This is because, in the case of truly novel problems, the particular processor or coalition of processors that may find a solution *cannot be specified in advance*. Perhaps the most impressive example of this ability of the nervous system to access unpredictable sets of processors comes from the extensive literature on conscious feeback in the control of either single neurons or, apparently, any population of neurons (Chase 1974). The feedback signal must always be conscious—we would not expect people or animals to learn feedback tasks if they were distracted, habituated to the feedback signal or asleep.

Comparisons to other models

Global Workspace theory shows a striking amount of agreement with other approaches, as well as some significant differences. It is important to note that the theory defines a *class* of models, rather than just a single one. One can imagine many different instantiations. McClelland (1986) has shown that connectionist networks can make up a global workspace configuration. It is possible to interpret the brainstem reticular formation as a hierarchy of increasingly global workspaces, culminating in a single high-level workspace corresponding to consciousness (Baars 1988, p 132). A set of global workspaces corresponding to mutually inhibitory perceptual systems is also attractive for understanding perceptual consciousness (Baars 1988, p 105, Baars & Newman 1992). In principle, such workspaces could be instantiated in the brain by modulation of rapid, correlated waveforms (as suggested by Crick & Koch 1980), by 'multiregional retroactivation' (Damasio 1989), by a 'cortical focus' (Kinsbourne 1988), by 're-entrant signalling' (Edelman 1989), or by 'multiple drafts' (Dennett 1991, Dennett & Kinsbourne 1992).

However, some important differences should be noted. Approaches to consciousness seem to be separable into those that emphasize the parallel and distributed nature of neural functioning, and those that emphasize limited capacity mechanisms. In the first category are models suggested by Dennett (1991), Dennett & Kinsbourne (1992), Damasio (1989) and John (1976). Models emphasizing limited capacity include those of Baddeley (1992a), Shallice (1978), Norman & Shallice (1986), Crick (1984) and Crick & Koch (1990). The point of this paper is that *both* distributed and limited capacity aspects of consciousness must be accounted for in a single, unified model (cf. Kinsbourne 1988).

A possible neural substrate

Given the defining properties of global workspace systems, we can study the neuroscience literature to see if analogous properties exist in the brain. Two defining properties are (a) competition for input to a neural global workspace, and (b) global distribution of its output (Baars & Newman 1992).

Two neural mechanisms associated with conscious experience (in the sense that their absence results in loss of consciousness) show competition between different input modalities. These are the brainstem reticular formation (Magoun 1962, Hobson & Brazier 1980) and the nucleus reticularis of the thalamus (Scheibel 1980). The reticular formation is thought to modulate the activity of many higher-level neural structures, notably the neocortex; the nucleus reticularis is believed to control thalamic 'gatelets' that can open or close sensory tracts on their way to the cortex. Lesions in either structure result in a loss of consciousness.

The problem with both of these systems is that their output bandwidth does not seem to be large enough to carry the information for a conscious visual scene, for example. Further, phenomena like blindsight suggest that primary cortical projection areas are needed for conscious perceptual experiences, because abolition of striate cortex leads to a loss of normal conscious vision without abolishing object representation. The situation can therefore be summarized as follows:

(1) Activities in the reticular formation and the nucleus reticularis seem to be necessary but not sufficient for conscious experience;

(2) Stimulus representation in primary sensory projection areas also seems to be necessary but not sufficient for conscious perceptual experience (Weiskrantz 1988).

The simplest hypothesis is that *both* components together are necessary *and* sufficient to support conscious perceptual experience. For consciousness of a visual object, like a coffee cup, one plausible account is that a thalamocortical feedback loop, along the lines of Edelman's 're-entrant signalling loop' (1989), may be necessary in order to establish a specific cortical focus corresponding to the stimulus (Kinsbourne 1988). Once the loop is established, information from primary visual cortex can be broadcast via massive connections from striate cortex to subcortical mechanisms via the thalamus, and to other cortical areas via massive connections, such as the arcuate fasciculi, long and short association fibres, commissural tracts to the contralateral hemisphere, and possibly through the 'feltwork' of layer I of the cortex (Baars & Newman 1992). Thus, once the stimulus is maintained long enough in primary sensory cortex, there are massive opportunities for global broadcasting to other parts of the brain.

Summary and conclusions

Any adequate theory of consciousness must account for both limited capacity, integrative mechanisms and wide-spread, distributed intelligence. Global workspace architectures have both features, are practical for solving problems that need to combine specialized autonomous systems, and provide a natural way to think about consciousness. The global workspace approach discussed here can model perceptual consciousness, conscious components of problem-solving and conscious involvement in action control. This approach resembles other accounts of the role of consciousness in the nervous system, but is not reducible to them. Global workspace architectures can be instantiated in many different ways, but all of them involve competition between global workspace input, and global dissemination of output. Brain structures that are required for normal conscious experiences can carry out these functions.

Acknowledgements

The theoretical framework presented here has been in development since 1978, greatly aided by a Sloan Foundation Cognitive Science Scholar appointment (1979–1980) at the Center for Human Information Processing, University of California at San Diego, and by a Visiting Scientist appointment (1985–1986) at the John D. and Catherine T. MacArthur Foundation Program on Conscious and Unconscious Mental Processes, University of California at San Francisco. I am especially grateful to Donald A. Norman, David Galin and Katherine McGovern.

References

Baars BJ 1983 Conscious contents provide the nervous system with coherent, global information. In: Davidson R, Schwartz G, Shapiro D (eds) Consciousness and self regulation. Plenum Publishing Corporation, New York, vol 3:45–76

Baars BJ 1988 A cognitive theory of consciousness. Cambridge University Press, New York

Baars BJ 1992 The psychology of human error: implications for the architecture of voluntary control. Plenum Publishing Corporation, New York

Baars BJ, Newman J 1992 A neurobiological interpretation of the Global Workspace theory of consciousness. In: Revonsuo A, Kamppinen M (eds) Consciousness in philosophy and cognitive neuroscience. Routledge, London, in press

Baddeley AD 1992a Working memory. Science (Wash DC) 255:556–559

Baddeley AD 1992b Consciousness and working memory. Consci & Cognit 1:3–6

Chase MH (ed) 1974 Operant control of brain activity. University of California Press, Berkeley, CA

Crick FHC 1984 Function of the thalamic reticular complex: the searchlight hypothesis. Proc Natl Acad Sci USA 81:4586–4593

Crick FHC, Koch C 1990 Towards a neurobiological theory of consciousness. Semin Neurosci 2:263–275

Damasio AR 1989 Time-locked multiregional retroactivation: a systems-level proposal for the neural substrates of recall and recognition. Cognition 33:25–62

Dennett D 1991 Consciousness explained. Little, Brown, Boston, MA

Dennett D, Kinsbourne M 1992 Time and the observer: the where and when of consciousness in the brain. Behav Brain Sci 15:175–220

Edelman G 1989 The remembered present: a biological theory of consciousness. Basic Books, New York

Gazzaniga MS 1988 Brain modularity: towards a philosophy of conscious experience: In: Marcel AJ, Bisiach E (eds) Consciousness in contemporary science. Oxford University Press, Oxford

Geschwind N 1979 Specializations of the human brain. Sci Am 241:180–201

Haier RJ 1992 Regional glucose metabolic changes after learning a complex visuospatial/ motor task: a positron emission tomography study. Brain Res 570:134–143

Hayes-Roth B 1985 A blackboard architecture of control. Artif Intell 26:251–351

Hobson JA, Brazier MAB 1980 The reticular formation revisited: specifying function for a non-specific system. Raven Press, New York

John ER 1976 A model of consciousness. In: Schwartz G, Shapiro D (eds) Consciousness and self-regulation. Plenum Publishing Corporation, New York, p 6–50

Kinsbourne M 1988 Integrated field theory of consciousness. In: Marcel AJ, Bisiach E (eds) Consciousness in contemporary science. Oxford University Press, Oxford

Lassen NA, Ingvar DH, Skinhøj E 1978 Brain function and blood flow. Sci Am 239:50–59

Libet B 1981 Timing of cerebral processes relative to concomitant conscious experiences in man. In: Adam G, Meszaros I, Banyai EI (eds) Advances in physiological science. Pergamon Press, Oxford

Libet B 1993 The neural time factor in conscious and unconscious events. In: Experimental and theoretical studies of consciousness. Wiley, Chichester (Ciba Found Symp 174) p 123–146

Luria AR 1980 Higher cortical functions in man, 2nd edn. Basic Books, New York (Russian language edition 1969)

Marcel AJ 1983 Conscious and unconscious perception: an approach to the relations between phenomenal experience and perceptual processes. Cognit Psychol 15:238–300

Marcel AJ 1993 Slippage in the unity of consciousness. In: Experimental and theoretical studies of consciousness. Wiley, Chichester (Ciba Found Symp 174) p 168–186

McClelland JL 1986 The programmable blackboard model of reading. In: McClelland JL, Rumelhart DE and the PDP Group (eds) Parallel distributed processing—explorations in the microstructure of cognition, vol 2: Psychological and biological models. MIT Press, Cambridge, MA, p 122–169

Magoun WH 1962 The waking brain, 2nd edn. Thomas Publishers, Springfield, IL

Mountcastle VB 1978 An organizing principle for cerebral function: the unit module and the distributed system. In: Edelman GM, Mountcastle VB (eds) The mindful brain. MIT Press, Cambridge, MA, p 7–50

Norman DA, Shallice T 1986 Attention to action: willed and automatic control of behavior. In: Davidson RJ, Schwartz GE, Shapiro D (eds) Consciousness and self-regulation. Plenum Publishing Corporation, New York, vol 4:1–18

Posner MI 1992 Attention as a cognitive and neural system. Curr Dir Psychol Sci 11:11–14

Scheibel AB 1980 Anatomical and physiological substrates of arousal. In: Hobson JA, Brazier MA (eds) The reticular formation revisited. Raven Press, New York, p 55–66

Shallice T 1978 The dominant action system: an information-processing approach to consciousness. In: Pope KS, Singer JL (eds) The stream of consciousness: scientific investigations into the flow of experience. Plenum Publishing Corporation, New York, p 117–153

Shiffrin RM, Dumais ST, Schneider W 1981 Characteristics of automatism. In: Long J, Baddeley A (eds) Attention and performance IX. Erlbaum Associates, Hillsdale, NJ, p 223–238 (Atten Perform Ser)

Weiskrantz L 1988 Some contributions of neuropsychology of vision and memory to the problem of consciousness. In: Marcel AJ, Bisiach E (eds) Scientific approaches to consciousness. Oxford University Press, Oxford, p 183–199

DISCUSSION

Harnad: Your model faces more problems than Jeffrey Gray's (this volume), for the following reason. His model first accounts for a good deal of behavioural and neurobiological data, then it has the interpretative problem represented by Hemsley's move: are some of the components which are interpreted as conscious or as referring to consciousness justifiably interpreted as such? Your model, by contrast, is only interpretation; indeed, it seems to me to be mostly *post hoc* interpretation of other people's models and of known facts about the nervous system.

Baars: What could be more relevant to consciousness than an experimental design in which consciousness is a variable? When Libet (1981) records somatosensory activity due to a supraliminal stimulus to the skin for 30 ms, no consciousness is reported. After 100 ms or longer, depending on the intensity of the stimulus, consciousness of the stimulus is reported. It seems to me that such a result has implications for perceptual consciousness *as such*.

Dozens of other cases allow direct comparisons between very similar conscious and unconscious phenomena. In stimulus habituation, the identical stimulus is presented before and after it fades from consciousness. There is independent evidence that the stimulus continues to be represented in the primary sensory projection area even after conscious access fades (Sokolov 1963, Thatcher & John 1977). Again, we can compare very similar conditions in which people are either conscious of the stimulus or not.

We are not looking just at single studies here, but at entire research literatures, both psychological and neurobiological. There is much evidence about threshold phenomena, such as those studied by Ben Libet, stimulus habituation, automaticity of practised skills, selective attention, incubation in problem-solving, episodic forgetting and recall, mental imagery and inner speech, all of which differentiate between similar conscious and unconscious processes.

All these lines of evidence impose strong empirical constraints on any adequate theory of conscious experience. It seems to me that there is nothing radical or unusual about this claim. It is exactly the way we go about collecting evidence on any other empirical phenomenon.

Marcel: With all due respect, the Global Workspace theory cannot be the case, because from Helmholtz onwards the whole point is that those processes that are pre-conscious, which give you illusions, for instance, are exactly the processes which themselves actually take inputs from different modalities. That's how you get illusions—the effects of vision on touch give a tactile illusion because something non-conscious takes input from different sources or modalities. If *non*-conscious processes exhibit the properties that you attribute to the conscious 'global workspace', how is a global workspace a theory of *consciousness*?

Baars: I agree that an adequate theory must deal with cross-modal as well as higher-level abstract contents of consciousness. I try to do this in my book (Baars 1988).

Carr: Your talk provides an opportunity to summarize what I see as the progress we have made during the symposium and some of the questions that remain to be answered. At the end of the first day we were left in a very pessimistic state. Many people generally agreed with one form or another of Searle's proposal that consciousness arises in some sense as an integral property of nervous system operations, but it was accepted that we have no notions at all about what a theory of how that property arises might look like. However, there are three proposals that represent the beginnings—just the very beginnings—of such a theory. We have heard about constraints on such a theory (for example, Tony Marcel's interesting results) and also about methods for investigating it empirically (such as Bill Newsome's work with monkeys and now Bernie Baars' discussion of the method of comparing the same processes when they are conscious and when they are not). I'll talk a little about these three proposals for a theory of the structure and origins of consciousness, and then return to Baars' work.

The first proposal is the single-structure theory (Posner 1992, Edelman 1989). There is a privileged structure in the brain and when that gets activated, you are conscious. This proposal doesn't tell us how the activation of that structure makes the consciousness or what aspect of its operation is the consciousness. Nor does it tell us the ontological substance or the ontological character of that consciousness. (Remember Marcel's smart distinction between the setting conditions for consciousness and the nature of what arises.) But it does begin to provide the outlines of a potential structure of a neural theory of how consciousness arises. The single-structure proposal didn't get much shrift; some people take it seriously, many don't.

The second proposal is the Kinsbourne–Dennett view that there could be many different processes, or sets of processes, going on that are capable of giving rise to consciousness at any given point of time (Kinsbourne, this volume). The process that occupies the largest portion of the brain somehow will provide the conscious experiences—consciousness has something to do with the largest mass of tissue involved in processing at any given time.

The third proposal is also associated with Dennett and with others, including Marcel. In this proposal, there are lots of different consciousnesses around. It's a little unclear to me which one is going to be in control at any given time: that presumably is one of the questions one would have to answer with such a theory.

Now, Bernie Baars has described a method that might be able to choose among these candidates by comparing the same processes when they are conscious and when they are unconscious. One example involves skilled performance. When we are learning a task, it seems to occupy our attention, but when we are practised it doesn't any more. At the level of general description, this is anecdotal truth among cognitive theory. However, it is not clear exactly what it means to be 'conscious' or 'fully occupied' in the one sense, and 'not conscious' in the other. One is not *unconscious* when performing a skill; one may be conscious of different aspects of the task in different ways.

Baars proposed that one could do a neural analysis of this situation and look, say using positron emission tomography (PET), at a novel performance and a skilled performance. One such PET study was done by Julie Fiez and the Washington University neurology group (communicated by Marc Raichle 1990). Unpractised subjects are asked to perceive a series of nouns; in response to each noun they generate the appropriate verb. The nouns are presented at one per second, so this is a demanding task. The PET scan shows that a region in left inferior prefrontal cortex 'lights up', indicating increased blood flow. This area shows increased activity during the performance of several other tasks related to word meanings. The anterior cingulate also lights up, as do some areas in the basal ganglia and an area in the cerebellum, relative to baselines that control for the motor performances and speech. With practice in this task, people become fluent: they now produce the same verb in response to each noun, whereas they might not early in the trial, and they do it very quickly and easily. Fiez has not collected careful phenomenal reports of what the subjects are thinking, but we do see these same characteristics in many skilled performances. The PET scan of a practised subject shows that the left anterior prefrontal activation is no longer above control conditions; neither is the anterior cingulate activation. The basal ganglia activation is still there, as is some cerebellum activation, but a component of it has disappeared. The component that remains is one that is shared with the activity of simply naming a list of words presented visually. A new area of activation has now risen above baseline—the set of structures around the temporal–parietal junction that is also activated when one names words.

So we have behavioural evidence that performance becomes fluent; we have neural evidence that the brain structures involved in fluent performance are different from the one involved in novice performance. What does that say about the three candidate theories of consciousness? Take first the single-structure theory. If we believe that one is fully conscious at the beginning in a way that one is not after practice, then we must see some structure that's active in the one case and not in the other. There are such structures. What about the view of multiple consciousnesses? To the extent that we believe the character of conscious experience changes, there are different structures that become activated in the two situations. So there is a basis for believing in multiple consciousnesses, each giving rise to a different sort of conscious experience. What about the 'mass of tissue' theory? There is no good evidence from this study that consciousness depends on mass of tissue *per se*, because the total amount of tissue activated has not clearly changed, but possibly you can't make the judgement from these PET data. There are other PET studies in which the total amount of activation does appear to change.

So, we have three candidates for this 'setting condition' theory—the theory of the evidentiary conditions about which aspects of neural and cognitive processing are associated with consciousness, and which are not. We have the beginnings of methods for investigating the merits of these theories. In particular, the candidate theories differ in terms of how consciousness might be distributed—where, in either the information-processing system or the neural system, consciousness might arise. We have techniques for studying how the distribution of consciousness might change, at least in the neural systems (that's what Baars and I have been talking about). Yesterday, Pat Wall (this volume) described ways of showing how the organization of conscious processes might influence neurophysiology. Bill Newsome showed how the organization of the neurophysiology might influence conscious experience. Thus, in addition to candidate theories, we have concrete examples of several relevant and promising empirical methodologies.

Are we therefore able to distinguish among these candidates for allocating consciousness to neural cognitive processes? Not yet, but we do have some clear directions and some methods that we can apply. Do we have anything to speak to the second question, the ontological substance, and the necessity of that particular substance, once we know the setting conditions and the processes giving rise to it? Not yet, and there is much debate about the difference between those two things. So, even though we haven't answered all the questions, we have made a lot of progress and we should not leave feeling pessimistic.

Gray: I would like to utter a cautionary word about the way in which a PET scan is interpreted. The glucose utilization method reflects the activity of, principally, the nerve terminals in a particular region. But those nerve terminals are just as likely to be inhibitory as excitatory terminals, and the energy consumption is going to be the same. Have you taken that problem into account?

Carr: I appreciate your point. However, the general logic of the point I was trying to make in that context doesn't necessarily depend on whether a structure is more excited when its blood flow is increased, or less. Whichever occurred, you know that the structure was working harder. For a more detailed interpretation, you have to know what kinds of information the structure was sending via facilitation and via inhibition. Similarly, when a structure fails to show increased blood flow after practice, is that because it's no longer involved or because it has become so good at its job that the job is now really easy? There are questions that remain to be answered about how to interpret PET scans; no method is perfect. But if we apply several methods, with different strengths and weaknesses, we will ultimately answer the question.

Baars: I agree with Jeffrey Gray's caution about the PET scan data. One reason the PET scan results are so attractive is that they appear to support the results on event-related potentials (ERPs) reported by Thatcher & John (1977).

They implanted multiple electrodes in the brain of an awake cat and found ERP readings all over the brain before habituation. After stimulus habituation, ERPs were found only in the stimulated modality. The same pattern has now been reported in a study of cerebral blood flow (see Haier et al 1992). The range of stimuli and tasks in these studies is very wide.

Wall: There is a real bias in this discussion, namely that sensory processing is related only to the input. Hardly anyone has mentioned processing that might be going on in relation to the output. In rat hippocampus there are cells that fire only when the animal is in a particular location (O'Keefe & Nadel 1978). It has been asked experimentally if these cells signal the animal's present location (the input) or whether they signal the location in relation to the goal (the future output). These cells would generally serve the input processing that has been the basis of most discussion here.

But, as Nick Humphrey asked me yesterday, what's so odd about pain? I listed a series of sensory events, such as pain, hunger, thirst, sleepiness, which contain a strong prediction of the future. I would like to suggest that there are some processes going on which are primarily about what you are going to do, rather than what is happening. Since you have only one option in what you may do at any one time, for example you can't turn right and left simultaneously, this limitation might solve part of the question as to why you have an apparently limited process going on in an apparently unlimited structure.

Marcel: In my paper (this volume), the first set of experiments exactly illustrates the dependency of one's experience on one's action.

Nagel: Pat, may I ask about the reticular formation hypothesis? You asked, why all this focus on the cortex? Are you sceptical about any location, or do you really have in mind that something in the brainstem is more essential?

Wall: You invite me to point a finger at some structure and to assign to it the entire monopoly of one sensory function. That version of phrenology is no more valid for deep structures than it is for the cortex. A sensory function may reach a single conclusion such as 'my foot hurts me', but it has done so by a sequence of processes distributed in space and time. All the experimental evidence now points to the process (and, for that matter, the conclusion) being an interactive pattern in time and in many structures, both cortical and deep.

Baars: I think the reticular formation is involved, plus the nucleus reticularis of the thalamus; from studies on patients with blindsight it looks as if the primary visual projection area is required for conscious visual experience. I think a first approximation neural model must include those structures. You can show quite straightforwardly that the neuroanatomy is at least compatible with the global workspace interpretation.

Lockwood: Suppose we had a thalamus and reticular formation in a vat, and we supplied them artificially with the same kind of stimulation they would be getting if there were a cortex and all the rest. Do you think that, phenomenologically, we would then get the whole show?

Baars: This is a question for Dan Dennett and John Searle; they have thought much more about the philosophical issues. I have my hands full just trying to understand the simplest evidence that is clearly relevant to conscious experience.

Lockwood: Dan doesn't think this is a meaningful question.

Marcel: There is an interesting point about certain types of functionalist approaches to consciousness. Several information-processing theories (including Bernie Baars') add a box and postulate that access to that box is what gives you consciousness. In principle, there is no reason why access to another information-processing stage should yield consciousness or phenomenal experience. However, there is another type of theoretical move one can make. In order to get into that box or to have access, you may need a certain type of content. For David Rosenthal (1990), it is the type of content that will support higher-order thoughts about such content. But note that once you have this special type of content, you don't need an extra box or access—you already have what you wanted, namely consciousness. Information-processing approaches don't take content seriously.

Baars: I take the issue of content very seriously. It is obviously of primary psychological importance.

Marcel: If you have a change in content, why do you need an extra box?

Baars: It's just a way of describing the flow of information.

Marcel: You don't need it.

Shevrin: I have what I think is a logical problem. Whether you have the notion, as Bernie Baars is suggesting, of some centralized conceptual locus for consciousness, or that consciousness is distributed over a variety of systems, you have to presuppose some invariant characteristic, or characteristics, that accounts for consciousness, which is the issue that we are trying to address. So in the broad conceptual sense we have to talk about a consciousness system, whether it's distributed over various drafts or localized in an anatomical centre.

Baars: I was trying to make a functional point, but I think it has implications for brain.

Shevrin: I think the question that Dan Dennett would need to answer is: what are the invariant properties of these distributed drafts across the brain that actually produce consciousness?

Dennett: I don't like the way you put it as 'producing' consciousness, but I agree that I have to say by virtue of what properties of what's going on in the brain do certain contents become conscious.

I want to give some advice to the scientists here about how to proceed with their business, while John Searle and I proceed with ours. Let me point out a few facts which I think are uncontentious. When zombies are given a novel and difficult task, their zombie global workspace is more extensively activated than when they perform a practised task. When zombies are pseudo-schizophrenic, they fail to utilize previous memories in order to avoid the 'this is novel' response, which then generates pseudo-hallucinations of pseudo-delusional pseudo-belief. When zombies do biofeedback, the signal has to enter their pseudo-conscious global workspace in order for it to work. That's one way of putting the facts. Or, if I were right, you could say that we were actually talking about consciousness all along. The point is that you can go ahead and work out your models and your theories, and leave this issue, which has now been very well articulated, aside. In 10 years, you can come back and find out whether you have been using a theory of pseudo-consciousness or a theory of consciousness.

Singer: Most of the examples given at this symposium have dealt with external inputs. Bill Newsome's study of the input to the monkey's brain is an exception, and is fascinating for that reason (Newsome & Salzman, this volume). When we talk about consciousness and conscious experience, it is not just saying 'I see a light flickering over here'; an awful lot of it is remembering things from our past or thinking about the future. How do we think such centrally generated phenomena relate to some of the brain models presented here?

Baars: Your work (Singer, this volume) is absolutely central to the issue of externally versus internally generated conscious content. I have struggled with this in my own thinking about these issues. One thing that strikes me is the extent to which internal processes have quasi-perceptual features: you can make slips of the tongue in inner speech that are very similar to overt slips of the tongue that occur in normal speech (Dell & Repka 1992). Finke (1980) and others have shown that the domain of visual imagery is very similar to visual perception. So one of the things that seems unmotivated by any psychological function that I know, and which therefore may be an evolutionary phenomenon, is the strong resemblance between conscious perception of the outer world and internally generated conscious processes, such as visual imagery, inner speech and fantasy.

Shevrin: In the work that we have heard, which is highly representative of the work going on in these fields, one is dealing with essentially purely cognitive processes. These are cognitive processes under certain constrained conditions. There is a default condition concerning the endogenous state of the subject. One assumes that the subject's task is defined entirely by the experimenter's instructions. But, there are other factors: the task as the subject understands it and is motivated to perform it, cooperatively or not.

Can the interesting things that have been discovered, or the questions that are posed, be generalized to states of the organism under different conditions of endogenous stimulation, of heightened or different motivations? Motivation hasn't been raised at all, yet we would all agree, unlike behaviourists, that motivation is very much a part of everything that we do, and of what the rat does.

My other concern relates to what Bernie Baars has just been saying, and also what Tony Marcel was calling our attention to, namely that we ignore content. For example, the serial nature of consciousness may be a function of the fact that in cognitive research we deal with only one state of consciousness, usually of the alert, awake, cooperative subject. What if we were to be dealing with states of intoxication, psychosis or dreaming? Our daily experience tells us that often we can't put into words all of what we are actually consciously experiencing. There may be more than a half a dozen contents present at a time and we may, in fact, experience confusion as a result. At such times, words fail us, because language is intrinsically temporal and serial. So I wonder if what we are discovering can be generalized to these other states of consciousness that we have barely touched upon.

Dennett: Let me try to draw a connection between a remark that Tom Nagel made some years ago (Nagel 1979, p 35) and a question that Peter Fenwick raised earlier (p 118). Tom said that as we keep subtracting the circumstances that surround an action, we work back until we get to a point where the responsible agent seems to reside, and this is viewed as an ominous theoretical trend. Peter Fenwick was really speaking to the same thing when he discussed the issue of responsibility. As we learn more and more about the brain, mechanistically, what is going to happen to our notion of responsibility?

In my book *Elbow Room* (Dennett 1984, p 143) I said that if you make yourself really small, you can externalize just about everything. Michael Gazzaniga was asked earlier: 'Why are you putting the self in the left hemisphere?' He didn't want to say, 'That's where the ego is': he said the machinery is in there, and without that machinery you don't have a self. But it isn't just in the left hemisphere; it has to have the rest of the system around it in order for it to be conscious. Michael Lockwood asked: 'What happens if you put the reticular formation of the thalamus in a box?' But if you supply that system with all the inputs that we normally receive, then you have a larger system where you simply restore all the things that have to be there. The idea that you want to shrink the self or the consciousness down to a little spot is a mistake.

My response to Peter Fenwick is this. We already know how to resist the encroaching diminution of selfhood—you keep yourself large. We spoke yesterday about the locus of control. I want to suggest that the locus of control is the whole brain: there isn't any one place which is headquarters. A responsible agent knows about limitations, knows about not getting drowsy, about trying to protect himself or herself from the circumstances where control is going to be more difficult. In the same way that we worry about keeping our external environment free from obstacles that will prevent us from doing what we ought to do, we also worry about keeping our internal envioronmental free from obstacles that will prevent us from doing what we have to do. That's why the whole brain is the locus of control.

Lockwood: By the same argument, why stop at the brain? Why not take the whole body? Why not take the whole world? The argument you are using would make it arbitrary to stop at the boundaries of the brain.

Dennett: To some extent that's true.

Fenwick: I understand this as follows. You say the locus of control is the whole brain, and you then talk about a responsible agent, which you seem to equate with the whole brain. The philosophical point is: what happens to responsibility when one sub-system is forcing behaviour in a particular direction, which the responsible agent can't help? It could be argued that if brain and mind are identical, then any set of behaviours is totally determined by brain function: change brain function and you change behaviour. There is no question of responsibility. I exploit this concept all the time with my patients when I give them antidepressants. I change their perceived world and their actions in a very specific way. Is the whole of mind conditioned in this molecular way? If so, there can be no responsibility in the accepted sense of the word. Can we allocate responsibility simply to the global nature of the system? Surely mind is beyond that.

Dennett: To the extent I understand it, there are these opponent systems—not one, but many. A healthy individual is one who exploits, and of course *is*, the collection of opponent systems that gets the job done. If one such system gets completely out of balance, then you have somebody who is no longer responsible.

Searle: Dan Dennett is worried that the philosophers didn't address Peter Fenwick's question. I feel no guilt at all in not addressing it—it's the subject matter for another conference. To address that, I would have to talk about freedom of choice, causation of behaviour, how reasons for action relate to responsibility—I couldn't begin to do that here. And the worst thing you can do in a discussion like this is give the impression that you have answered a question when you haven't.

Nagel: It is also a question that simply cuts across these others, because a dualist faces the problem of free will as much as a materialist does.

Van Gulick: There seem to be at least two very different ways of thinking about consciousness. One is to focus on the phenomenal, subjective, felt, experiential aspect. The other is to view consciousness as involved in a lot of very sophisticated, higher-level, cognitive, informational activities, such as Michael Gazzaniga's theory that consciousness constructs an ongoing interpretative narrative, or Dan Dennett's view that it spins a heterophenomenological narrative, or Bernie Baars' theory of consciousness as a global workspace. There is a kind of tension, because we imagine that the touchy, feely, subjective aspect is present in very simple creatures, even in some that have virtually no cortex. These creatures are capable of no metacognition, very little cognition and only simple information processing.

We need to figure out how, in the human case, these two aspects of consciousness (the experiential and the metacognitive) get knitted together. Perhaps, in our biological heritage, things that had an initial 'felt' aspect have been recruited into structures which have come, in humans, to play a much higher cognitive role. There may be creatures or systems, biological or artificial, that are capable of all the high information processing, and metacognition, without any felt, subjective aspect at all. But the mind–body problem, if it is focused on the subjective, has to explain how subjective experience provides the basis for higher cognition in humans.

One place where there might be a connection is the unity of consciousness. John Searle mentioned unity. There are many unities; there is unity at a single time (e.g. how things in the visual field get united into a single visual experience), or the unity of different sensations (e.g. how tactile and visual sensations are united); there is unity across time. Each, in a sense, involves the construction of a narrative. Different pieces of information, or different aspects of our representation of the world, are brought into contact with one another to build a more unified and transparently coherent picture of the world.

With regard to the subjective aspects, consider a single visual perception at a moment. The ethologist, Konrad Lorenz, in his book on the evolution of consciousness, *Behind the Mirror* (Lorenz 1973), looked at different lineages of animal systems. He talked about the distinction between animals that have orienting responses or taxes but don't have any general overall visual information or spatial information, and birds such as starlings which have multiple pharotaxes, and can traverse any route whatsoever through their environment—they have all the information about the spatial surround available. What you need from the subjective side is some way to construct an overall visual representation of your environment using a continuous sensory manifold. Those manifolds are the same things that have the visual qualia, but they are playing a very strong informational role. If we can begin to understand how this is the kind of representation we need to integrate visual information, then perhaps we can see how other aspects of higher cognition and greater information processing involve building a larger and larger structure in which the visual is one piece. When we have visual experience, it's not just the visual modality that's involved—it's the visual modality interacting with all of these other systems.

So I see these two poles, the subjective and the higher cognitive, as closely connected. We need to work more on the link; that's what I would call functionalist theorizing.

Harnad: Ben Libet's challenge concerning *content* is a valid challenge to the kind of position that Tom Nagel and John Searle and, to a certain extent, I and Michael Lockwood appear to share. The simple way to describe it is this. If at the end of the day you have a theory like Jeffrey Gray's that accounts for all the data and that can or cannot be given a mental interpretation, then you either give it a mental interpretation, in which case various states will have a qualitative content, or you do not. Ben Libet seems to have a point when he says: if you don't give it a mental interpretation, you have an awful lot of what looks like otherwise useless extraneous baggage. I do not agree with him completely, I just want to contrast it with the cases that kept on getting contrasted here—the case of life and the case of ordinary physics.

Ordinary physics is the most instructive. (This time, instead of using quarks, I'll use superstrings.) A complete physical theory at the end of the day will also contain some funny things. Suppose it contains superstrings. With these, it can account for all the data. Suppose you try to 'deinterpret' the theory by asking: 'What if, in reality, there are no superstrings?' The theory collapses; it does not work (i.e. it does not successfully predict and explain all the data) unless there are superstrings. You can say: 'Maybe there's a universe in which zombie superstrings replace real superstrings', but that's not interesting any more. Either the superstrings or the zombie superstrings are needed, irrespective of what you want to call them, otherwise the theory doesn't work. By contrast, no working physical theory requires an 'élan matériel' in order to work, any more than any working biological theory requires an élan vital, such that, if you take it out, the theory collapses. That's why biology is no different from physics or engineering in this respect.

Now, what about qualitative content (qualia—élan mental?) in a complete neurobiological theory? I think Tom Nagel and John Searle are too generous when they say that if we indeed arrive at a *complete* neurobiological theory, that's all they want. I am still asking this separate question: is the mentalistic interpretation of the theory—positing and drawing upon the qualia—optional or not? If it's not optional, then there's nothing special about the case of mind science either (but then I'd like to know precisely *why* it's not optional).

Searle: I think there's a rather simple answer to this question. Dan Dennett's picture is typical of what a lot of people, both in science and philosophy, have thought for a long time; it goes as follows. Science is objective, therefore at the end of the day when we have a complete science of the brain/mind, it will be as objective as physics, and all of this touchy feely stuff will retreat to a vanishing point. As Dan says, we would just get bored with the idea that there might be something else, something more than objective third-person phenomena.

My answer to that is very simple. There is a pun on 'objective'. We need to distinguish between ontological subjectivity and objectivity on the one hand, and epistemic subjectivity and objectivity on the other. Science aspires to *epistemic* objectivity—which means truths that we can all agree on. That Van Gogh is a better painter than Matisse is subjective. That Matisse at one time lived in Nice is objective. Besides epistemic subjectivity and objectivity, there is a form of *ontological* subjectivity, which is what we are talking about when we discuss consciousness. We are talking about entities that really exist; hence statements about them have epistemic objectivity, but the mode of their existence is this first-person, touchy, feely, 'what it's like', mode of existence. We can't pretend that such phenomena don't exist; you have to feign anaesthesia to pretend that you don't have a subjective experience when you feel a pain.

Here, then, is the answer. The complete science of the brain doesn't leave anything out, because one of the terms in a complete science of the brain is the touchy, feely, 'what it feels like', quality of conscious phenomena. In the complete science of the brain, you will have terms like pain, tickle, itch, and you will mean those in the full sense.

How did we ever get into this bind? There is an historical obstacle we need to overcome. Aristotle would not have had this worry. It is strictly a local worry that arose in Europe after the 17th century. I believe we are repeating mistakes that originated with Descartes in the 17th century. Descartes, Copernicus and Galileo separated the conscious observer from the ontologically objective world that was being observed. At that time, this was a pragmatically useful separation. Physics could not have advanced without making that separation. But now it's become an obstacle to our investigations. What I am urging is that the ontologically subjective phenomena should become part of the subject matter of an objective science of the brain—nothing should be left out.

Descartes thought it was mysterious that hitting your thumb with a hammer could cause you to feel a pain. After all, the thumb and the hammer are physical and the pain is mental. Nowadays, we have just moved Descartes' mystery into the brain. We no longer worry about the fact that hitting your thumb with a hammer causes you to feel pain, but to many people it seems mysterious that neuron firings can cause sensations of pain. But it's important to recognize this: as a matter of plain biological fact, neuron firings do cause sensations of pain. Of course, in one sense all causal relations can seem miraculous. Electromagnetism and gravity seem amazing, and in a sense they are amazing. But consciousness is no more amazing than are electromagnetism and gravity, and it is as much a part of the world as are electromagnetism and gravity.

Gray: I would like to make essentially the same point in a way that I find easier to understand. The problem that arises about consciousness seems to me to have nothing to do with history; it's built in. It is built in for this reason. As a scientist, any terms about conscious experience that I choose to use are necessarily theoretical words, about other people and about animals. From that point of view, conscious experience is a theory word, just as élan vital was a theory word. If Dan Dennett wanted to get rid of it in his functionalist analysis, he could. But we have also, each of us inside our head, conscious experiences as data. We are also pretty convinced that we are all sufficiently alike that everybody else is having those same data. Those data need explanation, so you can't just get rid of them as you could get rid of élan vital.

References

Baars BJ 1988 A cognitive theory of consciousness. Cambridge University Press, New York

Dell GS, Repka RJ 1992 Errors in inner speech. In: Baars BJ (ed) Experimental slips and human error: exploring the architecture of volition. Plenum Publishing Corporation, New York, p 235–262

Dennett DC 1984 Elbow room: the varieties of free will worth wanting. MIT Press, Cambridge, MA

Edelman G 1989 The remembered present: a biological theory of consciousness. Basic Books, New York

Finke R 1980 Levels of equivalence in imagery and perception. Psychol Rev 87:113–132

Gray JA 1993 Consciousness, schizophrenia and scientific theory. In: Experimental and theoretical studies of consciousness. Wiley, Chichester (Ciba Found Symp 174) p 263–281

Haier RJ, Sieger JR, MacLachlan A, Soderling E, Lottenberg S, Buchsbaum MS 1992 Regional glucose metabolic changes after learning a complex visuospatial/motor task: a positron emission tomographic study. Brain Res 570:134–143

Kinsbourne M 1993 Integrated cortical field model of consciousness. In: Experimental and theoretical studies of consciousness. Wiley, Chichester (Ciba Found Symp 174) p 43–60

Libet 1981 Timing of cerebral processes relative to concomitant conscious experiences in man. In: Adam G, Meszaros I, Banyai EI (eds) Advances in physiological science. Pergamon Press, Oxford

Lorenz K 1973 Behind the mirror. Harcourt Brace Jovanovich, New York

Marcel AJ 1993 Slippage in the unity of consciousness. In: Experimental and theoretical studies of consciousness. Wiley, Chichester (Ciba Found Symp 174) p 168–186

Nagel T 1979 Mortal questions. Cambridge University Press, Cambridge

Newsome WT, Salzman CD 1993 The neuronal basis of motion perception. In: Experimental and theoretical studies of consciousness. Wiley, Chichester (Ciba Found Symp 174) p 217–246

O'Keefe J, Nadel L 1978 The hippocampus as a cognitive map. Oxford University Press, Oxford

Posner MI 1992 Attention as a cognitive and neural system. Curr Dir Psychol Sci 11:11–14

Rosenthal D 1990 A theory of consciousness. ZIF Report No 40. Zentrum für Interdisziplinäre Forschung, Bielefeld, Germany

Singer JL 1993 Experimental studies of ongoing conscious experience. In: Experimental and theoretical studies of consciousness. Wiley, Chichester (Ciba Found Symp 174) p 100–122

Sokolov EN 1963 Perception and the conditioned reflex. Macmillan, New York

Thatcher RW, John ER 1977 Foundations of cognitive processes. Harper & Row, New York

Wall PD 1993 Pain and the placebo response. In: Experimental and theoretical studies of consciousness. Wiley, Chichester (Ciba Found Symp 174) p 187–216

Summary

T. Nagel

Department of Philosophy, New York University, 503 Main Building, Washington Square, New York, NY 10003, USA

I found this conference very illuminating. I do think that this subject moves more rapidly on the scientific side than it does on the philosophical side. Michael Gazzaniga asked me whether it is really necessary to have a philosophical conference more frequently than every 10 years! Probably not. We are like ageing prize fighters constantly exchanging the same punches. But even that process, given that none of us seems to fall down, may serve some function.

This is one of those areas in which the relation between very abstract and philosophical consideration of the subject, and empirical science, has been fruitful for both sides. I am struck by the influence of philosophical controversies over the last 20–25 years on scientific discussions, and vice versa.

John Searle says from time to time, 'I want to get this problem out of philosophy and into science, where it belongs'. My reply would be that in a scientific treatment there is a very important place for philosophical reflection and philosophical disagreement of precisely the kind we have been having. What kind of scientific theory would count as a theory of consciousness will be determined by theoretical considerations that are essentially philosophical. That's really the nub of the dispute between Dan Dennett and John Searle: what are the adequacy conditions of such a scientific theory.

The main question is whether one should be aiming for a theory that contains as primitive terms some variant of the kind of mental concepts we are familiar with, having characteristically linked first- and third-person applications, or whether we should be aiming for a theory which essentially replaces those concepts with a third-person description of the behaviour of those who employ them and to whom they apply, and provides an explanation of all of that. I myself remain convinced that we cannot even talk about consciousness, and therefore cannot have a theory of it, without using concepts that are not just third personal.

In general, it makes sense to look for reductionist theories of familiar things, and such theories will not employ all the familiar concepts which we ordinarily use to describe those things. For example, it is true that chairs are composed of atoms. This means you can, in principle, explain the physical properties of any particular chair and what will happen to it under different conditions in terms of physics and chemistry. However, the proposition that chairs are composed of atoms is not itself a proposition of physics, and the concept 'chair' will not appear in any of these explanations or theories. Chairs are treated by physics simply as combinations of atomic structures.

But there is a question left over: what kind of truth is it that chairs are composed of atoms? We can answer that question by observing that the proposition contains a concept which is embedded in human life and human activities, but which can be used to refer to things that can also be described from the standpoint of physics. So the significance of the proposition, as well as its truth, depends on the existence of the human practices and perspective from which the concept gets its life. In this case, we can pass the buck to the human perspective to account for the meaningfulness of the reductionist thesis.

But what should we do when the subject of a scientific theory is the human perspective and human consciousness itself? Even if we were able to provide a physicochemical theory which explained all the observable behaviour of the organism, there is again a question left over: we still have to provide some interpretation of the proposition that such a creature is conscious. And now we can no longer pass the buck to the human perspective, because that is what we are analysing. Functionalists believe that if the behaviour explained includes all the behaviour on the basis of which we ascribe consciousness to others, that is all we need to account for the meaning of the crucial proposition. Antireductionists believe that this proposition involves concepts of a different logical type, whose direct employment cannot be eliminated from the story without making it no longer possible even to express the thought that certain organisms are conscious. So we are left, not surprisingly, with the disagreement over whether it is possible to formulate a scientific theory of conscious mental life which does not employ any concepts that are subjective in something logically like the way that prescientific phenomenological concepts are subjective and the concepts of existing physical science are not.

To move to another issue, closer to specific problems of empirical research, it became clear in our discussions that there is no general agreement on how to tell whether or not a given mental event is conscious. (This came up in reference to the papers of Shoemaker, Kihlstrom, Libet and Newsome.) In various circumstances, both normal and pathological, subjects will react to a stimulus while denying any conscious awareness of it. There seem to be two distinct possible interpretations of such cases: either the stimulus produced a behavioural or cognitive result without any conscious sensory effect along the way; or there was a conscious event, but it failed to register in short-term memory or in some other way failed to make a connection with the type of second-order introspective awareness that results in first-person reports of one's own conscious states. An important task, I think, is the exploration of the kind of evidence that would enable us to decide which of these things had happened in a given case. We clearly cannot rely simply on verbal testimony, since in any case this is absent in infants and in other animals. On the other hand, we cannot simply take every capacity to discriminate or respond to stimuli as evidence of conscious awareness. If there is to be anything worthy of being called a scientific treatment of consciousness, this basic conceptual question requires more work.

A related unresolved issue which surfaced in our discussions concerned the relation between conscious and unconscious mental states. Most of us seem comfortable with the concept of an unconscious mental state, even if only for things like beliefs which we are not currently thinking about. But there seems to be a division between those who think that the only legitimate conception of this sort is one that can be analysed in terms of a disposition to have the corresponding conscious experiences under certain conditions, and those who think, as Freud did, that it is legitimate to speak of unconscious mental phenomena, provided they operate in causing action and other mental events in ways sufficiently similar to those of the states of which we can become introspectively aware. Such states could be mental even though permanently unconscious. (Freud himself thought they were all physical states of the central nervous system, but that we could in the present state of knowledge describe them only by means of a mentalistic theory.) Here again, it seems to me that the scientific study of consciousness should include more discussion, to which philosophers may be able to contribute, of the place of consciousness in the larger domain of the mental, and of the extent of that domain and the relations, logical and otherwise, between its conscious and unconscious aspects.

The final issue I wish to mention, which kept coming up and which clearly calls for extensive reflection, is that of the so-called unity of consciousness and its relation to the study of highly specific aspects or components of experience. (Many participants raised it: Kinsbourne, Marcel, Wall, Gazzaniga, Gray, Baars.) It is natural to attempt a bottom-up approach to the understanding of how a complex system like an animal or a conscious mind operates—gradually accumulating information about the neurophysiological conditions of such things as particular perceptual features, and then trying to see how they are put together into experiential wholes. But it is clear from many of the experimental results presented here that a top-down approach is at least as important, and that we cannot in general understand how specific aspects of conscious experience arise without referring to the contribution of the brain or mind as a whole in the creation of a mental response to specific stimuli. It appears that the unity of consciousness is not only one of the most puzzling things that a theory has to explain, but that it, or something corresponding to it, plays a fundamental explanatory role as well as a role in determining the contents of consciousness. Though some proposals have been offered, it remains difficult to imagine, from a logical point of view, what a theory of this kind would look like; but empirical data of the sort presented by many of the contributors to this symposium, both about the ordinary functioning and, illuminatingly, about the possibilities of breakdown, of the mental mechanisms of integration, call out for more discussion than we were able to give them here.

Index of contributors

Subject index